Horringer, Parish

Horringer Parish Registers

Baptisms, Marriages and Burials

Horringer, Parish

Horringer Parish Registers

Baptisms, Marriages and Burials

Inktank publishing, 2018

www.inktank-publishing.com

ISBN/EAN: 9783747750957

HORRINGER

PARISH REGISTERS.

Baptisms, Marriages, and Burials,

WITH

APPENDIXES AND BIOGRAPHICAL NOTES.

1558 to 1850.

———:o:———

Woodbridge:
GEORGE BOOTH, CHURCH STREET.
1900.

CONTENTS.

—:o:—

ILLUSTRATIONS.

—:o:—

PREFACE.

THIS is not the place in which to attempt to give any history of Horringer, but one or two things may be jotted down.

I. ITS NAME.—Horningsworth, Horningserth, Horninger, Horringer. These forms of the name will be found in successive use during the last 800 years. As time runs on names, like other things, will undergo slight changes, and those changes generally follow certain unwritten laws. In the change from Horningsworth to Horningserth, and from Horningserth to Horninger, and from Horninger to Horringer, the usual law is followed. There are other cases in which *worth* is corrupted into *er*. I have heard my father say that Ickworth used often to be called Icker, and I have heard it so called by an old man within the last few months.

But apparently in the course of the 18th century the form Horningsheath came into use, and it still more or less survives and holds the field with Horringer.

Now Horningsheath is as bad as it can be, and the sooner it is got rid of the better. For it is neither the original name, nor is it a legitimate, natural, and regular corruption of the original name. It proceeds from a mistaken idea and from false etymology. When the old English word *worth* dropped out of the language and people ceased to know that there had been such a word in it, then they began to think that the last syllable of Horningserth represented heath, and so they took to calling it Horningsheath. But the Domesday book of 800 years ago, and other early documents show positively that the last syllable of the name was *worth* and not *heath*. Therefore Horningsworth is right, because it is what men originally called it: Horningserth, Horninger, and Horringer are right because they are the natural and regular corruptions of the original name; but Horningsheath is wrong because it is neither the one nor the other, but the result of a false notion.

II. MEANING OF THE NAME.—The first two syllables must represent the name of some early owner. I presume that his time lay between the rather wide limits of A.D. 500 and 900. Possibly he was an emigrant from the shores of the Baltic, and Horningsea in Cambridgeshire may be another of his possessions. The last syllable, worth, is an early English word meaning an estate of some sort.

There are certain syllables one or other of which will often be found at the end of the names of villages, such as worth, ton, stead, field, ham, and others. And it is curious to notice how these syllables will often be found in groups. Without going out of this immediate neighbourhood one can see this. In Hawstead, Whepstead, Stanstead, and Boxsted we have a group of steads. In Cockfield, Stansfield, Stanningfield, and the three Bradfields we have a group of fields. In Cavenham, Icklingham, Tuddenham, Heigham, Saxham, Denham, Dalham, we have a group of hams. And in Ickworth, Horningsworth, and Bedericksworth we have three contiguous worths. The force of this last instance is not weakened by the fact that Bedericksworth has changed its original name for that of Bury St. Edmunds.

III. DIVISION INTO TWO PARISHES.—At some time or other Horringer was divided into two, Great and Little. There were two halls or manor houses, two churches, two rectors. Mr. Gage says that this division seems to have been made at some time between the Norman Conquest and the death of Henry II, *i.e.* between 1066 and 1189. The two parishes were consolidated in 1528. In Appendix VI I have given a list of the rectors of each Horringer from 1300 to 1528, and of the rectors of the two amalgamated Horringers from 1528 to the present time. The church of Great Horringer which is still doing duty to-day is dedicated to St. Leonard. The church of Little Horringer which is clean gone was dedicated to St. Peter. It stood not far from Little Horringer hall, and I imagine that a spade and a pick axe could easily discover what was its length and breadth and shape.

IV. THE OWNERS. — Of that early owner whose name remains embedded in the name of the village, like the bones of an extinct animal embedded in a rock, I can say nothing. Perhaps he was a Viking, who sailed from the shores of the Baltic, landed somewhere on the coast of Suffolk, and fought his way inland as far as the worth which still bears his name.

The earliest owner whom one can see with any distinctness is Theodred, an East Anglian Bishop and afterwards Bishop of London. He died somewhere about A.D. 960. Mr. Gage prints his will in full. By it he gave his land at Ickworth, Horringer, Nowton, and Whepstead to the newly-founded abbey at Bury St. Edmunds.

The next owners then are the Abbots of Bury. When once lands got into the possession of an abbey, there they remained as long as the abbey went on, for the abbey neither died nor sold nor gave.* So the manors of Great and Little Horringer remained in the possession of the Abbots of Bury for nearly 600 years after the death of Bishop Theodred.

In 1537 the monasteries were dissolved and their vast landed possessions came before long into the market. The reformation changed the religion of the people and the services in their churches. But it did more than that. It set free an enormous quantity of land which had been locked up for centuries in the possession of the Church, and sent it into the market.

After the dissolution of the monasteries in 1537 the manors of Great and Little Horringer did not keep company but got parted for a time, and so we must follow them separately.

GREAT HORRINGER.—In 1546 this manor and advowson were granted by the Crown to Sir Thomas Darcy, afterwards Lord Darcy of Chick. In 1549 Sir Thomas sold it to Sir Robert Southwell, Master of the Rolls, whose grandson, Sir Robert, sold it in 1583 to Sir Robert Jermyn of Rushbrooke, so that henceforth it became part of the Rushbrooke estate.

The Jermyn family possessed it for the next 125 years, their representatives being as follows :—

1. Sir Robert who first obtained it was he who made that curious marriage with Judith Blagge of Little Horringer. (See Blagge in Biographical Notes.) He died in 1614 and was succeeded by his son

2. Sir Thomas. This was he who was the friend and patron of William Bedell. (See Bedell in Biographical Notes.) He had two sons, of whom Henry the younger was created Earl of St. Albans, and is said to have been privately married to Queen Henrietta Maria, the widow of Charles I. Sir Thomas died in 1644, and was succeeded by his eldest son

3. Thomas. This Thomas had two sons, Thomas No. 4 and Henry No. 5, and died in 1659.

4. Thomas. This Thomas became Baron Jermyn on the death of his uncle, the Earl of St. Albans, in 1683. His only son Thomas was killed in 1692 by the mast of a ship falling on him on the Thames. (See Diary of John, Lord Bristol, under Dec., 1692.) Lord Jermyn died in 1703 leaving five daughters and co-

* Ickworth was an exception to this rule. It only remained in the possession of the abbey for about an hundred years, and then was exchanged for Elvedon and became private property. See Gage's Thingoe Hundred, p. 276.

heiresses, of whom Mary, the eldest, was married to Sir Robert Davers of Rougham, and brought the Rushbrooke estate to the Davers family.

5. Henry, the younger brother of No. 4, was created Lord Dover in 1685, and succeeded his brother as Lord Jermyn in 1703. He died in 1708 without children, and both baronies then became extinct. The article on him in the Dictionary of National Biography says that "most of his property passed to Sir Jermyn Davers, who had married his niece." This is incorrect, as it was Sir Robert, the father of Sir Jermyn, who married his niece. It is not quite clear whether Horringer passed to the Davers' family on the death of Thomas, Lord Jermyn, in 1703, or on the death of Henry, Lord Jermyn, in 1708.

Either in 1703 or in 1708 the manor of Great Horringer passed by inheritance from the Jermyns to the Davers family, who had it for just 100 years. I have given some account of the origin of this ill-fated family in the Biographical Notes. Their representatives as owners of the manor of Great Horringer were as follows:—

1. Sir Robert Davers, 2nd Bart., married Mary, one of the five daughters and co-heiresses of Thomas, Lord Jermyn, and died in 1722. He was succeeded by his son

2. Sir Robert, who died s. p. in 1723, and was succeeded by his brother

3. Sir Jermyn, who died in 1742, and was succeeded by his son

4. Sir Robert. This Robert is always ignored, but at p. 320 I have given my authority for his existence, which is supported by the fact that the Institution books at the Diocesan Registry at Norwich set down Mr. French as being presented to the rectory in 1758 by Sir Robert and not Sir Charles. (See p. 254.) He died in America in 1763 and was succeeded by his brother

5. Sir Charles, who was in the army and represented Bury St. Edmunds in Parliament continuously from 1774 to 1802, and died without legitimate issue in 1806. Sir Charles had two sisters, Mary and Elizabeth. Mary died unmarried in 1805 at her house on the Angel Hill at Bury St. Edmunds, adjoining the Abbey gate. Elizabeth was married to Frederick Hervey, Earl of Bristol and Bishop of Derry (see Fred: Hervey in Biographical Notes), and died at Ickworth Lodge in 1800. This marriage brought the Rushbrooke estate (including Great Horringer) to the Hervey family. On the death of Sir Charles in 1806 his nephew, Frederick William Hervey, 5th Earl and afterwards 1st Marquis of Bristol, by right of his mother succeeded to it. He sold Rushbrooke hall to the

Rushbrooke family who now possess it, but Horringer has since then kept company with Ickworth, and belongs to-day to his grandson.

So much for the manor of Great Horringer, which for now over 300 years has passed by right of inheritance from owner to owner. As the Abbots of Bury had previously possessed it for nearly 600 years, it will be seen that its changes through a thousand years in this world of change have not been many, and that the auctioneer has not had many opportunities of pointing out its merits.

With regard to the hall or manor house, in the days of Bury Abbey the abbots occasionally resided there. But I imagine that since it became part of the Rushbrooke estate it has been a farm-house. The present tenant, Mr. Moore, has kindly shown me over every corner of it, but I cannot see anything that I could put down to the times of the abbots. There are some indications of a moat, but they are not very clear. Mr. Gage mentions John Pryck as being a tenant of it in the latter days of the abbots. Pryck, recently always spelt Pryke, is an old Ickworth and Horringer name which has only lately died out there.

LITTLE HORRINGER.—We must now pass on to notice the successive owners of this manor. The complications of land tenure in the middle ages are so fearful that it is sometimes difficult to make out who is the real owner of land. But apparently the Abbots of Bury owned Little as well as Great Horringer. They certainly presented to both livings, and one of them built Little Horringer hall. This hall was built by John Melford *alias* Reeve *alias* Noel, the last of the abbots, who only survived the fall of his abbey a few months, and died at Bury in 1540. It was pulled down by George, 2nd Earl of Bristol, and nothing remains of it but the moat and that indescribable something which always remains, even though every brick be hauled away.

Mr. Gage tells us that after the dissolution of the monasteries Little Horringer was granted by the Crown to Sir Thomas Darcy, who in 1549 sold it to Sir Robert Southwell, who in 1550 sold it to John Moore of Peckham, Co. Kent, who in 1552 sold it to Thomas Lucas of Horsecroft, who in 1562 sold it to Sir Ambrose Jermyn of Rushbrooke, the father of Sir Robert Jermyn who bought Great Horringer.

It is curious that though both Great and Little Horringer were in the possession of the Elizabethan Sir Robert Jermyn and are now in the possession of the Victorian Marquis of Bristol, yet they have not gone together but have travelled from the one to the other by totally different routes. While Great

Horringer has always passed by right of inheritance Little Horringer has been frequently coming into the market. The auctioneer may have had chances of puffing the one while he has had no chance whatsoever of puffing the other.

From Sir Robert Jermyn the manor passed by some process or other, gift or exchange or purchase, to the Blagge family, with whom he was connected by more than one marriage. The Blagges have helped to fill the registers, and some account of them will be found in the Biographical Notes. They were there from about 1570 to about 1640.

After the Blagges came the Gipps family, who I presume bought it. They were there from about 1640 to about 1720. Some account of them will be found in the Biographical Notes.

After the Gipps family came Admiral Thomas Davers, a younger son of Sir Robert Davers of Rushbrooke, who I presume bought it, though possibly he may have inherited it. Some account of him will be found in the Biographical Notes.

In 1752 the widow and son of Admiral Davers sold it to George, Lord Bristol, who gave £6,600 for it. He pulled down the hall, and with the materials built the present farm-house just outside the moat.

Since then Little Horringer has kept company with Ickworth, which it joined some 50 years earlier than Great Horringer.

Of its church nothing is visible above ground, but the site is known, and I presume that the foundations remain untouched.

In following the descent of these two manors it must not be supposed that they included every house and every acre in the parish. They included the advowson, the mansion house, a certain amount of land, a certain number of houses, and various manorial rights, but there was a certain amount of land which either never had been part of the manor or had got detached from it at some time or other, as planets have been detached from the sun, as comets have been detached from the earth. One of the charges brought against the last Abbot of Bury was that he spent too much time at his granges and that he converted divers farms into copyholds.

Both John, 1st Earl of Bristol, and his grandson and successor, George, bought up such of these smaller estates in Horringer as they could, and I imagine that some of them were thrown into Ickworth park. In a manuscript book George, who succeeded his grandfather in 1751, has entered an account of "Purchases made by me since the death of my grandfather."

To Mr. George Boldero for houses and lands belonging to Mr. Moyle in the Parish of Horringer, £840.

To Mr. Johnson for his house in the churchyard at Bury, which house I afterwards exchanged with Lady Ann Hervey for her house and estate in Horringer Parish, £525.

To Mr. Symonds for his estate in Horringer, £4,500.

To Mr. Sparke, Mrs. Sparke and Mrs. Kedington for their lands in Horringer, £850.

To Mr. Neville, Mr. and Mrs. Syer for their lands in Horringer, £1,950.

I cannot identify any of these estates, but as both Mr. Moyle and Mr. Symonds were connected by marriage with the Jermyn and Davers families, their estates may have been detached portions of the manor of Great Horringer.

And besides those estates there was that one, now represented by Horringer house, which belonged to the Covels in the 17th century, and others of various sizes. Horsecroft (see Lucas in Biographical Notes) appears never to have formed part of the manor of either Horringer.

V. THE INHABITANTS.—These registers show us little more than their bare names and their duration of life, but I presume that during the whole period their occupation was mainly agricultural. For about ten years, viz., from 1695 to 1704, both in the register of Baptisms and of Burials, the occupation is given, farmer, labourer, woolcomber, shepherd, as the case may be. But except during those ten years no occupation is mentioned till 1813, when in the register of Baptisms it begins to be given regularly. The building of the great house at Ickworth, which was begun near about 1790, must have brought a large number of carpenters and bricklayers into the village, some of whom seem to have permanently settled there, and I presume their children are there to-day. The bricks required for that building must also have given considerable employment for a time, as they appear to have been made on the spot. Sixty years earlier, in the time of John, Lord Bristol, Horringer hands had made Ickworth bricks for the Court house at Bury St. Edmunds. Thirty years earlier still, viz., in 1702, Ickworth bricks were needed for Ickworth Lodge, but as there was then a village of Ickworth, Horringer hands need not have been required to the same extent. (Letters of John, Lord Bristol, Nos. 204, 206, 1019, 1021, 1023.)

The population of Horringer as given in the decennial census returns is as follows. I have not got the figures for each return.

1801	543	1831 ...	586	1891 ...	599
1811	523	1871 ...	691		
1821	539	1881 ...	662		

The following table shows the number of entries which I have printed here in each period of fifty years from 1558 to 1850. The first period is eight years short of fifty.

	Baptisms.	Marriages.	Burials.
1558 to 1600	340	117	167
1601 to 1650	442	144	282
1651 to 1700	433	88	291
1701 to 1750	451	123	408
1751 to 1800 ...	799	166	470
1801 to 1850	958	235	559
Total...	3423	873	2177

THE OLD RECTORY HOUSE.

VI. THE RECTORS.—I have given a list of the Rectors in Appendix VI and of the Curates in Appendix XI, and have added there and in the Biographical Notes anything that I could find out about them. It will be seen that three of the Rectors became Bishops, viz., Bedell and Womack in the 17th century and Lord Arthur Hervey in the 19th. The view of the old Rectory house here given shows it as it is to-day. I imagine that in its general outline and appearance it does not look very different to what it did when Bedell entertained his parishioners there and planted and grafted and inoculated and dug in its garden. The sash windows of course belonged to a later date. It ceased to be the rectory house when the new one was built in 1873, and is now a Village Club and Institute.

VII. THE VILLAGE.—It must be enough to say under this heading that the centre of Horringer is about two miles from the centre of Bury St. Edmunds. On its boundary line lie successively Bury St. Edmunds, Westly, Little Saxham (?), Ickworth, Whepstead, Hawstead, Nowton, Hardwick, and so back to Bury. (See Appendix V.) The church standing on the Green which affords a healthy play-ground for the neighbouring school, Ickworth park peeping in through the park gates, the wide village street with wide margins on either side, the comfortable looking cottages set well back from the road and standing in ample gardens, everything wide, ample, fresh, airy, and clean, make it at any rate in its outward appearance a model village. The squalor which disgraces many English villages, the narrow, cribbed, confined, unhealthy look which some of them have and which makes them more like the slums of a town than like a country village, every bit of ground within the minimum legal number of feet from the centre of the road grabbed by somebody's greed, the squalid gardenless houses touching the very road, so that open windows, if such there should be, receive within not air but dust, all this is happily not to be seen in Horringer street.

VIII. THE ORIGINAL REGISTERS.—These are mostly in fair condition and have been fairly well kept. From the beginning in 1558 to 1622 the writing is very fine and as fresh as if done yesterday, the regnal year of the sovereign being given on one side of the page while the year of our Lord is given on the other. I have left off printing with the end of 1850, so that we have in these volumes the record of three centuries, or to be exact 293 years. In the Baptisms there are no gaps. In the Marriages and Burials there are one or two short gaps during the troublous times of the 17th century. But though there are hardly any gaps of whole years, it is clear that many entries have been omitted. When entries were not made in the Register at the time but only jotted down on any scrap of paper and copied into the book at the end of the year, it is very likely that the scraps of paper would be lost and the entries never be made. And it is clear that this has often happened. This carelessness went on even to within this present century. However, we have got a good deal and must be thankful for that.

As the contents of the two earliest existing volumes are rather mixed, I will set them out here. The letters are of my giving.

A. Baptisms, Feb. 5, 1558, to Dec. 16, 1624.
Marriages, 1558, to Sept. 21, 1623.
Burials, Nov. 22, 1558, to June 22, 1624.
2 pages with list and notices of Rectors.
Baptisms, Dec. 28, 1624, to July, 1700.
Marriages, April 13, 1625, to Feb. 17, 1730.
Burials, March 25, 1625, to July 29, 1682.
Baptisms, April 6, 1731, to end of 1812.
Burials, May 15, 1731, to end of 1812.

B. 10 pages of Briefs. (Printed in Appendix I.)
Births, May 17, 1695, to Dec. 15, 1704.
Births, Sept. 4, 1698, to Nov. 6, 1700.
1 Marriage, 1698. 5 Marriages, 1653–54. 3 Burials, 1653.
Loose leaf, containing Baptisms, Marriages, and Burials, 1702.
Baptisms, Aug. 30, 1700, to Feb. 25, 1730.
Burials, 1673, to March 16, 1730.
Loose leaf, containing Burials from Aug., 1695, to July, 1700.

It will be seen that for a few years on either side of 1700 there are duplicate copies of entries, which do not always exactly agree. This is what I refer to when I mention "duplicate."

In 1679 an Act of Parliament was passed for the encouragement of the woollen trade. By the Act an affidavit had to be sworn to and brought to the Minister within eight days of burial, declaring that the deceased had been buried in woollen. The penalty was £5. Accordingly every entry of burial from 1679 to 1760 or soon after states that the affidavit had been received. Now and then it is stated that it was received after the specified time. I have not thought it worth while to print the words "affidavit received," but content myself with saying here that the words are there in every case.

From 1776 to 1785 the date of birth is given as well as that of baptism. I have printed this at the end of each entry.

Towards the close of the last century it appears to have been the common custom for children to be privately baptized at home immediately after birth, and afterwards (sometimes 2 or 3 years afterwards) received into the Church. Sometimes the entry was made at the time of the private baptism, sometimes at the time of reception, and sometimes at both times. I have left out the second entry when I happened to notice it. There is a good deal of confusion in the chronological order of the entries, which I have tried to diminish.

In 1789 begins the very useful custom of giving the mother's maiden name. This I have printed in brackets in the Register of Baptisms.

When there are two surnames in brackets the other one is hers by a former marriage.

It must not be forgotten that till 1751 the year is reckoned to begin at March 25.

There only remains for me to express my thanks to the Rev. James Giddens for the help he has given me in many ways.

S. H. A. H.

28, Angel Hill, Bury St. Edmunds,
July, 1900.

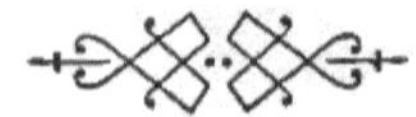

Abbreviations and Explanations.

———:o:———

These abbreviations will be found in the Marriage entries from 1725 onwards:—L for licence. P for parish. S for single. W for widow or widower.

In the Baptismal entries 1776 to 1786 the date at the end of the entry is the date of birth.

In Baptisms and Burials from 1789 onwards the surname in brackets is the mother's maiden name.

In Marriages 1837 to 1850, "single," "of this parish," and "labourer," are implied where it is not otherwise stated. Also, the profession after the bride's name is that of her father.

HORRINGER PARISH REGISTERS.

BAPTISMS.

Nomina omnium ac singulorum qui a nato Christo anno 1558 decimoque septimo Novembris (quo *nmicam*[1] *aie*[1] illustrissima ac nunquam satis laudibus celebranda princeps D. Elizabetha regium munus feliciter inibat Christianaque in Anglia Reipub: curam suscipiebat,) in ecclesia parochiali de Hornincher alias Horningsherth magna, cæmiteriove ejusdem, vel sacra Baptismatis aqua abluti, vel matrimonio rite conjuncti, vel terræ mandati atque sepulti sunt, ex ejusdem serenissimæ piisimæque Elizabethæ principis mandato in perpetuam *rer*[2] memoriam ad bonum commune ac publicum pergameno fideliter commissa.

BAPTISMES.

1558.	Feb.	5.	Henrie the sonne of Henrie Mahwe.
1559.	April	2.	John the sonne of John Man.
	April	27.	Margaret the daughter of Stephen Bully.
	Aug.	20.	Margaret the daughter of Robert Wellom.
	Oct.	17.	William the sonne of William Lilly.
	Jan.	18.	Ann the daughter of Mr. Jaslin.
	March	17.	John the sonne of John Godfrie.
	March	24.	Marie & Francis the daughters of John Turner.
1560.	March	30.	Elizabeth daughter of Martin Rooding.
	April	9.	William the sonne of Edmund Kent.
	April	9.	John the sonne of John Lilly.
	Maie	1.	Elizabeth daughter of Elizabeth Marten.
	Maie	12.	Edmond sonne of John Wellom.
	Aug.	15.	Ann daughter of William Wellom.
	Aug.	4.	Elizabeth daughter of John Hande.
	Oct.	10.	John the sonne of Barnabie Smith.
	Nov.	22.	Anne daughter of Cuthbert Smith.
	Dec.	8.	George sonne of George Mayo.
	Jan.	26.	John the sonne of John Kent.

[1] I cannot interpret these two words. The second may be "die."

[2] Quære "rerum."

1561.	Maie	6.	Margaret daughter of Henrie Mayo,
	and		Margaret daughter of Robert Wellom.
	Maie	15.	Thomas the sonne of Edward Bardwel.
	Dec.	21.	Elizabeth daughter of Thomas Barker.
	Jan.	25.	Stephen the sonne of Stephen Bully.
	Jan.	26.	Isabel daughter of Thomas Norman.
	Feb.	7.	Rose daughter of William Lilly.
	March	24.	Marie daughter of John Overen.
1562.	March	25.	Simon the sonne of John Hande.
	March	30.	Margaret daughter of John Lilly.
	April	12.	Joane daughter of John Wellom borne, and buried the 13th of the same moneth.
	Maie	17.	Edward sonne of Edward Bardwel.
	Maie	24.	Sara daughter of Marten Rooding.
	June	28.	Rainolde sonne of Thomas Brett.
	Oct.	2.	Elizabeth daughter of John Godfrie.
	Nov.	10.	Elizabeth daughter of Thomas Draklon.
	Jan.	17.	Ann daughter of John Gylman.
	Jan.	21.	Robert sonne of Cuthbert Smith.
	March	7.	William sonne of Henrie Mayo.
	March	10.	William sonne of Eustace Hayward.
1563.	April	21.	Frauncis sonne of Edward Bardwel.
	Maie	12.	Joane daughter of John Wellom.
	June	17.	James sonne of Austin Neweport.
	Julie	11.	Robert sonne of Robert Newegate.
	Aug.	1.	Alice daughter of John Buckenam.
	Oct.	4.	Thomas the sonne of William Cooke.
	Oct.	28.	Henrie the sonne of Thomas Barker.
	Feb.	6.	Judith the daughter of Thomas Birde.
1564.	April	4.	Robert the sonne of Thomas Brett.
	April	22.	Elizabeth daughter of Thomas Largeaunt. [Sargeaunt ?]
	Maie	7.	John the sonne of Edward Bardwel.
	Maie	14.	Margaret the daughter of Robert Spalding.
	Maie	28.	Amie daughter of Henrie Parkin.
	June	4.	Richard the sonne of John Hande.

	Nov.	19.	William sonne of John Lilly.
	Dec.	24.	Bridget daughter of Thomas Norman.
	Jan.	21.	Elizabeth daughter of John Coppin.
	Jan.	28.	Nicholas sonne of William Austin.
	Feb.	2.	Thomas sonne of Eustace Hawarde.
	Feb.	2.	John the sonne of Anthonie Butler.
	Feb.	25.	John the sonne of Austin Neweport.
	March	18.	Rose daughter of George Mayo.
1565.	March	25.	John the sonne of William Lilly.
	March	25.	John sonne of Henrie Mayo.
	April	24.	Hester daughter of Edward Bardwel.
	Maie	6.	Margaret daughter of John Godfrie.
	Maie	13.	John the sonne of John Spinke.
	Aug.	12.	Elizabeth daughter of Robert Wellom.
	Nov.	25.	Ann daughter of William Hall.
	Nov.	25.	Elizabeth daughter of Thomas Drakelon.
	Dec.	16.	Elizabeth daughter of Benet Elmar.
	Jan.	13.	John the sonne of Thomas Brett.
	Jan.	13.	William sonne of Thomas Birde.
	Feb.	17.	Thomas sonne of Roger Parker.
1566.	Sept.	15.	Anthonie sonne of Anthonie Butler.
	Sept.	28.	Marie daughter of William Fynn.
	Oct.	15.	Edward sonne of John Hande.
	Dec.	22.	Thomas the sonne of John Turner.
	Dec.	27.	Richard sonne of Austin Neweport.
	Jan.	1.	Elizabeth daughter of Thomas Brett.
	Feb.	2.	Henrie sonne of Eustace Haward.
	Feb.	16.	Christopher sonne of Thomas Norman.
	Feb.	23.	Henrie sonne of John Godfrie.
1567.	June	8.	Agnes daughter of John Lilly.
	June	8.	John the sonne of William Austin.
	Aug.	5.	John the sonne of Thomas Draklon.
	Aug.	30.	John the sonne of Thomas Birde.
	Sept.	6.	John the sonne of Leonard Staps.
	Sept.	14.	Barbara daughter of John Edmondes,

	Jan.	18.	Margerie daughter of Bennet Elmar.
1568.	April	19.	Robert & Joane the children of William Lilly.
	Julie	25.	Elizabeth daughter of Edward Barret.
	Julie	25.	Jane daughter of William Haul.
	Oct.	3.	Agnes daughter of William Fynn.
	Oct.	12.	John the sonne of John Bucchenham.
	Oct.	30.	Robert sonne of John Gylman.
	March	12.	Margaret daughter of Thomas Brett.
1569.	April	17.	Susan daughter of John Godfreie.
	Aug.	21.	Alice daughter of Richard Cooper.
	Sept.	20.	Agnes daughter of John Lilly.
	Oct.	30.	Edward sonne of William Austen.
	Nov.	6.	Edward sonne of Robert Spalding.
	Nov.	18.	Margerie daughter of John Turner.
	Dec.	25.	John the sonne of John Mayo.
	March	2.	Edmond the sonne of William Haul.
1570.	April	16.	William the sonne of Thomas Birde.
	June	18.	Dorothie the daughter of Richard Godfrie.
	Julie	25.	Katharine daughter of William Man.
	Julie	30.	Elizabeth daughter of John Edmondes.
	Oct.	29.	John the sonne of John Edhouse.
	Feb.	2.	Katharine the daughter of Edward Sillet.
	March	4.	John the sonne of Richard Cooper.
	March	4.	Margaret the daughter of John Mayo.
1571.	April	1.	Ann daughter of Robert Brett.
	April	1.	John the sonne of John Cooke.
	June	1.	Jermyn Duke gent. baptized.
	Nov.	11.	Edmonde sonne of Eustace Haward.
	Jan.	20.	Elizabeth daughter of William Austin.
	Feb.	18.	Katharine daughter of William Fynn.
	March	9.	Jane the daughter of John Gylman.
1572.	March	29.	Audrie the daughter of John Edmondes.
	Maie	4.	Susan the daughter of John Lilly.
	Julie	6.	Thomas the sonne of John Cooke.
	Julie	20.	Elizabeth daughter of John Mayo.

	Aug.	3.	John the sonne of Jefferie Berrie.
	Oct.	20.	Richard the sonne of Richard Godfrie.
	Nov.	30.	John the sonne of Ralfe South.
	Dec.	14.	Susan the daughter of Thomas Norman.
1573.	Oct.	11.	Frauncis the sonne of John Maio.
	Nov.	1.	Alice daughter of Thomas Brett.
	Nov.	13.	John the sonne of John Eddouse.
	Jan.	6.	John the sonne of Edward Sillet.
1574.	June	6.	Elizabeth daughter of William Durrant.
	Julie	4.	John the sonne of John Cooke.
	Julie	30.	Alice the daughter of John Edmondes.
	Aug.	22.	Richard the sonne of John Cooke.
	Sept.	19.	Dorotheie the daughter of Henrie Blagge Esquire.
1575.	Maie	15.	Thomas the sonne of Jefferie Berrie.
	Aug.	6.	Frauncis the daughter of John Mayo.
	Sept.	25.	Margaret the daughter of William Page.
	Oct.	28.	Dorothie the daughter of Thomas Brett.
	Feb.	14.	Jane daughter of William Fynn.
	March	2.	Jefferie sonne of John Cooke.
	March	18.	Richard the sonne of Thomas Norman.
1576.	April	17.	Thomas sonne of William Godfrie.
	Aug.	8.	Joane daughter of Richard Sillet.
	Sept.	7.	Marie daughter of John Edmondes.
	Sept.	16.	Elizabeth daughter of Edward Cocke.
	Dec.	13.	John the sonne of John Mayo.
	Dec.	24.	Thomas the sonne of Richard Godfrie.
	Dec.	30.	Edward sonne of Edward Sillet.
1577.	April	14.	Richard sonne of John Godfrie.
	April	14.	Bridget daughter of William Fynn.
	June	23.	Alice daughter of William Barom.
	Julie	7.	Alice daughter of John Goose.
	Aug.	25.	Robert sonne of John Page.
	Oct.	23.	Marie daughter of John Eddouse.
	Nov.	10.	Margaret daughter of Jeffrie Berrie.
	Nov.	27.	Thomas sonne of John Bud.

	Jan.	20.	John the sonne of William Rogers.
	Feb.	10.	Penelope daughter of Thomas Beningfild.
	March	24.	Edward sonne of John Cooke.
1578.	Sept.	28.	John the sonne of John Godfrie.
	Oct.	5.	Elizabeth daughter of John Bud.
	Nov.	6.	Ann daughter of John Gips.
	Dec.	26.	Richard sonne of Richard Sillet.
	Feb.	25.	Lyon sonne of Richard Goodrick gent.
	March	15.	William the sonne of William Page.
1579.	Maie	31.	Edmond the sonne of Frauncis Cale.
	Maie	31.	William the sonne of Richard Godfrie.
	June	22.	Marie daughter of Rice, or Witherbie, or.*
	June	24.	John the sonne of John Wellam.
	Julie	26.	Joane the daughter of John Mayo.
	Aug.	29.	Josua the sonne of James Bower.
	Aug.	30.	Elizabeth daughter of Edmunde Gosnolde.
	Oct.	4.	Jeremie the sonne of William Durrant.
	Oct.	17.	Alice daughter of John Godfrie.
	Feb.	10.	Bridget the daughter of Edward Sillet.
	Feb.	15.	Elizabeth daughter of John Goose.
	Feb.	28.	Thomas the sonne of Henrie Blagge esquire.
	March	12.	Susan the daughter of William Rogers.
1580.	April	17.	Thomas the sonne of William Barom.
	Sept.	4.	Margaret the daughter of John Edmondes.
	Sept.	4.	Thomas of Settys, base.
	Oct.	9.	Agnes the daughter of Jerome Goose.
	Oct.	23.	Prudence the daughter of John Mayo.
	Oct.	23.	Richard sonne of John Cutmare.
	Nov.	6.	Agnes the daughter of Thomas Kendal.
	March	20.	Frauncis daughter of John Eddouse.
1581.	March	27.	Thomas the sonne of Richard Sillet.
	Julie	15.	William sonne of John Cooke.
	Julie	30.	Margaret the daughter of Richard Godfrie.

* The entry is certainly as I have copied it. I imagine that another alias was accidentally omitted.

	Oct.	18.	Thomas the sonne of Thomas Barker.
	Oct.	22.	Frauncis the sonne of Edward Sillet.
	Nov.	1.	Marie the daughter of James Sillet.
	Nov.	26.	Thomas the sonne of Thomas Wellam.
	Nov.	26.	Thomas the sonne of Nicholas Friet.
	Feb.	11.	John the sonne of Henrie Bucchenham.
	Feb.	25.	Edward sonne of John Godfrie.
	Feb.	25.	Adrian the daughter of Philip Newegate.
	March	15.	Edward the sonne of William Page.
	March	24.	Margaret the daughter of John Yonge.
1582.	April	1.	Rose the daughter of John Gipse.
	June	17.	Frauncis the sonne of William Godfrie.
	Nov.	11.	Agnes the daughter of John Goose.
	Jan.	20.	Marie the daughter of Jerome Goose.
1583.	Julie	28.	Marie the daughter of John Thurston.
	Sept.	10.	Susan the daughter of John Eddouse.
	Sept.	15.	Marie the daughter of William Barom.
	Oct.	13.	William the sonne of James Sillet.
	Nov.	24.	John the sonne of Philip Newegate.
	Dec.	1.	Bridget the daughter of Richard Sillet.
	March	8.	Margaret the daughter of John Godfrie,
	&		Susan the daughter of John Edmondes,
	&		Agnes daughter of John Cutmare.
	March	22.	Isabel daughter of Henrie Bucchenham.
1584.	April	26.	John the sonne of Thomas Scot.
	Aug.	17.	William the sonne of William Sawier.
	Oct.	20.	Elizabeth the daughter of William Fuller.
	Nov.	17.	Josias the sonne of Edward Sillet.
	Nov.	26.	Thomas the sonne of Thomas Deiton esquire.
	Dec.	26.	Robert sonne of Robert Larner.
1585.	June	13.	Agnes daughter of Henrie Bennet.
	Julie	11.	Epinetus the sonne of William Page.
	Oct.	3.	Ann the daughter of Thomas Scot.
	Dec.	5.	Joseph the sonne of Philip Newegate.
	Dec.	12.	Alice the daughter of John Thurston.

	Jan.	27.	Margaret the daughter of William Barom.
	March	19.	Henrie the sonne of Henrie Mahwe,
	&		Edward the sonne of James Sillet,
	&		Dorothie the daughter of John Godfrie.
1586.	June	12.	Henrie sonne of Henrie Bucchenham.
	Sept.	18.	Henrie sonne of Hester Bardwell, singlewoman.
	Oct.	14.	Robert sonne of John Cutmare.
	Dec.	11.	Ursula the daughter of John Godfrie.
	Dec.	26.	Alice the daughter of John Godfrie the miller.
	Jan.	6.	William the sonne of Thomas Scot.
	Feb.	12.	Clement the sonne of Richard Sillet.
	Feb.	16.	Thomas the sonne of John Edmondes.
1587.	April	30.	John the sonne of William Fuller.
	Julie	16.	Thomas the sonne of William Sawier.
	Oct.	8.	John the sonne of Robert Larner.
	Oct.	8.	Margaret the daughter of James Sillet.
	Nov.	23.	Marie daughter of William Barton.
	Jan.	21.	Margaret the daughter of John Eddouse.
	Jan.	28.	Richard the sonne of Peter Diggel.
	Feb.	18.	Margaret the daughter of Henrie Mahue.
1588.	April	8.	Marie the daughter of William Page,
	&		Marie the daughter of Philip Newegate.
	Maie	12.	Marie the daughter of John Godfrie the miller.
	Maie	19.	John the sonne of James Maio.
	Oct.	6.	Ann the daughter of John Foorde.
	Dec.	2.	Edward sonne of William Barom.
	Dec.	8.	Mary daughter of Thomas Scot.
	Dec.	15.	Elizabeth daughter of Nicholas Friet.
	Feb.	17.	Christopher the sonne of Thomas Norman.
1589.	June	22.	John the sonne of John Godfrie the miller.
	Julie	6.	John the sonne of Clement Lucas gent.
	Sept.	13.	James the sonne of James Sillet.
	Oct.	5.	Henrie the sonne of Nicholas Bucchenham.
	Oct.	12.	Robert the sonne of Thomas Rogers.
	Dec.	21.	Merri-woe daughter of John Godfrie th' elder.

	Dec.	21.	Bridget the daughter of Henrie Mahue.
	Feb.	15.	Agnes the daughter of Robert Larner.
	Feb.	22.	Elizabeth daughter of Richard Smith.
	March	1.	John the sonne of William Sawier.
1590.	April	26.	Edward sonne of Peter Diggle.
	June	28.	Marie the daughter of John Godfrie of litle Hor:
	Julie	12.	Agnes the daughter of Richard Dearson.
	Oct.	11.	Elizabeth daughter of John Eddouse.
	Jan.	17.	William the sonne of Holofernes Tolar.
	Jan.	24.	John the sonne of Thomas Norman the yonger.
	Feb.	7.	Bridget the daughter of William Page.
	March	14.	John the sonne of William Fishen.
	March	21.	Amie daughter of John Foorde.
1591.	April	25.	Margaret the daughter of John Calowe
	Maie	2.	Joan the daughter of William Fynn.
	Maie	16.	Clement sonne of Clement Lucas gent.
	Sept.	19.	Lettes the daughter of Thomas Scot.
	Nov.	21.	Agnes the daughter of Barnabie Lilly.
	Jan.	15.	Ann the daughter of Gregorie Birchinal.
	Jan.	22.	Marie daughter of John Godfrie the millar.
1592.	April	9.	John the sonne of Henrie Mahue.
	Oct.	8.	Robert the sonne of Robert Newegate.
	Nov.	5.	John the sonne of James Sillet.
	Dec.	17.	Marie the daughter of Richard Dearson.
	Jan.	21.	Eedie the daughter of William Barom.
	Feb.	5.	John the sonne of Barnabie Lilly.
	March	10.	Rose the daughter of Peter Diggle.
1593.	April	8.	Gilbert sonne of Holofernes Tolar.
	April	29.	Roger the sonne of William Sawier.
	Sept.	16.	Robert the sonne of Robert Adams.
	Nov.	11.	Alice daughter of John Foorde.
	Dec.	30.	John the sonne of William Page.
	Feb.	25.	Robert sonne of Henrie Mahue.
1594.	Aug.	11.	John the sonne of Edmund Haward.
	Jan.	5.	Thomas the sonne of James Sillet.

	Feb.	9.	William the sonne of Robert Lilly.
	March	23.	Elizabeth daughter of Barnabie Lilly.
1595.	May	25.	Richard the sonne of Richard Dearson.
	June	1.	Ann daughter of Austin Cooper.
	June	8.	Frauncis daughter of William Cowel.
	Julie	6.	Ann daughter of William Fishen.
	Aug.	17.	Edmond sonne of Thomas Garret.
	Sept.	28.	Richard sonne of John Godfrie the miller.
	Dec.	7.	Alice the daughter of Edmond Haward.
	Feb.	last.	John the sonne of John Foord.
1596.	March	28.	Rose the daughter of Henrie Mahue.
	Nov.	21.	William the sonne of John Lilly.
	Feb.	13.	Thomas the sonne of Robert Lilly.
	March	13.	Alice the daughter of Thomas Pilgrime.
1597.	Maie	8.	Bridget the daughter of Barnabie Lilly.
	Julie	13.	William the sonne of William Barom the yonger.
	Oct.	16.	Elizabeth daughter of William Cowel.
	Oct.	29.	William the sonne of Edmund Haward.
	Nov.	13.	Philips the sonne of James Sillet.
	Dec.	26.	Robert sonne of William Barom th' elder.
	Feb.	5.	John the sonne of John Lilly.
	Feb.	19.	William the sonne of William Fishen.
	March	5.	William the sonne of Henrie Mahue.
1598.	Maie	28.	Robert the sonne of John Foord.
1599.	April	2.	Susan daughter of Edmund Haward.
	April	22.	Joane the daughter of Barnabie Lilly.
	Maie	6.	Thomas the sonne of John Lilly.
	Maie	17.	Agnes the daughter of Katharine Fynn, singlewoman.
	Aug.	19.	Marie the daughter of William Barom the yonger.
	Oct.	21.	Barbara the daughter of Henrie Haward.
	Dec.	9.	William the sonne of William Cowel.
	Feb.	10.	Elizabeth the daughter of Robert Lilly.
	March	9.	Marie the daughter of Henrie Mahewe.
1600.	April	13.	Barbara the daughter of William Fishen.
	Aug.	3.	Thomas the sonne of Robert Breate.

	Aug.	17.	William the sonne of Richard Deareson.
	Sept.	28.	Frauncis the daughter of John Godfrie.
	Oct.	5.	Richard the sonne of James Sillet.
	Oct.	27.	Edward the sonne of John Lillie.
	Jan.	11.	John the sonne of John Engoll.
	Feb.	15.	Marie the daughter of John Foorde.
	March	15.	Richard the sonne of Barnabie Lillie.
1601.	April	14.	William the sonne of Robert Newegate.
	Maie	17.	John the sonne of Edmond Haward.
	June	21.	Robert the sonne of Thomas Moore.
	Aug.	23.	Susan the daughter of William Emmyns.
	Dec.	17.	James the sonne of James Baldwin.
	Jan.	10.	Ann the daughter of Thomas Bull.
1602.	April	25.	Elizabeth the daughter of Henrie Mahewe.
	June	3.	John the sonne of Robert Breate.
	June	10.	Richard the sonne of George Steagle.
	June	26.	Margerie the daughter of Thomas Stanton of Hardwyke.
	Dec.	5.	Alise the daughter of Henrie Haward.
	Feb.	20.	John the sonne of Henrie Froste.
	March	19.	Susan the daughter of John Foorde,
	&		Bridget the daughter of John Lillie.
1603.	Maie	22.	John the son of Robert Lillie.
	Julie	24.	Marie the daughter of William Haward.
	Julie	31.	Sebastian the sonne of James Sillet.
	Oct.	30.	Henry the sonne of William Fishen.
	Nov.	23.	Elizabeth the daughter of William Emmyns.
	Dec.	26.	Edmund the sonne of Edmund Haward.
	Feb.	14.	Harveie the sonne of William Rookes.
	Feb.	16.	Rose the daughter of John Engoll.
	Feb.	26.	Frederick the sonne of John Godfreie.
	March	5.	Bridget the daughter of John Adams.
1604.	April	25.	Marke the sonne of John Dysing.
	May	1.	Susan the daughter of John Lillie.
	May	13.	Edward the sonne of Robert Newegate.
	May	20.	Bridget the daughter of Thomas Bull.

	June	24.	Luke the sonne of Henrie Mahewe.
	Nov.	15.	Debora the daughter of Robert Emyns.
	Dec.	23.	Ann the daughter of Stephen Godfrie.
1605.	May	19.	Thomas the sonne of William Cowel.
	Julie	7.	Sara the daughter of William Bull.
	Nov.	17.	George the sonne of George Jaques.
	Nov.	24.	Elizabeth the daughter of Edmund Haward.
	March	17.	Richard the sonne of John Lilly.
1606.	Sept.	14.	William the sonne of William Page.
	Oct.	5.	Thomas the sonne of William Baron.
	Oct.	19.	Bacchavil the sonne of John Cheston.
	Oct.	26.	William the sonne of Henrie Haward.
	Nov.	16.	John the sonne of Theodore Walker.
	Nov.	16.	Robert the sonne of John Dysing.
	Feb.	1.	Bridget the daughter of Edward Sillet.
1607.	April	19.	Mary the daughter of John Lilly.
	May	26.	Alse the daughter of Ambrose Gouldsmith.
	May	31.	Bridget the daughter of Robert Everet.
	Aug.	9.	Martha the daughter of Edward Godfreie.
	Nov.	8.	Robert the sonne of Thomas Bull.
	Feb.	last.	Bridget the daughter of Robert Lilly.
1608.	March	28.	Elizabeth the daughter of Steeven Godfreie.
	April	3.	Margaret the daughter of John Cheston.
	April	23.	Henry the sonne of Thomas Stanton.
	Maie	15.	Bridget the daughter of Fraunces Manning a singlewoman.
	Maie	25.	Ann the daughter of William Page.
	Maie	29.	Thomas the sonne of George Jaques.
	Oct.	16.	Edward the sonne of Edward Sillet.
	Nov.	30.	Ann the daughter of Isaac Trumble.
	Dec.	11.	Martha the daughter of Robert Brett.
	Feb.	5.	Ann the daughter of John Lillie.
	Feb.	12.	Martha the daughter of William Varvie.
	Feb.	27.	Jane the daughter of John Engol.
1609.	March	25.	Ann the daughter of George Stegol.
	April	19.	Lucie the daughter of William Lucas gent.

	April	23.	Rose the daughter of Robert Everard.
	Maie	21.	John the sonne of Roger Howton.
	Sept.	3.	William the sonne of William Lynge.
	Sept.	17.	George the sonne of John Bucchenam.
	Oct.	1.	Margaret the daughter of Edward Godfrey.
	Nov.	19.	Harry the sonne of Ambrose Goldsmith.
	Nov.	26.	Jone the daughter of John Silvester.
	Jan.	14.	Susan the daughter of William Fishon.
	Jan.	18.	Harrie the sonne of Ambrose Blagge esq.
	Feb.	11.	Henry the sonne of Henry Howe.
	Feb.	25.	Alse the daughter of Alse Frost singlewoman.
1610.	April	9.	Eede the daughter of Theodore Walker.
	May	20.	Rose the daughter of John Langley.
	June	3.	John the sonne of William Simondes.
	Dec.	9.	William the sonne of William Bailie.
	Feb.	7.	Elizabeth the daughter of William Baron.
	Feb.	17.	Elizabeth the daughter of William Vardie.
1611.	April	14.	Dorothie the daughter of John Bucchenham.
	April	28.	Mary & Susan the daughters of Edmund Haward.
	Maie	8.	Christian the daughter of William Lucas gent.
	June	25.	George the sonne of Ambrose Blagge esq.
	Julie	4.	Francis the sonne of Edward Sillet.
	Aug.	4.	Margaret the daughter of Robert Lillie.
	Oct.	6.	Eedie the daughter of Theodore Walker.
	Jan.	5.	Dorothie the daughter of Edward Godfrie.
	March	1.	Audrie the daughter of John Lillie.
	March	20.	Joseph the sonne of Henrie Howe.
1612.	April	13.	Margaret the daughter of William Page the yonger.
	Maie	20.	Sara the daughter of Edmund Barbar.
	June	14.	William the sonne of William Bayly.
	Julie	5.	John the sonne of Ambrose Goldsmith.
	Aug.	9.	John the sonne of William Lyng.
	Aug.	30.	Mary the daughter of John Engol.
	March	7.	Frauncis the sonne of William Varvie.
	March	25.	Joane the daughter of John Bucchenham.

1613.	May	23.	Christian the daughter of John Lilly.
	Julie	13.	Thomas the sonne of Ambrose Blagge esq.
	Sept.	12.	Margaret the daughter of Edward Sillet.
	Sept.	19.	Robert the sonne of William Page the yonger.
	Feb.	13.	Theodore the sonne of Edmund Haward.
	March	10.	Thomas the sonne of William Lucas esq.
1614.	April	17.	Margaret the daughter of Thomas Cropley.
	April	25.	Martha the daughter of William Fishon.
	Maie	1.	Judith the daughter of Edward Godfreie.
	Julie	31.	James the sonne of Stephen Godfreie.
	Sept.	25.	Robert the sonne of Henrie Wellom.
	Oct.	16.	Elizabeth the daughter of William Bayly.
	Oct.	23.	Thomas the sonne of John Dysing.
	Nov.	20.	Thomas the sonne of Thomas Talbot.
	Nov.	22.	Katarine the daughter of Ambrose Blagge esq.
	Dec.	11.	Thomas the sonne of Thomas Bull.
	Feb.	12.	John the sonne of John Bucchenham.
	Feb.	26.	Robert the sonne of Ambrose Goldsmith.
1615.	Julie	11.	Harrie the sonne of Edmund Haward.
	Sept.	7.	Elizabeth the daughter of Robert Houghton.
	Sept.	17.	Elizabeth the daughter of John Engol.
	Oct.	1.	Marie the daughter of Edward Sillet.
	Nov.	19.	Hannah alias Anna the daughter of William Skott.
	Dec.	3.	Richard the sonne of John Drue.
	Dec.	17.	Marie the daughter of William Page.
	March	5.	Gipson sonne of William Lucas Esquire.
1616.	April	17.	Elizabeth out of the house of William Verve.
	July	18.	William Croply.
	Nov.	17.	Sara the daughter of Edward Godfry.
	Nov.	19.	Susan the daughter of Thomas King.
	Jan.	23.	John the sonne of William Verve.
	March	9.	Alice the daughter of William Bayly.
1617.	Aug.	28.	Elizabeth the daughter of Gregory Borham.
	Sept.	14.	Thomas the sonne of Henry Welham.
	Sept.	28.	William the sonne of Robert Manning.

	Oct.	12.	William the sonne of Ambrose Goldsmith.
	Nov.	2.	Simon the sonne of Edmund Hayward.
	Jan.	4.	Thomas the sonne of Edward Payne.
	Jan.	11.	Elizabeth the daughter of Thomas Wiffin.
	March	1.	Thomas the sonne of Richard Dearson.
	March	15.	Thomas the sonne of John Ingold.
1618.	March	31.	Thomas the sonne of Edward Syllet.
	May	1.	Robert the sonne of Robert Howton.
	May	10.	Bridget the daughter of Stephen Godfry.
	May	28.	Thomas the sonne of William Page.
	Dec.	28.	Robert the sonne of Robert Steward.
	Feb.	7.	John the sonne of John Cheston.
	Feb.	14.	Robert the sonne of Thomas Talbot.
	Feb.	14.	Elizabeth the daughter of Richard Church.
	March	21.	Ambrose the sonne of William Bedell.
1619.	May	2.	Rebekah the daughter of Edward Godfry.
	May	27.	Susan the daughter of William Vervie.
	June	9.	Sarah the daughter of Robert Spark.
	June	16.	Anne the daughter of Ambrose Blagg Esq.
	July	28.	William the sonne of William Lucas Esq.
	Oct.	10.	Amy the daughter of John Buckenham.
	Dec.	5.	William the sonne of William Wiffin.
1620.	April	4.	Mary the daughter of Nicholas Barber gent.
	April	17.	Jacob the sonne of Henry Howe.
	May	7.	Anne the daughter of William Bayly.
	May	14.	John the sonne of William Cole.
	June	9.	John the sonne of Richard Dearson.
	Oct.	15.	Thomas the sonne of Ambrose Goldsmith,
	&		Thomas the sonne of Alice Frost.
	Nov.	5.	John the sonne of Edward Payne.
	Nov.	22.	Judith the daughter of Ambrose Blagg Esq.
	Dec.	21.	Richard the sonne of William Page.
	Jan.	14.	Elizabeth the daughter of Edward Sillet.
	Jan.	31.	Mary the daughter of Robert Spinck.
1621.	May	10.	Lydia the daughter of William Lucas Esq.

	May	13.	Alice the daughter of Thomas Bull.
	May	20.	William the sonne of William Toller.
	June	3.	Susan the daughter of Robert Howton.
	July	6.	Grace the daughter of John Fiston.
	July	17.	Henrie the sonne of Edward Godfry, at home.
	July	29.	Susan the daughter of Robert Steward.
	Aug.	9.	Martha the daughter of William Sadleton.
	Oct.	14.	Etheldred or Audry the daughter of Edmund Hayward.
	Oct.	21.	Henry the sonne of Thomas Talbot.
	Nov.	4.	Nicholas the sonne of John Buckenham.
	Dec.	2.	John the sonne of John Gedge.
	Feb.	17.	Anne the daughter of Gilbert Toller.
	Feb.	26.	Nicholas the sonne of Nicholas Barber gent.
	March	5.	Mary the daughter of Robert Sparke.
	March	17.	William the sonne of John Ingold.
	March	23.	Martha and Mary the daughters of Vincent Handler.
1622.	March	31.	Susan the daughter of Henry Howe.
	Sept.	4.	Elizabeth the daughter of James Wiard.
	Sept.	8.	Frances the daughter of William Baylie.
	Sept.	22.	Sara the daughter of Edward Mason.
	Oct.	20.	John the sonne of John Larner.
	Oct.	26.	Martha the daughter of Ambrose Blagge Esquire.
	Jan.	1.	Jane the daughter of Robert Spinck.
	Jan.	26.	John the sonne of John Guy.
	Feb.	16.	Holophernes the sonne of William Toller,
	&		Joane the daughter of Edward Payne.
1623.	April	3.	Bridget the daughter of Richard Sillet the younger.
	April	14.	Mary the daughter of Vincent Handler.
	Oct.	1.	Thomas the sonne of Thomas Hempsted.
	Nov.	2.	Anne the daughter of Ambrose Goldsmith.
	Jan.	11.	Edward the sonne of Edward Godfry.
	Feb.	15.	John the sonne of Edward Sillet.
1624.	April	11.	Robert the sonne of Robert Hood.
	April	18.	Elizabeth the daughter of John Bokenham.
	April	25.	John the sonne of John Church.

	April	27.	Anne the daughter of Nicholas Barber gent.
	May	2.	Anne the daughter of Edmund Hayward.
	July	4.	William the sonne of John Fiston.
	Aug.	13.	Humfry the sonne of Ambrose Blagge Esquire.
	Sept.	12.	Mary the daughter of Robert Steward,
	&		Joane the daughter of Gilbert Toller.
	Oct.	6.	Henry the sonne of Richard Deareson.
	Oct.	17.	William the sonne of Robert Howton.
	Oct.	31.	William the sonne of Thomas Talbot.
	Nov.	3.	Sarah the daughter of Samuel Allen.
	Nov.	7.	Thomas the sonne of Francis Redgwell.
	Dec.	16.	Jasper the sonne of William Lucas Esquire.
	Dec.	28.	Vincent the sonne of Vincent Handler.
	Jan.	2.	Robert the sonne of John Ingold.
	Feb.	6.	Anne the daughter of George Wiffin.
	Feb.	27.	Robert the sonne of Robert Sparke.
	March	15.	James the sonne of James Wiard.
	March	20.	Robert the sonne of William Towler.
1625.	March	25.	William the sonne of John Gedge.
	May	1.	Dorothe the daughter of Richard Sillet.
	May	15.	John the sonne of John Spark.
	June	19.	Margaret the daughter of Robert Booty.
	Sept.	20.	William the sonne of John More.
	Sept.	30.	William the sonne of Thomas Cornish.
	Oct.	5.	Mary the daughter of William Ruggle.
	March	19.	Anable the daughter of Robert Adams.
1626.	April	12.	Thomas the sonne of Robert Spinck.
	April	25.	Katherine the daughter of Robert Cooke.
	May	9.	Marie the daughter of William Lucas Esq.
	May	29.	James the sonne of John Hayward.
	June	12.	Ambrose the sonne of Ambrose Blagge Esq.
	Sept.	6.	Christian the daughter of Robert Sparke.
	Sept.	10.	Lidia the daughter of Samuel Allen.
	Sept.	17.	Marie the daughter of Edward Godfry.
	Jan.	6.	Edward the sonne of Edward Payne,

1627.	May	15.	Marie the daughter of John Fiston.
	July	25.	William Covill.
	Aug.	26.	John Cooper and John Redgin.
	Sept.	9.	William Ruggles.
	Sept.	27.	Elizabeth Dearson.
	Dec.	23.	Leah Ingold.
	Jan.	24.	Henry the sonne of James Wiard.
	March	13.	Thomas the sonne of Thomas Bret.
1628.	May	8.	William the sonne of Robert Spinck.
	May	25.	William the sonne of Edward Payne.
	June	3.	Richard the sonne of Richard Sillet.
	June	15.	John the sonne of John Hayward.
	Sept.	2.	Elizabeth daughter of Robert Steward.
	Oct.	26.	John sonne of John Titmouse,
	&		Elizabeth daughter of John Titmouse,
	&		Anne daughter of Robert Cooke.
	Nov.	30.	Henry sonne of Ambrose Blagge.
	Dec.	10.	Alice daughter of William Covill.
	Feb.	1.	Mary daughter of Thomas Tabott.
1629.	April	16.	Alese daughter of Robert Sparke.
	May	10.	John the sonne of John Fiston.
	June	7.	Grace the daughter of Robert Adames.
	Sept.	13.	Josias the son of John Write.
	Nov.	1.	John the son of William Ruggles.
	Dec.	6.	Alice daughter of Vincent Handler.
	Jan.	1.	Robert the son of Robert Spinke.
	Feb.	7.	Rodger the son of Ambrose Mayes.
1630.	April	7.	Edmund sonne of Ambrose Blague.
	May	2.	Robert sonne of Edward Godfree.
	May	11.	Elizabeth daughter of Richard Cooper.
	July	12.	Edmund the sonne of John Hayward.
	Aug.	17.	William the sonne of James Wyard.
	Aug.	22.	Edward the sonne of Edward Payne.
	Sept.	5.	Marie the daughter of Richard Derson.
	Nov.	11.	Elizabeth daughter of William Covell.

	Nov.	19.	William sonne of Henery Chapman.
	Dec.	22.	George the sonne of George Kiddington.
	March	4.	An the daughter of Fredericke Godferye.
1631.	May	4.	Thomas the sonne of Robert Cotton.
	May	29.	Francis the daughter of Robert Cooke.
	June	5.	Mary the daughter of Robert Spinke.
	June	19.	Susan Rouleson.
	Aug.	7.	Samuel the sonne of William Ruggle.
	Sept.	28.	Katharine the daughter of Robert Sparke.
	Dec.	3.	Thomas the sonn of Thomas Parker.
	Dec.	4.	Edward the sonne of Edmund Hayward.
	Feb.	9.	Marie the daughter of Henry Sillet.
	Feb.	26.	John the sonne of John Wright.
1632.	May	26.	Bridget the daughter of Bridget Bull.
	Aug.	4.	Stephen the sonn of Stephen Wiffen.
	Jan.	1.	Ann the daughter of Richard Cooper.
	Feb.	10.	Ann the daughter of Henry Sillet.
	Feb.	24.	Marie the daughter of Gilbert Towler.
	March	24.	Josias the son of William Stanfeild.
1633.	April	7.	Ann daughter of John Fisson.
	May.	7.	Hester the daughter of James Wyard.
	June	11.	William the sonn of John Hayward.
	Aug.	18.	Martha the daughter of Paul Adames.
	Aug.	25.	Lydia the daughter of Richard Dearson.
	Sept.	29.	Margaret the daughter of Robert Spinke.
	Oct.	2.	Robert the sonne of George Kerington.
	Oct.	13.	John the sonn of Robert Adames.
	Feb.	2.	Ralph the son of William Prior.
1634.	April	3.	William the son of Vincent Handler.
	April	10.	Edward the son of John Sparke.
	April	20.	Abigall the daughter of Robert Cooke.
	April	24.	Robert the son of Robert Sparke.
	May	4.	Marie the daughter of William Ruggles.
	Julie	23.	Thomas the sonne of William Covill.
	Oct.	19.	John the sonne of William Bumsterd.

	Dec.	14.	John the sonne of John Eurn.
	Feb.	1.	Joane the daughter of Henery Sillet.
1635.	April	5.	James the sonne of James Drumm.
	April	16.	Dorothy the daughter of Stephen Wiffen.
	May	17.	Jane the daughter of Jane Ingoll.
	May	31.	Edward the sonne of Edward Payne.
	June	2.	Marie the daughter of Richard Cooper.
	June	18.	Thomas the sonne of Thomas Chinnery.
	Aug.	19.	Thomas the sonne of James Wiarde.
	Oct.	25.	William the sonne of Paul Addams.
	Nov.	22.	George the sonne of John Hayward.
	Dec.	1.	Margaret the daughter of Ambrose Blagge Esq.
1636.	April	13.	Abigall the daughter of George & Susan Adkin.
	April	29.	Anne the daughter of Robert & Frances Spinke.
	June	5.	Robert the sonne of Robert & Grace Addames.
	July	6.	William the sonne of John & Frances Euen.
	Sept.	18.	Martha the daughter of Thomas & Anne Brewster.
	Oct.	18.	John the sonne of Thomas & Adry Chinery.
	Nov.	9.	Anne the daughter of William & Alice Covell.
	Jan.	22.	Henry the son of Thomas & Joane Parker.
	Jan.	26.	John the son of Robert & Barbarie Turner.
	March	12.	Robert the son of Robert & Bridget Cooke.
	March	19.	Elizabeth the daughter of Thomas & Elizabeth Wellam.
1637.	Oct.	22.	Martha the daughter of William & Elizabeth Rugle.
	Nov.	8.	Martha the daughter of Edmund & Martha Astey.
	Nov.	30.	Elizabeth the daughter of Thomas & Anne Brewster.
	Jan.	21.	Richard the sonne of Robert & Margaret Goodrick.
	Feb.	16.	William the sonne of Thomas & Margaret Godfrie.
	March	18.	Lawrence the sonne of John & Barbarie Hayward.
1638.	April	14.	John the son of William & Alice Covell.
	May	13.	Thomas the son of George & Susan Adkin.
	June	17.	Mary the daughter of John & Frances Ewen.
	July	3.	Frederick the son of Robert & Frances Spinke.
	July	.	Gyles the son of Edmund & Amye Hayward.
1639.	March	8.	Anne the daughter of Robert & Margaret Goodrick.

	July	7.	Henry the son of Stephen & Elizabeth Wiffen.
	Aug.	14.	John the sonne of Thomas & Margaret Godfrie.
	Aug.	25.	Thomas son of John & Triphena Sore.
	Feb.	2.	Francis sonne of Thomas & Priscilla Talbot.
	March	8.	Frances daughter of John & Frances Ewen.
	March	13.	Susan daughter of Thomas & Jone Parker.
	March	22.	Richard son of Robert & Bridget Cooke.
1640.	April	19.	Edward son of Edward & Grace Finsham.
	April	26.	Thomas son of Thomas & Adric Chinery.
	May	18.	Thomas sonne of Robert & Margaret Goodrick.
	June	14.	Thomas sonne of William & Rose Manning.
	Jan.	12.	Francis daughter of William & Francis Nunne.
	Jan.	23.	Anne daughter of William & Elizabeth Bernard.
	Jan.	24.	Elizabeth daughter of William & Elizabeth Ruggles.
	March	14.	Martha daughter of Robert & Frances Spinke.
1641.	April	1.	Robert son of Robert & Margaret Goodricke.
	May.	1.	John son of George & Susan Adkin.
	June	13.	Barbarie daughter of John & Frances Euin.
	June	29.	Elizabeth daughter of Robert & Mary Bilham.
	June	30.	Zara daughter of Thomas & Elizabeth Wiffin.
	Aug.	5.	Edward sonne of Edward & Grace Finsham.
	Feb.	20.	Sicely daughter of Thomas & Jone Parker.
	March	6.	William sonne of William & Rose Manning.
	March	20.	Margaret daughter of John & Margaret Smithe.
1642.	Aug.	10.	Frances daughter of Robert & Elizabeth Sparrow.
	Aug.	19.	Margaret daughter of Robert & Margaret Goodrick.
	Nov.	1.	Sarah daughter of Robert & Sarah Goldsmith.
	Dec.	4.	James sonne of John & Triphyna Sore.
	Dec.	14.	Anne daughter of Abraham & Anne Coppin.
	Jan.	28.	Frances daughter of Edmund & Alice Talbot.
	Feb.	20.	William sonne of William & Dorcas Hammond.
1643.	May	7.	Anne daughter of William & Rose Manning.
	May	17.	Anne daughter of Thomas & Adrie Chinery.
	July	25.	James sonne of John & Barbara Ewyn.
	Aug.	7.	William sonne of Gibson & Elizabeth Lucas

	Sept.	4.	Henery sonne of Robert & Margaret Goodrick.
	Sept.	20.	Rebecca daughter of Edward & Grace Finsham.
	Oct.	20.	Samuel sonne of Robert & Bridget Cooke.
	Jan.	4.	William sonne of Ambrose & Elizabeth Goldsmith.
	Jan.	13.	John sonne of John & Margaret Smith.
	Feb.	22.	Susan daughter of Clement & Elizabeth Heigham.
	March	24.	Thomas sonne of Thomas & Elizabeth Reggin.
1644.			Rebecca daughter of Jane Engold.
	May	16.	Dorcas daughter of William & Dorcas Hammond.
	July	25.	Anne daughter of William & Mary Towler.
	Sept.	5.	Frances daughter of John & Frances Ewen.
	Oct.	3.	Elizabeth daughter of Robert & Elizabeth Sparrow.
	Jan.	1.	Elizabeth daughter of Robert & Margaret Goodrick.
	Jan.	29.	Margaret daughter of Thomas & Elizabeth Parker.
	Feb.	21.	William sonne of William & Rose Manning.
1645.	April	27.	Margaret daughter of Edward & Grace Finsham.
	May	18.	Susan daughter of John & Susan Noble.
	May	27.	Benjamin sonne of John & Triphæna Sore.
	July	30.	Margaret daughter of Richard & Martha Gipps.
	Aug.	22.	Benninfield sonne of Clement & Elizabeth Heigham.
	Sept.	7.	Anne daughter of John & Katharine Senning.
	Dec.	15.	Jeremy sonne of Henry & Frances Sparrow.
	Dec.	17.	Anne daughter of Robert & Sarah Goldsmith.
	Jan.	4.	Thomas sonne of John & Margaret Smith.
	Feb.	12.	Joane daughter of Thomas & Joane Bennold.
	March	1.	Nathaniel sonne of Robert & Margaret Goodrick.
	March	22.	James sonne of William & Dorcas Hammond.
1646.	April	16.	Gibson sonne of Gibson & Elizabeth Lucas.
	May	3.	Susan daughter of Thomas & Elizabeth Wiffen.
	May	3.	Francis sonne of Thomas & Elizabeth Reggin.
	June	5.	Richard sonne of Richard & Martha Gipps.
	July	16.	James sonne of James & Alice Linge.
	Oct.	12.	William sonne of William & Mary Towler.
	Oct.	12.	Jonathan sonne of John & Frances Ewen.
	Nov.	22.	Sarah daughter of William & Rose Manning.

	Jan. 15.	William sonne of Clement & Elizabeth Heigham.
	Jan. 18.	Sarah daughter of Edward & Grace Fensham.
1647.	March 31.	Thomas sonne of Thomas & Elizabeth Parker.
	April 17.	Christian daughter of Gibson & Elizabeth Lucas.
	Aug. 12.	John sonne of Richard & Martha Gipps.
	Sept. 5.	Robert sonne of Robert & Elizabeth Sparrow.
1648.	March 26.	Mary daughter of William & Dorcas Hammond.
	May. 7.	Thomas son of Thomas & Elizabeth Reggin.
	Aug. 10.	Robert sonne of John & Margaret Smith.
	Sept. 22.	Caleb son of Thomas & Mary Sillet.
	Oct. 22.	Ellen daughter of Edward & Grace Finsham.
	Oct. 22.	Hannah daughter of Henry & Francis Sparrow.
	Dec. 9.	Elizabeth daughter of John & Elizabeth Ewen.
	Dec. 26.	Thomas son of Thomas & Hester Gardner.
	Jan. 21.	Thomas son of Thomas & Joan Bennold.
	Feb. 15.	John son of Robert & Margaret Goodrick.
	Feb. 20.	Elizabeth daughter of Thomas & Elizabeth Parker.
	Feb. 21.	Robert son of Robert & Sarah Goldsmith.
1649.	Dec. 12.	Richard son of Gibson & Elizabeth Lucas.
	Feb. 3.	Vincent son of William & Marie Towler.
1650.	March 26.	Thomas son of Richard & Martha Gipps.
	April 10.	William son of William & Susan Goldsmith.
	May 9.	Joshua son of Thomas & Mary Sillet.
	May 13.	Edward son of Arthur & Susan Goodchild.
	June 6.	Lawrence son of Lawrence & Alice Border.
	Sept. 10.	John son of Thomas & Sarah Wadkin.
1651.	March 13.	Christopher son of William & Elizabeth Prick.
	April 10.	Vincent son of Vincent & Barbara Handler.
	April 17.	Rose daughter of William & Rose Manning.
	June 8.	Elizabeth daughter of Richard & Martha Gipps.
	June 11.	Philip daughter of John & Philip Cowper.
	Aug. 14.	Thomas son of Gibson & Elizabeth Lucas.
	Sept. 21.	Elizabeth daughter of Thomas & Elizabeth Ridgin.
	March 4.	Edmund son of Edmond & Mary Hayward.
1652.	May 13.	James son of James & Margaret Wyard.

June 17. Thomas son of Robert & Sarah Goldsmith.
June 18. George son of Richard & Martha Gipps.
Aug. 24. Elizabeth daughter of John & Philip Cowper.
Oct. 15. Edward son of Thomas & Hester Gardiner.
Oct. 15. John son of John & Rebecca Smith.
Feb. 16. Mary daughter of Thomas & Mary Sillet.
Feb. 19. Mary daughter of Edward & Grace Finsham.
Feb. 20. Christian daughter of Gibson & Elizabeth Lucas.
March 6. Margaret daughter of William & Marie Towler.
1653. March 24. Marie daughter of Henry & Joane Godfrie.
Sept. 15. Richard son of Richard & ——— Sillet.
Nov. 3. Thomas son of Thomas & Marie Goldsmith.
Nov. 24. Sarah daughter of Thomas & Sarah Wadkin.
Dec. 1. Christian daughter of Edward & Grace Finsham.
Jan. 16. Anne daughter of William & Joane Handler.
Feb. 3. Judith daughter of Robert & Margaret Goodrick.
——— Thomas son of John & Rebeccah Smith.
March 22. Rose daughter of Thomas & Elizabeth Ridgin.
[Torn.] daughter of Thomas & Cadman.
1654. July 6. Elizabeth daughter of James & Margaret Wyard.
Aug. 1. Martha daughter of Richard & Martha Gippes.
Sept. 28. Robert son of Robert & Anne Towler.
Nov. 7. Elizabeth daughter of Josiah & Ester Wright.
Jan. 6. John son of Gibson & Elizabeth Lucas.
Jan. 6. Thomas son of Thomas & Elizabeth Skinner.
Feb. 1. Edward son of Edward & Elizabeth Godfrey.
Feb. 5. John son of John & Philip Cowper.
March 1. Mary daughter of William & Susan Goldsmith.
March 4. Anne daughter of John & Dorothy Hayward.
1655. June 15. Mary daughter of William & Rose Manning.
Jan. 13. William son of William & Joane Handler.
Jan. 23. John son of William Prick.
Jan. 25. John son of John & Mary Manteau.
Feb. 4. Holofernes son of William & Mary Towler.
March 23. John son of Thomas & Elizabeth Ridgin.

1656. June 22. James sonne of Josiah & Esther Wright.
Aug. 3. Elizabeth daughter of William & Elizabeth Guttridge.
Aug. 14. Mary daughter of Richard & Martha Gippes.
Aug. 15. Clement son of Gibson & Elizabeth Lucas.
Sept. 23. Mary dauter of Thomas & Mary Gouldsmith.
Oct. 5. Rebeccah daughter of John & Rebeccah Steward.
Nov. 5. Katharine daughter of Thomas & Katharine Sergeant.
Dec. 8. John son of John & Jane Gervase.
Jan. 12. Henry son of Thomas & Elizabeth Skinner.
1657. April 26. Susan daughter of William & Susan Goldsmith.
May 10. Joseph son of Henry & Jone Godfrey.
Aug. 21. Elizabeth daughter of Thomas & Mary Wellam.
Sept. 27. Isaac son of John & Margaret Smith.
Feb. 7. Alice daughter of Robert & Sarah Goldsmith.
Feb. 16. Elizabeth daughter of Richard & Martha Gippes.
March 21. Sache son of Gibson & Elizabeth Lucas.
1658. Aug. 12. Sherman son of John & Mary Manteau.
Jan. 6. William son of Thomas & Elizabeth Skinner.
Jan. 6. Sarah daughter of John & Marie Robinson.
March 4. Thomas son of Thomas & Katharine Sergeant.
1659. April 26. Anne daughter of William & Elizabeth Guttridge.
Aug. 19. Margaret daughter of James & Margaret Wyard.
Sept. 30. John son of John & Philip Cooper.
Oct. 10. Frederick son of John & Jane Jarvis.
Nov. 2. Esther daughter of Josias & Esther Wright.
Nov. 26. Martha daughter of Henry & Joane Godfrey.
Jan. 2. George son of Robert & Anne Kerrington.
March 20. Sulyard son of Mr. Valentine & Jane Gipps.
1660. April 13. Mary daughter of John & Dorathy Hayward.
Nov. 1. Walter son of William & Elizabeth Prick.
1661. June 2. Samuel son of John & Jane Jarvis.
July 28. Elizabeth daughter of William & Susan Goldsmith.
Aug. 25. Sarah daughter of Thomas & Elizabeth Skinner.
Oct. 6. Charles sonn of Gibson Lucas, Professor of Theologie, and Elizabeth his wife.

	Dec.	1.	Edward son of Edward & Katharine Fincham junior.
	Jan.	4.	George son of Mr. Valentine & Jane Gipps.
1662.	May	19.	Anne daughter of William & Mary Towler.
	May	29.	Richard son of John & Philip Cowper.
	June	29.	Thomas son of Josias & Esther Wright.
	July	13.	Mary daughter of Robert & Sarah Goldsmyth.
	Oct.	19.	Leah daughter of Thomas & Leah Manning.
	Nov.	2.	Robert son of John & Joan Gervase.
	Nov.	5.	Robert son of Robert & Anne Kerrington.
	Jan.	12.	Mary daughter of John & Mary Manteau.
	March	12.	John son of William & Mary Covell.
	March	22.	Thomas son of William & Mary Godfry.
1663.	April	10.	John son of John & Mary Robinson.
	May	21.	Mary daughter of William & Elizabeth Gutteridge.
	Aug.	8.	James & Gricyll, children of James & Gricyll Bland.
	Oct.	22.	Susan daughter of Roger & Susan Baker.
	Oct.	28.	Edward son of John & Joan Gervase.
	Jan.	8.	Clement son of Gibson Lucas, Professour of Divinity, & Elizabeth his wife.
	March	11.	Margaret daughter of Thomas & Leah Manning.
	March	13.	John son of John & Dorothy Hayward.
1664.	April	22.	William son of William & Mary Godfry.
	May	1.	Elizabeth daughter of Thomas & Elizabeth Spurling.
	Aug.	21.	Henry son of Henry & Joan Godfrey.
	Oct.	6.	Ann daughter of Mr. William & Mary Covell.
	Oct.	11.	Ambrose son of William & Susan Goldsmyth.
	Nov.	18.	Robert son of Thomas & Catherin Sergeant.
	Dec.	2.	Margaret daughter of Josias & Hester Wright.
	Jan.	6.	Ann daughter of Robert & Ann Kerrington.
	Jan.	12.	Elizabeth daughter of Henry & Elizabeth Wiffen.
	Jan.	30.	Robert son of Thomas & Elizabeth Skinner.
1665.	April	5.	Paul sonn of William & Alice Addames.
	April	12.	Edmund sonn of Thomas & Marie Everred.
	May	29.	Marie dauter of Gipson & Elizabeth Lucas.
	July	4.	Susan dafter of William & Susan Herrington.

	Aug.	21.	Ann dauter of Larrance & Ann Womack.
	Sept.	9.	Frances dauter of William & Elissibeth Ewen.
	Nov.	6.	Hannah dauter of William & Hannah Wyerd.
	Dec.	1.	Steven son of Thomas & Elisebeth Spurlin.
	Jan.	13.	Margeret daughter of Thomas & Margeret Adkin.
1666.	March	30.	William son of William & Elisibeth Goodritch.
	June	1.	Hinry son of Hinry & Jone Godfry.
	Oct.	5.	Ann dauter of William & Faith Spinke.
	Nov.	7.	Mary dauter of John & Phillup Cooper.
	Nov.	7.	Elisebeth dauter of William & Elisibeth Ewen.
	Dec.	6.	Thomas sonn of William & Mary Covell.
	Dec.	21.	Thomas sonn of William & Mary Godfry.
	Dec.	28.	Margeret dawter of Hinry & Elisibeth Wiffen.
	Jan.	20.	John sonn of William & Susan Goldsmith.
	Feb.	2.	Mary dauter of Roger & Mary Baker.
	Feb.	25.	Thomas sonn of Thomas & Margaret Wiffon.
	March	2.	Josias sonn of Josias & Ester Wright.
1667.	April	6.	Rebecke dauter of John & Dorythye Heywerd.
	April	12.	John sonn of John & Frances Noble.
	May	7.	Elisebeth dauter of William & Susan Herrington.
	Sept.	23.	William sonn of William & Hannah Weyerd.
	Sept.	3.	John sonn of William & Elisebeth Ewen.
	Sept.	20.	Mary dauter of Robert & Ann Kerington.
	Oct.	17.	Susan dauter of Thomas & Margeret Adken.
	Nov.	17.	Frances sonn of Frances & Frances Frost.
	Jan.	18.	William sonn of William & Cristian Cater.
	Feb.	14.	Edmund sonn of Edmund & Mary Hemsted.
1668.	May	10.	Elisebeth dauter of John & Frances Noble.
	June	21.	John sonn of Thomas & Elisebeth Scinner.
	July	24.	Allce dauter of John & Allce Smith.
	Aug.	28.	Josyas sonn of Josyas & Ester Right.
	Sept.	7.	Ritchard sonn of William & Mary Covell.
	Oct.	8.	William sonn of William & Susan Herrington.
	Jan.	15.	Frances dauter of William & Hannah Weyerd.
1669.	May	9.	John sonn of John & Margeret Ewen.

	Sept.	26.	Steven son of John & Priscilla Cooper.
1671.	June	13.	Thomas son of Robert & Ann Kerrington.
	Sept.	14.	Rachel daughter of William & Hannah Wiard.
	Oct.	1.	Christian daughter of William & Elizabeth Ewen.
	Nov.	21.	Richard son of William & Mary Covell.
	Jan.	30.	William son of William & Susannah Lilly.
	Feb.	2.	Robert son of William & Susannah Goldsmith.
	Feb.	12.	Mary daughter of George & Elizabeth Cadney.
	March	5.	Elizabeth daughter of Thomas & Elizabeth Skynner.
	March	15.	John son of John & Alice Smith.
1672.	June	29.	William son of John & Priscilla Cooper.
1673.	May	8.	Mary daughter of John & Margarett Almond.
	Sept.	8.	Richard son of Thomas & Margarett Wiffin.
	Jan.	1.	Susannah daughter of William & Elizabeth Ewen.
	Jan.	2.	Thomas son of Thomas & Anne Chinery.
	Jan.	18.	Mary daughter of Lawrence & Anne Perkins.
	Jan.	22.	Grace daughter of George & Mary Nelson.
	March	2.	Anne daughter of John & Anne Peachy.
	March	22.	Abigail daughter of Thomas & Margarett Atkins.
1674.	March	29.	Alice daughter of William & Alice Adams.
	May	24.	Hannah daughter of John & Margarett Ewen.
	June	12.	Margarett daughter of William & Susan Lilly.
	June	21.	James son of Edmund & Mary Hemsted.
	July	12.	Anne daughter of Thomas & Anne Jaggard.
	Oct.	30.	Anne daughter of John & Mary Robinson.
	Nov.	3.	George son of George & Elizabeth Cadney.
	Jan.	24.	Anne daughter of William & Elizabeth Ewen.
	Feb.	21.	Gibson son of William & Margarett Lucas.
	March	7.	William son of Josias & Hester Wright.
	March	7.	Mary daughter of Thomas & Bridgett Chinery.
1675.	April	24.	Elizabeth daughter of William & Mary Prigg.
	May	7.	Mary daughter of Thomas & Elizabeth Skinner.
	July	18.	Thomas son of William & Christian Cater.
	Aug.	15.	Mary daughter of Thomas & Anne Chinery.
	Sept.	17.	James son of William & Hannah Wiard.

Dec. 27. Katharine daughter of John Skelton Esq. & the Lady Payton, his wife.
Dec. 28. Mary daughter of John & Joan Hockle.
1676. April 9. Martha daughter of John & Martha Noble.
May 23. Lawrence son of Lawrence & Elizabeth Howard.
May 26. John son of William & Anne Newport,
& Elizabeth daughter of John & Margarett Ewen.
July 1. William son of Thomas & Margarett Wiffin.
Aug. 26. William son of William & Mary Prigg.
Aug. 27. Alice daughter of William & Elizabeth Ewen.
Sept. 12. John son of Lawrence & Anne Perkins.
Oct. 12. Elizabeth daughter of William & Anne Lucas.
Dec. 12. Anne daughter of Thomas & Bridgett Chinery.
Dec. 14. Elizabeth daughter of Henry & Elizabeth Gray.
Jan. 28. Elizabeth & Susannah, twin daughters of John & Joan Hockly.
Feb. 8. Sarah daughter of James & Sarah Ewen.
Feb. 10. John son of Thomas & Margarett Atkins.
March 6. Thomas son of William & Hannah Wiard.
March 8. Thomas son of John & Anne Peachy.
March 13. Barbara daughter of Thomas & Barbara Ford.
March 17. Elizabeth daughter of George & Rose Jarrold.
1677. June 8. Thomas son of Thomas & Elizabeth Gardiner.
July 21. James son of William & Elizabeth Ewen.
Aug. 9. Martha daughter of George & Mary Nelson.
Oct. 18. Ellen daughter of Thomas & Elizabeth Ling.
Nov. 8. Mary daughter of William & Susannah Lilly.
Nov. 13. Christian daughter of William & Anne Lucas.
Nov. 15. John son of Lawrence & Elizabeth Howard.
Nov. 29. Susannah daughter of Thomas & Anne Chinery,
& William son of Edward & Susannah Cheavely.
Dec. 2. Mary daughter of Francis & Frances Frost.
Dec. 27. Richard son of Sir Richard & the Lady Elizabeth Gipps
Jan. 2. John & Elizabeth children of John & Margarett Arnold.
Jan. 22. Margarett daughter of Henry & Elizabeth Gray.

	Feb.	15.	Joseph son of William & Christian Cater.
	March	10.	Mary daughter of John & Martha Noble.
1678.	April	12.	Martha daughter of Thomas & Barbara Ford.
	April	13.	John son of John & Joan Hockly.
	May	9.	Abigail daughter of Lawrence & Anne Perkins.
	July		James son of James & Elizabeth Wiard of Ikworth.
	Sept.	10.	James son of William & Mary Prigg.
	Oct.	12.	Natthaniell son of Natthaniell & Anne Goodrick.
	Dec.	19.	Henry son of Henry & Elizabeth Gray.
	Jan.	30.	John son of William & Elizabeth Ewen.
	Feb.	13.	Sarah daughter of Thomas & Bridgett Chinery.
	Feb.	22.	Elizabeth daughter of John & Elizabeth Prigg.
	March	16.	Thomas son of Thomas & Elizabeth Ling.
1679.	June	5.	Elizabeth daughter of Sir Richard & the Lady Elizabeth Gipps.
	June	5.	Robert son of Robert & Anne Goldsmith.
	July	18.	Elizabeth daughter of Laurence & Elizabeth Howard.
	Nov.	10.	Francis sonne of Francis & Jone Hockley.
	Dec.	11.	Thomas son of Thomas & Barbara Ford.
	Dec.	28.	Grace daughter of George & Elizabeth Cadny.
	Jan.	16.	William son of William & Anne Lucas.
	Feb.	1.	John son of William & Susannah Lilly.
	Feb.	2.	Ralph son of William & Alice Adams.
	Feb.	8.	Anne daughter of ——— & Margaret Atkins.
	Feb.	25.	Elizabeth daughter of William & Christian Warren of Hargett house in Suffolke.
	March	11.	Sarah daughter of John & Anne Peachy.
1680.	Aug.	1.	Charles son of John & Martha Noble.
	Oct.	31.	Christian daughter of Robert & Anne Goldsmith.
	Jan.	23.	William sonne of Francis & Frances Frost.
	Jan.	31.	Edmund sonne of Anthony & Catharine Horrinx.
	Feb.	17.	Elizabeth daughter of Thomas & Elizabeth Ling.
	March	18.	Richard son of Thomas & Elizabeth Gardiner.
1681.	Aug.	13.	Susan daughter of Laurence & Ann Perkins.
	Sept.	11.	Elizabeth daughter of Thomas & Bridget Chinery.

	Jan.	3.	Katherine daughter of Sir Richard & Elizabeth Gibbs.
	Jan.	20.	Henry son of Henry & Mary Cosens.
	Feb.	9.	Leonard son of John & Martha Jackson.
1682.	March	26.	Robert son of Thomas & Ann Jaggard.
	May	22.	Thomas son of John & Martha Noble.
	May	26.	Georg son of Georg & Mary Nelson.
	June	6.	John son of Thomas & Elizabeth Garner.
	June	23.	Ann daughter of Robert & Ann Goldsmith.
	June	25.	Henry sonn of John & Mary Folkes.
	Aug.	16.	James sonn of John & Mary Reve.
	Oct.	16.	Thomas son of Thomas & Barbary Ford.
	Dec.	30.	William son of William & Elizabeth Alderton.
	Jan.	6.	Matthew son of William & Abigail Prick.
	March	18.	James son of John & Susan Wyers.
1683.	July	15.	Elizabeth daughter of Henry & Mary Cosens.
	Sept.	14.	Elizabeth daughter of Thomas & Elizabeth Ling.
	Oct.	9.	—— son of George & Mary [Cadny. ?]
	Nov.	24.	Margaret daughter of Thomas & Barbary Ford.
	Dec.	6.	Mary daughter of George & Rose Gerald.
	Jan.	24.	Thomas son of Thomas & Bridget Chinery.
1684.	March	25.	John son of William & Abagaile Prick.
	March	25.	Ann daughter of Thomas & Ann Chinery.
	March	30.	Mary daughter of Henry & Mary Folkes.
	April	3.	Chris: daughter of William & Elizabeth Alderton.
	April	18.	Edward son of Edward & Susan Hempstead.
	June	1.	Mary daughter of John & Ann Petchy.
	July	17.	Elizabeth daughter of John & Mary Reeve.
	Oct.	9.	Mary daughter of Thomas Smith, Rector, and Eleanor his wife.
	Dec.	11.	Sarah daughter of Thomas & Barbary Ford.
	Jan.	30.	Rose daughter of George & Rose Gerald.
1685.	July	21.	Hester daughter of Thomas & Bridget Chinery.
	Sept.	6.	Ann daughter of Robert & Leah Jarvis.
	Sept.	17.	Susan daughter of Edward & Susan Hempstead.
	Nov.	5.	John son of Richard & Susan Ernesby.

	Nov.	14.	Henry son of Henry & Mary Cosens.
	Nov.	24.	Robert son of Thomas & Elizabeth Ling.
	Dec.	13.	Elizabeth daughter of John Godfrey.
	March	22.	Elizabeth daughter of Thomas & Barbary Ford.
1686.	March	26.	James son of James & ——— Mortlock.
	June	2.	Thomas son of Thomas Smith, Rector, & Eleanor his wife.
	Aug.	26.	Elizabeth daughter of Thomas & Elizabeth How.
	Sept.	16.	John son of William & Elizabeth Alderton.
	Sept.	24.	Robert son of Robert & Leah Jarvis.
	Nov.	25.	John son of John & Mary Sparrow.
	Feb.	24.	John son of Edward & Susan Hempsted.
1687.	April	4.	Hester daughter of Richard & Susan Ernesby.
	July	31.	Mary daughter of John & Mary Reeve.
	Nov.	2.	Mary daughter of Edmund & ——— Willingham.
	Nov.	5.	Katherine daughter of Anthony & Katherine Hallux.
	Dec.	18.	Mary daughter of James & Mary Mortlock.
	Jan.	15.	Robert son of John & Martha Noble.
	Feb.	9.	Thomas son of Thomas & Bridget Chinery.
	Feb.	10.	John son of John & Lydia Godfry.
	Feb.	28.	Mary daughter of Thomas & Elizabeth How.
	March	2.	Robert son of William & Elizabeth Alderton.
1688.	May	24.	William son of John & Rachel Lait.
	June	22.	Ling Gibliddy. [?]
	July	5.	Charles son of William & Ann Lucas.
	July	27.	Robert son of Thomas Smith, Clerk, & Eleanor his wife.
	July	29.	Robert son of John & Ann Petchy.
	Aug.	30.	Hester daughter of Thomas & Elizabeth Gardiner.
	Sept.	4.	Thomas son of Henry & Mary Cosens.
	Oct.	30.	Ann daughter of Thomas & Elizabeth Wiffen.
	Dec.	20.	John son of John & Susan Clerke.
1689.	April	11.	Antony son of Thomas & Barbary Ford.
	May	20.	Michael son of James & ——— Mortlock.
	May	31.	Hannah daughter of William & Elizabeth Alderton.
	July	26.	Ann daughter of Edmund & Alice Bray.
	Aug.	4.	William son of John & Martha Noble.

	Aug.	6.	Mountjoy son of Edmund & Ann Rose.
	Aug.	16.	Sarah daughter of John & Sarah Wright.
	Dec.	5.	Thomas son of Edmund & —— Willingham.
	Dec.	12.	Frances daughter of Thomas & Elizabeth How.
	Jan.	4.	Mary daughter of Henry & Mary Cosens.
1690.	May	1.	Samuel son of Richard & Sarah Edgely.
	May	15.	Robert son of John & Susan Clerke.
	Aug.	9.	William son of William & Mary Herrington.
	Dec.	26.	Susanna daughter of Thomas & Elizabeth Ling.
1691.	April	3.	Thomas son of John & Susan Clerk.
	April	4.	Thomas son of Henery & Ann Sorrell.
	April	16.	Isaac son of Thomas & Bridget Chinery.
	Sept.	20.	Mary daughter of John & Susan Covell.
	Oct.	12.	Ann daughter of Thomas & Elizabeth How [?].
	Nov.	2.	Susan daughter of Robert & Susan Talbot.
	Nov.	26.	John son of John & ——. Hallux.
	Jan.	15.	Rachel daughter of John & Rachel Laite.
	Jan.	24.	Sarah daughter of Richard & —— Edgely.
	Jan.	30.	Thomas son of John & Ann Ling.
	Feb.	4.	Sarah daughter of William & Elizabeth Alderton.
	Feb.	7.	Antony son of Thomas Smith, Rector, & Eleanor his wife.
	March	13.	Else daughter of Edmund & —— Willingham.
1692.	March	27.	Samuel son of Samuel & Alice Bray.
	May	11.	William son of Henery & Mary Cosens.
	May	22.	John son of John & Susan Clerke.
	Oct.	6.	John son of Thomas & Ann Ling.
	Dec.	15.	Thomas son of Thomas & Elizabeth Wiffen.
	Jan.	22.	Frances daughter of Lewis & —— Mortlock.
	March	14.	Elizabeth daughter of Robert & Susan Talbot.
1693.	April		Hannah daughter of John & Hannah Wiseman.
	June	17.	William son of Theodore & Mary Wix.
	July	12.	Susan daughter of John & Susan Clerke.
	July	30.	Joseph son of Joseph Alexander, clerke, & Frances his wife.
	Aug.	17.	Susan daughter of Stephen & —— Cooper.
	Aug.	18.	Mary daughter of Thomas Smith, clerke, & Ellinor his wife.

	Nov.	24.	Sarah daughter of Thomas & Elizabeth How.
	Dec.	11.	Alice daughter of William & Elizabeth Alderton.
1694.	April	10.	Ann daughter of John & Ann Ling.
	Sept.	1.	Elizabeth daughter of Thomas & Elizabeth Gardner.
	Sept.	7.	Mary daughter of Robert & Ann Jaggard.
	Sept.	22.	Mary daughter of Edward & Sarah Parker.
	Sept.	27.	John son of John & Hannah Wiseman.
	Oct.	25.	Mary daughter of Henery & Mary Everade.
	Jan.	22.	Elizabeth daughter of William & Martha Cooper.
	Jan.	27.	Mary Robinson, a bastard child.
1695.	April	1.	Edmund son of Edmund & Mary Willingham.
	April	29.	Mary daughter of Elizabeth Bowes.
	May	17.	Hugh son of Hugh & Mary Pattle, farmer.
	June	—	Thomas son of John & Rachel Lait, labourer.
	June	16.	Laurence son of Thomas & Elizabeth Wiffen, labourer.
	July	21.	John Covel son of John & Elizabeth Kittle, farmer.
	July	24.	Mary daughter of Joseph & Mary Crowch, labourer.
	July	28.	Elizabeth daughter of Robert & Leah Jarvis, labourer.
	Oct.	7.	Jane daughter of Thomas Smith, clerke, & Eleanor his wife.
	Nov.	22.	Thomas son of Samuel & Alice Bray, labourer.
	Nov.	22.	Susan daughter of William & ——— Lilly, labourer.
	Dec.	6.	Frances daughter of Joseph & Frances Alexander, clerke.
	Dec.	12.	Mary daughter of Theodore & Mary Wix, woolcomber.
	Feb.	28.	John son of *James & Mary Mortlock, labourer.
1696.	April	3.	Elizabeth daughter of Richard & Elizabeth Elsden, woolcomber.
	May	31.	Rachel daughter of John & Susan Clerke, labourer.
	June [?]	4.	Thomas son of John & Hannah Wiseman, woolecomber.
	Aug.	29.	John son of John & Hannah Smith junior, labourer.
	Aug.	30.	Mary daughter of Henery & Elizabeth Cornwall, labourer.
	Oct.	19.	Hannah daughter of Thomas & Susan Wiseman, woolcomber.
	Oct.	22.	William son of William & Martha Cooper, labourer.
	Feb.	5.	Katherine daughter of John & Elizabeth Kittle, farmer.

*Called Lewis in the duplicate.

1451358

	Feb.	25.	Elizabeth daughter of John & Elizabeth Hern, labourer.
1697.	March	26.	Elizabeth daughter of Hugh & Mary Pattle, labourer.
	April	15.	Mary daughter of Joseph & Mary Bunting, labourer.
	May	16.	Sarah daughter of Edward & Sarah Parker, labourer.
	Aug.	8.	Elizabeth daughter of James & Elizabeth Frost, labourer.
	Aug.	9.	Mary Lilly, a bastard child.
	Aug.	31.	Isabella daughter of Richard & Elizabeth Elsden, labourer.
	Oct.	22.	John son of William & Elizabeth Newport, farmer.
	Nov.	19.	John son of John & Ann Wiseman, labourer.
	Jan.	9.	Mary daughter of Henery & Elizabeth Cornwall, labourer.
	March	7.	—— daughter of Edmund & Mary Willingham, labourer.
1698.	July	24.	Thory son of Thory [Theodore] & Mary Wix, woolcomber.
	Sept.	23.	Thomas son of John & Hannah Wiseman, woolcomber.
	Sept.	30.	James son of James & Elizabeth Frost, labourer.
	Oct.	30.	John son of William & Martha Cooper, labourer.
	Dec.	28.	Joseph son of Joseph & Mary Bunting, labourer.
	Jan.	3.	Elizabeth daughter of John & Elizabeth Kittle, farmer.
	Jan.	17.	Frances daughter of Henry & Frances Harvy, shipherd.
	Feb.	2.	Lewis son of James & —— Mortlock, labourer.
1699.	March	30.	Ann daughter of William & Elizabeth Newport, labourer.
	April	21.	Richard son of Richard & Elizabeth Elsden, woolcomber.
	May	12.	William son of William & —— Limmer, farmer.
	May	14.	Philip son of Henry & Elizabeth Cornwall, labourer.
	July	16.	John son of John & Else Bensted, labourer.
	July	30.	Sarah daughter of Samuel & Alice Bray, labourer.
	Aug.	27.	Francis son of Francis & Ann Frost, labourer.
	Oct.	18.	William son of Robert & Ann Potter, labourer.
	Dec.	17.	Mary daughter of Ambrose & Margaret Freind, labourer, [In the duplicate it is Ambrose Freeman.]
	Dec.	26.	Stephen son of Francis & Sarah Foreman, labourer.
	Feb.	4.	Elizabeth daughter of Edward & Sarah Parker, labourer.
	—	—	A child of Boss, labourer. [In Register of Births only.]
1700.	April	3.	Jonathan son of John & Susan Clerke, labourer.
	July	20.	John son of John & Alice Bensted, labourer.
	Aug.	—	Richard son of William & Martha Cooper, labourer.

	Aug.	30.	Richard son of Richard & Elizabeth Elsdon, labourer.
	Sept.	19.	Ann daughter of Robert & Ann Potter, labourer.
	Sept.	21.	Frances daughter of Henry & Frances Harvy, labourer.
	Sept.	26.	Mary daughter of John & Elizabeth Hern, labourer.
	Nov.	1.	Thomas son of John & Hannah Smith, labourer.
	Nov.	5.	John son of James & Elizabeth Frost, labourer.
	Nov.	22.	William son of William Lilly junior, labourer.
	Nov.	28.	Susan daughter of Henery & Elizabeth Cornwall, labourer.
	Jan.	30.	Francis son of Francis & Sarah Foreman, labourer.
	March	16.	Elizabeth daughter of Joseph Bunting, labourer.
	March	20.	Henry son of Henry & Martha Musket, tradesman.
	March	24.	Betty daughter of William and Elizabeth Newport, labourer.
1701.	July	10.	Mary daughter of John and Hannah Wiseman, woolcomber.
	Oct.	21.	Susanna daughter of John & Susan Clerke, labourer.
	Jan.	15.	William son of William & Martha Nicolls, labourer.
	Feb.	19.	William son of John & Alice Bensted, labourer.
	Feb.	22.	Samuel son of Samuel & Ann Battely, gentleman.
	March	7.	Susanna daughter of Henry & Elizabeth Cornwall, labourer.
	March	8.	Sarah daughter of Widow Petchy.
1702.	June	19.	Thomas son of Robert & Leah Jarvis, labourer.
	Sept.	9.	A daughter of Joseph Alexander, clerke. [Amongst births only.]
	Sept.	13.	Bridget daughter of John & Elizabeth Hern, labourer.
	Oct.	2.	Robert son of Robert & Ann Potter, labourer.
	Oct.	18.	Mary daughter of James & Mary Frost, labourer.
	Oct.	29.	A son of Ralf Adams, labourer. [Among births only.]
	Nov.	8.	Susan daughter of John & Martha Booman, shiphard.
	Nov.	20.	Daughter of Ambrose Freind, woolcomber. [Births only.]
	Nov.	29.	Ann daughter of Joseph & Mary Bunting, labourer.
	Dec.	30.	Mary daughter of William & Mary Harrington, woolcomber.
	Feb.	23.	Elizabeth daughter of Thomas and Elizabeth Wiffen, labourer.
1703.	April	12.	Susanna daughter of John & Sarah Pitches, labourer.
	May	2.	Mary daughter of Francis & Sarah Foreman, labourer.
	May	20.	Margat daughter of William Cooper, labourer,

	July	11.	Thomas son of Henry & Elizabeth Cornwall, labourer.
	July	22.	Mary daughter of Richard & Elizabeth Elsden, labourer.
	July	30.	Thomas son of Thomas & Elizabeth Bass.
	Sept.	12.	William son of William & Ann Hawes, labourer.
	Sept.	20.	Samuel son of Francis & Else Shaw.
	Oct.	17.	Sarah daughter of Edward & Sarah Parker, labourer.
	Oct.	24.	Elizabeth daughter of John & Carr Brooke, labourer.
	Nov.	11.	William son of William & Elizabeth Newport, labourer.
	Dec.	28.	Mary daughter of Robert & Mary Sandcroft.
	Dec.	7.	Thomas son of Henry & Amy How.
	Jan.	29.	Frank son of James & Elizabeth Frost, labourer.
	March	23.	Hannah daughter of John Ewen, farmer.
1704.	April	4.	Mary daughter of William & Margat Holland, labourer.
	May	11.	John son of William & Mary Harrington, woolcomber.
	June	13.	Ralfe son of Ralfe & Sarah Adams, labourer.
	Aug.	20.	Ann daughter of Francis & Ann Frost, labourer.
	Sept.	7.	Katherine daughter of John & Susan Clerke, labourer.
	Oct.	15.	Elizabeth daughter of Francis & Else Shaw, labourer.
	Nov.	12.	Samuel son of Joseph & Mary Bunting.
	Dec.	11.	Sarah & Elizabeth twin daughters of Robert & Mary Sondcroft.
	Dec.	21.	Ann daughter of Edward Forster, clerke, deceased, & Hester his wife.
	Jan.	22.	John & Elizabeth twins of Robert & Ann Potter.
	Feb.	11.	Elizabeth daughter of Thomas & Elizabeth Bass.
	Feb.	25.	James son of William & Ann Hawes.
	Feb.	26.	Thomas son of James & Elizabeth Frost.
1705.	May	28.	William son of John & Mary Rolfe.
	June	25.	Marian daughter of Ambrose & Margaret Freind.
	Aug.	3.	Edward son of Edward & Rachel Parker.
	Nov.	27.	Else daughter of Francis & Else Shaw.
	Jan.	23.	Dyllavera daughter of John & Ewen.
	Jan.	24.	Daniel son of Francis & Sarah Foreman.
	Feb.	2.	Charles son of John & Car Brooke.
1706.	April	11.	Thomas son of William & Elizabeth Newport.

	April	12.	Isabella daughter of Richard & Elizabeth Elsden.
	June	7.	John son of Ralfe & Sarah Adams.
	June	30.	Charles son of Charles Web.
	July	21.	John son of Francis & Ann Frost.
	Aug.	2.	Ann daughter of Robert & Ann Potter.
	Oct.	27.	Robert son of Robert & Mary Sondcroft.
	Nov.	10.	Thomas son of William & Ann Hows.
	Dec.	6.	Ann daughter of Thomas & Elizabeth Bass.
	Dec.	27.	John son of Edward & Rachel Parker.
	Dec.	31.	Francis son of Francis & Else Shaw.
	Feb.	22.	Richard son of Richard & Sarah Gardiner.
1707.	July	20.	Anthony son of Henry & Susan Smith.
	Aug.	14.	William son of John & Ann Ewen.
	Aug.	24.	——— — of John & Car Brooke.
	Aug.	28.	James son of Robert & Elizabeth Cooke.
	Sept.	21.	William son of James & Elizabeth Frost.
	Nov.	14.	Else daughter of Ralfe & Sarah Adams.
	Jan.	6.	Hannah daughter of John & Hannah Smith.
	March	12.	Hannah daughter of Edward & Rachel Parker.
	March	13.	Daniel son of Francis & Sarah Foreman.
1708.	April	2.	Samuel son of Robert & Ann Potter.
	June	17.	Ambrose son of Ambrose & Margaret Freind.
	Oct.	24.	John son of John Sparrow.
	Nov.	28.	Ann daughter of James & Ann Spalden.
	Jan.	28.	Ann daughter of Francis & Else Shaw.
1709.	April	18.	Richard son of Richard & Sarah Gardiner.
	Feb.	19.	Samuel Went, bastard child.
1710.	April	20.	George son of George & Susan Nellson.
	Sept.	3.	Ann daughter of Henry & Susan Smith.
	Sept.	21.	John son of John & Elizabeth Bray.
1711.	April	8.	Hannah daughter of Edward & Rachel Parker.
	April	24.	John son of Thomas & Rebecca Gardiner.
	June	30.	Gabriel Hallux, bastard child.
	July	29.	Rachel daughter of Ralf & Sarah Adams.
	Oct.	19.	Richard son of Francis & Sarah Foreman.

	Oct.	19.	Thomas son of John Sparrow.
	March	13.	Susan daughter of John & Ann Ewen.
1712.	July	6.	Robert son of John & Carr Brook.
	July	13.	John son of James & Elisabeth Frost.
	Aug.	14.	Elisabeth daughter of William & Elisabeth Harrington.
	Oct.	16.	Hannah daughter of John Sparrow.
	Dec.	30.	Mary daughter of Thomas & Mary Murton.
	Jan.	1.	Susanna daughter of Isaac & Susan Bartlet.
	Jan.	24.	Susan daughter of John & Susan Ong.
1713.	April	30.	Robert son of John & Elisabeth Bray.
	Sept.	6.	Henry son of Henry & Susan Cosens.
	Oct.	10.	Elisabeth daughter of William & Elisabeth Lait.
	Nov.	8.	Sarah daughter of Michael & Elisabeth King.
	Jan.	15.	William son of Edward & Rachel Parker.
	March	19.	Mary daughter of John & Ann Ewen.
1714.	April	14.	James & Mary, twin children of James & Ann Spalden.
	April	17.	Elisabeth daughter of —— & —— How.
	April	18.	James son of Francis & Sarah Foreman.
	Oct.	16.	John son of Henry & Susan Cosens.
	Dec.	28.	Hannah daughter of John & Susan Ong.
	Jan.	13.	William son of John & Elisabeth Bray.
	March	2.	Paul son of Ralf & Sarah Adams.
	March	4.	Francis son of Charlas Web.
1715.	May	15.	Elisabeth daughter of Thomas & Katherine Crack.
	May	23.	John son of Mr. John Battely, clerk, & Ann his wife.
	June	19.	Katherine daughter of Thomas Crack.
	June	26.	Robert son of Robert & Judeth Clerk.
	Oct.	11.	Robert son of Robert & Susan Pain.
	Nov.	27.	Elisabeth daughter of Josuah & Elisabeth Bunting.
	Feb.	19.	Sarah daughter of Edmund & Sarah Hempsted.
	March	15.	Elisabeth daughter of Henry & Susan Cosens.
1716.	April	12.	Samuel son of Mr. John Battely, Rector of Trorson, & Ann his wife.
	July	1.	Elisabeth daughter of John & Elisabeth Spicer.
	Aug.	10.	Isaac son of Isaac & Mary Chinery.

	Nov.	4.	John son of John & Susan Ong.
	Dec.	26.	Rachel daughter of William & Elisabeth Lait.
	Dec.	30.	Rebecca daughter of Thomas & Rebecca Gardiner.
	Feb.	8.	Elisabeth daughter of John & Ann Ewen.
	March	24.	Jonathan son of Edmund & Sarah Hempsted.
1717.	April	14.	Sarah daughter of John & Elisabeth Bray.
	June	29.	John son of Thomas & Katherine Crack.
	Oct.		Ann daughter of John & Ann Battely.
	Nov.	17.	Mary daughter of ——— How.
	Dec.	6.	John son of John & Elisabeth Spicer.
	Jan.	19.	Thomas son of Isaac & Mary Chinery.
1718.	May	12.	John son of John & Carr Brook.
	June	7.	Thomas son of Henry & Susan Cosens.
	July	24.	Mary daughter of Thomas & Mary Mortlock.
	Oct.	26.	Katherine daughter of Mr. John Battely, clerk, & Ann his wife.
	Nov.	16.	Thomas son of Joshuah & Elisabeth Bunting.
	Nov.	23.	Randal son of Edmund Lemmon.
1719.	April	26.	Mary daughter of John & Elisabeth Spicer.
	June	24.	Robert son of James Frost.
	Sept.	21.	Thomas son of Thomas & Katherine Crack.
	Oct.	10.	Elisabeth daughter of Robert & Susan Pain.
	Dec.	13.	Susan daughter of Henry & Susan Cosens.
	Dec.	17.	Susan daughter of William & Elisabeth Lait.
	Feb.	25.	Richard son of Francis & Else Shaw.
	Feb.	28.	Thomas son of Thomas & Frances How.
	March	10.	John son of Mr. John & Ann Battely.
	March	13.	William son of William & Ann Lias.
1720.	April	2.	Mary daughter of Stephen & Mary Lemmon.
	July	10.	Else daughter of Thomas & Else Willingham.
	Sept.	29.	Mary daughter of John & Elisabeth Bray.
	Oct.	2.	James & John, twin children of James & Mary Mortlock.
	Dec.	28.	Mary daughter of Henry & Susan Cosens.
	Jan.	6.	Rachel daughter of Robert & Judith Clerk.
1721.	June	15.	Charles son of John & Ann Battely.

	July	28.	John son of John & Mary Oatly.
	Sept.	21.	Susan daughter of George & Susan Nelson.
	Oct.	21.	Elisabeth daughter of Thomas & Else Willingham.
	Nov.	3.	Mary daughter of William & Mary Harvy.
	Dec.	14.	John son of William & Ann Oliver.
	Jan.	27.	Mary daughter of John & Marial Sparrow.
	March	18.	Ann daughter of William & Ann Lias.
1722.	April	14.	Mary daughter of Josuah Bunting.
	June	12.	Susan daughter of Robert & Susan Pain.
	Nov.	26.	William & Ann, twin children of William & Ann Oliver.
	Jan.	1.	——— son of John & Esther Clerk.
	Jan.	25.	Margat daughter of Edmund & Beatley Willingham.
	Feb.	11.	Katherine daughter of James & Mary Mortlock.
	Feb.	21.	William bastard child of Bridget Hern.
	March	6.	Ann daughter of Henry & Susan Cosens.
1723.	April	20.	Thomas son of John & Mary Oately.
	May	20.	Elizabeth daughter of John & Ann Battely.
	July	24.	Hugh son of Hugh & Mary Spencer.
	Nov.	13.	Thomas son of William & Elizabeth Lait.
	March	1.	Elisabeth daughter of John & Marial Sparrow.
1724.	Aug.	21.	Thomas son of William & Ann Oliver.
	Sept.	22.	Lewis son of James & Mary Mortlock.
	Oct.	11.	Mary daughter of Hugh & Mary Spencer.
	Dec.	31.	Mary daughter of John & Elisabeth Spicer.
	Jan.	30.	Mary daughter of John & Mary Oatly.
	Feb.	13.	Elisabeth daughter of Joseph & Frances How.
	March	20.	Thomas son of Thomas & Alice Willingham.
1725.	March	30.	Mary daughter of Edmund & Beatley Willingham,
	&		Thomas son of William & Elizabeth Lait.
	May	17.	Thomas son of Thomas & Elizabeth Pain.
	June	4.	John son of Thomas & Catherine Crack.
	June	25.	Eleanor Patridge daughter of William & Anne Lias.
	July	18.	Isabella daughter of William & Anne Oliver.
	Aug.	27.	Nicolas son of John & Anne Battely.
	Nov.	28.	John son of Samuel & Sarah Pond.

	Feb.	12.	Oliver son of John & Marial Sparrow.
	Feb.	24.	Hugh son of Hugh & Mary Spencer.
1726.	April	11.	Richard son of Richard & Jane Elsden.
	June	29.	Elizabeth (Gates),* a foundling.
	Dec.	28.	Jermyn son of John & Mary Symonds.
	Jan.	6.	Ann daughter of Thomas & Ann Pleasance.
	March	24.	Ann daughter of John & Elizabeth Spicer.
1727.	April	4.	John son of Richard & Mary How.
	April	20.	George son of William & Ann Oliver.
	April	27.	Mary daughter of William & Elizabeth Lait.
	May	11.	William son of John & Ann Battely.
	May	18.	Christian daughter of John & Mary Oatly.
	May	22.	Thomas son of James & Mary Frost.
	—	—	Elizabeth daughter of Thomas & Elizabeth Pain.
	Nov.	10.	John son of John & Christian Dykes.
	Jan.	7.	Susan daughter of Joshua & Elizabeth Bunting.
	Feb.	10.	John & Thomas, twin children of John & Mary Symonds.
	Feb.	12.	Rebecca Wymock, a child of Rebecca Wymock & Thomas Sergeant.
1728.	April	11.	Mary daughter of Thomas & Alice Willingham.
	June	16.	Ann daughter of John & Marial Sparrow.
	Nov.	16.	William son of Samuel & Sarah Pond.
	Jan.	29.	Mary daughter of John & Mary Symonds.
	Feb.	6.	Sarah daughter of William & Elizabeth Lait.
	March	3.	Thomas son of Thomas & Rose Gardiner,
	&		Elizabeth daughter of William Hempsted.
1729.	May	7.	John (Porch),† a foundling child.
	June	20.	Thomas son of Thomas & Ann Bird.
	June	22.	Christian daughter of John & Christian Dykes.
	Oct.	20.	Thomas son of Thomas & Mary Frost.
	Dec.	3.	Michael son of Michael & Hannah Houghton.
	Jan.	9.	Elizabeth daughter of James & Mary Frost.

* The name is in brackets in the original, and was probably given to the child from its being found at the Park or Church gates. See also May 7, 1729.—S. H. A. H.

† See June 29, 1726, and note.—S. H. A. H.

	Feb.	19.	Edmund son of Thomas & Alice Willingham.
	Feb.	19.	John son of John & Mary Symonds.
1730.	April	9.	Priscilla daughter of Thomas & Priscilla Cornwall.
	April	17.	Hannah daughter of Robert & Hannah Kendal.
	May	1.	Isabella daughter of Hugh & Mary Spencer.
	July	5.	Rose daughter of Thomas & Rose Gardiner.
	Jan.	28.	Timothy son of Samuel & Sarah Pond.
	Feb.	25.	George son of Richard & Elizabeth How.
1731.	April	6.	Robert son of Thomas & Elizabeth Pain.
	April	29.	Thomas son of Thomas & Ann Pleasance.
	June	8.	Potter son of William & Ann Frost.
	July	13.	Richard son of John & Sarah Miller,
	&		Robert son of Robert & Hannah Kendal.
	Aug.	10.	Thomas son of Rev[d] John Symonds & Mary his wife.
	Aug.	24.	William son of Richard & Jane Elsden,
	&		James son of John & Christian Dykes.
	Jan.	1.	Michael son of Michael & Hannah Howton.
	Jan.	8.	Susan daughter of John & Marial Sparrow.
	Feb.	20.	Robert son of Robert Brook & Rachel Willingham.
	Feb.	28.	Thomas son of Thomas & Mary Frost.
	March	22.	Elizabeth child of William Daniel & Elizabeth Brook.
1732.	April	3.	Mary daughter of James & Mary Frost.
	May	.	Sarah child of Thomas Till & Sarah How, both of Read.
	June	.	Mary daughter of Samuel and Sarah Pond.
	July	22.	John son of William & Elizabeth Lait.
	Sept.		Thomas son of Thomas & Ann Pleasance.
	Oct.	.	Mary daughter of Thomas Davers Esq. & Catharine his wife.
	Oct.	.	Ann daughter of William & Ann Frost.
	Jan.	.	Delariviere daughter of Rev.[d] John Symonds & Mary his wife.
	Feb.	.	Hannah daughter of Joseph & Mary How.
1733.	April	7.	Roger son of Thomas & Elizabeth Pain.
	June	19.	Hannah daughter of Robert & Hannah Kendal.
	Aug.	1.	Elizabeth daughter of Thomas & Priscilla Cornwell.
	Aug.	25.	John son of Thomas & Rose Gardner.

Sept. 1. Susan daughter of Robert & Elizabeth Daniel.
Feb. 16. John son of Thomas & Mary Frost.
1734. March 25. Robert son of William & Ann Frost.
June 10. Rachel daughter of Thomas & Rachel Marchell.
June 14. Mary daughter of Joseph & Mary How.
June 27. Elizabeth daughter of Samuel & Sarah Pond.
July 6. Frances daughter of James & Mary Frost.
July 14. Elizabeth daughter of John & Marial Sparrow.
July 25. James son of John & Mary Ottley.
Oct. 5. Elizabeth daughter of John & Elizabeth Hye of Thetford.
Jan. 12. John son of Rachel Willingham.
Feb. 15. John son of John & Margaret Hibble.
March 3. Thomas son of Richard & Jane Elsden.
March 8. Joseph son of Joseph & Elizabeth Hammond.
1735. April 20. James son of Robert & Hannah Greenwood.
April 24. Thomas son of Robert & Hannah Kendal.
April 30. Mary daughter of Thomas Davers Esq. & Catharine his wife.
May 26. John son of John & Mary Cook.
June 7. Zachariah son of Joseph & Mary How.
July 3. Elizabeth daughter of Thomas & Ann Pleasance.
Aug. 21. John son of Michael & Hannah Howton.
Oct. 16. William son of Thomas & Alice Willingham.
Dec. 11. William son of William & Ann Frost.
Jan. 27. Elizabeth child of Elizabeth Spicer.
Feb. 12. Mary daughter of John & Mary Brown.
March 19. Samuel son of John & Mary Otley.
1736. March 26. John son of David & Margaret Hill.
May 24. Thomas son of Thomas & Priscilla Cornwall.
July 17. Jane daughter of John & Margaret Hibble.
Aug. 7. George son of Stephen & Hannah Sparrow.
Sept. 9. Samuel son of Samuel & Sarah Pond.
Nov. 5. Robert son of Robert & Hannah Greenwood.
Nov. 29. Henrietta daughter of Thomas Davers Esq. & Catharine his wife.

	Dec.	2.	Abraham son of Giles & Sarah Tray.
	Dec.	10.	Mary daughter of Robert & Mary Jacob.
	Feb.	25.	Frances daughter of James & Mary Frost.
	Feb.	28.	Sarah daughter of John & Mary Cook.
1737.	April	2.	Mary daughter of Thomas & Mary Frost.
	April	17.	Joseph son of Joseph & Mary Cater.
	May	29.	William son of William & Susan Holden.
	Aug.	5.	Edward son of Edward & Isabella Woodruff.
	Nov.	24.	Susan daughter of Samuel & Sarah Pond.
	Nov.	27.	John son of John & Mary Brown.
	Dec.	27.	Elizabeth daughter of William & Ann Frost.
	Jan.	14.	William son of William & Elizabeth Cater.
1738.	April	3.	John son of Robert & Hannah Kendal.
	April	6.	Abraham son of Thomas & Priscilla Cornwell.
	May	5.	Sarah daughter of Thomas & Alice Willingham.
	May	27.	James son of Michael & Hannah Howton.
	July	20.	Martin son of William & Susan Holden.
	Aug.	6.	William son of John & Christian Dykes.
	Sept.	17.	William son of Thomas & Ann Pleasance.
	Oct.	16.	Mary daughter of Thomas Davers Esq. & Catharine his wife.
	Nov.	5.	Susan daughter of John & Mary Cook.
	Feb.	1.	Thomas son of Samuel & Sarah Firmin.
	Feb.	20.	William son of Joseph & Mary Cater.
1739.	July	12.	Mary reputed the base child of Elizabeth Warden.
	Aug.	11.	John son of John & Elizabeth Swan.
	Aug.	24.	John son of William & Susan Holden.
	—	—	Samuel son of Samuel & Sarah Pond.
	Oct.	14.	Edmund son of James & Mary Frost.
	Jan.	1.	Thomas son of Thomas & Diana Secker.
	Feb.	2.	Edmund son of William & Ann Frost.
	March	9.	William son of William & Ann Layt.
	March	21.	Valentine reputed the base child of Elizabeth Warden.
1740.	April	5.	Elizabeth daughter of John & Mary Brown.
	April	14.	John son of John & Ann Bray.
	May	15.	John son of John & Mary King.

May 22. William son of John & Elizabeth Wymock.
Oct. 11. Mary daughter of Thomas & Priscilla Cornwell.
Jan. 11. John son of Robert & Hannah Greenwood.
Feb. 15. Jane daughter of John & Mary Cook.
March 2. Timothy & Ann, twin children of Samuel & Sarah Pond.
March 5. James son of Joseph & Mary Cater.
March 13. Elizabeth daughter of William & Abigail Peach.
March 24. Edward son of Isaac & Mary Ely of Thurston.
1741. May 17. Elizabeth daughter of Robert & Mary Jacob.
June 23. Ann daughter of Charles Southgate.
Sept. 3. Diana daughter of Thomas & Diana Secker.
Nov. 22. Thomas son of William & Susan Holden.
Jan. 17. Mary daughter of John & Mary King.
Feb. 4. Anna Maria daughter of the Revd Dr Symonds & Mary his wife.
March 1. William son of John & Ann Bray.
March 12. Charles reputed the base child of Catharine Mortlock.
1742. March 26. William son of John & Mary Otley.
June 4. Rebecca daughter of Thomas & Rose Gardner.
June 8. Mary daughter of William & Ann Frost.
July 4. Elizabeth daughter of Richard & Elizabeth Cobbin.
Aug. 1. Stephen son of Stephen & Mary Leader.
Oct. 9. Ann daughter of Samuel & Sarah Pond.
Oct. 19. William son of William & Abigail Peach.
Jan. 10. Mary daughter of William & Ann James.
Jan. 18. Isabella daughter of Thomas Davers Esq. & Catharine his wife.
Jan. 20. Henry son of Thomas & Diana Secker.
Jan. 23. Hannah daughter of Thomas & Priscilla Cornell.
1743. June 24. Sarah daughter of Edward & Mary Roffe.
July 31. Robert son of Stephen & Mary Leder.
Sept. 11. Richard son of Richard & Elizabeth Cobing.
Sept. 22. William son of William & Ann Bunton.
Sept. 23. Mary daughter of Thomas & Mary Murton.
Sept. 29. Frances son of Joseph & Mary Cater.

	Oct.	2.	Henrietta Maria daughter of John & Mary King.
	Oct.	8.	John & Jane, children of John & Elizabeth Brown.
	Nov.	6.	Thomas son of Nathanael & Margaret Atkins.
	Jan.	13.	Elizabeth daughter of William & Elizabeth Cater.
	Feb.	12.	Thomas son of John & Ann Bray,
	&		Martha daughter of Samuel & Sarah Pond.
	Feb.	24.	Thomas son of Thomas & Elizabeth Elsden.
	March	1.	Mary daughter of John & Mary Cooper.
	March	2.	Susan daughter of William & Ann James.
1744.	April	1.	John son of William & Ann Frost.
	May	22.	Alice daughter of Thomas & Diana Secker.
	June	2.	Mary daughter of John & Elizabeth Swan.
	June	3.	Joseph son of Joseph & Mary How.
	July	8.	Charles son of Robert & Hannah Greenwood.
	Aug.	10.	Delariviere daughter of John & Rebecca Bunton.
	Sept.	29.	Susan daughter of William & Susan Lilly.
	Sept.	30.	Mary daughter of Michael & Hannah Houghton.
	Oct.	27.	Samuel son of George & Grace Avis.
	Dec.	28.	Thomas son of Charles & Sarah Southgate.
	Jan.	26.	Margaret & Mary daughters of Stephen & Mary Leader.
	Feb.	17.	Henry son of William & Abigail Peach.
1745.	June	8.	Samuel son of William & Susan Holden.
	June	27.	Philip son of Thomas & Priscilla Cornwall.
	June	29.	Edward son of Edward & Mary Roffe.
	July	23.	Sarah daughter of Thomas & Diana Secker.
	Sept.	20.	Elizabeth daughter of Thomas & Elizabeth Elsden.
	Oct.	1.	Ann daughter of Able & Ann Newman.
	Oct.	11.	Thomas son of Joseph & Mary Cater.
	Oct.	23.	John son of John & Rebecca Bunting.
	Jan.	6.	Robert son of William & Ann James.
	Feb.	15.	Thomas son of Thomas & Mary Murton.
	March	14.	John son of Richard & Elizabeth Cobbing.
1746.	March	29.	Henry son of William & Elizabeth Cater.
	July	11.	Bridget daughter of Castell & Susan Goodchild.
	July	27.	Mary daughter of George & Grace Avis.

	Sept.	21.	William son of Charles & Sarah Southgatt.
	Sept.	27.	Sarah daughter of John & Mary Brown.
	Dec.	7.	Sarah reputed child of Sarah May.
	Jan.	18.	Elizabeth daughter of Stephen & Mary Leader,
	&		Abigail daughter of William & Abigail Peach.
	Jan.	30.	Timothy son of Samuel & Sarah Pond.
	Feb.	23.	Hannah daughter of Robert & Hannah Greenwood.
	March	20.	Elizabeth daughter of Abel & Ann Newman.
	March	22.	Mary daughter of Edward & Mary Roffe.
1747.	May	16.	Thomas son of Thomas & Elizabeth Frost.
	June	11.	Francis son of John & Mary Cooper.
	July	30.	Sarah daughter of William & Ann Frost.
	Aug.	27.	Francis son of Edward & Susan Drew.
	Oct.	4.	Susan daughter of William & Susan Holden.
	Nov.	23.	Thomas Coppinger son of Thomas Moyle Esq. & Sarah his wife.
	Dec.	19.	Sarah daughter of Thomas & Mary Merton.
	Jan.	26.	William Jermyn son of William & Ann Gallant.
1748.	April	6.	Grace daughter of John & Grace Avis.
	Aug.	6.	George William son of Constantine Phipps Esq. & Lepel his wife.
	Oct.	9.	Hannah daughter of Christopher & Susan Rosbrock,
	&		Stephen son of Stephen & Mary Leader.
	Oct.	17.	John son of John & Mary Cater.
	Nov.	20.	William son of William & Elizabeth Hempstead.
	Dec.	30.	Thomas son of William & Elizabeth Cater.
	Jan.	27.	Amy Claudia Susanna daughter of Henry & ? Argent.
	Feb.	18.	Abel son of Abel & Ann Newman.
	March	6.	Elizabeth daughter of Thomas & Elizabeth Frost.
1749.	May	6.	Mary daughter of Oliver & Mary Sparrow.
	June	6.	John son of Edward & Susan Drew.
	June	13.	John son of George & Grace Avis.
	July	31.	Joseph son of William & Ann Gallant.
	Aug.	2.	Isabella daughter of Thomas & Sarah Moyle.
	Sept.	27.	Elizabeth daughter of John & Elizabeth Swan.

	Oct.	8.	Ann daughter of John & Mary Brown,
	&		Robert son of William & Abigal Pache.
	Oct.	30.	Ann daughter of John & Ann Miller.
	Dec.	22.	Thomas son of Thomas & Elizabeth Elsden.
	Jan.	23.	Francis son of Robert & Hannah Greenwood.
	Feb.	2.	Charlotte daughter of Thomas & Mary Mutton.
	March	22.	Catharine daughter of Francis & Jane Gooch.
1750.	April	1.	Thomas son of Stephen & Mary Leader.
	April	15.	Robert son of Edward & Mary Roffe.
	April	22.	Mary daughter of Robert & Mary Seaman.
	June	17.	Samuel son of Samuel & Lydia Dearsly.
	July	8.	Sarah daughter of Edmund & Sarah Payn.
	Sept.	23.	William son of William & Susan Holden.
	Nov.	3.	Elizabeth daughter of William & Elizabeth Hempstead.
	Nov.	4.	Mary daughter of Joseph & Mary Cater.
	Dec.	30.	Mary daughter of John & Rebecca Bunting.
1751.	(Henceforth the year begins on Jan. 1 instead of March 25. S. H. A. H.)		
	Jan.	11.	Elizabeth daughter of William & Ann Gallant.
	Jan.	12.	Elizabeth daughter of John & Elizabeth Swan,
	&		Sarah daughter of Edward & Susan Drew.
	Feb.	3.	Mary daughter of Francis & Elizabeth Talbot.
	Feb.	4.	Mary daughter of Thomas & Elizabeth Frost.
	March	29.	Mary daughter of William & Elizabeth Cater.
	April	4.	Elizabeth daughter of Samuel & Mary Turner.
	May	2.	Henry son of Joseph & Susan Prick.
	May	6.	Mary daughter of Giles & Mary Frost.
	July	20.	Edmund child of Ann Winney.
	July	22.	Sarah daughter of John & Ann Smith.
	Dec.	19.	William son of Samuel & Lydia Dearsley.
	Dec.	25.	Thomas child of Mary Hammond.
	Dec.	30.	John son of Stephen & Mary Leader.
1752.	Feb.	13.	Thomas son of James & Katharine Finch.
	March	29.	Martha daughter of John & Mary Brown.
	April	18.	Mary daughter of John & Ann Miller.
	April	20.	Thomas son of George & Grace Avis.

	May	22.	Thomas son of Thomas & Susan Allen.
	May	29.	Charles son of Robert & Mary Simmons.
	June	13.	Betty daughter of Edmund & Sarah Payn.
	Aug.	16.	Margaret daughter of William & Elizabeth Hempstead.
	Aug.	19.	Lyas son of Abel & Ann Numan.
	Oct.	1.	Charles son of Charles & Mary Vear.
	Nov.	6.	William son of Giles & Mary Frost.
1753.	Feb.	4.	James son of James & Mary Marchil.
	April	20.	John son of John & Ann Smith.
	June	24.	Frances daughter of Thomas & Elizabeth Frost.
	July	1.	Mary daughter of Edward & Susan Drew.
	Aug.	4.	Hannah daughter of William & Ann Gardiner.
	Sept.	9.	Hannah daughter of William & Hannah Smith.
	Sept.	2.	Elizabeth daughter of James & Katherine Finch.
	Oct.	18.	John son of John & Mary Brooks.
	Nov.	18.	John Dearson son of John Dearson Miller & Ann his wife.
	Dec.	11.	Rose daughter of Joseph & Susan Prick.
	Dec.	29.	Abraham son of Richard & Susan Smith.
1754.	Feb.	10.	Edmund son of Edmund & Sarah Willingham.
	Feb.	17.	Mary daughter of Robert & Mary Norman.
	Feb.	18.	Katherine daughter of Edmund & Sarah Payn.
	Feb.	19.	Margaret daughter of William & Elizabeth Hempstead.
	March	29.	Elizabeth child of Mary Smith.
	April	25.	Thomas son of Thomas & Alice Jackson.
	May	16.	Elizabeth daughter of William & Elizabeth Cater.
	June	23.	Humfrey & Frederick, sons of Charles & Mary Varow.
	June	27.	Elizabeth child of Susan Bunting.
	July	21.	William son of William & Ann Miller.
	Aug.	5.	William son of Edward & Mary Roffe.
	Oct.	1.	Martha daughter of Charles & Martha Abbot.
	Nov.	11.	Thomas son of John & Mary Brown.
	Nov.	17.	Alice daughter of Thomas & Mary Willingham.
	Dec.	6.	John son of William & Susan Osborn.
	Dec.	16.	William son of John & Susan Tweed.
1755.	Jan.	22.	William son of John & Rebecca Bunting.

Feb. 4. James son of James & Mary Marchil.
Feb. 28. James son of John & Ann Smith.
May 29. John son of Thomas & Susan Allen.
June 26. William son of William & Elizabeth Beleman.
Aug. 1. Giles son of Giles & Mary Frost.
Sept. 10. John son of John & Mary Thompson.
Sept. 29. Richard son of Richard & Susan Smith.
Oct. 25. George son of ye honourable & Revd Frederick Hervey & Elizabeth his wife.
Nov. 10. Joseph son of William & Hannah Smith.
Nov. 29. John son of Thomas & Elizabeth Frost.
Dec. 15. Robert son of Robert & Mary Norman.
1756. Jan. 18. Sarah daughter of James & Sarah Haselwood.
March 6. Richard son of Richard & Ann Crack.
March 12. Samuel son of William & Elizabeth Hempstead.
March 28. Mary daughter of Edmund & Sarah Payn.
June 13. Elizabeth Sibbellar daughter of Revd William & Susannah Tong.
July 8. Sarah daughter of William & Elizabeth Cater.
Sept. 25. Alice daughter of Joseph & Susan Prick.
Oct. 3. Thomas son of Edmund & Sarah Willingham.
Oct. 15. William son of William & Ann Miller.
Oct. 16. John son of William & Ann Miller.
Oct. 18. William son of John & Ann Smith.
Oct. 25. Mary daughter of Thomas & Mary Holden.
Nov. 27. Susan daughter of John & Susan Tweed.
1757. Jan. 29. John Augustus son of ye Honble & Revd Frederick Hervey & Elizabeth his wife.
March 13. Edmund son of Thomas & Mary Willingham.
April 25. Elizabeth daughter of John & Elizabeth Swan.
May 24. Mary daughter of James & Mary Marchil.
May 29. John son of William & Elizabeth Beleman.
June 4. Susan daughter of Oliver & Mary Sparrow.
June 5. Elizabeth daughter of Robert & Mary Norman.
July 8. Joseph son of John & Mary Thomson.

	July	10.	William son of Edward & Susan Drew.
	July	7.	Phebe daughter of Richard & Susan Smith.
	Oct.	13.	Susannah Maria daughter of Rev[d] M[r] & Susannah Tong.
	Oct.	22.	Mary daughter of Edmund & Sarah Payn.
1758.	Jan.	5.	James son of James & Sarah Haselwood.
	Feb.	12.	Mary daughter of Thomas & Mary Holden.
	March	21.	Thomas son of Thomas & Martha Bedell.
	March	25.	William son of Thomas & Elizabeth Frost.
	May	13.	Elizabeth Christiana daughter of ye Hon[ble] & Rev[d] Frederick Hervey & Elizabeth his wife.
	May	29.	Ann daughter of John & Elizabeth Swan.
	July	28.	Thomas & William sons of Joseph & Susan Prick.
	Aug.	13.	John son of William & Elizabeth Hempsted.
	Aug.	14.	Elizabeth daughter of Joseph & Margaret Hammond.
	Oct.	15.	Ann daughter of William & Ann Miller.
	Dec.	17.	Margaret daughter of John & Susan Tweed.
1759.	March	25.	John son of Richard & Susan Smith.
	May	29.	John son of Charles & Mary Varo.
	June	24.	William son of John & Sarah Smith.
	July	1.	Joseph son of James & Sarah Haselwood.
	July	15.	Simon son of Ambrose & Mary Sale.
	Sept.	16.	Abram son of Thomas & Ann Richardson.
	Nov.	11.	John son of James & Mary Marchil.
	Dec.	16.	George son of William & Elizabeth Cater.
	Dec.	27.	Mary daughter of Thomas & Mary Willingham.
1760.	March	16.	Elizabeth daughter of William & Ann Polly.
	March	23.	Nathanel son of Nathanel & Abigal Adkin.
	April	1.	Almond & Frances, twin daughters of Robert & Mary Norman.
	April	6.	Elizabeth daughter of William & Elizabeth Hempsted.
	April	13.	Benjamin son of Joseph & Susan Prick.
	April	20.	Sarah daughter of Richard & Sarah Ablot.
	May	11.	Elizabeth daughter of William & Elizabeth Billeman.
	May	18.	William son of Edmond & Sarah Willingham.
	June	1.	Joseph son of Joseph & Margaret Hammond.

	June	8.	John child of Jane Heble.
	June	11.	Sarah daughter of John & Susan Tweed.
	July	27.	James son of Thomas & Elizabeth Frost.
	Sept.	14.	Mary daughter of John & Mary Oswell.
	Oct.	10.	Ann daughter of Charles & Sary Rushbrook.
	Nov.	9.	Samuel son of Richard & Susan Smith.
	Dec.	24.	Susan daughter of Thomas & Sarah Houlden.
1761.	Feb.	27.	Martha daughter of Thomas & Martha Bedell.
	May	24.	Deborah daughter of William & Elizabeth Hempsted.
	June	7.	Thomas son of John & Sarah Smyth.
	June	29.	Frederick Clayton son of Frederick & Elizabeth Hervey.
	Oct.	4.	Robert reputed child of Susan Cook.
	Oct.	18.	Susan daughter of Thomas & Susan Allen.
	Oct.	25.	John son of John & Mary Adams.
	Nov.	15.	Edmund son of Edmund & Mary Pain.
	Dec.	25.	John son of Ambrose & Mary Seall.
	Dec.	27.	Mary daughter of James & Sarah Hazlewood.
1762.	Jan.	10.	Isaac reputed child of Elizabeth Jacob.
	Feb.	24.	Edmund son of Robert & Mary Norman.
	March	26.	Mary daughter of John & Susan Tweed.
	May	1.	William son of Richard & Susan Smyth.
	May	16.	Thomas son of Thomas & Ann Richarson.
	June	24.	William son of Thomas & Mary Willingham.
	July	4.	Rebecca daughter of John & Anne Rushbrook.
	Aug.	24.	Susan daughter of William & Susan Miller.
	Oct.	28.	Susan daughter of Nathaniel & Abigail Attkin,
	&		Sarah daughter of Thomas & Elizabeth Frost.
	Nov.	5.	Elizabeth daughter of Thomas & Elizabeth Sharp.
	Nov.	8.	Mary daughter of Joseph & Margaret Hammond.
	Dec.	25.	George Fuller reputed child of Elizabeth Pleasants.
1763.	Feb.	16.	Ann daughter of John & Sarah Smith.
	March	4.	William son of Robert & Sarah Frost.
	May	8.	Mary daughter of William & Elizabeth Billman.
	June	17.	Thomas Major son of Thomas & Mary Holden.
	July	1.	John reputed child of Susan Herrington.

	July	1.	Mary daughter of John & Mary Cooper.
	Aug.	8.	Lucy daughter of Joshua & Jane Grigby.
	Aug.	9.	Edward son of William & Mary Hempsted.
	Sept.	4.	Sarah daughter of John & Ann Rasbrook.
	Sept.	4.	Elizabeth daughter of Joseph & Susan Underwood.
	Oct.	9.	Susan daughter of Richard & Susan Smith.
	Oct.	23.	Robert son of Ambrose & Mary Sall.
	Oct.	30.	Joshua son of William & Susan Miller.
	Nov.	13.	John son of Thomas & Martha Bedell.
1764.	Feb.	24.	Elizabeth daughter of John & Elizabeth Bell.
	April	8.	John son of James & Sarah Haslewood.
	April	15.	Elizabeth daughter of Edmund & Sarah Willingham.
	May	6.	Mary daughter of Francis & Mary Smith.
	June	10.	John son of John & Susan Tweed.
	Aug.	16.	Martha daughter of Edmund & Mary Payne.
	Sept.	20.	Mary daughter of John & Mary Cooper.
	Sept.	21.	Stephen son of Isaac & Mary Brook.
	Oct.	17.	Charlotte daughter of William & Sarah Bray.
	Nov.	4.	John son of William & Martha Adams.
	Nov.	16.	George son of George & Sarah Challiss.
	Dec.	7.	John son of John & Mary Frost.
	Dec.	16.	Robert son of Robert & Ann Sutton.
1765.	Jan.	25.	James son of Ambrose & Mary Sall.
	Feb.	2.	Kitty daughter of Thomas & Elizabeth Frost.
	Feb.	3.	Charles son of Charles & Susan Rasbrook.
	Feb.	10.	John son of Thomas & Ann Richardson.
	Feb.	24.	Christopher son of Christopher & Elizabeth Rasbrook.
	March	17.	Thomas son of Richard & Susan Smith.
	March	31.	Elizabeth daughter of John & Sarah Smith.
	April	7.	James son of Thomas & Elizabeth Bird.
	May	31.	William son of Robert & Sarah Frost.
	June	16.	Thomas son of Thomas & Elizabeth Sharp.
	July	23.	Susan daughter of William & Susan Miller.
	Sept.	1.	Robert son of Richard & Elizabeth Smith.
	Oct.	13.	John son of Francis & Mary Smith.

Dec. 8. Thomas son of Robert & Mary Norman.
Dec. 9. James & Gardiner, sons of James & Rebecca How.
Dec. 15. Mary Margaret Elizabeth daughter of William & Mary Hempsted.
Dec. 22. Martha daughter of James & Martha Polle.
1766. Jan. 19. Sarah daughter of William & Sarah Bray.
Jan. 27. Ann daughter of John & Elizabeth Bell.
Feb. 3. Mary daughter of William & Ann Polle.
Feb. 6. William son of Joseph & Susan Underwood.
Feb. 28. Georgina Mary Caroline daughter of Andrew & Mary Fartier.
March 1. Lucy daughter of Thomas & Ann Durrant.
March 20. Sarah daughter of Thomas & Mary Holden.
April 27. Sarah daughter of George & Sarah Challice.
May 21. Elizabeth daughter of John & Elizabeth Bray.
May 25. John son of William & Mary Evett.
June 29. Jeremiah son of Christopher & Elizabeth Rashbrook.
July 8. Mary daughter of John & Mary Frost.
July 20. Edmund son of James & Martha Spolden.
Sept. 7. Thomas son of John & Susanna Tweed.
Sept. 14. Mary daughter of John & Mary Nun.
Sept. 19. Arabella daughter of Isaac & Mary Brookes.
Nov. 9. Samuel son of James & Mary Marshall.
Dec. 14. Joseph son of Joseph & Elizabeth Prick.
Dec. 25. John son of Thomas & Martha Beddell.
1767. Jan. 16. Ann daughter of Thomas & Elizabeth Sharp.
Jan. 22. Ann daughter of James & Sarah Haslewood.
Feb. 19. Samuel son of John & Sarah Smith.
March 25. James son of George & Margaret Sparke.
April 6. Robert son of Richard & Susanna Smith.
April 15. Hannah daughter of Thomas & Elizabeth Frost.
June 5. Ann daughter of Robert & Sarah Frost.
June 7. Betty daughter of John & Mary Cooper.
July 14. Thomas son of John & Sarah Gardiner.
Aug. 30. Elizabeth daughter of Charles & Martha Levit.
Sept. 13. Ann daughter of William & Ann Lillie.

	Sept.	20.	John son of Charles & Susan Rosbrook.
	Nov.	1.	Joseph son of John & Mary Frost.
	Nov.	22.	John son of John & Elizabeth Bray.
	Nov.	29.	Mary daughter of William & Mary Hempsted.
1768.	Jan.	11.	James son of James & Sarah Crack.
	Jan.	17.	Delaravier daughter of Thomas & Mary Willingham.
	Feb.	3.	Ann daughter of Thomas & Ann Orridge.
	Feb.	21.	Elizabeth daughter of Christopher & Elizabeth Rosbrook.
	March	5.	Sarah daughter of John & Mary Nunn.
	March	6.	Gardiner son of James & Rebecca How.
	March	20.	Susan daughter of Joseph & Susan Underwood.
	April	1.	John son of John & Constant Durrant.
	April	10.	Sarah daughter of Richard & Elizabeth Smith.
	April	17.	William son of Thomas & Ann Richardson.
	May	22.	Catharine daughter of Thomas & Elizabeth Bird.
	June	12.	John son of Henry & Elizabeth Cater.
	July	24.	Mary daughter of James & Martha Polle.
	July	25.	Nancy daughter of Isaac & Mary Brookes.
	Oct.	14.	Peter son of Peter & Elizabeth Pask.
	Nov.	20.	Lydia daughter of William & Sarah Bray.
	Nov.	27.	Mary daughter of John & Mary Frost.
	Dec.	4.	William son of John & Sarah Mariah Gardiner.
1769.	Jan.	7.	John son of Thomas & Ann Durrant.
	Jan.	8.	Mary daughter of John & Mary Adams.
	Jan.	12.	Ann Potter daughter of Robert & Sarah Frost.
	Jan.	29.	James son of Richard & Susanna Smith.
	Jan.	31.	William son of William & Susan Parsons.
	Feb.	5.	Hannah daughter of George & Sarah Challice.
	March	23.	George son of Rev[d] George & Elizabeth Rogers.
	March	29.	Martha daughter of James & Martha Pitt.
	April	23.	James son of Robert & Mary Norman.
	May	18.	Augustus William son of Andrew & Mary Fartier.
	June	4.	James son of John & Susan Tweed.
	June	18.	Mary daughter of John & Sarah Smith.
	July	2.	Ambrose son of James & Sarah Haslewood.

	July	23.	Mary daughter of Thomas & Elizabeth Sharpe.
	Sept.	24.	Sarah daughter of James & Martha Spolden.
	Oct.	8.	William son of Ambrose & Mary Sale,
	&		Charles child of Mary Fuller.
	Oct.	15.	Mary daughter of John & Elizabeth Bray,
	&		Hannah daughter of Christopher and Elizabeth Rosbrook.
	Nov.	11.	Richard reputed child of Sarah Death.
	Nov.	19.	Mary daughter of Thomas & Martha Beddell.
	Nov.	26.	Thomas son of John & Mary Frost.
	Dec.	11.	Edmund son of Edmund & Elizabeth Nunn.
1770.	Jan.	7.	William son of Henry & Elizabeth Cater,
	&		John son of John & Mary Nunn.
	Jan.	15.	Rose daughter of James & Rebecca How.
	Feb.	21.	Sarah daughter of Thomas & Ann Richardson.
	Feb.	24.	Sarah daughter of James & Mary Marshall.
	Feb.	25.	Sarah daughter of Joseph & Susan Underwood.
	March	1.	William son of Isaac & Mary Brookes.
	April	1.	Micah reputed child of Mary Boram.
	April	8.	Mary daughter of John & Mary Holden.
	May	20.	William son of William & Ann Lillie.
	June	3.	Elizabeth daughter of James & Martha Polle.
	June	4.	Susan daughter of Thomas & Elizabeth Frost.
	June	6.	Elizabeth daughter of Rev[d] George & Elizabeth Rogers.
	June	6.	John son of John & Sarah Frost.
	July	22.	Mary daughter of John & Sarah Browne.
	Aug.	3.	Daniel son of William & Susan Parsons.
	Aug.	5.	Thomas son of Thomas & Hannah Frost.
	Oct.	21.	Edward son of William & Mary Hempsted.
	Nov.	19.	John & Thomas, twin sons of James & Sarah Crack.
	Nov.	26.	Charlotte child of Elizabeth Pear.
	Dec.	2.	William son of John & Mary Frost.
	Dec.	9.	William son of William & Sarah Bray.
1771.	March	3.	John son of James & Rebecca How.
	March	17.	Ambrose son of James & Sarah Haslewood.
	March	26.	John son of John & Sarah Gardiner,

	March	26.	Elizabeth daughter of William & Susan Ransom.
	May	19.	Sarah & Ann daughters of John & Mary Cooper.
	June	9.	James son of James & Rebecca Pitt.
	June	1.	John & William, twin sons of George & Sarah Challice.
	June	15.	Robin son of Christopher & Elizabeth Rosbrook.
	June	16.	Samuel son of John & Mary Adams.
	Aug.	11.	Elizabeth daughter of John & Elizabeth Bray.
	Sept.	22.	Walter son of John & Susan Tweed.
	Oct.	1.	Sarah daughter of William & Sarah Adams.
	Nov.	14.	William son of William & Sarah Frost.
	Nov.	23.	Thomas son of Henry & Elizabeth Cater.
	Dec.	16.	Robert son of Robert & Elizabeth Hitchcock.
1772.	Feb.	3.	Richard son of Edmund & Elizabeth Nunn.
	Feb.	11.	Mary daughter of Thomas & Mary Orridge.
	Feb.	29.	Ann daughter of John & Mary Nunn.
	March	20.	Peter son of Rev[d] George & Elizabeth Rogers.
	March	28.	John son of John & Sarah Browne.
	March	28.	John & William, twin sons of Robert & Mary Norman.
	March	29.	Sarah daughter of Ambrose & Mary Sale.
	April	24.	William son of Isaac & Mary Brookes.
	April	26.	Susan daughter of William & Ann Lilly.
	May	10.	James son of James & Martha Polly.
	May	17.	George son of Richard & Susan Smith.
	June	22.	Francis son of Richard & Elizabeth Smith.
	Aug.	23.	Edmund son of James & Martha Spolden,
	&		James son of Thomas & Martha Bedell.
	Sept.	6.	Elizabeth daughter of John & Elizabeth Downing.
	Nov.	9.	Susan daughter of William & Susan Parsons.
	Nov.	22.	Abraham son of John & Sarah Smith.
	Dec.	27.	Ann daughter of John & Mary Frost.
1773.	Jan.	31.	William son of Christopher & Elizabeth Rosbrook.
	March	2.	Sarah daughter of Thomas & Elizabeth Sharpe.
	March	31.	Grace daughter of Robert & Elizabeth Hitchcock.
	April	4.	Edward, Francis & William, sons of Edward & Elizabeth Drew, were all born on April 4 and baptized the same day.

April 11. Ann daughter of William & Sarah Bray.
May 2. Isaac son of Thomas & Ann Richardson.
May 2. Ann daughter of Henry & Elizabeth Cater.
May 23. Elizabeth daughter of James & Sarah Crack.
June 6. Ann daughter of John & Mary Cooper.
June 13. Isaac son of John & Elizabeth Bray.
July 4. William son of James & Sarah Haslewood.
Sept. 4. Ann child of Tammatha Wright.
Sept. 26. Frances child of Mary Fuller.
— — Susan daughter of George & Sarah Challice.
Nov. 14. Mary child of Mary Frost.
Dec. 8. James son of James & Hannah Otley.
Dec. 12. William son of John & Mary Adams.
Dec. 13. Rose Ann daughter of James & Rebecca Howe.
1774. March 29. Edward son of Rev.[d] George & Elizabeth Rogers.
April 21. Arthur John son of Isaac & Mary Brookes.
June 19. Betty daughter of William & Ann Lilly.
June 24. John son of John & Mary Swan.
July 3. George William son of John & Elizabeth Downing.
July 17. Susan daughter of John & Mary Frost.
July 31. Sarah daughter of William & Susan Parsons.
Aug. 10. William son of Edward & Elizabeth Nunn.
Sept. 10. Sarah daughter of William & Sarah Frost.
Nov. 18. William son of Robert & Mary Norman.
Nov. 21. Ezra son of Joseph & Susan Underwood.
Dec. 23. Rose daughter of John & Sarah Gardiner.
1775. Jan. 15. Jonathan son of Thomas & Martha Beddell.
Jan. 29. James & Susan, children of William & Mary Polly.
Feb. 2. Hannah daughter of James & Hannah Ottley.
Feb. 14. Charles son of John & Mary Holden.
March 7. Robert son of John & Mary Spolden.
April 4. Charles son of Henry & Elizabeth Cater.
April 5. James son of Thomas & Mary Sparkes.
June 5. Frederick son of James & Rebecca How.
June 6. George son of Edward Drew jun & Elizabeth his wife.

June 12. Mary daughter of James & Rebecca Pitt.
June 24. Susan daughter of John & Elizabeth Bray.
July 16. Ann daughter of Thomas & Ann Richardson.
Aug. 3. Thomas son of Thomas & Elizabeth Alvis.
Aug. 16. John & Mary Lilly, twin children of John & Ann Adams.
Aug. 27. Ann daughter of James & Martha Spolding.
Sept. 3. Ann daughter of John & Sarah Browne.
Oct. 1. William son of George & Abigail Challice.
Oct. 15. Lydia daughter of Richard & Elizabeth Smith.
Oct. 29. John son of Christopher & Elizabeth Rosbrook.
Nov. 5. William son of William & Elizabeth Hempsted.
Nov. 15. Alice daughter of John & Sarah Smith.
Dec. 17. Thomas son of William & Sarah Bray.
1776. Feb. 9. Thomas son of John & Mary Frost. Feb. 2.*
Feb. 14. Thomas son of Rev. George & Elizabeth Rogers. Feb. 10.
March 22. Sarah daughter of James & Sarah Crack. Dec. 13, 1775.
May 5. Tabitha daughter of John & Elizabeth Brewster.
May 9. Mary daughter of James & Elizabeth Bull.
June 10. William son of William & Sarah Frost. June 9.
June 16. Mary daughter of Edmund & Mary Willingham.
July 12. Betty daughter of William & Ann Lyng. July 12.
July 14. Joseph child of Mary Fuller. July 7.
July 16. John son of Edmund & Elizabeth Nunn. July 7.
July 21. Anthony Salt child of Mary Payne.
Aug. 4. Mary daughter of William & Mary Polley. July 23.
Sept. 1. Elizabeth daughter of John & Mary Nunn. Aug. 14.
Nov. 2. Henry son of William & Sarah Adams. Nov. 2.
Nov. 2. Mary daughter of Richard & Ann Adams. Nov. 2.
Nov. 16. Richard son of Thomas & Mary Spark. Nov. 14.
Dec. 20. John son of William & Ann Lilly.
1777. Jan. 17. Samuel son of Robert & Elizabeth Hitchcock. Jan. 5.
Jan. 10. Thomas son of James & Hannah Otley. Jan. 2.
Jan. 20. Elizabeth daughter of John & Susanna Tweed. Jan. 11.
Feb. 6. Mary daughter of Joseph & Susan Underwood. Feb. 3.

* The date at the end of the entry is the date of birth.—S. H. A. H.

March 5. Elizabeth daughter of Henry & Elizabeth Cater. March 2.
March 12. Lucy daughter of Rev. George & Elizabeth Rogers. March 6.
March 30. George son of Thomas & Elizabeth Avis. March 3.
April 21. Elizabeth daughter of John & Mary Spolding. April 16.
April 28. John son of John & Susan Warren. April 28.
June 8. Ann daughter of James & Ann Copsey. April 25.
June 23. Thomas son of James & Rebecca How.
June 24. Thomas son of Thomas & Ann Orridge. June 24.
July 19. Frances daughter of Thomas & Frances Frost. July 15.
Aug. 12. William son of Thomas & Mary Cater. Aug. 10.
Aug. 17. Mary daughter of William & Susan Parsons. July 30.
Aug. 17. James son of John & Mary Frost. Aug. 6.
Aug. 28. Lewis son of Christopher & Elizabeth Rosbrook. Aug. 28.
Sept. 22. William son of William & Mary Candler. Sept. 22.
Oct. 18. John son of John & Dillarivier Rolfe. Oct. 18.
Oct. 28. John child of Mary Moore. Oct. 28.
Nov. 16. William son of William & Elizabeth Ambrose.
1778. Jan. 15. Frances child of Frances Frost. Jan. 14.
Feb. 11. Susan daughter of John & Sarah Browne.
April 19. Mary daughter of Samuel & Elizabeth Avis. April 4.
May 2. Sarah daughter of John & Elizabeth Brewster. May 1.
May 16. Susan child of Susan Garrard. May 14.
May 24. Susan daughter of William & Ann Lyng.
May 24. Joseph son of Joseph & Lydia Holt. May 24.
June 12. Elizabeth daughter of James & Sarah Hazlewood. June 2.
June 21. Edmund son of Edmund & Mary Willingham. May 19.
July 7. William son of Jeremiah & Sarah Ashman.
Aug. 11. Edward son of Edward & Elizabeth Drew. Aug. 9.
Sept. 5. Mary Willingham child of Ann Death.
Sept. 18. Michael son of James & Sarah Crack. Sept. 1.
Dec. 5. William son of Thomas & Ann Orridge. Dec. 4.
Dec. 19. James son of James & Ann Copsey. Dec. 18.
1779. Jan. 9. John son of Robert & Elizabeth Hitchcock. Jan. 8.
Feb. 16. Thomas son of Isaac & Mary Brookes. Jan. 24.
March 8. Rebecca daughter of John & Susan Tweed. March 6.

March 22. John son of John & Mary Underwood. March 18.
March 23. Henry son of Henry & Elizabeth Cater. March 20.
April 1. Mary daughter of William & Sarah Frost.
April 4. William son of John & Mary Nunn. Dec. 2, 1778.
April 11. Joseph son of William & Mary Polley. March 31.
May 6. Sarah daughter of William & Sarah Frost. May 4.
June 14. Sarah daughter of Richard & Ann Adams. June 12.
June 19. James son of Rev. George & Elizabeth Rogers. June 12.
June 27. Mary daughter of Thomas & Mary Sparke.
Aug. 15. Ann daughter of William & Elizabeth Ambrose. July 24.
Sept. 1. William son of John & Susan Warren. Aug. 29.
Sept. 19. Mary daughter of John & Mary Frost. Sept. 11.
Sept. 19. James son of John & Dillarivier Rolfe. Sept. 6.
Sept. 28. John son of Thomas & Frances Frost. Sept. 27.
Oct. 6. Susan daughter of William & Mary Goldsmith. Sept. 18.
Oct. 8. Alice daughter of William & Alice Parsons. Oct. 5.
Oct. 24. Lewis son of Christopher & Elizabeth Rosbrook.
Nov. 11. Sophy daughter of Thomas & Elizabeth Avis. Nov. 11.
Dec. 29. Sarah daughter of Thomas & Sarah Mason. Dec. 23.
1780. Feb. 21. Mary daughter of Samuel & Elizabeth Avis. Feb. 20.
Feb. 24. Mary daughter of Thomas & Elizabeth Lyng. Feb. 21.
March 21. Ann daughter of William & Ann Coe. March 20.
April 1. John son of Thomas & Mary Bannock. March 31.
April 2. Henry son of Thomas & Mary Cater. March 14.
April 18. Susanna daughter of William & Susanna Bray. April 5.
May 18. Lucinda daughter of Isaac & Mary Brookes.
June 11. Sarah child of Martha Golding. June 2.
July 24. John son of John & Sarah Avis. July 19.
Oct. 4. Alice daughter of Edmund & Alice Willingham. Oct. 4.
Oct. 25. Charlotte daughter of John & Mary Cooper.
Nov. 12. Mary daughter of Edmund & Alice Willingham. Oct. 23.
Nov. 12. William son of William & Elizabeth Willingham. Nov. 7.
Dec. 31. James son of James & Susan Ramplin. Dec. 23.
1781. Jan. 14. Robert son of James & Ann Copsey. Dec. 29, 1780.
Jan. 30. William son of John & Mary Wymock. Jan. 29.

	March	13.	Martha child of Susan Dew. March 10.
	March	18.	Charles son of Christopher & Elizabeth Rosbrook. March 3.
	March	22.	William son of Thomas & Francis Frost. March 19.
	April	15.	Mary daughter of John & Elizabeth Brewster. March 29.
	June	5.	Elizabeth daughter of William & Elizabeth Ambrose. May 21.
	June	11.	Elizabeth daughter of William & Mary Polley. Feb. 28.
	July	25.	Christopher son of John & Mary Underwood. July 15.
	July	29.	Elizabeth daughter of Thomas & Alice Richardson. July 12.
	July	30.	John son of William & Alice Parsons. July 28.
	Aug.	2.	John son of William & Mary Goldsmith. July 22.
	Aug.	6.	Robert son of John & Sarah Avis. July 24.
	Aug.	5.	Ann daughter of William & Mary Lyng. July 23.
	Aug.	26.	George William son of Ann Lilly. Aug. 11.
	Nov.	1.	Ann daughter of Joseph & Susan Underwood. Oct. 26.
	Nov.	1.	Mary daughter of John Dearson & Mary Miller. Oct. 19.
	Dec.	2.	Mary child of Mary Sharpe. Nov. 20.
	Dec.	15.	Robert son of James & Ann Copsey. Dec. 12.
1782.	Jan.	12.	Robert son of Rev. George & Elizabeth Rogers. Jan. 9.
	Jan.	20.	Sarah child of Mary Cooper. Jan. 19.
	Jan.	23.	Mary daughter of Henry & Elizabeth Cater. Jan. 22.
	Feb.	1.	Frances daughter of Samuel & Susan Evered. Jan. 18.
	Feb.	12.	John & William, twin sons of William & Mary Pettit. Feb. 11.
	March	1.	Mary Anne daughter of Thomas & Mary Bannock. March 1.
	March	27.	Thomas son of William & Sarah Frost. March 27.
	?	19.	Sarah daughter of Samuel & Elizabeth Avis. ? 13.
	April	20.	Rebecca daughter of John & Sarah Avis. April 16.
	April	26.	Mary Ann daughter of Joseph & Elizabeth Prick. April 17.
	May	7.	Joseph son of Edmund & Elizabeth Nunn.
	May	19.	Dillariviere daughter of John & Sarah Brown. April 28.
	June	9.	Ann daughter of Richard & Ann Adams. June 8.
	June	9.	Elizabeth child of Elizabeth Marton. Dec. 25, 1781.
	June	15.	Susan daughter of James & Phœbe Lyng. June 11.
	Aug.	25.	Edmund son of William & Elizabeth Willingham. Aug. 15.
	Sept.	5.	Elizabeth daughter of John & Sarah Marchill.
	Oct.	3.	Mary daughter of Edmund & Alice Willingham. Sept. 28.

Nov. 27. Mary daughter of John & Mary Spolden. Nov. 21.
Dec. 22. Elizabeth daughter of Edmund & Mary Willingham. Dec. 5.
1783. Jan. 12. Benjamin son of Thomas & Sarah Mason. Dec. 19, 1782.
Feb. 16. Sarah daughter of John & Elizabeth Brewster. Jan. 14.
Feb. 21. Ann daughter of William & Mary Polley.
March 4. John son of Thomas & Mary Cater. March 3.
April —. Elizabeth daughter of Thomas & Elizabeth Ling.
April 27. Susan daughter of James & Susan Ramplin. April 11.
May 11. William son of William & Ann Lyng. May 3.
June 1. James son of Charles & Mary Corston. May 5.
June 5. Elizabeth daughter of William & Mary Layt.
June 9. Martha Maria daughter of Rev. George & Elizabeth Rogers, born June 7.
Sept. 13. Edward son of Thomas & Ann Orange.
Sept. 24. Thomas posthumous child of William & Susan Bray.
Nov. 24. William son of Thomas & Ann Byford. Nov. 24.
Dec. 14. Henry Brunning child of Elizabeth Willingham.
Dec. 22. Jonathan Waller son of John & Sarah Marshall. Dec. 8.
Dec. 28. Sarah daughter of John Dearson & Mary Meller. Dec. 17.
1784. Feb. 19. Sarah daughter of William & Mary Polley.
March 24. Elizabeth daughter of George & Elizabeth Holden. March 24.
April 9. Hannah daughter of Henry & Elizabeth Cater. April 4.
April 11. Francis Henry son of Thomas & Mary Bannock. April 7.
April 24. Mary daughter of James & Ann Copsey. April 10.
May 18. Thomas son of William & Alice Parsons. May 9.
May 20. Elizabeth daughter of Anthony & Elizabeth Crick. May 15.
Aug. 3. Mary daughter of Thomas & Frances Frost. Aug. 1.
Aug. 8. Sarah daughter of Joseph & Sarah Farrance.
Aug. 28. George son of George & Matthew Cater. Aug. 26.
Oct. 10. Charles son of Charles & Alice Ward. Sept. 16.
Oct. 17. Thomas son of William & Elizabeth Willingham. Oct. 15.
Oct. 28. Elizabeth daughter of James & Hannah Otley. Oct. 14.
1785. March 20. William son of Richard & Elizabeth Smith.
April 21. Rebecca daughter of James & Rebecca Howe. April 12.
April 22. Susan daughter of John & Elizabeth Brewster. April 15.

April 24. Elizabeth daughter of Thomas & Sarah Mason. April 10.
May 8. Sarah daughter of William & Ann Ling. March 22.
June 17. Mary & Frances, twin daughters of Thomas & Ann Byford.
July 3. Ann daughter of John & Ann Frost. May 4.
July 3. Thomas son of Edmund & Mary Willingham. June 21.
July 4. William son of John & Sarah Alvis. June 23.
Aug. 5. Henry son of Charles & Susan Coe.
Aug. 9. Sophia daughter of John & Sarah Marshall. June 23.
Aug. 14. George son of George & Elizabeth Holden.
Aug. 14. Ann daughter of Richard & Ann Adams.
Nov. 3. Francis William son of Edward & Elizabeth Drew. Nov. 10, 1783.
Nov. 16. John Dearson son of John Dearson & Mary Miller.
Nov. 20. Robert son of Abigail Wilden.
Dec. 26. Robert son of William & Mary Polly.
1786. Jan. 9. Susan daughter of Anthony & Elizabeth Crick.
Jan. 29. Thomas son of Thomas & Mary Cater.
Feb. 7. Susan daughter of Thomas & Susan Last.
Feb. 28. Ann daughter of Henry & Elizabeth Cater.
May 30. Elizabeth daughter of Henry & Mary Everard.
June 4. Delariviere daughter of Edmund & Alice Willingham.
June 13. Robert son of John & Mary Spalding.
June 15. William son of Samuel & Elizabeth Alvis.
June 16. Anna Maria daughter of Thomas & Mary Bannock.
June 18. James son of Charles & Mary Cawston.
July 8. Martha daughter of George & Martha Cater.
July 22. James son of John & Delariviere Rolfe.
Aug. 30. Alice daughter of Charles & Alice Ward.
Nov. 18. Maria daughter of John & Elizabeth Adkin.
Nov. 26. Ann daughter of Thomas & Sarah Mason.
1787. Jan. 16. George son of John & Sarah Alvis.
Feb. 20. Susan daughter of George & Elizabeth Holden.
May 3. George son of Henry & Elizabeth Cater.
May 17. Charles son of Richard & Elizabeth Sparrow.
May 20. Rose daughter of John & Elizabeth Brewster.

	May	20.	Sarah daughter of William & Elizabeth Willingham.
	July	29.	Thomas & Mary, children of George & Martha Cater.
	Aug.	19.	William son of John & Catharine Death.
	Sept.	16.	Mary daughter of Margarett Daines.
	Sept.	30.	Thomas son of Richard & Elizabeth Smith.
	Oct.	21.	Sarah daughter of Christopher & Elizabeth Rosbrook.
	Dec.	3.	Mary daughter of John & Mary Ellis.
	Dec.	25.	Mary Ann daughter of Anthony & Elizabeth Crick.
1788.	April	8.	Ann daughter of Robert & Dorcas East.
	April	8.	Francis son of Edward & Elizabeth Drew.
	May	13.	Lucy daughter of William & Mary Goldsmith.
	May	18.	Mary daughter of James & Sarah Norton.
	May	18.	Joseph son of Joseph & Sarah Farrance.
	May	19.	Maria daughter of William & Alice Pearson.
	May	25.	Delariviere daughter of Edmund & Mary Willingham.
	May	25.	William son of Thomas & Elizabeth Ling.
	June	4.	Thomas son of Thomas & Susan Last.
	Aug.	10.	Edmund son of Charles & Alice Ward.
	Aug.	17.	John son of John & Mary Goldson.
	Aug.	17.	Robert son of John & Mary Spalding.
	Aug.	24.	Elizabeth daughter of Mary Beddle.
	Aug.	31.	George son of John & Delariviere Rolfe.
	Sept.	23.	Sarah daughter of John & Sarah Marshall.
	Sept.	21.	Martha daughter of Richard & Elizabeth Butcher.
	Nov.	30.	John son of Mary Rowland.
1789.	Feb.	18.	John son of John & Mary Marking.
	Feb.	18.	Hannah daughter of John & Elizabeth Brewster.
	April	12.	John son of John & Catharine Death.
	April	19.	John son of John & Sarah King.
	April	21.	Caroline More daughter of Ann Smith.
	May	3.	George John son of George & Elizabeth Lanham.
	May	27.	Elizabeth daughter of Edward & Elizabeth (Cooper) Drew.
	June	14.	Lucy daughter of Ann Lofts.
	June	15.	Robert son of Robert & Dorcas (Rudling) East.
	July	5.	Edmund son of Edmund & Alice (Goodchild) Willingham.

	July	11.	Mary daughter of Thomas & Sarah (Moss) Mason.
	Aug.	8.	Martha daughter of Richard & Elizabeth (Pawsey) Sparrow.
	Aug.	29.	Thomas son of the late John Ward & Ann (Spink) his wife.
	Oct.	28.	James son of Thomas & Mary (Sparrow) Cater.
	Nov.	1.	Stephen son of George & Catharine (Smith) Knock.
	Nov.	24.	John son of John & Mary (Garwood) Ellis.
	Dec.	10.	Frances daughter of John & Mary (Clark) Spalding.
	Dec.	25.	John son of John & Elizabeth (Smith) Adkin.
1790.	Feb.	4.	Edward son of Charles & Alice (Willingham) Ward.
	Feb.	4.	Edmund son of William & Elizabeth (Layt) Willingham.
	Feb.	6.	Delariviere daughter of Edmund & Mary (Bunting) Willingham.
	Feb.	22.	Ann daughter of Henry & Elizabeth (Mahew) Cater.
	Feb.	27.	John & Mary, twin children of John & Mary (Wallace) Goldson.
	March	3.	Ann daughter of Samuel & Elizabeth (Pear) Alvis.
	March	7.	John son of John & Elizabeth (Pattle) Brewster.
	March	14.	John son of Elizabeth Cooper.
	April	11.	Sarah daughter of John & Mary (Humphry) Marshall.
	June	16.	Alice daughter of Edward & Elizabeth (Cooper) Drew.
	June	16.	William son of George & Martha (Beddle) Cater.
	July	5.	Robert son of Ann Frost.
	Aug.	8.	Isaac Cropley son of John & Delariviere (Bunting) Rolfe.
	Aug.	10.	Bet daughter of Richard & Elizabeth (Clarke) Butcher.
	Sept.	10.	Mary Ann daughter of Joseph & Sarah (Deed) Farrance.
	Nov.	24.	Susan daughter of Charles & Susan (Page) Coe.
1791.	Jan.	22.	Mary daughter of John & Catharine (Frost) Death.
	Jan.	23.	William son of William & Ann (Nunn) Ling. Jan. 1788.
	Jan.	23.	Thomas son of William & Ann (Nunn) Ling.
	Jan.	26.	Mary daughter of John & Sarah (Garnham) Billerman.
	March	10.	Isaac & Robert, twins of John & Mary (Baker) Marking.
	March	26.	John son of William & Elizabeth (Layt) Willingham.
	March	31.	Alicia daughter of George & Elizabeth (Lyes) Lanham.
	April	17.	Elizabeth Canham daughter of Elizabeth Davy.
	June	18.	Thomas son of John & Mary (Wallace) Goldson.

July 13. William son of Thomas & Mary (Jackson) Bannock.
July 31. Daniel son of John & Mary (Garwood) Ellis.
Sept. 18. George son of George & Catharine (Smith) Knock.
Sept. 22. Mary daughter of James & Mary (Eagle) Goodchild.
Sept. 29. George son of John & Ann (Rosbrook) Cockle.
Oct. 18. Susan daughter of James & Ann (Howe) Copsey.
Dec. 3. James son of John & Mary (Clark) Spalding.
1792. Jan. 31. William son of George & Elizabeth (Grice) Root.
March 13. Thomas son of John & Sarah (Bray) King.
March 29. Charles son of John & Elizabeth (Pattle) Brewster.
April 1. John & Mary twins of William & Dorothy (Reed) Richardson.
April 15. John son of Thomas & Ann (Bird) Byford.
June 1. Lucy daughter of William & Alice (Prick) Pearsons.
June 6. Mary Ann daughter of William & Hannah (Griggs) Lilly.
June 22. William son of Thomas & Susan (Cutmore) Last.
July 1. Charlotte daughter of John & Elizabeth (Smith) Atkin.
Nov. 4. George son of William & Mary (Hempsted) Emmett.
1793. Jan. 13. Susan daughter of Thomas & Elizabeth (Nunn) Lyng.
Jan. 27. John son of Charles & Alice (Willingham) Ward.
Feb. 3. George son of Sarah Spalding.
Feb. 7. Elizabeth daughter of John & Catharine (Frost) Death.
April 17. William son of William & Sarah (Richardson) Seal.
April 28. George son of George & Elizabeth (Lyes) Lanham.
June 9. Martha daughter of George & Martha (Beddle) Cater.
June 29. Elisabeth daughter of George & Elisabeth (Grice) Root.
Sept. 23. Mary daughter of Mary Beddle.
Oct. 13. Ann daughter of Joseph & Sarah (Cooper) Prick.
Oct. 17. Mary daughter of Thomas & Mary (Sparrow) Cater.
Dec. 12. William son of William & Sarah (Holden) Frost.
1794. Jan. 5. Jemima daughter of Elizabeth Butcher, widow.
Jan. 5. John son of James & Ann (Howe) Copsey.
Feb. 20. Richard son of John & Ann (Rosbrooke) Cockle.
Feb. 23. James son of William & Elizabeth (Layt) Willingham.
April 3. Mary daughter of William & Ann (Nunn) Ling.
May 18. Mary daughter of John & Grace (Taylor) Marshall.

	May	27.	Elizabeth daughter of John & Mary (Garwood) Ellis.
	June	10.	Sarah daughter of Isaac & Elizabeth (Brooks) Brooks.
	Aug.	6.	Mary daughter of Thomas & Ann (Bird) Byford.
	Aug.	17.	Hannah daughter of William & Hannah (Griggs) Lilly.
	Sept.	19.	James son of Thomas & Susan (Cutmore) Last.
	Sept.	21.	Sophia daughter of Charles & Alice (Willingham) Ward.
	Oct.	3.	Samuel son of John & Elizabeth (Pattle) Brewster.
	Oct.	8.	James son of Thomas & Amy (Pryke) Sylverston.
	Nov.	23.	Charles son of Charles & Susan (Page) Coe.
	Dec.	4.	Hannah Armstrong daughter of William & Hannah (Sylverston) Sylverston.
	Dec.	7.	Hannah Maria daughter of Abraham & Hannah (Hagreen) Elsden.
1795.	Jan.	4.	Thomas son of John & Catharine (Frost) Death.
	Jan.	7.	Mary daughter of George & Elizabeth (Grice) Root.
	April	26.	Samuel & Thomas sons of John & Sarah (Allerton) Ranner.
	May	10.	William son of John & Elizabeth (Smith) Adkin.
	May	26.	Susan daughter of Thomas & Lucy (Hilton) Tweed.
	May	28.	Sally daughter ofWilliam & Hannah (Sylverston) Sylverston. Received into the Church.
	July	12.	Mary Ann daughter of Edward & Susan (Underwood) Johnson.
	July	14.	Isaac son of Isaac & Elizabeth (Brooks) Brooks.
	Aug.	9.	Mary daughter of John & Grace (Taylor) Marshall.
	Aug.	18.	John son of John & Mary (Wallace) Goldson.
	Oct.	14.	Winnifred daughter of Caleb & Margarett (Morley) Lee.
	Oct.	22.	Henry son of John & Mary (Baker) Marking.
	Nov.	4.	William son of William & Ann (Malton) Last.
1796.	March	3.	Sarah daughter of William & Sarah (Holden) Frost.
	March	13.	Robert son of Robert & Alice (Haylock) Sharpe.
	May	29.	Hannah daughter of Edward & Hannah (Rosbrook) Crack.
	June	4.	Mary Anne daughter of William & Elizabeth (Bullard) Norman.
	June	6.	Robert son of William & Alice (Prick) Pearson.
	June	15.	Elizabeth daughter of Edward & Sarah (Wing) Gooch.

June 19. James son of John & Mary (Garwood) Elliss.
July 1. Joshua son of Joseph & Sarah (Cooper) Prick.
July 3. James son of Elizabeth Tweed.
Aug. 4. Mary daughter of James & Mary (Eagle) Goodchild.
Aug. 15. Abraham son of Abraham & Ruth (Dutton) Cobbin.
Aug. 21. Sarah daughter of John & Martha (Nunn) Nunn.
Aug. 21. Maria daughter of George & Elizabeth (Lyes) Lanham.
Aug. 21. Edward son of William & Elizabeth (Layt) Willingham.
Sept. 4. Maria daughter of William & Mary (Rickwood) Musk.
Oct. 7. Charles son of Samuel & Hannah (Elsden) Mizen.
Oct. 10. Mary Ann daughter of Edward & Mary (Bradley) Musk.
Oct. 31. Louisa daughter of Michael & Ann (Parker) Sturgeon.
Dec. 9. George son of George & Elizabeth (Grice) Root.
Dec. 25. Simon son of Thomas & Susan (Cutmore) Last.
1797. Feb. 10. James son of Thomas & Ann (Bird) Byford.
April 7. Joseph son of William & Sarah (Sexton) Leech.
May 7. Mary daughter of George & Elizabeth (Ling) Cook.
July 21. James son of John & Grace (Taylor) Marshall.
July 23. Mary & Fanny, daughters of John & Sarah (Bray) King.
July 30. Frederick son of John & Elizabeth (Smith) Adkin.
Oct. 9. Caroline daughter of William & Hannah (Griggs) Lilly.
Oct. 15. Tammy daughter of James & Ann (Howe) Copsy.
Nov. 27. Isaac son of William & Alice (Prick) Pearsons.
Dec. 17. Ann daughter of Ann Martin.
Dec. 31. John son of William & Bell (Finch) Frost.
1798. Jan. 7. Elizabeth daughter of George & Martha (Beddle) Cater.
Jan. 7. James son of James & Elizabeth (Bray) Taylor.
Jan. 21. Fanny daughter of William & Ann (Nunn) Ling.
Feb. 11. John son of John & Hannah (Paine) Tricker.
Feb. 11. William son of Mark & Ann (Cole) Hammond.
March 25. John son of Abraham & Ruth (Dutton) Cobbin.
April 15. Susan daughter of William & Sarah (Richardson) Seale.
April 29. Mary Ann daughter of William & Temperance (Elliss) Ebbon.
May 20. John son of John & Sarah (Underwood) Ridgen.
May 27. James son of John & Catharine (Frost) Death.

	July	15.	Edward son of Edward & Hannah (Rosbrook) Crack.
	July	22.	George son of John & Matthew (Nunn) Nunn.
	July	23.	Joshua son of George & Elizabeth (Lyes) Lanham.
	Aug.	12.	Mary daughter of John & Ann (Smith) Brown.
	Aug.	12.	Frederica daughter of Michael & Ann (Parker) Sturgeon.
	Aug.	19.	Ann daughter of James & Mary (Eagle) Goodchild.
	Sept.	16.	Elizabeth daughter of Edward & Mary (Bradley) Musk.
	Nov.	4.	Mary Ann daughter of John & Elizabeth (Wellham) Pearsons.
	Nov.	11.	Robert son of Edward & Sarah (Wing) Gooch.
	Nov.	18.	George son of William & Elizabeth (Layt) Willingham.
	Nov.	25.	Mary Ann daughter of James & Ann (Crack) Last.
	Dec.	30.	Robert son of John & Mary (Wallace) Goldston.
1799.	Jan.	1.	Sarah daughter of John & Elizabeth (Sharpe) Lanham.
	Jan.	13.	Isaac son of William & Sarah (Sexton) Leech.
	Jan.	20.	William Nunn son of Sarah Spalding.
	Jan.	21.	James son of William & Hannah (Sylverston) Sylverston.
	Feb.	17.	Ann daughter of Anthony & Sarah (Clark) Osborn.
	Feb.	24.	John son of George & Elizabeth (Grice) Root.
	Feb.	24.	Simeon son of Henry & Elizabeth (Death) Briggs.
	Feb.	24.	Elizabeth daughter of John & Mary (Garrard) Elliss.
	April	14.	Mary daughter of Joseph & Sarah (Cooper) Prick.
	April	19.	Samuel son of William & Ann (Malton) Last.
	May	26.	Mary Anne daughter of Edward & Susan (Underwood) Johnson.
	July	7.	Abraham son of Ann Cooper.
	Aug.	4.	William son of William & Temperance (Elliss) Ebbon.
	Oct.	27.	George William son of Anthony & Elizabeth (Prick) Crick.
	Oct.	27.	Louisa daughter of Elizabeth Lilly.
	Nov.	17.	Rachael daughter of Jonas & Rachael (Bray) Row.
1800.	Feb.	8.	William son of William & Hannah (Griggs) Lilly.
	Feb.	23.	William son of John & Hannah (Paine) Tricker.
	March	9.	John son of George & Elizabeth (Ling) Cook.
	May	4.	Sophia daughter of John & Ann (Smith) Brown.
	May	30.	Harriet daughter of William & Ann (Malton) Last.
	June	1.	William son of William & Mary (Leech) Rosbrook.

July 1. Samuel son of Samuel & Hannah (Elsden) Miseman.
July 12. William son of James & Sarah (Alvis) Bullas.
July 14. John Double son of John & Clementina (Double) Reynolds.
Aug. 3. Stephen son of Edmund & Mary (Bradley) Musk.
Aug. 28. William son of William & Sarah (Sexton) Leech.
Oct. 26. Eliza daughter of James & Ann (Crack) Last.
Nov. 25. Maria daughter of William & Mary (Grimwood) Edwards.
Nov. 26. Henry son of George & Martha (Biddle) Cater.
Dec. 21. Robert son of William & Temperance (Elliss) Ebbon.
1801. Jan. 25. Martin son of Robert & Alice (Haylock) Sharpe.
Feb. 22. George son of John & Sarah (Underwood) Ridgen.
March 8. Harriet daughter of William & Susan (Richardson) Seale.
March 15. William son of Anthony & Sarah (Clark) Osborne.
April 12. Thomas son of George & Elizabeth (Lyes) Lanham.
May 10. Thomas son of Jonas & Rachael (Bray) Row.
May 23. Sarah daughter of William & Mary (Frost) King.
June 9. John son of Michael & Ann (Parker) Sturgeon.
June 14. Mary daughter of Edward & Hannah (Rosbrook) Crack.
June 28. Thomas son of Ann Richardson.
Aug. 7. Phebe daughter of James & Mary (Harrington) Cook.
Aug. 16. Alice daughter of James & Mary (Eagle) Goodchild.
Sept. 13. Harrison son of Mark & Ann (Cole) Hammond.
Oct. 4. Isaac son of William & Elizabeth (Layt) Willingham.
Oct. 4. William son of Elizabeth Lilly.
Oct. 6. Alice daughter of William & Hannah (Sylverston) Sylverston.
Dec. 20. Susan daughter of John & Elizabeth (Sharpe) Lanham.
1802. Jan. 10. William & John, sons of Abraham & Mary (Clark) Elsden.
Jan. 19. James son of John & Ann (Smith) Browne.
Jan. 28. Robert son of John & Hannah (Paine) Tricker.
Jan. 31. Amy daughter of Ann Martin.
Feb. 21. John son of John & Mary (Petitt) Warren.
Feb. 28. Martha daughter of William & Ann (Nunn) Ling.
March 28. Benjamin son of James & Ann (Crack) Last.
April 16. Mary daughter of Joseph & Sarah (Cooper) Prick.
June 13. John son of Edward & Sarah (Wing) Gooch.

July 19. Frances daughter of John & Catharine (Frost) Death.
Sept. 26. George son of William & Dinah (Cocksedge) Hazelwood.
Oct. 17. John son of Roger & Sophia (Alvis) Adams.
Oct. 24. John son of William & Hannah (Griggs) Lilly.
Dec. 5. Betty daughter of George & Betty (Ling) Cook.
1803. Jan. 23. Lewis son of William & Mary (Leech) Rosbrook.
Feb. 20. Thomas son of James & Mary (Eagle) Goodchild.
Feb. 27. Sarah daughter of Jacob & Sarah (Sparrow) Richardson.
March 6. Phœbe daughter of William & Ann (Ling) King.
March 6. Joseph son of William & Mary (Grimwood) Edwards.
March 13. John son of Edmund & Mary (Turner) Revell.
March 20. Harriet daughter of Susan Rampling.
April 10. Jeremiah son of William & Temperance (Elliss) Ebbon.
April 24. Harriet daughter of John & Hannah (Paine) Tricker.
May 12. James David son of Thomas & Lucy (Hilton) Tweed. Feb. 11, 1801.
May 29. Sarah daughter of Edward & Hannah (Rosbrook) Crack.
May 29. Ann daughter of William & Sarah (Richardson) Sale.
June 12. John son of James & Mary (Spalden) Wratham.
June 19. Isaac son of John & Clementina (Double) Reynolds.
July 31. Edmund son of George & Dilly (Calf) Harrington.
Aug. 28. Jonas son of Jonas & Rachael (Bray) Rowe.
Aug. 30. John son of Edward & Honor (Tunbridge) Drew.
Sept. 4. George son of Edmund & Mary (Bradley) Musk.
Sept. 4. James son of Nathaniel & Elizabeth (Waits) Flack.
Sept. 18. John son of Samuel & Sarah (Mizeman) Mizeman.
Oct. 2. John son of James & Mary (Harrington) Cook.
Oct. 30. Elizabeth & Mary, daughters of John & Matthew (Nunn) Nunn.
Nov. 6. Lucinda daughter of Robert & Alice (Pearsons) Copsey.
Nov. 27. William son of John & Ann (Smith) Browne.
Dec. 11. William son of Ruth Cobbin, widow of Abraham Cobbin.
1804. Feb. 26. Mary daughter of George & Elizabeth (Lyes) Lanham.
March 15. Ann daughter of Michael & Ann (Parker) Sturgeon.
May 26. William son of William & Mary (Willingham) Orridge.

May 27. William son of William & Dinah (Cocksedge) Hazelwood.
June 24. Harriet & Sarah, twin daughters of James & Lydia (Wells) Howe, received. Priv: bapt: June 26, 1803.
July 14. John son of James & Sarah (Alvis) Bullas.
July 29. Mary daughter of Ann Cooper.
Sept. 24. Elijah son of Joseph & Sarah (Cooper) Prick.
Sept. 30. Susannah daughter of Edward & Sarah (Wing) Gooch.
Sept. 30. Mary daughter of Anthony & Sarah (Clark) Osborn.
Oct. 10. Samuel George son of Roger & Sophia (Alvis) Adams.
Oct. 14. John son of John & Sarah (Mason) Barrell.
Dec. 2. John son of William & Ann (Ling) King.
Dec. 25. Susan daughter of Edward & Hannah (Rosbrook) Crack.
Dec. 25. Rachael daughter of William & Hannah (Griggs) Lilly.
Dec. 25. Anna Maria daughter of William & Susan (Mullinger) Ambrose.
Dec. 30. Eliza daughter of William & Mary (Rickwood) Musk.
1805. Jan. 6. John son of Frances Green.
Feb. 9. Maria daughter of William & Mary (Leech) Rosbrook.
Feb. 10. Joseph son of Samuel & Sarah (Mizeman) Mizeman.
Feb. 10. John son of John & Elizabeth (Wellham) Pearsons.
Feb. 17. Milla daughter of James & Mary (Spalden) Wratham.
March 13. John son of William & Mary (Grimwood) Edwards.
May 19. Susan daughter of Elizabeth Butcher, widow.
June 2. George son of George & Mary (Nunn) Sillett, received. Priv: bapt: at Bradfield.
June 5. Susan daughter of George & Elizabeth (Grice) Root.
June 23. Ann daughter of George & Elizabeth (Ling) Cook.
June 30. George son of John & Ann (Bullen) Kemp.
July 7. William son of Thomas & Susan (Ramplin) Newman.
July 7. James son of Elizabeth Lilly.
Aug. 11. Alexander son of William & Temperance (Ellis) Ebbon.
Aug. 25. Harriet daughter of Archibald & Mary (Cater) Davis.
Aug. 25. Susannah daughter of John & Catharine (Frost) Death.
Sept. 29. George son of James & Mary (Harrington) Cook.
Nov. 24. William son of James & Mary (Eagle) Goodchild.

Nov. 24. Susan daughter of Edward & Sarah (Wing) Gooch.
Dec. 8. William & Frederick, twin sons of William & Rose Ann (Howe) Smith.
Dec. 12. Mary Ann daughter of George & Mary Ann (Naylor) Double.
Dec. 29. John son of James & Ann (Crack) Last.
1806. Jan. 3. Harriet daughter of John & Hannah (Paine) Tricker.
March 2. John son of Mark & Ann (Cole) Hammond.
May 11. James son of Jonas & Rachael (Bray) Rowe.
May 25. Susan daughter of Henry & Elizabeth (Tweed) Hart.
June 29. Mary daughter of Abraham & Mary (Clarke) Elsden.
July 4. Thomas son of William & Mary (Willingham) Orridge.
July 13. William son of Edmund & Mary (Bradley) Musk.
July 20. William son of William & Lucy (Dutton) Brewster or Bruce.
Oct. 19. Maria daughter of John & Mathew (Nunn) Nunn.
Oct. 26. Lucy daughter of John & Ruth (Cobbin) Fenner.
Nov. 7. George William son of George William & Ann (Howard) Lilly.
Nov. 9. Mary Ann daughter of George & Mary (Nunn) Sillett.
Nov. 10. John Hagreen son of Elizabeth Bull.
Nov. 30. Sarah daughter of Joseph & Sarah (Cooper) Prick.
1807. March 1. Ann daughter of William & Hannah (Griggs) Lilly.
March 1. George son of John & Ann (Smith) Browne.
March 22. George son of Thomas & Lucy (Hilton) Tweed.
March 29. Martha daughter of James & Ann (Crack) Last.
April 7. James son of James & Alice (Byatt) Hardy.
April 26. Harriet daughter of Edward & Sarah (Wing) Gooch.
May 3. James son of George & Elizabeth (Lyes) Lanham.
May 3. Rhoda daughter of William & Temperance (Elliss) Ebbon.
May 10. James son of James & Ann (Spalding) Salisbury, received: priv: baptized Aug. 11, 1804.
May 10. John son of George & Biddy (Woods) Crack.
May 11. George Scarfe son of George Scarfe & Mary Ann (Naylor) Double.
May 31. Matthew son of Samuel & Sarah (Mizeman) Mizeman.
June 28. John son of William & Rose Ann (Howe) Smith.

	Aug.	2.	Robert son of William & Mary (Grimwood) Edwards.
	Aug.	2.	Thomas son of Thomas & Mary (Osborne) Middleditch.
	Aug.	16.	Sarah daughter of John & Sarah (Sharpe) Tricker.
	Aug.	16.	HenryWilliam son of William & Susan (Mullinger)Ambrose.
	Aug.	16.	William son of William & Ann (Ling) King.
	Aug.	16.	James son of James & Mary (Eagle) Goodchild.
	Sept.	13.	Robert son of Edward & Honor (Tunbridge) Drew.
	Sept.	17.	Thomas Grice son of Thomas & Ann (Double) Adkin.
	Nov.	15.	Isaac son of Isaac & Sarah (Willingham) Race.
	Dec.	20.	Charles son of Hannah Shelver.
1808.	Jan.	10.	Maria daughter of James & Sarah (Ling) Warren.
	Feb.	23.	Mary daughter of John & Charlott (Sarjent) Alvis.
	Feb.	28.	Henry son of Lewis & Elizabeth (Cater) Rosbrook.
	March	27.	William son of Anthony & Sarah (Clark) Osborn.
	June	5.	George son of George & Bet (Ling) Cook.
	June	12.	James son of Mary Coe.
	June	19.	Harriet daughter of Edward & Hannah (Rosbrook) Crack.
	Nov.	13.	Harriet daughter of Mark & Ann (Cole) Hammond.
	Nov.	27.	William son of Jonas & Rachael (Bray) Row.
	Dec.	13.	William son of William & Elizabeth (Naylor) Bilson.
1809.	Jan.	1.	Susan daughter of Edmund & Mary (Bradley) Musk.
	Jan.	22.	Ann daughter of James & Mary (Harrington) Cook.
	April	23.	Lucy daughter of John & Elizabeth (Welham) Pearsons.
	Aug.	24.	Robert son of George & Mary Ann (Naylor) Double.
	Aug.	27.	Harriet daughter of William & Rose Ann (Howe) Smith.
	Sept.	24.	Sarah daughter of Samuel & Sarah (Mizeman) Mizeman.
	Oct.	1.	Elizabeth daughter of William & Susan (Mullinger) Ambrose.
	Oct.	1.	Harriet daughter of Mary Cater.
	Oct.	15.	James son of Abraham & Matthew (Copsey) Rooks.
	Dec.	25.	Samuel son of James & Ann (Crack) Last.
	Dec.	27.	Jeremiah son of James & Ann (Spalding) Salisbury.
1810.	Jan.	7.	Elizabeth daughter of Isaac & Sarah (Willingham) Race.
	Feb.	18.	Fanny daughter of John & Matthew (Nunn) Nunn.
	Feb.	18.	Elizabeth daughter of Maria Adkin.
	March	25.	Lucy daughter of Robert & Mary (Parfrey) Alvis.

May 6. Robert son of William & Mary (Grimwood) Edwards.
May 20. Frederick son of William & Ann (Ling) King.
July 1. Mary Ann daughter of John & Sarah (Sharpe) Tricker.
July 2. Elizabeth Mary daughter of William & Elizabeth (Naylor) Bilson.
July 15. James son of Edward & Sarah (Wing) Gooch.
Aug. 19. James & Samuel twins of James & Sarah (Ling) Warren.
Sept. 16. Henry James son of James & Sarah (Alvis) Bullas.
Dec. 2. Sarah daughter of John & Charlott (Searjant) Alvis.
1811. Feb. 17. Eliza daughter of Mark & Ann (Cole) Hammond.
March 17. Emily daughter of William & Mary (Rickwood) Musk.
March 21. William son of William & Sarah (Bryant) Greene.
March 22. James Matthew son of James & Mary (Simpson) Scarling.
April 5. Johnson William son of George & Mary Ann (Naylor) Double.
May 5. Jane daughter of Edward & Hannah (Rosbrook) Crack.
May 28. Thomas Cook son of Frances Double.
May 28. Melmoth son of Charles Hill Hall & Augusta (Browning) his wife. April 26.
June 5. Anna Maria daughter of Charles & Hannah (Cater) Double.
June 17. Frederick Naylor son of John & Margarett (Naylor) Salisbury.
July 30. Nancy daughter of Thomas & Lucy (Hilton) Tweed.
July 21. Sarah daughter of Edmund & Mary (Bradley) Musk.
Sept. 2. Esau son of Charles & Charlott (Crick) Rosbrook.
Sept. 2. Sarah daughter of William & Hannah (Griggs) Lilly.
Sept. 5. Mary Ann daughter of John & Elizabeth (Nunn) Baker.
Oct. 21. Mary Ann daughter of Benjamin & Elizabeth (Palmer) Pryke.
Oct. 31. Jermyn son of James & Esther (Welby) Lewis.
Nov. 24. James son of James & Ann (Crack) Last.
Dec. 25. Thomas son of John & Elizabeth (Wellham) Pearsons.
Dec. 29. Samuel son of Jonas & Rachael (Bray) Rowe.
1812. Feb. 16. Lucy daughter of James & Sophia (Crack) Ramplin.
March 17. Mary Ann daughter of William & Mary (Elmer) Baker.
March 19. William Charles son of Charles & Hannah (Cater) Double.

April 19. Thomas son of William & Rose Ann (Howe) Smith.
May 17. Sarah daughter of Isaac & Sarah (Willingham) Race.
June 28. Robert son of Abraham & Matthew (Copsey) Rooks.
June 28. Mary daughter of Samuel & Sarah (Mizeman) Mizeman.
Aug. 2. Frederick son of Mark & Ann (Cole) Hammond.
Aug. 9. Lucy daughter of John & Charlott (Searjeant) Alvis.
Aug. 23. Susan daughter of William & Temperance (Elliss) Ebbon: priv: baptized March 1, 1810.
1813. Jan. 24. Mary Ann daughter of Sarah Rosbrook. June 7, 1812.
Feb. 3. Charlotte dau: of James & Sarah Bullas, labourer.
Feb. 16. William Naylor son of George & MaryAnn Double, publican.
March 14. Henry son of Robert & Mary Alvis, labourer.
April 11. Arthur son of Matthew & Jane Gostwick, labourer.
May 28. Sydney son of Charles Hill & Augusta Hall, gentleman.
May 30. Susan dau: of George & Bett Cook, labourer.
June 20. Mary dau: of Simon & Susanna Mansfield, labourer.
July 11. William Charles son of William & Susan Ambrose, shoemaker.
July 11. Robert son of Robert Barrell & Catharine Heyhoe, servants.
Aug. 29. George son of Michael & Sarah Crack, labourer.
Sept. 19. George son of late John & Frances Buckle, soldier. Dec. 1, 1807.
Nov. 21. George son of John & Mary Greenwood, labourer.
1814. April 16. Edward son of William & Sarah (Bryant) Green, labourer. Sept. 18, 1813.
May 22. Mary Anne daughter of Caroline Smith.
June 13. Frances dau: of Abraham & Martha (Copsey) Rooks, labourer.
July 10. Sophia dau: of Jeremiah & Drusilla (Pryke) Jermyn, labourer, of Ickworth.
Aug. 25. John William son of Mary Banham.
Sept. 28. Betty dau: of Edward & Mary (Brewster) Willingham, labourer.
Oct. 21. Thomas son of Mary Ling.
Nov. 14. James son of James & Sophia (Crack) Ramplin, labourer.

1815. Jan. 15. Elizabeth daughter of Elizabeth Bull.
Jan. 29. Mary dau : of William & Lydia (Stagg) Arnold, labourer.
Jan. 8. Henry son of William & Mary (Grimwood) Edwards, wheelwright.
March 28. Louisa Browning dau: of Charles Hill & Augusta (Browning) Hall, esquire.
April 9. Edward son of John & Elizabeth (Double) Mower, labourer.
April 16. Theodosia dau: of Matthew & Jane (Balls) Gossick, shepherd.
April 16. Rebecca dau: of Isaac & Sarah (Willingham) Raice, labourer.
April 16. Thomas son of Sarah Risbrooke.
April 23. George son of John & Charlotte (Serjeant) Avis, labourer.
May 14. Mary daughter of Michael & Sarah (Markwell) Crack, labourer.
May 21. Isaac son of Jonas & Rachel (Bray) Rowe, labourer.
May 30. Martha, wife of James Scarling jun. and dau: of Neville & Ann (Cooper) Fuller, gentleman.
June 4. Lionel son of William & Rose Anne (Howe) Smith, woolcomber.
July 31. Lucina dau: of Benjamin & Elizabeth (Palmer) Pryke jun., blacksmith.
Aug. 6. Elizabeth dau: of Roger & Sophia (Alvis) Adams, shoemaker. Oct. 2, 1813.
Aug. 13. George son of William & Sophia (Middleditch) Cater, labourer.
Aug. 25. Elizabeth dau: of Charles & Hannah (Cater) Double, labourer.
Sept. 24. William son of George & Elizabeth (Lynn) Cooke, labourer.
Nov. 12. Elizabeth Mary Anne dau: of William Bacon & Mary Anne (Cooke) Wigson of Horsecroft, gent.
Dec. 24. George son of William & Mary (Cater) Rutter, labourer.
Dec. 25. Susan dau: of James & Anne (Crack) Last, labourer.
1816. Jan. 28. Elizabeth dau: of William & Tabitha (Copsey) Root, carpenter.
March 21. Charles son of George & Mary Anne (Double) Scarff, innkeeper.

April 7. James son of James & Sophia (Crack) Ramplin, labourer.
June 30. Eliza daughter of Sarah Arborn.
July 8. William son of Robert & Ann Spalding, labourer.
Aug. 13. Jane dau: of Robert & Mary (Stearn) Durrant, labourer.
Sept. 1. James son of Maria Lanham.
Sept. 14. James son of James & Sarah (Alvis) Bullass, labourer.
Sept. 22. Mary daughter of Mary Death.
Dec. 25. Henry son of James Sharp of Nowton & Maria Last, labourer.
1817. Jan. 12. John son of Abraham & Martha (Copsey) Rooks, labourer.
Feb. 2. John son of Thomas & Martha (Cater) King, labourer.
Feb. 23. John son of John & Elizabeth (Double) Mower, labourer.
March 9. Martha Susanna dau: of James & Martha Susanna (Fuller) Scarling, gent.
March 17. Eliza dau: of Lewis & Rebecca (Norman) Rushbrooke, labourer.
March 17. Thomas son of William & Sarah (Rushbrooke) Gorlstone, labourer.
April 2. Eliza dau: of John & Charlotte (Serjeant) Alvis, labourer.
April 13. Mary dau: of Charles & Elizabeth (Bull) Coe, labourer.
April 20. Elizabeth dau: of William & Sarah (Thoroughgood) Willingham, labourer.
May 4. Isaac son of James & Mary (Copsey) Boreham, labourer.
May 18. Maria dau: of Isaac & Sarah (Willingham) Raice, labourer.
May 25. Marianne dau: of Edmund & Mary (Brewster) Willingham, labourer.
July 19. Robert son of William & Esther (Saunders) Cooke, labourer.
Aug. 3. Frances daughter of Mary Ling.
Oct. 19. Mary dau: of Matthew & Jane (Balls) Gostwick, shepherd.
Nov. 28. William son of William Bacon & Mary Anne (Cooke) Wigson of Horscroft, gent.
Dec. 12. Elizabeth dau: of John & Elizabeth (Nunn) Baker, labourer.
Dec. 25. George son of William & Tabitha (Copsey) Root, carpenter.
1818. Jan. 6. Charles Browning son of Charles Hill & Augusta (Browning) Hall, esquire.

Jan. 18. Robert son of John & Mary (Cooke) Copsey, labourer.
Feb. 1. Thomas son of John & Sarah (Lewis) Ridnall, carpenter.
Feb. 8. Rebecca dau: of William & Rosanne (Howe) Smith, wool-comber.
March 8. Fanny dau: of George & Bett (Ling) Cooke, labourer.
April 12. Mary Ann dau: of Charles & Elizabeth (Bull) Coe, labourer.
May 15. John son of Jonas & Rachel (Bray) Rowe, labourer.
May 15. Maria dau: of Henry & Mary (Sale) Grimwood, labourer.
May 17. Isaac son of James & Sophia (Crack) Ramplin, labourer.
June 7. John son of Nathaniel & Anne (Howard) Adkin, labourer.
Aug. 11. Charles son of William & Sarah (King) Palmer, labourer.
Sept. 7. William Swithin son of Thomas & Ann (Double) Adkin of Bury, innkeeper.
June 22. Eliza dau: of Lewis & Rebecca (Norman) Rosbrooke, labourer. Jan. 31, 1817.
Dec. 2. Mary Anne dau: of William & Mary Anne (Grimwood) Edwards, wheelwright.
Dec. 17. Mary Anne dau: of Robert & Mary (Stearne) Durrant, labourer.
Dec. 20. James son of Michael & Sarah (Markwell) Crack, labourer.
Dec. 22. Esther dau: of Isaac & Sarah (Willingham) Race, labourer.
1819. Jan. 2. William son of Louis & Rebecca (Norman) Rosbrooke, labourer.
Jan. 6. William son of Simon & Mary (Ling) Last, labourer.
March 6. Mary Anne dau: of William Bacon & Mary Anne (Cooke) Wigson of Horsecroft, gent.
March 21. Mary Anne dau: of George & Mary Anne (Gooch) Farrents, blacksmith.
May 9. Mary Anne dau: of William & Sally (Husbandman) Willingham, labourer.
May 13. Mary dau: of William & Esther (Saunders) Cooke, labourer.
May 16. Ann dau: of Abraham & Hannah (Crack) Cooper, labourer.
May 23. Thomas son of Robert & Sarah (Boyce) Wells, wheelwright.
July 4. Abraham son of Abraham & Martha (Copsey) Rooks, labourer.

F

Sept. 12. William son of Sarah Rosbrooke.
Sept. 18. Edmund son of Edward & Mary (Brewster) Willingham, labourer.
Sept. 19. James son of John & Martha (Ling) Goldstone, labourer.
Sept. 26. Eliza dau: of James & Mary (Copsey) Boreham, labourer.
Oct. 10. Susanna Maria dau: of John & Charlotte (Serjeant) Alvis, labourer.
Nov. 7. Mary Emily dau: of James & Sarah (Alvis) Bullass, labourer.
Nov. 28. Mary daughter of Mary Coe.
1820. Jan. 31. John son of Robert & Mary (Musk) Gooch, labourer.
May 7. Henry Gardiner son of William & Rosa Ann (Howes) Smith, woolcomber.
July 9. Mary dau: of William & Sarah (King) Palmer, labourer.
May 21. Matthew son of Matthew & Jane (Balls) Gostwick, shepherd.
May 21. William son of Lewis & Rebecca (Norman) Rosbrooke, labourer.
July 16. William son of James & Sophia (Rolfe) Ramplin, labourer.
Aug. 6. James son of Isaac & Sarah (Willingham) Race, labourer.
Aug. 28. Emma dau: of William Bacon & Mary Anne (Cooke) Wigson of Horsecroft, gent.
Nov. 13. Thomas son of Abraham & Hannah (Crack) Cooper, labourer.
1821. Feb. 27. James son of John & Mary (Cooke) Copsey, labourer. Feb. 24, 1820.
Feb. 25. Susan dau: of Simon & Mary (Ling) Last, labourer.
Feb. 27. Susan dau: of William & Thomasin (Copsey) Root, labourer.
March 1. Sarah dau: of George & Mary (Gooch) Farrents, blacksmith.
March 7. James son of Robert & Mary (Stern) Durrant, labourer.
March 21. Lehabin dau: of Francis & Elizabeth (Thompson) Double, labourer.
April 8. Abraham son of Abraham & Sophy (Wright) Steed of West Wratting, Cambridgeshire, blacksmith.
April 8. Mary Anne dau: of Robert & Anne (Bedlington) Spalding, labourer.
April 22. David son of William & Esther (Saunders) Cook, labourer.

	June	3.	Mary Anne dau: of Charles & Elizabeth (Bull) Coe, labourer. April 7, 1818.
	June	3.	James son of Charles & Elizabeth (Bull) Coe. May 24, 1821.
	June	10.	Thomas son of Michael & Sarah (Markwell) Crack, labourer.
	Aug.	12.	Robert son of Robert & Sarah (Blowess) Wells, labourer.
	Sept.	30.	Mary daughter of Ann Martin.
	Sept.	30.	Amy dau: of William & Sophy (Middleditch) Cater, labourer.
	Sept.	30.	Henry Marjoram son of Zechariah & Sarah (Batley) Fenton, gardiner.
	Nov.	14.	John son of John & Martha (Ling) Goldestone, labourer.
	Dec.	5.	John son of William & Sarah (King) Palmer, labourer.
	Dec.	9.	George son of James & Mary (Gout) Cater, labourer.
1822.	Jan.	17.	William son of James & Elizabeth (Marshall) Arborn of Chevington, labourer.
	Jan.	27.	Rebecca dau: of William & Rose Anne (Howe) Smith, woolcomber.
	Jan.	27.	William son of James & Mary (Copsey) Boreham, labourer.
	Feb.	10.	George Edward son of James & Mary Ann (Lilly) Wallaker, labourer.
	Feb.	10.	George son of Robert & Mary Ann (Musk) Gooch, bricklayer.
	April	28.	Jane dau: of Matthew & Jane (Balls) Gostwick, shepherd.
	May	2.	Sophy dau: of John & Charlotte (Serjeant) Alvis, labourer.
	May	4.	Henry son of James & Sophia (Crack) Ramplin, labourer.
	May	26.	William son of William & Sarah (Thoroughgood) Willingham, labourer.
	June	9.	Abraham son of Isaac & Sarah (Willingham) Race, labourer.
	July	7.	Henry son of Abraham & Mary (Crack) Cooper, labourer.
	July	18.	Henry son of Thomas Brown of Dalham & Eliza Last.
	July	28.	James son of Thomas & Eliza (Last) Brown of Dalham, labourer.
	Aug.	18.	Elizabeth dau: of William & Sarah (Rosbrooke) Goldestone, labourer.
	Aug.	25.	John son of Lewis & Rebecca (Norman) Rosbrooke, labourer.
	Sept.	22.	Mary Ann dau: of John & Mary Copsey, labourer.

Oct. 27. David son of William & Hester (Saunders) Cooke, labourer.
Nov. 14. Sarah dau : of John Goldestone & Mary Crack, labourer, of Walsham.
1823. Feb. 25. Mary Ann dau : of Simon & Mary (Ling) Last, labourer.
March 30. Mary Ann dau : of William & Tabitha (Copsey) Root, labourer.
March 30. Robert son of Robert & Sophia (Hambling) Mayes, labourer.
April 6. John son of David & Maria (Langham) Smith, labourer.
April 27. Thomas son of Robert & Elizabeth (Cater) Catchpole, shepherd.
May 11. Mary dau : of Thomas & Mary (Pettit) Leonard, of Ickworth, groom.
June 1. Frederick son of Zachariah & Sarah (Battley) Fenton, gardener.
July 27. Elizabeth dau : of George & Jane (Nelson) Musk, labourer.
Aug. 17. Henry Cameron son of Henry Curtis & Anne Alicia (Cameron) Cherry, clergyman.
Aug. 24. Elizabeth dau : of Michael & Sarah (Markwell) Crack, labourer.
Sept. 7. David son of Robert & Mary (Sterne) Durrant, labourer.
Oct. 20. Henry Cooke son of William Bacon & Mary Ann (Cooke) Wigson of Horsecroft, gent.
Dec. 25. Susannah dau : of John & Mary (Langham) Winch of Ickworth, labourer.
1824. Jan. 1. Elizabeth dau : of George & Mary (Gooch) Farrants, blacksmith.
Jan. 11. Elizabeth dau : of John & Mary (Cook) Copsey, labourer.
Feb. 8. Henry son of John & Fanny (Pickering) Simkin, thatcher.
Feb. 22. Maria dau : of James & Sophia (Rolfe) Ramplin, labourer.
Feb. 22. George son of George & Mary (Osborn) Greenwood, labourer.
Feb. 22. Sophia dau : of Robert & Sarah (Bloyse) Wells, wheelwright.
Feb. 22. James son of William & Elizabeth (Fitch) King, labourer.
March 3. William son of William & Sarah (King) Palmer, labourer.
March 17. Michael son of Robert & Peggy (Drake) Ridnell, labourer.

March 27. Eliza dau: of Robert & Elizabeth (Crow) Winch, labourer.
April 16. Sophia dau: of Thomas & Kezia (Rayner) Pryke, blacksmith.
May 2. Harriett dau: of James & Mary (Copsey) Boreham, labourer.
May 23. Stephen son of Stephen & Elizabeth (Cutting) Saunders, shoemaker.
June 6. Elizabeth dau: of Matthew & Jane (Balls) Gostwick, shepherd.
June 20. Frederick son of Abraham & Hannah (Crack) Cooper, labourer.
July 4. Sophia dau: of William & Sophia Cater, labourer.
Aug. 1. James son of William & Rose Ann (Howe) Smith, Parish Clerk.
Aug. 8. Henry Curtis son of Henry Curtis & Anne Alicia (Cameron) Cherry, clergyman.
Oct. 3. Jonathan son of Isaac & Sarah (Willingham) Race, labourer.
Oct. 17. Mary Elizabeth dau: of Robert & Mary (Musk) Gooch, bricklayer.
Oct. 30. Thomas son of William Bacon & Mary Ann (Cooke) Wigson of Horsecroft gent.
Nov. 5. Hannah dau: of John & Charlotte (Sarjeant) Alvis, labourer.
1825. Jan. 2. James son of Charles & Mary (Middleditch) Golding, labourer.
Feb. 3. Elizabeth dau: of John & Mary Ann (Garwood) Kemp, farmer. Feb. 4, 1824. Baptized at Chevington, christened here.
Feb. 20. David son of David & Maria (Lanham) Smith, labourer.
Feb. 24. Daniel son of James & Sarah (Winter) Ellis, labourer.
April 10. William son of William & Esther (Saunders) Cooke, gardener.
May 8. Eliza dau: of William & Sarah Willingham, labourer.
May 8. William son of George & Mary (Gooch) Farrents, blacksmith.
May 15. Edward son of Edward & Elizabeth (Ebbing) Brown, servant.
May 19. Simon son of Simon & Mary (Ling) Last, labourer.
July 27. Maria dau: of Sarah Rosbrooke.
Aug. 21. William son of John & Mary (Cooke) Copsey, labourer.
Oct. 2. Sarah dau: of Robert & Elizabeth (Cater) Catchpole, shepherd.

Oct. 9. Sarah Elizabeth dau: of George & Jane (Nelson) Musk, labourer.

Nov. 13. Sarah dau: of William Read & Mary Etherington, cabinet-maker. Jan. 6, 1823.

Nov. 20. Kezia dau: of Thomas & Kezia (Rayner) Pryke, blacksmith.

Dec. 4. John William son of Robert & Elizabeth (Crow) Winch, labourer.

Dec. 4. Thomas son of Abraham & Martha (Copsey) Rooks, labourer.

Dec. 18. Harriet dau: of William & Tabitha (Copsey) Root, carpenter.

Dec. 20. John Charles son of John & Mary Ann (Garwood) Kemp, farmer.

1826. Jan. 3. Robert son of William & Sarah (King) Palmer, labourer.

Feb. 13. Emily Alicia dau: of Henry Curtis & Anne Alicia (Cameron) Cherry, clergyman.

Feb. 21. Mary dau: of William & Mary (Howlet) Plum of Ickworth, gamekeeper. June 15, 1822.

& Elizabeth do. do. do. May 25, 1824.

Feb. 26. Edward John son of Edward & Sarah (Langham) Crack, labourer.

March 2. James son of James & Sarah (Winter) Elliss, labourer.

April 16. Susan dau: of Thomas Pearsons, horse dealer, & Mary Coe.

April 23. Rebecca dau: of Lewis & Rebecca (Norman) Rosbrook, labourer.

May 28. Henry son of Henry & Rachel (Rowe) Cater, labourer.

May 29. Esther dau: of William & Esther (Saunders) Cooke, gardener.

June 9. William son of Abraham & Hannah (Crack) Cooper, labourer.

June 26. Richard son of William Bacon & Mary Ann (Cooke) Wigson, of Horsecroft gent.

July 30. Susan dau: of Michael & Sarah (Markwell) Crack, labourer.

Oct. 8. Eliza dau: of Daniel Douglas, stone mason, & Maria Edwards.

Dec. 3. George son of John & Harriet (Powell) Short, stone mason.

Dec. 10. Thomas son of Philip & Anne (Goodchild) Meadows, labourer.

	Dec.	24.	Sarah dau : of Robert & Sarah (Drake) Ridnell, labourer.
1827.	Jan.	7.	James son of Robert & Sarah (Blois) Wells, labourer.
	Jan.	7.	Susanna dau : of Rachel Hammond.
	Jan.	7.	Amelia dau : of John & Mary (Winch) Rolfe, carpenter.
	Feb.	4.	Charlotte dau : of Charles & Charlotte (Crick) Rushbrooke, labourer.
	March	5.	Ellis Maria dau : of Robert & Anne (Plum) Pearsons, farmer.
	March	10.	William son of John & Fanny (Pickering) Simkin, thatcher.
	May	11.	William son of John & Frances (Clarke) Miseman, labourer.
	May	11.	Isaac son of James & Sarah (Winter) Ellis, labourer.
	May	20.	Lucy Moyse dau : of Benjamin & Sarah (Steed) Pryke, blacksmith.
	May	24.	Mary Ann Parsons dau : of Thomas & Lydia (Pearson) Pryke, blacksmith.
	May	29.	Thomas son of Simon & Mary (Ling) Last, labourer.
	June	3.	Jonathan son of Mathew & Jane (Balls) Gostwick, labourer.
	June	3.	Mary Ann dau : of Mary Ann Crack.
	June	15.	Martha dau : of George & Sarah (Sexton) Braine, servant.
	June	22.	Robert son of William & Sarah (King) Palmer, labourer.
	July	15.	William son of George & Jane (Nelson) Musk, labourer.
	July	15.	Edward son of Robert & Mary (Musk) Gooch, labourer.
	July	26.	Mary Ann dau : of Henry & Mary (Sale) Grimwood, labourer.
	Aug.	5.	Sophia dau : of James & Mary (Copsey) Boreham, labourer.
	Sept.	30.	Eliza dau : of James & Sophia Ramplin, labourer.
	Dec.	2.	Mary Ann dau : of Philip & Ann (Goodchild) Meadows, labourer.
	Dec.	23.	Eliza dau : of William & Tabitha (Copsey) Root, labourer.
1828.	Jan.	6.	Hannah dau : of William & Elizabeth (Fitch) King, labourer.
	Jan.	13.	Mary Ann dau : of Stephen & Elizabeth (Cutting) Saunders, shoemaker.
	Jan.	27.	Jane dau : of William & Esther (Saunders) Cook, labourer.
	Feb.	1.	Emma Eliza dau : of John & Mary Ann (Garrard) Kemp, farmer.
	March	14.	John son of George & Mary (Gooch) Farrants, blacksmith.

April 6. Emily dau: of Lewis & Rebecca (Norman) Rosbrooke, farmer.
April 13. James son of Edward & Sarah (Lanham) Crack, labourer.
April 17. Henry son of Joseph & Elizabeth (Grimwood) Edwards, labourer.
May 25. Jane dau: of Robert & Ann (Bedlington), Spalding, labourer.
May 25. Thomas & Harriet, children of John & Mary (Crack) Goldstone of Walsham, labourer.
May 25. Mary Ann dau: of John & Mary (Boreham) Limmarks, labourer.
Aug. 10. Caroline dau: of Sarah Tricker.
Aug. 31. Rachel dau: of William & Rachel (Cater) Elsden, servant.
Sept. 7. Henry son of John & Mary (Cooke) Copsey, labourer.
Oct. 4. Ellen dau: of John & Charlotte Serjeant, servant.
Nov. 16. Sarah dau: of Mathew & Jane (Balls) Gostwick, labourer.
Nov. 23. John Arthur son of William & Harriet (Cater) Bullas, labourer.
Dec. 21. William son of John & Hannah (Cockle) Bull, labourer.
Dec. 23. Elizabeth Martha dau: of John & Elizabeth (Adkins) Moss, builder.
1829. Jan. 27. Louisa dau: of — & Ann (Sale) Levett, labourer.
Feb. 6. Harriet dau: of Abraham & Hannah Cooper, labourer.
March 1. Susan dau: of Isaac & Sarah Race, labourer.
March 29. Jane dau: of William & Harriot (Burgess) Eade, servant.
April 9. Benjamin son of Thomas & Keziah (Rayner) Pryke, blacksmith.
May 25. Mary Ann dau: of John & Frances (Fanny) (Pickering) Simkin, thatcher.
June 10. Thomas son of William & Sarah (King) Palmer, labourer.
June 15. Ann dau: of Simon & Mary (Ling) Last, labourer.
June 21. Harriet dau: of John & Harriet (Powell) Short, labourer.
July 10. Frederick Turnor son of William Bacon & Mary Ann (Cooke) Wigson, gent.
Sept. 6. Robert son of Robert & Mary (Musk) Gooch of Bury St. Edmunds, bricklayer.

Sept. 6. James Cook son of Joseph & Ann (Cook) Miseman, labourer.
Sept. 13. William son of Robert & Sarah (Blose) Wells, labourer.
Sept. 20. Caroline dau: of John & Mary (Pryke) Elsden, labourer.
Oct. 18. Betsy dau: of Robert & Peggy (Drake) Ridnell, labourer.
Nov. 1. Emma dau: of James & Sophia (Last) Ramplin, labourer.
Nov. 1. Alice dau: of Philip & Anne (Goodchild) Meadows, labourer.
Nov. 4. Mark son of Theodorus & Mary (Steed) Harrison, bricklayer. April 19, 1825.
Dec. 14. Ann dau: of John & Mary (Lanham) Winch, labourer.
Dec. 27. Elias son of James & Sarah (Winter) Elliss, labourer.
1830. Jan. 3. Harriet dau: of George & Sarah (Bird) Tweed, labourer.
Jan. 17. Elizabeth Emma dau: of Charles & Harriet (Sale) Nunn, servant.
Jan. 17. James Josiah Tregellas son of Sophia Hammond.
Feb. 12. Maria dau: of John & Elizabeth (Adkin) Moss, joiner.
April 11. Marianne dau: of Phillis Lennard.
May 30. Jane dau: of Richard & Susan (Crack) Cockerill, labourer.
May 30. Susannah dau: of William & Sarah (Thorogood) Willingham, labourer.
July 4. Marianne dau: of William & Elizabeth (Fitch) King, labourer.
July 31. Anne dau: of William & Esther (Saunders) Cook, labourer.
Aug. 2. Susan dau: of Stephen & Sarah (Sharp) Musk, labourer.
Aug. 15. George son of George & Susan (Nelson) Musk, labourer.
Aug. 22. Lucy Adalaide dau: of Henry & Mary (Sale) Grimwood, wheelwright.
Oct. 6. Penelope Heigham dau: of Edward & Mary Anna Penelope (Heigham) Gould, clerk.
Oct. 24. Maria dau: of William & Tabitha (Copsey) Root, carpenter.
Oct. 25. Valentine John son of John & Sarah (Green) Edwards, wheelwright.
Oct. 31. Ann dau: of Thomas & Mary (King) Goodchild, labourer.
Nov. 8. Susannah dau: of John & Mary (Last) Wing, labourer.
1831. Jan. 9. Lucy dau: of George & Sarah (Bird) Tweed, labourer.
Jan. 22. William son of William & Rachel (Cater, Rowe) Elsden, labourer.

Jan. 28. Elijah son of Thomas & Keziah (Raynham) Pryke, blacksmith.
Feb. 22. Harriet dau: of Richard & Susan (Crack) Cockeril, labourer.
April 11. Amy dau: of William & Sarah (King) Palmer, labourer.
May 8. Amelia dau: of John & Charlotte (Newman) Sergeant, labourer.
May 8. James son of George & Mary (Gooch) Farrents, blacksmith.
May 21. Harriet dau: of Robert & Peggy (Drake) Ridnall, labourer.
May 22. James son of Simon & Mary (Ling) Last, labourer.
May 22. Eliza dau: of Thomas & Ann (Boyce) Thompson, shoemaker.
May 23. William son of Robert & Ann (Plumb) Pearson of Ickworth, farmer.
June 1. William son of George & Sarah (Tricker) Cooper, dealer.
June 5. Frederick son of Zechariah & Sarah (Martin) Mayes, labourer.
June 19. James son of James & Mary (Long) Langham, shepherd.
June 23. Sarah dau: of William & Frances (Death) Wheeler, labourer.
June 25. Emma dau: of William Bacon & Mary Ann (Cooke) Wigson, gent. July 23, 1822,
& Ann do. do. Born March 31, 1828,
& Adelaide Jane do do. Born April 24, 1831.
July 31. Thomas son of John & Mary (Cook) Copsey, labourer.
Sept. 4. William son of William & Jane (Burgess) Eade, servant.
Sept. 11. Emma dau: of William & Tabitha (Copsey) Root, labourer.
Sept. 18. Susannah dau: of Matthew & Jane (Balls) Gostwick, shepherd.
Nov. 13. Catharine Maria dau: of Edward & Mary Anna Penelope (Heigham) Gould, clerk.
Dec. 1. Robert son of Jeremiah & Mary (Liles) Ebbens, servant.
Dec. 5. Jane dau: of Joseph & Ann (Cook) Miseman, labourer.
Dec. 25. Maria dau: of John & Elizabeth (Payne) Smith, labourer.
Dec. 25. Henry son of William & Anne (Arbon) Sale, labourer.
Dec. 25. Benjamin Pearman son of James & Hannah (Pearman) Pryke of Mildenhall, blacksmith.
1832. Jan. 16. Eliza dau: of William & Marianne (Palfrey) Brown, labourer.

Jan. 22. Marianne dau: of John & Harriet (Rutter) Bullass.
Feb. 6. Thomas son of John & Frances (Pickering) Simkin, thatcher.
Feb. 14. William Gardiner son of Harriet Smith.
Feb. 19. Mary Ann dau: of Sarah Windward.
Feb. 21. Susan dau: of Isaac & Caroline (Linge) Race, labourer.
March 13. Charles son of Matthew & Marianne (Boggis) Miseman, labourer.
April 1. Maria dau: of Robert & Sarah (Blois) Wells, labourer.
April 15. William son of George & Anna Maria (Ambrose) Brewster, stonemason.
April 22. Jane dau: of Robert & Mary (Cater) Elsden, labourer.
May 4. Sarah Elizabeth dau: of Stephen & Sarah (Sharp) Musk, labourer.
June 3. Charles son of James & Sophia (Crack) Ramplin, labourer.
June 10. Louisa dau: of Robert & Anne (Boyce) Thompson, shoemaker.
June 17. James son of John & Mary (Pryke) Elsden, labourer.
June 26. Sarah dau: of Thomas & Mary (King) Goodchild, labourer.
July 30. John son of Abraham & Hannah (Crack) Cooper, labourer.
Aug. 15. James son of Philip & Anne (Goodchild) Meadows, labourer.
Sept. 2. Marianne dau: of James & Sarah (Winter) Elliss, labourer.
Sept. 12. Harriet dau. of Thomas & Kezia (Rayner) Pryke, blacksmith.
Sept. 16. Ada Georgiana dau: of Henry & Maria (Creed) Watson, gent.
Nov. 1. John Elsden son of Susan Death, of Borley, Essex.
Nov. 4. Maria dau: of James & Susannah (Lanham) Byford, farmer.
Nov. 11. Maria dau: of George & Jane (Nelson) Musk, labourer.
Dec. 7. Thomas son of George & Sarah (Bird) Tweed, labourer.
Dec. 25. Jane dau: of John & Harriet (Powel) Short, stonemason.
1833. Jan. 7. Septimus Seaven son of William Bacon & Mary Anne (Cooke) Wigson, gent.
Feb. 8. Susan dau: of Stephen & Sophy (Flack) Paske, labourer.
Feb. 16. James son of James & Esther (Hustler) Death, labourer.
Feb. 24. Anna Maria dau: of John & Charlotte (Newman) Sergeant, servant.

March 11. Maria dau: of Simon & Mary (Ling) Last, labourer.
March 31. Sophia dau: of William & Tabitha (Copsey) Root, labourer.
April 1. Lucy dau: of William & Esther (Saunders) Cook, labourer.
May 12. Sophy dau: of William & Elizabeth (Fitch) King, labourer.
May 26. Liddy dau: of William & Sarah (King) Palmer, labourer.
June 9. Jane dau: of Stephen & Sarah (Sharp) Musk, labourer.
July 7. William son of Zechariah & Sarah (Martin) Mayes, labourer.
July 13. Mary Eliza Merelina dau: of Edward & Mary Anna Penelope (Heigham) Gould clerk.
July 21. Sarah dau: of William & Rachel (Cater, Rowe) Elsden, labourer.
July 27. Ellen dau: of John & Mary Anne (Bullock) Heigho, labourer.
Aug. 11. Robert son of William & Sarah (Bailey) Lilley, labourer.
Oct. 20. Jane dau: of John & Mary (Lanham) Winch, labourer.
Oct. 27. Hannah dau: of John & Mary (Goldson, Crack) Pallant of Walsham.
Oct. 31. Elizabeth dau: of Philip & Anne (Goodchild) Meadows, labourer.
Nov. 25. Elizabeth dau: of Joseph & Mary (Cumming) Bridgman, labourer.
Dec. 25. William son of Richard & Susan (Crack) Cockerill, labourer.
Dec. 25. Elizabeth Jane dau: of William & Anne (Arbon) Sale, labourer.
1834. Jan. 19. Sophia dau: of William & Mary Ann (Palfrey) Brown, labourer.
Feb. 14. Kenelm William son of John & Sarah (Green) Edwards, wheelwright.
March 2. Marianne dau: of Joseph & Marianne (Sillet) Mayhew, publican.
March 21. James Matthias son of James Matthias & Abigail (Lloyd) Brewster, stonemason.
March 30. Robert David son of John & Harriet (Rutter) Bullass, labourer.
April 13. George son of Roger & Eliza (Ponder) Dakin, bricklayer.
May 18. Thomas son of Robert & Peggy (Drake) Ridnall, labourer.

May 18. Robert James son of Robert & Anne (Boyce) Thompson shoemaker.
May 20. George son of Matthew & Marianne (Boggis) Mison, labourer.
May 25. Jane dau: of Ezekiel & Charlotte (Naylor) Durrant, labourer.
June 8. Sarah dau: of Jeremiah & Mary (Liles) Ebbens, labourer.
June 9. Lucy dau: of William & Marianne (Mison) King, labourer. July, 1832.
June 15. Jane dau: of George & Jane (Nelson) Musk, labourer.
July 13. Sarah dau: of James & Esther (Hustler) Death, labourer.
Aug. 10. Marianne dau: of Henry & Susan (Musk) Crooks, servant.
Aug. 17. Eliza dau: of John & Mary (Pryke) Elsden, labourer.
Aug. 20. Marianne dau: of George & Sarah (Tricker) Cooper, dealer.
Aug. 24. Rebecca dau: of Isaac & Caroline (Ling) Race, labourer.
Sept. 7. Anna Maria dau: of John & Frances (Pickering) Simpkin, thatcher.
Sept. 7. Emma Eliza dau: of Mary Mison.
Sept. 21. George William son of Charles & Sarah (Lilly) Canham, gamekeeper.
Oct. 5. George son of James & Sophia (Last) Ramplin, labourer.
Oct. 19. Thomas son of Thomas & Keziah (Rainer) Pryke, blacksmith.
Oct. 26. Martha dau: of James & Mary Anne (Smith) Blencowe of Horsecroft, labourer.
Nov. 7. George son of George & Sophia (Bailey) Buckle, labourer.
Nov. 23. Sophia dau: of James & Lucy (Ramplin) Boreham, labourer.
Nov. 29. Susan dau: of John & Mary (Cooke) Copsey, labourer.
Dec. 25. Daniel son of James & Sarah (Winter) Ellis, labourer.
Dec. 28. Anne Elizabeth dau: of George & Anna Maria (Ambrose) Brewster, stonemason.
1835. Feb. 16. John son of John & Charlotte (Newman) Sergeant, labourer.
March 8. Stephen son of Stephen & Sophia (Flack) Paske, labourer.
March 15. Sarah Anne dau: of Joseph & Anne (Cooke) Mison, labourer.
March 25. Marianne dau: of David & Elizabeth (Harris) Hammond, labourer.

April 2. Memorandum from certificate. May 12, 1831, Baptized at the English Episcopal Chapel, Elizabeth dau: of Isaac & Charlotte Brooke of St. Servan, Department of Ille & Vilaine, by J. T. Mansel, Off: Min: of St. Servan.

April 2. Memorandum from Certificate. Nov. 11, 1832, Arthur George son of Isaac & Charlotte Brooke of St. Helier in the Island of Jersey, by C. Hue, Rector of St. Helier.

April 5. Emma dau: of Joseph & Marianne (Sillet) Mayhew, publican.

April 17. Henry William son of Robert & Charlotte (Offord) Edwards, wheelwright.

May 13. George son of George & Elizabeth (Bull) Crack, labourer.

June 7. Mary dau: of Thomas & Mary (King) Goodchild, labourer.

June 28. Henry James son of William & Sarah (King) Palmer, labourer.

July 12. Maria dau: of John & Maria (Cable) Bridges, labourer.

Aug. 2. Edmund John son of William & Cordelia (Death) Kirrage, bricklayer.

Aug. 23. Susan dau: of George & Sarah (Bird) Tweed, labourer.

Aug. 23. Sarah Anne dau: of Zechariah & Sarah (Mountain) Mayes, labourer.

Oct. 18. Henry son of William & Sarah (Bailey) Lilly, labourer.

Oct. 18. George son of Abraham & Hannah (Crack) Cooper, labourer.

Nov. 17. Richard Edgar son of John & Elizabeth (Edgar) Sturgeon, farmer.

Dec. 3. Ezekiel son of Ezekiel & Charlotte (Naylor) Durrant, labourer.

Dec. 13. Susan dau: of Matthew & Mary Anne (Boggis) Mison, labourer.

Dec. 18. Elizabeth dau: of Simon & Mary (Ling) Last, labourer.

Dec. 20. Elizabeth dau: of James & Esther (Hustler) Death, labourer.

Dec. 27. Agnes dau: of William & Tabitha (Copsey) Root, labourer.

1836. Jan. 17. John son of John & Mary (Everet) Lanham, labourer.

Feb. 2. George son of Robert & Harriet (Tweed) Petch, gardener.

Feb. 8. Marianne dau: of William & Rachel (Cater, Rowe) Elsden, labourer.

Feb. 22. Marianne dau: of Richard & Susan (Crack) Cockerill, labourer.

March 10. Thomas son of John & Harriet (Rutter) Bullass, labourer.

April 12. Eliza Ann dau: of James Mathew & Eliza (Lowe) Scarling, gent.

May 15. Mary Anne dau: of Robert & Anne (Boyce) Thompson, shoemaker.

May 22. Sarah dau: of William & Ann (Arborn) Sale, labourer.

June 3. Eliza dau: of Isaac & Caroline (Linge) Race, labourer.

June 3. William son of George & Sophia (Bayley) Buckle, labourer.

July 17. Susan dau: of Henry & Susan (Musk) Brooks, shoemaker.

Aug. 24. Ann Elizabeth dau: of William & Mary Anne (Mison) King, labourer.

Aug. 28. Emma dau: of James & Susanna (Lanham) Byford, carter.

Sept. 5. Sarah Ann dau: of Thomas & Keziah (Rayner) Pryke, blacksmith.

Sept. 18. Eliza dau: of Robert & Eliza (Crowe) Hammond, labourer.

Oct. 30. Frederick son of James & Ann (Double) Vincent of Bury, labourer.

Nov. 27. James Anthony son of Anthony & Mary Anne (Pryke) Michnelly of London, plasterer.

Dec. 6. Jane dau: of Thomas & Agnes (Attree) Turner, farmer.

Dec. 19. Sarah dau: of Jermyn & Sarah (Wells) Lewis, shoemaker.

Dec. 28. Sarah Anne dau: of Robert & Elizabeth (Willingham) Cooke, labourer.

1837. Jan. 15. Anna Maria dau: of Thomas Grimwood & Elizabeth (Ambrose) Saunders, wheelwright.

March 9. Johnson son of Joseph & Mary Ann (Sillett) Mayhew, inn-keeper.

March 12. Rebekah dau: of James & Sarah (Winter) Ellis, labourer.

March 19. Maria dau: of George & Jane (Nelson) Musk, labourer.

March 25. Thomas Orgill son of Susanna Partridge. March 1, 1836.

March 26. Mary Anne dau: of Thomas & Sophia (Hammond) Catchpole, labourer.

March 26. John son of David & Elizabeth (Harris) Hammond, labourer.

March 26. Sophia dau: of James & Lucy (Ramplin) Boreham, labourer.
April 2. Jeremiah, born Dec. 11, 1814: William, Sept. 3, 1817: Elizabeth, Nov. 9, 1819: Mary, Nov. 9. 1819: George, May 12, 1821: children of Jeremiah & Mary (Grimwood) Saunders, shoemaker.
April 2. Sarah dau: of Edward & Jane (Arbon) Green, labourer.
April 2. Charles son of John & Mary (Pryke) Elsdon, labourer.
April 4. Georgiana dau: of John & Mary Ann (Garwood) Kemp, farmer.
April 16. Thomas Grimwood son of Jeremiah & Mary (Grimwood) Sanders, shoemaker. Jan. 11, 1814.
April 16. Josiah son of do do do. Feb. 28, 1816.
May 7. Thomas son of James & Esther (Hustler) Death, labourer.
June 5. Mary Anne dau: of John & Mary (Cook) Copsey, labourer.
June 11. Martha Susanna dau: of William & Sarah (King) Palmer of Westley, labourer.
June 18. Jane dau: of John & Maria (Cable) Bridge, labourer.
June 18. James Cuming son of Joseph & Mary (Cuming) Bridgman, butcher. May 29, 1836.
July 9. Caroline dau: of do do do. Dec. 2. 1828.
July 16. Joseph Edmund son of John & Elizabeth (Edgar) Sturgeon, farmer.
July 23. Sarah Ann dau: of John & Frances (Pickering) Simpkin, thatcher.
Aug. 6. James son of Robert & Elizabeth (Perry) Gooch, bricklayer.
Aug. 20. Sophia dau: of Zechariah & Sarah (Martin) Mayes, labourer.
Aug. 20. Jane dau: of Stephen & Sophia (Flack) Pask, labourer.
Oct. 2. James Henry son of James Matthew & Eliza (Lowe) Scarling, gent.
Oct. 22. John Baker son of Robert & Mary Ann (Baker) Rooks, labourer.
Dec. 25. Sarah Charlotte dau: of John & Harriet (Rutter) Bullass, labourer.
1838. Jan. 28. Marianne dau: of John & Harriet (Smith) Green, carpenter.
Feb. 14. Arabella dau: of John & Sarah (Green) Edwards, wheelwright.
March 25. Alice dau: of Thomas & Mary (King) Goodchild, labourer.

April 1. Alfred son of Robert & Harriet (Tweed) Petch, gardener.
June 8. Esther wife of John Stutter gent. & dau: of Thomas & Mary Gill, gent. of Bury St. Edmunds.
June 17. John son of William & Mary (Coe) Spalding, labourer.
Aug. 26. William son of George & Anne (Goodliffe) Cater, labourer.
Sept. 2. Emma dau: of Jermyn & Sarah (Wells) Lewis, shoemaker.
Sept. 7. Thomas son of Thomas & Agnes (Attree) Turner, gent.
Sept. 30. Robert son of William & Sarah (Thorogood) Willingham, labourer.
Sept. 30. Esther dau: of Robert & Elizabeth (Willingham) Cooke, labourer.
Oct. 28. Emily dau: of James & Hannah (Holmes) Clarke, labourer.
Nov. 4. Maria dau: of Edward & Jane (Arbon) Green, labourer.
Dec. 9. Elizabeth dau: of James & Suzanna (Langham) Byford, carter.
Dec. 16. Emma dau: of William & Tabitha (Copsey) Root, labourer.
Dec. 23. Mary Anne dau: of William & Sarah (Bailey) Lilley, labourer.
Dec. 23. Thomas William son of Thomas & Elizabeth (Ambrose) Saunders, wheelwright.
1839. Jan. 13. Joseph son of Joseph & Mary Anne (Sillett) Mayhew of Bury, innkeeper.
Jan. 27. Thomas son of John & Mary (Everet) Langham, labourer.
Feb. 10. Maria dau: of George & Sarah (Tricker) Cooper, butcher.
March 10. John Thomas son of Thomas & Amy (Martin) Parker, brickmaker.
March 31. William Nunn son of William & Eliza (Nunn) Makup, labourer.
April 7. George son of William & Rachel (Rowe) Elsden, labourer.
June 16. Charles son of John & Frances (Pickering) Simpkin, thatcher.
June 16. Sarah dau: of Henry & Suzan (Musk) Crooks, shoemaker.
June 26. James son of Isaac & Caroline (Linge) Race, labourer.
July 7. Maria dau: of William & Anne (Arborn) Sale, labourer.
July 17. Mary Anne dau: of Robert & Mary Anne (Baker) Rooks, labourer.

G

July 28. Abraham son of John & Mary (Pryke) Elsden, labourer.
Aug. 11. Maria dau: of Simon & Mary (Ling) Last. Jan. 21, 1833.
Aug. 11. Elizabeth dau: of do do. Sept. 14, 1835.
Aug. 11. James son of do do. June 24, 1839.
Aug. 24. Joseph son of John & Maria (Cable) Bridge, labourer.
Sept. 22. Emma dau: of James & Sarah (Winter) Ellis, labourer.
Sept. 26. Susan dau: of Thomas & Mary (King) Goodchild, labourer.
Oct. 6. Joseph son of Joseph & Elizabeth (Winch) Farrants, blacksmith.
Oct. 6. George son of William & Mary Anne (Palfrey) Brown, labourer.
Nov. 5. Edward son of George & Jane (Nelson) Musk, labourer.
Nov. 10. George son of Richard & Susan (Crack) Cockrill, labourer.
Nov. 24. Martha dau: of Thomas & Sophia (Hammond) Catchpole, labourer.
1840. Jan. 12. Jane dau: of Daniel & Harriet (Evered) Jolly, labourer.
Feb. 9. Harriet Martha dau: of John & Harriet (Rutter) Bullass, labourer.
Feb. 9. William son of Henry & Emily (Doel), Cater, labourer.
Feb. 23. Sarah dau: of Sarah Buckle.
March 1. Elizabeth dau: of John & Charlotte (Newman) Sergeant, labourer.
March 22. Anne dau: of William & Mary (Coe) Spalding, labourer.
April 19. Henry Harrold son of Thomas & Sarah (Ridnall), Wade, labourer.
April 26. John Michael son of John & Elizabeth (Edgar) Sturgeon, farmer.
April 26. Elizabeth dau: of Thomas & Elizabeth (Ambrose) Saunders, wheelwright.
May 17. Emily dau: of Zachariah & Sarah (Martin) Mays, labourer.
June 21. Amos Green son of John & Sarah (Green) Edwards, wheelwright.
July 5. Esther dau: of Isaac & Caroline (Linge) Race, labourer.
Sept. 6. Amy Sabina dau: of John & Elizabeth (Root) Bowers, wheelwright.

Sept. 28. Amy dau : of George & Sarah (Bird) Tweed, shopkeeper.
Oct. 13. Charles son of Robert & Anne (Cater) Cobbing, labourer.
Oct. 14. Louisa Harriot dau: of George Innes & Rachel (Bevan) Bevan, gent.
Nov. 8. Margaret Anne dau: of James & Susannah (Langham) Byford, carter.
Nov. 29. Eliza dau : of William & Eliza (Nunn) Makup, labourer.
Dec. 24. Elizabeth dau: of Joseph & Elizabeth (Winch) Farrants, blacksmith.
1841. Jan. 20. Phœbe dau : of Cornelius & Clare (Boswell) Smith, of no regular abode, Hargrave parish, tinker.
Feb. 14. Betsy dau : of Isaac & Mary (Cage) Boreham, labourer.
March 28. Amy dau : of Mary Cook.
April 13. Thomas Underwood son of John & Elizabeth Ann (Underwood) Josslyn, innkeeper.
May 2. William Henry son of Mary Anne Willingham.
June 13. William son of George & Sarah (Tricker) Cooper, jobber.
July 20. Thomas Ramsey son of William & Emily (Ramsey) Gardiner of Bury, farmer.
Aug. 8. Jane Elizabeth dau : of John & Elizabeth (Edgar) Sturgeon, farmer.
Aug. 22. Charles son of James & Lucy (Rampling) Boreham, labourer, Sept. 12, 1838.
Aug. 22. Richard son of do do do. March 28, 1841.
Aug. 22. Anne dau : of William & Mary Anne (Spalding) Boreham, labourer.
Aug. 29. Robert son of Elijah & Louisa (Lambert) Deacon, brickmaker.
Sept. 12. Mary Anne dau: of Jermyn & Sarah (Wells) Lewis, shoemaker.
Sept. 19. James son of William & Anne (Arbon) Sale, labourer.
Oct. 3. William son of Robert & Dorothy (Cawston) Avis, labourer.
Oct. 3. Edward Stephen son of George & Jane (Nelson) Musk labourer.
Oct. 24. Fanny dau: of John & Frances (Pickering) Simpkin, thatcher.

Nov. 7. James son of William & Mary Anne (Palfrey) Brown, labourer.

Nov. 14. Henry son of Thomas Grimwood & Elizabeth (Ambrose) Saunders, wheelwright.

Nov. 14. Helen dau: of William & Elizabeth (Bailey) Lilly, labourer.

1842. Jan. 2. Caroline dau: of George & Harriet (Harrold) Brown, labourer.

Jan. 2. Henry son of John & Mary (Evered) Langham, labourer.

Jan. 15. Eliza dau: of William & Mary Anne (Wyard) Last, labourer.

Jan. 23. Elizabeth dau: of James & Sarah (Winter) Elliss, labourer.

March 27. Amos Lionel son of John & Harriet (Smith) Green, carpenter.

April 3. John son of William & Rachel (Rowe) Elsden, labourer.

April 24. Anne dau: of William & Mary (Coe) Spalding, labourer.

May 23. George Buchanan son of George Innes & Rachel (Bevan) Bevan, esquire.

May 29. Matilda dau: of John & Eliza (Maclean) Hitchings, of Bury, plasterer. Jan. 15, 1840.

May 29. Byron son of do do. Dec. 2, 1841.

July 10. Harriet dau: of Henry & Emily (Doel) Cater, labourer.

July 31. Elizabeth dau: of Zechariah & Sarah (Martin) Mays, labourer.

Aug. 7. William son of William & Mary (Saunders) Payne, shoemaker.

Aug. 4. Anne dau: of Enoch & Mary Anne (Aldrich) Martin, groom.

Sept. 4. Elizabeth dau: of Henry & Susan (Musk) Crooks, shoemaker.

Sept. 11. Anne dau: of Isaac & Mary Anne (Cage) Boreham, shoemaker.

Sept. 18. Sarah dau: of John & Maria (Cable) Bridge, labourer.

Oct. 15. Sarah dau: of William & Caroline (Cooper) Sanders, tailor.

Oct. 30. Obadiah son of John & Sarah (Green) Edwards, wheelwright.

Nov. 29. Emma Anne dau: of William & Sarah (King) Palmer of Westley, labourer.

Dec. 25. John son of Thomas & Sarah (Ridnall) Wade, labourer.

1843. Jan. 1. Henry son of John & Elizabeth (Root) Bowers, labourer.

Jan. 8. George son of William & Suzan (Flack) Nunn, labourer.
Jan. 15. John son of James & Mary (Cook) Boreham, labourer.
Feb. 5. Mary Anne dau: of Henry & Mary Anne (Willingham) Last, labourer.
Feb. 20. Emily Wayte dau: of William & Emily (Ramsey) Gardiner, farmer.
March 19. Emma dau: of John & Charlotte (Newman) Sergeant, labourer.
March 19. Katharine dau: of John & Sarah Anne (Simpson) Debenham, blacksmith.
March 26. Caroline dau: of William & Mary Anne (Palfrey) Brown, labourer.
April 4. Rebecca dau: of Thomas & Elizabeth (Ambrose) Saunders, wheelwright.
April 23. Harriet dau: of Thomas & Amy (Martin) Parker, labourer.
April 20. Hercules son of Joiner & Sarah (Smith) Buckley, of no regular abode, tinker & grinder.
May 21. Emily dau: of James & Lucy (Ramplin) Boreham, labourer.
May 28. Mary dau: of Robert & Anne (Cater) Cobbing, labourer.
June 4. Hannah dau: of William & Tabitha (Copsey) Root, carpenter.
June 4. Eliza Helen dau: of Jonathan & Jemima (Champ) Bugg, bailiff.
July 23. Lucy dau: of Robert & Dorothy (Cawston) Avis, labourer.
Aug. 8. Charles son of George & Susan (Coe) Brown, servant.
Aug. 13. Anna Louisa and Frederick William, twin children of John & Elizabeth (Edgar) Sturgeon, farmer.
Aug. 20. William son of George & Mary (Last) Cater, labourer.
Sept. 17. Rebecca dau: of John & Mary (Pryke) Elsden, labourer.
Oct. 1. Henry son of William & Eliza (Nunn) Makup, groom.
Oct. 29. Sophia dau: of Thomas & Sophia (Hammond) Catchpole, labourer.
Nov. 5. Susanna dau: of Joseph & Elizabeth (Winch) Farrants, blacksmith.
Dec. 22. William son of Charles & Anne (Sale) Levett, labourer.

Dec. 24. Louisa dau: of Isaac & Mary Anne (Cage) Boreham, shoemaker.

Dec. 24. Joseph William son of William & Mary (Spalding) Boreham, labourer.

Dec. 25. William son of John & Elizabeth (Root) Bowers, wheelwright.

Dec. 25. Frederick William son of George & Emily (Pleasants) Root of Bury, carpenter.

1844. Jan. 24. Edward son of George Innes & Rachel (Bevan) Bevan, esquire.

Feb. 11. Robert son of Stephen & Sophia (Flack) Pask, labourer.

March 3. Thomas son of William & Ann (Arborn) Sale, labourer.

April 24. Thomas son of Thomas & Ann (Crack) Goodchild, labourer.

April 29. Harriet dau : of William & Emily (Ramsey) Gardiner, farmer.

May 5. George son of James & Susan (Langham) Byford, carter.

May 19. Sarah Anne dau : of Robert & Mary (Perrey) Gooch of Bury, bricklayer.

May 27. Charlotte Mary dau : of Robert & Charlotte (Offord) Edwards of Bury, wheelwright.

June 9. Isaac son of Isaac & Caroline (Ling) Race, labourer.

June 18. Anne dau : of John & Frances (Pickering) Simpkin, thatcher.

June 23. Susanna dau : of Jermyn & Susan (Flack) Lewis, shoemaker.

July 28. John Elijah son of William & Mary (Coe) Spalding, labourer.

Sept. 15. Sophia dau : of James & Sarah (Winter) Ellis, labourer.

Oct. 6. Anne dau : of Edward & Eliza (Talbot) Swan, labourer.

Oct. 6. Arthur son of Thomas & Sarah (Ridnal) Wade, labourer.

Oct. 13. Elizabeth dau : of John & Mary (Evered) Langham, labourer.

Nov. 3. George son of John & Maria (Cable) Bridge, labourer.

Dec. 3. Susanna dau : of Samuel & Elizabeth (Cook, Willingham) Rowe, labourer.

Dec. 29. William son of Enoch & Marianne Martin, groom.

1845. Jan. 5. Maria dau : of Henry & Mary Ann Last, labourer.

Jan. 5. James son of George & Susan Brown, labourer.

Feb. 5. Arthur Joseph son of Robert & Martha (Smith) Pettitt, labourer.

March 2. Mary Ann dau: of Zachariah & Sarah (Martin) Mayes, labourer.
March 2. Amos son of William & Susan (Flack) Nunn, labourer.
April 6. Emily dau: of Henry & Emily (Dewell) Cater, labourer.
May 4. Emma dau: of William & Mary Ann (Palfrey) Brown, labourer.
May 11. Henry son of Jonathan & Jemima (Champ) Bugg, bailiff. Dec. 18, 1843.
May 11. John son of do do. Dec. 3, 1844.
May 30. Mary Alice dau: of George Innes & Rachel (Bevan) Bevan, esquire.
June 8. Harriet dau: of James & Mary (Cooke) Boreham, labourer.
June 29. Eliza dau: of Henry & Eliza (Watts) Edwards, wheelwright.
July 6. Harriet dau: of Isaac & Mary Ann (Cage) Boreham, labourer.
July 6. James son of George & Mary Ann (Last) Cater, labourer.
July 13. Fanny dau: of George & Susan (Cox) Petch, labourer. April, 15, 1842.
July 20. John Henry son of John & Harriet (Smith) Green, carpenter.
Sept. 7. William son of Reuben & Susan (Garrard) Alston, policeman.
Sept. 7. David son of Robert & Dorothea (Cawston) Avis of Horse-croft, labourer.
Sept. 25. William Allen son of William & Emily (Ramsey) Gardiner, farmer.
Oct. 5. Betsy dau: of George & Mary (Wright) Ridgeon, labourer.
Nov. 2. Ellen dau: of John & Sarah (Simpson) Dedman, blacksmith.
Nov. 9. Joseph son of Joseph & Elisabeth (Winch) Farrents, black-smith.
Dec. 7. Charles son of John & Esther (Vero) Garwood, labourer.
1846. — — Henry son of John & Mary (Pryke) Elsden, labourer. Oct. 16, 1845.
May 3. James Patrick son of Thomas & Mary Ann (Durrant) Finch, labourer.
May 3. Walter son of Walter & Amelia (Watkinson) Boreham, labourer.
May 3. Abigail dau: of John & Charlotte (Newman) Sergeant, labourer.
June 9. George son of James & Mary (Cook) Boreham, labourer.

Aug. 2. Louisa dau : of John & Harriet (Gill) Rowe, labourer.
Aug. 2. James son of Stephen & Sophy (Flack) Paske, labourer.
Aug. 16. Jane dau : of Isaac & Susan (Ridgeon) Ramplin, labourer.
Aug. 23. Anne dau : of Thomas & Sarah (Ridnal) Wade, labourer.
Aug. 23. Harold son of Benjamin & Elizabeth (Wade) Fayrs of Hartest, carpenter.
Aug. 23. Robert son of John & Elizabeth (Root) Bowers, wheelwright.
Aug. 30. George son of William & Mary (Spalding) Boreham, labourer.
Sept. 6. Robert son of William & Ann (Arborn) Sale, labourer.
Sept. 6. Amy dau : of John & Hannah (Orriss) Palmer, labourer.
Oct. 4. Joseph son of John & Mary (Evered) Lanham, labourer.
Oct. 4. William son of William & Marianne (Palfry) Brown, horse-keeper.
Nov. 1. Marianne dau : of Benjamin & Caroline (Emmett) Bolingbrook, labourer.
Dec. 20. Elisabeth dau : of George & Susan (Coe) Brown, labourer.
1847. Jan. 4. Lydia dau: of Isaac & Mary Ann (Cage) Boreham, shoemaker.
Jan. 4. Harry son of George & Jane (Nelson) Musk, labourer.
Feb. 7. Arthur son of William & Eliza (Nunn) Metcalf, labourer.
Feb. 7. Eliza dau : of Samuel & Elizabeth (Willingham) Rowe, labourer.
Feb. 14. Delariviere Susan dau : of Thomas & Susan (Root) Orridge, labourer.
Feb. 21. Rachel Georgina dau : of George Innes & Rachel (Bevan) Bevan, esquire.
Feb. 21. Harry son of Edward & Betsey (Talbot) Swan of Horsecroft.
Feb. 21. Hannah dau : of Robert & Dorothea (Cawston) Avis of Horsecroft, labourer.
Feb. 22. Elisabeth dau : of Elisabeth Paske of Depden, servant.
March 7. Mary Ann dau : of Isaac & Caroline (Linge) Race, labourer.
March 21. John Tricker son of George & Sarah (Tricker) Cooper, labourer.
April 11. Isabella dau : of Jermyn & Sarah (Sillett) Lewis, shoemaker.
May 2. Alfred son of Robert & Charlotte (Shave) Osborn, labourer.

June 6. John son of Henry & Mary Ann (Willingham) Last, labourer.
June 6. Henry James son of James & Susanna (Langham) Byford, carter.
June 6. Eliza dau: of Henry & Emily (Doel) Cater, labourer.
June 20. John son of George & Mary Ann (Last) Cater, labourer.
Sept. 5. James son of Stephen & Sophia (Flack) Pask, labourer.
Sept. 5. Walter son of Walter & Amelia (Watkinson) Boreham, labourer.
Oct. 3. John son of John & Fanny (Pickering) Simpkin, labourer.
Nov. 7. Harry son of Robert & Dorothea (Cawston), Alvis, labourer.
1848. Jan. 3. George son of William & Emily (Ramsey) Gardiner, farmer.
Feb. 6. Ann dau: of Thomas & Elizabeth (Ambrose) Saunders, wheelwright.
Feb. 6. Caroline dau: of Zachariah & Sarah (Martin) Mayes, labourer.
Feb. 6. John son of George & Harriet (Boreham) Gooch, labourer.
April 21. William son of William Gardiner & Susanna (Winch) Edwards, wheelwright.
May 7. Ernest George son of George Innes & Rachel (Bevan) Bevan, esquire.
June 4. James son of William & Harriet (Root) Fenton, labourer.
June 4. Sarah dau: of John & Hannah (Orriss) Palmer, labourer.
July 16. Frederick son of Jonathan & Jemima (Champ) Bugg. Dec. 5, 1846.
July 16. Emily dau: of do do. March 20, 1848.
July 26. Katharine dau: of John & Harriet (Gill) Rowe, labourer.
July 30. James son of Isaac & Susan (Ridgeon) Rampling, labourer.
Aug. 5. Henry Charles son of Henry & Eliza (Watts) Edwards, wheelwright.
Aug. 6. Susan dau: of John & Elizabeth (Root) Bowers, wheelwright.
Sept. 3. Henry son of Edward & Elizabeth (Talbot) Swann, labourer.
Oct. Amy dau: of Isaac & Mary Ann (Cage) Boreham, labourer.
Nov. 5. Jonathan son of Benjamin & Caroline (Emmet) Bolingbroke.
Dec. 24. Elizabeth dau: of James & Mary (Cooke) Boreham, labourer.
1849. Jan. 7. Marianne dau: of John & Mary (Pryke) Elsden, labourer.

Jan. 7. Henry son of Henry & Marianne (Willingham) Last, labourer.

Jan. 7. William son of Thomas & Adeliza (Eden) Crack, labourer.

Jan. 14. Anne dau : of John & Elisabeth (Root) Bowers, wheelwright.

March 4. Marianne dau : of William & Marianne (Palfrey) Brown, labourer.

April 21. Elizabeth dau : of George & Susan (Coe) Brown, labourer.

May 20. Emma Ann dau : of John & Elisabeth (Root) Bowers, wheelwright.

May 27. Rachel dau : of Samuel & Elisabeth (Cooke, Willingham) Rowe, labourer.

May 27. Eliza Elisabeth dau : of Thomas & Mary Anne (Durrant) Finch, labourer,

& Robert William son of do do. Twins.

June 3. James son of William & Charlotte (Garwood) Nunn, labourer.

June 3. Charles son of John & Sarah (Simpson) Debenham, blacksmith. Jan. 21, 1848.

June 3. Abraham son of Robert & Marianne (Baker) Rooks, labourer. June, 12, 1842,

& Martha Elisabeth dau : of do do. Oct. 11, 1844,

& Francis son of do do. June 12, 1847.

June 5. Harriet dau : of William & Emily (Ramsey) Gardiner, farmer. Aug. 14, 1848.

Aug. 5. Thomas son of George & Marianne (Last) Cater, labourer. Dec. 26, 1848.

Aug. 5. William Morley son of James & Anne (Cuthbert) Crack, labourer. Aug. 18, 1848.

Aug. 5. Marianne dau : of Henry & Emily (Dewell) Cater, labourer.

Aug. 5. Robert son of Robert & Dorothy (Cawston) Avis, labourer.

Sept. 2. Martha dau : of Isaac & Caroline (Linge) Race, labourer.

Sept. 2. Joseph son of Jonathan & Emma (Richardson) Race, labourer.

Sept. 2. Robert James son of Jermyn & Sarah (Wells) Lewis, shoemaker.

Sept. 2. Hannah dau : of John & Hannah (Orriss) Palmer, bailiff.

Sept. 2. Emily dau : of Joseph & Elizabeth (Winch) Farrants, smith.

Sept. 9. Walter James son of James Matthew & Caroline (Rogers) Scarlin, gent. Nov. 26, 1843,

& Caroline Elisabeth dau : of do do. Dec. 23, 1848.

Sept. 30. Arthur Henry son of Thomas & Anne (Nunn) Arborn, labourer.

Nov. 4. Frederick Niel son of George Innes & Rachel (Bevan) Bevan, esquire.

Dec. 26. William Henry son of William Henry & Anne Frances (Mathias) Rusbrooke, esquire.

1850. Jan. 6. Alfred Woods son of Richard & Augusta Sarah Hendy (Woods) Payne, horsekeeper.

Feb. 1. Georgiana dau : of George & Ann (Smith) Freestone, policeman.

Feb. 3. Henry son of Samuel & Marianne (Pask) Bowers of Bury, shepherd.

Feb. 3. Emily dau : of William & Harriet (Root) Fenton, labourer.

Feb. 3. Eliza dau : of James & Anne (Cuthbert) Crack, labourer.

March 3. James son of John & Elisabeth (Warren) Rowe, labourer.

May 5. Kezia dau : of Jonathan & Jemima (Clamp) Bugg, bailiff.

May 5. Emma dau : of Simon & Rachel (Elsden) Last, labourer.

May 5. Valentine son of William & Anne (Arbon) Sale, labourer.

May 19. Sarah dau : of Richard & Susan (Crack) Cockel, labourer. Dec. 18, 1847,

& Emma dau : of do do. Aug. 23, 1841,

& Mary Anne dau : of do do. May 5, 1835.

May 26. Emma dau : of Charles & Ann (Sale) Levett, shepherd. May 20, 1831.

June 2. Martin John son of John Gardner & Susannah (Winch) Edwards, wheelwright.

June 2. Eliza dau : of George & Susan (Coe) Brown, labourer.

July 6. Louisa dau : of Charles & Ann (Sale) Levett, shepherd. April 20, 1828.

Sept. 1. Ann Elizabeth dau : of Henry & Hannah (Root) Copsey, labourer.

Sept. 8. Edith Susan Rose dau : of James Matthew & Caroline (Rogers) Scarling, gent.

Sept. 8. Emma Ann dau : of Isaac & Susan (Ridgeon) Ramplin, labourer.

Oct. 6. William Herbert son of George & Caroline (Tricker) Pratt, wheelwright.

Nov. 3. George Thomas son of George Farrance & Jane (Hunt) Rolfe, farmer.

Nov. 17. Elizabeth dau : of John & Sarah (Simpson) Dedman,* blacksmith.

Dec. 25. Rachel dau : of John & Harriet (Gill) Rowe, labourer.

* Both here and in Nov., 1845, Dedman is a mistake in the original Register for Debenham.—S. H. A. H.

MARRIAGES.

Nullum omnino matrimonium hac in parochia celebratum A.D. 1558.

1559.	April	15.	John Turner	&	Christian Browne.
	June	1.	John Hande	&	Elizabeth Newegate.
	Julie	25.	William Wellam	&	Grace Mulley.
	Aug.	24.	John Wellam	&	Margaret Plummer.
	Oct.	1.	Robert Barret	&	Margaret Bulbrooke.
	Oct.	25.	Edmond Kent	&	Marian Hydon.
1560.	Sept.	17.	William Hall	&	Anne Reave.
1561.	June	8.	Eustace Haward	&	Joan Godfrie.
	Aug.	28.	Richard Baker	&	Anne Ease.
	Sept.	28.	Thomas Draklon	&	Joane Maio.
1562.	Julie	12.	Austin Neweport	&	Audrie Celie.
1563.	Maie	2.	John Allen	&	Katharine Nicolson.
	June	24.	John Austin	&	Dorothie Lilly.
	Nov.	22.	John Lilly	&	Margaret Emyn.
	Dec.	22.	William Fynn	&	Margaret Neale.
	Jan.	20.	William Austin	&	Margaret Golding.
1564.	June	2.	William Ostler	&	Joane Frauncis.
	Sept.	24.	Gyles Roote	&	Elenor Hill.
	Jan.	31.	John Spinke	&	Joane Arber.
	Feb.	8.	Bennet Elmer	&	Margaret Wellam.
1565.	Dec.	23.	Thomas Spinke	&	Dorothie Fastal.
1566.	Julie	4.	John Edmondes	&	Margaret Sillet.
	Oct.	29.	Richard Cooper	&	Elizabeth Bardwel.
	Nulli matrimonio copulati A.D. 1567.				
1568.	June	2.	Edward Paine	&	Katharine Stevens.

	Sept.	26.	William Braue	&	Elizabeth Moore.
	Jan.	27.	John Mayo	&	Emme Martin
1569.	Julie	28.	Robert Moody	&	Elizabeth Bucknam.
	Aug.	1.	Thomas Dytun gent:	&	Margaret Jermyn gent.
	Sept.	15.	Richard Godfrie	&	Philis Ease
	Oct.	3.	John Edmondes	&	Love Parman.
	Oct.	16.	Ralfe South	&	Jane Stanton.
	Nov.	30.	John Eddouse	&	Margaret Frauncis.
1570.	Oct.	17.	Nicholas Teuerson	&	Ann Stekel.
1571.	June	29.	William Page	&	Agnes Goose.
	Oct.	8.	Henrie Blagge esquire	&	Hester Jermyn gent.
	Oct.	22.	John Wrettam	&	Alice Wellam.
1572.	June	3.	John Godfrie	&	Tomasyn Saunders.
	June	19.	Anthonie White	&	Margerie Gurnie.
	June	26.	Robert Gipse	&	Isabel Goose.
	Julie	8.	Jefferie Berrie	&	Joane Lucas.
1573.	Maie	19.	Edward Cock	&	Agnes Emmyn.
	Aug.	6.	Thomas Wellam	&	Alice Maio.
1574.	Aug.	24.	Edmond Gosnolde	&	Marie Turner.
	Oct.	14.	William Godfrie	&	Alice Stanton.
	Oct.	20.	Thomas Mallinge	&	Thomasin Wetherbie.
	Feb.	4.	Laurance Jeffraie	&	Dorothie Austin.
1575.	June	14.	John Benningfield	&	Elizabeth Lucas.
	June	19.	John Goose	&	Alice Reuel.
	Julie	2.	Robert Potter	&	Katharine Harman.
	Julie	16.	Henrie Graiegoose	&	Joane Purkes.
	Oct.	9.	George Birde	&	Dennis Notte.
1576.	Oct.	6.	Henrie Hawkes	&	Alice Miller.
	Dec.	11.	Robert Scot	&	Elizabeth Lilly.
	Jan.	15.	Thomas Corder	&	Ann Fishon.
	Feb.	20.	John Godfrie	&	Margaret Wellam.
1577.	Maie	18.	George Norton	&	Rachel Gypse.
	Julie	1.	John Bud	&	Ann Marten.
	Julie	29.	John Gypse	&	Eden Mannyng.
	Oct.	6.	Robert Sanderson	&	Grace Barro.

	Oct.	7.	Robert Bragge	&	Margaret Folger.
1578.	June	22.	William Borne	&	Frauncis Stenne.
	Sept.	3.	Benet Howe	&	Ann Gipse.
	Sept.	28.	John Page	&	Margaret Booth.
	Feb.	22.	James Bouer	&	Rose Newegate.
1579.	Aug.	16.	John Rowland	&	Margerie Stokes.
	Sept.	20.	Thomas Barrum	&	Joane Jelly.
	Oct.	11.	Thomas Wellam	&	Marie Corder.
	Oct.	18.	Gyles Borde	&	Margerie Plesaunt.
1580.	June	23.	John Cutmer	&	Ann Burde.
	Julie	12.	Thomas Thurston	&	Margaret Carver.
	Sept.	18.	James Sillet	&	Marie Sillet.
	Nov.	20.	Thomas Barker	&	Margaret Boly.
1581.	June	18.	John Yonge	&	Margerie Godfrie.
	Julie	30.	Thomas Frauncis	&	Margaret Lilly.
	Dec.	10.	Henrie Buckenham	&	Joane Gipson.
1582.	April	17.	Luke Earle	&	Audrie Ashe.
1583.	June	24.	William Fuller	&	Elizabeth Spalding.
	Oct.	6.	William Sawier	&	Helen Edgerlie.
1584.	Sept.	21.	Adam Stevenson	&	Joane Starling.
	Oct.	19.	Robert Haul	&	Agnes Hart.
	Feb.	24.	Henrie Bennet	&	Elizabeth Wignol.
1585.	Aug.	24.	Henrie Mahue	&	Margaret Wellam.
1586.	Julie	4.	John Godfrie	&	Alice Swifte.
	Oct.	17.	Thomas Garret	&	Joane Paic-foote.
	Nov.	6.	Robert Perrie	&	Ann Maio.
	Feb.	21.	Robert Newegate	&	Elizabeth Buckenham.
1587.	June	3.	Thomas Leauer	&	Margerie James.
	Julie	28.	William Barten	&	Marie Turner.
	Oct.	22.	James Maio	&	Margaret Perrie.
1588.	Aug.	28.	Thomas Rogers	&	Bridget Wincol.
	June	16.	William Fishen	&	Barbara Sewel.
	Oct.	6.	William Tailor	&	Ann Brett.
	Dec.	19.	Richard Smith	&	Margaret Perrie.
	Jan.	6.	William Hawsted	&	Cicelie Froste.

Nulli matrimonio copulati A.D. 1589.

1590.	Maie	22.	Richard Dearson	&	Grace Dikes.
	Julie	14.	William Fynn	&	Joan Buckenam.
	Aug.	3.	Holofernes Toaler	&	Agnes Fynn.
1591.	Maie	9.	Gregorie Burchenal	&	Agnes Friet.
	Julie	12.	Barnabie Lilly	&	Elizabeth Wellam.

Nulli matrimonio copulati A.D. 1592.

1593.	April	16.	John Callowe	&	Alice Worldlie.
	Maie	1.	Edmond Haward	&	Alice Andrewes.
	June	25.	Robert Adams	&	Elizabeth Godfrie.
	Sept.	16.	Hugh Langham	&	Margaret Brantia.
	Nov.	1.	Edward Rose	&	Grace Snelling.
	Dec.	27.	Edward Cock	&	Emme Manning.
1594.	April	1.	George Clerk	&	Elizabeth Digersine.

Nulli matrimonio conjuncti A.D. 1595.

1596.	Sept.	2.	William Revel gent.	&	Margaret Short.
	Sept.	20.	John Sandes	&	Margaret Page.
	Oct.	15.	Thomas Pilgrime	&	Susan Godfrie.

Nullum matrimonium publicè initum A.D. 1597.

1598.	May	1.	John Lumpkin	&	Alice Cooper.
	June	4.	John Godfrie	&	Jane Godfrie.
	Sept.	10.	John Paman	&	Ann Web.
	Sept.	21.	Philip Sowter	&	Rose Maio.
1599.	Oct.	18.	John Engoll	&	Mary Eddouse.
1600.	Julie	13.	Robert Gawte	&	Marie Threddar.
	Oct.	1.	William Emmyns	&	Margaret Sowth.
	Oct.	19.	Edward Bulbrooke	&	Rose Lillie.
1601.	Julie	12.	William Haward	&	Alise Hobson.
	Sept.	21.	Robert Spinke	&	Marie Warde.
	Oct.	11.	Henrie Froste	&	Agnes Newegate.
	Oct.	29.	Thomas Bull	&	Alice Wellom.
1602.	June	8.	Edward Payne	&	Susan Tyler.
	Sept.	29.	Luke Say-wel	&	Bridget Browne.
	Sept.	29.	John Inhold	&	Margaret Deereman.
	Oct.	3.	Steeven Hardie	&	Bridget Friet.

	Feb.	24.	Richard Sillet	&	Tomazin Symondes.
	March	7.	William Brooke	&	Margaret Breate.
1603.	Oct.	23.	William Bull	&	Ann Greene.
	Nov.	16.	Isaac Trumble	&	Joan Moore.
	Jan.	31.	John Dysinge	&	Bridget Fynn.
	Feb.	2.	Steeven Godfreie	&	Marie Lodge.
1604.	June	24.	Ambrose Goldsmith	&	Ann Leach.
1605.	June	24	Henrie Wellom	&	Joan Sillet.
	Oct.	25.	Thomas Scot of Burie	&	Mercie Stock of Long Melford.
	Jan.	14.	John Wallis	&	Ursula Godfreie.
1606.	Julie	10.	Leonard Clerke	&	Alice Lillie.
	Oct.	6.	Edmond Yonges	&	Mary Sillet.
	Oct.	12.	George Steggel	&	Ann Clifford.
	Oct.	13.	Edward Godfrey	&	Dorothie Godfrey.
1607.	May	24.	John Button	&	Rose Page.
	June	29.	Robert Cuttin	&	Elizabeth Chinry.
	Sept.	21.	Thomas Goldsmith	&	Francis King.
	Feb.	8.	William Lyng	&	Prudence Sowth.
1608.	March	31.	Ambrose Blagge esquier	&	Martha Barbar.
	April	3.	Thomas Milbie	&	Ann Goose.
	April	18.	Thomas Baron	&	Amie Welles.
	June	27.	Robert Cooe	&	Ann Turner.
	June	29.	William Bailie	&	Frances Edhouse.
	Aug.	7.	William Vardie	&	Elizabeth Deareman.
	Oct.	3.	Henrie Mahewe	&	Barbara Hungerson.
	Oct.	17.	John Bucchenham	&	Dorothie Chinrey.
1609.	Maie	1.	Frauncis Tomson	&	Lettice Fletcher.
	Sept.	21.	Jhon Langley	&	Elizabeth Bucknam.
	Feb.	19.	Thomas Warner	&	Margaret B . . ffie.
1610.	June	5.	Humfrey Spinck	&	Grace Potter.
	Julie	1.	Robert Godfry	&	Margaret Wright.
	March	14.	Samuel Lyvermore	&	Grace Marram.
1611.	April	15.	Robert Howton	&	Susan Eddouse.
	June	9.	Edward Goldson	&	Mary Goose.

H

	Oct.	24.	Edmund Haward	&	Francis Rose.
	Jan.	16.	Antonie Fowler	&	Elizabeth Tyler.
1612.	June	28.	William Waters	&	Mary Spencer.
	Sept.	21.	Richard Bennol	&	Agnes Bennet.
	Jan.	16.	Stephan Garrat	&	Bridget Flander.
1613.	May	24.	Thomas Talbot	&	Mary Brooke.
	Aug.	29.	John Moore	&	Elizabeth Friet.
	Sept.	23.	Henry Mahewe	&	Susan Lilly.
	Oct.	19.	William Taylor	&	Margaret Eddouse.
1615.	May	29.	John Perkin	&	Bridget Page.
	Sept.	21.	Thomas Kinge	&	Elizabeth Eddouse.
	Oct.	9.	George Austin	&	Francis Hamand.
1616.	May	1.	Thomas May	&	Judith Wade.
	May	9.	Gilbert Towler	&	Anne Burchenall.
	Sept.	16.	Edward Paine	&	Joane Fynne.
1617.	June	9.	Robert Manning	&	Anne Newgate.
	June	16.	Thomas Wiffin	&	Anne Goose.
	July	14.	Thomas Trowle	&	Francis Manning.
	July	17.	John Church	&	Rose Bulbrooke.
	July	24.	Nicholas Barber gent.	&	Mary Birle.
	Jan.	8.	Josias Long	&	Susan Payne.
1618.	June	10.	Anthony Disborow	&	Susan Stalling.
	Oct.	14.	Robert Bret	&	Milesent Sharp.
	Oct.	28.	John Baker	&	Margaret Buckenham.
1619.	April	26.	Robert Spinck	&	Francis Godfry.
	June	24.	William Wiffin	&	Milesent Brett.
	Aug.	10.	Jasper Despotine	&	Susan Brand.
	Sept.	29.	John Fiston	&	Agnes Dearson.
1620.	May	15.	Josias Winter	&	Bridget Mayhew.
	June	15.	Robert Manning	&	Alice Stegall.
	July	16.	Thomas Gooday	&	Elizabeth Stegall.
	Sept.	20.	John Ingold	&	Elizabeth Fuller.
	Oct.	8.	Thomas Stephenson	&	Elizabeth Munson.
	Nov.	23.	John Larner	&	Joane Keeble.
	Feb.	1.	John Church	&	Abigael Threader.

1621.	May	10.	Benjamin Cooper gent.	&	Frances Dannock.
	Sept.	24.	Robert Hood	&	Dorothe Turner.
	Oct.	8.	William Sayer	&	Margaret Godfry.
	Oct.	11.	John Hayward	&	Katherine Cole.
	Nov.	8.	James Wiard	&	Elizabeth Covell.
	Jan.	21.	Vincent Handler	&	Barbara Bright.
	Jan.	31.	Henry Turner	&	Anne Clarke.
	March	5.	Thomas Bright gent.	&	Agatha Mileson.
1622.	Aug.	7.	Thomas Hempsted	&	Mary Baron.
1623.	July	28.	Thomas Baker	&	Susan Smith.
	Sept.	22.	Edmund Baker	&	Anne Wimple.
	Oct.	1.	John Church	&	Alice Frost.
	Sept.	21.	William Ruggle	&	Mary Hayward.
1625.	April	13.	John Sparke	&	Rose Ingold.
	May	23.	Robert Booty	&	Elizabeth Bokenham.
	May	26.	Robert Steward	&	Elizabeth Sparke.
	June	8.	Robert Adams	&	Grace Bland.
	Aug.	4.	John Hayward	&	Barbara Sere.
	Nov.	10.	Thomas Hamond	&	Alice Parker.
1626.	June	8.	Robert Cooke	&	Bridget Manning.
	Oct.	14.	Thomas Mainard	&	Rose Ward.
1627.	March	26.	Edmund Clerk	&	Frances Cutteris.
	Oct.	4.	Laurence Stebbing	&	Francis Peerson.
	Oct.	15.	John Titmouse	&	Elizabeth King.
	Oct.	15.	Philip Sturgeon	&	Prudence Coppin.
1628.	May	8.	Henry Wiard	&	Jane Godfry.
	Dec.	3.	John Sparke	&	Brigett Sillet.
1629.	Oct.	1.	William Chanefeild	&	Ann More.
	Feb.	1.	William Miller	&	Martha Godfrey.
1630.	Sept.	13.	John Mudd	&	Marie Derson.
1631.	July	7.	George Rouleson	&	Barbara Hayward.
	Oct.	10.	Henry Mayhewe	&	An Finne.
	Jan.	5.	Henrie Sillet	&	Ann Bouden.
1633.	Aug.	20.	John Blemell	&	Martha Gosnold.
	Sept.	30.	William Prior	&	Elizabeth Sparke.

	Oct.	3.	John Pocher	&	Alice Frost.
	Oct.	21.	William Newbery	&	Thomasin Fincham.
1634.	Julie	14.	John Eurn	&	Frances Watts.
	Nov.	3.	Edward Payne	&	Marie English.
1635.	Sept.	7.	Nicolas Brett	&	Eudolia Paris.
	Oct.	5.	George Adkin	&	Susan Elmer?
	Feb.	11.	Oliver Briant	&	Bridget Kerington.
1636.	June	7.	Edmund Hayward	&	Amie Albon.
1637.	Aug.	3.	Henery Sparke	&	Rebecca Boston.
	Jan.	17.	Edward Barret	&	Marie Tebbet.
1638.	July	4.	Thomas Talbot	&	Priscilla Parman.
	Aug.	14.	Benjamin Lilly	&	Dorothy Godfrye.
	Oct.	1.	Peter Manning	&	Jone Seber.
	March	21.	Richard Pepes	&	Mary Wincol.
1639.	Oct.	18.	James Wright	&	Frances Mortlemens.
1640.	Aug.	20.	Edmond Edwards	&	Elizabeth Clarke.
1641.	June	14.	John Smith	&	Margaret Rumbelow.
	Sept.	2.	John Taylor	&	Mary Mahue.
	Oct.	21.	Henry Mahue	&	Margaret Steward.
1642.	April	13.	John Cotton	&	Mary Martyn.
1643.	Aug.	10.	John Taylor	&	Ann Trumble.
	July	12.	John Smithe	&	Martha How.
	Sept.	28.	James Pleasance	&	Margaret Steward.
	Oct.	24.	Thomas Parker	&	Elizabeth Wyard.
	Oct.	31.	George Adkin	&	Margaret Huny? [or Hurry?]
	Nov.	5.	Stephen Bull	&	Katherine Gutteridge.
1644.	April	22.	Thomas Bennold	&	Joane Bucknam.
1645.	Oct.	2.	John Goldsmith	&	Anne Brett.
1646.	Sept.	24.	William Wiffen	&	Alice Clarke.
	Nov.	30.	Thomas Goldsmith	&	Joane Bucknam.
1647.	April	19.	Robert Sharpe	&	Susan King.
	June	23.	John Ewen	&	Elizabeth Toping.
1653.	Nov.	10.	Samuell Crame	&	Cristion Feltham.
	Nov.	14.	Robert Howton	&	Margrit Allet.

	Nov.	22.	Ralph Alpsley	&	Elezabeth Covell.
	Feb.	2.	Josias Wright	&	Hester Wyard.
1654.	May	16.	Francis Sebrooke	&	Elizabeth Cowper.
1660.	Jan.	31.	Thomas Turner	&	—— ——.
1661.	Sept.	23.	Thomas Macrow	&	Mary Dale.
1662.	May	15.	John Crick	&	Abigail Cooke.
	Sept.	25.	Thomas Gipps	&	Mary Bootie.
	Oct.	2.	George Smyth	&	Jane Ingall.
	Dec.	23.	Thomas Spurling	&	Elizabeth Bull.
	Feb.	16.	John Pentney	&	Susan Chinnery.
1663.	Oct.	4.	Edward Hutchinson	&	Elizabeth Tillot.
	Oct.	7.	Thomas Atkin	&	Margaret Halls.
	Nov.	19.	James Elsygood	&	Rebecca Haws.
1664.	May	15.	Beniamyn Johnson	&	Mary Towler.
	June	31.	William Ewen	&	Elizabeth Miller.
	July	30.	Robert Booty	&	Priscilla Talbot.
	Oct.	18.	Mr. Thomas Covell	&	Mrs. Judith Blagg.
1665.	Sept.	3.	Thomas Wiffen	&	Margaret King.
	Oct.	17.	William Spinke	&	Faith Potter.
	Nov.	18.	William King	&	Elisebeth Wiffen.
1667.	May	6.	William Cater	&	Cristian Bell.
	July	4.	John Norman	&	Jane Haryye.
	Sept.	18.	John Smith	&	Alce Meller.
1668.	March	30.	Thomas Sargeant	&	Constance Nicholls.
	Oct.	12.	Lawrence Perkins	&	Anne Potter.
1669.	May	6.	Lawrence Howard	&	Rebecca Ingold.
1671.	Aug.	24.	Thomas Gload	&	the Widdow Gardiner.
	—	—	John Howard	&	Elisabeth Edgely.
1673.	Sept.	22.	Thomas Prell	&	Anne Sharp.
	Oct.	2.	Thomas Jaggard	&	Anne Handler.
	Dec.	4.	Lawrence Howard	&	Elisabeth Manning.
1674.	April	30.	Robert Goodchild	&	Elisabeth Cooper.
	June	25.	William Prigg	&	Mary Day.
	Dec.	1.	John Hockle	&	Joane Copsey.
1675.	Nov.	24.	Thomas Gardiner	&	Elisabeth Wright.

	Jan.	25.	Thomas Nunne	&	Frances Finborough.
	Feb.	4.	Thomas Ling	&	Elizabeth Redgin.
1676.	April	6.	Edmund Howard of Hawsted	&	Susannah Sergeant of this parish.
	March	13.	Richard Patrick	&	Elizabeth Cresall of Bury.
1678.	June	10.	Thomas Goldsmith	&	the Widdow Gutridge.
	Nov.	30.	Isaac Peak	&	Katharine Jervise.
1679.	March	11.	William Gaynford	&	Margaret Wyard.
1680.	April	26.	Ambrose Orbell	&	Elizabeth Wyard.
	June	26.	Robert Beaumant	&	Sarah Chinrey.
	Oct.	19.	Robert Calond	&	Ann Pentney.
	Jan.	16.	John Jackson	&	Martha Ford.
1681.	Oct.	6.	Jonathan Mason	&	Elizabeth Mortlock.
1682.	Sept.	21.	Samuel Bray	&	Alice Goldsmith.
1683.	May	19.	Thomas Gee	&	Ann Acock.
	June	7.	John Welham	&	Ann Hudson.
	Oct.	3.	Richard Avis	&	Sarah Gault.
	Oct.	10.	Thomas Parker	&	Frances Robinson.
1684.	Nov.	20.	Robert Jarvis	&	Leah Manning.
	March	3.	Thomas How	&	Elizabeth Copping.
1685.	Feb.	3.	Samuel Smith of Stradford in Suffolk	&	Elizabeth Gelder of Bury.
1686.	Oct.	3.	John Cornwall	&	Alice Bennet.
	May	4.	George Bingley	&	Elizabeth Drury.
	April	5.	John Clerk	&	Susan Jarvis.
	Jan.	6.	Robert Cooper of Bury	&	Alice Cross of Saxam.
1687.	Jan.	15.	Thomas Wiffen	&	Elizabeth Parker.
1688.	Oct.	11.	John Wright	&	Sarah Drury.
	Nov.	13.	Mr. Henry Sorrell	&	Mrs. Ann Covell.
	Feb.	12.	John Stocken of Hawsted	&	Sarah Crowch of Horring-hearth.
1689.	Sept.	12.	William Gulston of Kertling	&	Rebecca Parker of Moulton.
	Oct.	3.	Henery Cornwall	&	Elizabeth Bennet.
1690.	June	30.	Robert Talbot	&	Susan Goldsmith.
1692.	Oct.		Edward Parker	&	Sarah Grigs.

1693.	June	4.	Henry Cosens	&	Widow Reeve.
	Sept.	21.	Robert White	&	Ann Jewers.
	Feb.	1.	Mr. John Hasel of Botsam	&	Mrs. Mary Covell.
1694.	Sept.	13.	Joseph Crowch	&	Mary Ling.
	Sept.	9.	William Newport	&	Elizabeth Goldsmith.
1695.	Sept.	24.	Richard Elsdon	&	Elizabeth King.
	Oct.	25.	John Bigsby	&	Mary Adams.
1696.	April.	2.	Mr. John Brown of Bury	&	Isabella Sharpe.
	Oct.	5.	John Linsted	&	Frances Sargant.
	Oct.	27.	John Indow, a soldier,	&	Martha Parce.
	Jan.	14.	John Wiseman of Mildenhall	&	Ann Jaggard.
1697.	Oct.	4.	Robert Pattle	&	Mary Roofe.
	Oct.	5.	William Sharpe	&	Frances Griggs.
	March	17.	John Sparrow	&	Mary Lanseter.
1698.	June	2.	Bartholomew Hunt	&	Hannah Ewen.
	Aug.	11.	William Basset	&	Ann Everadd.
	Oct.	20.	John Bensted, labourer,	&	Alice Smith.
1700.	Aug.	3.	Robert Harvy	&	Frances Langham.
	Oct.	3.	Timothy Hawkins	&	Susanna Chinery.
1701.	Jan.	6.	Marke Balls	&	Mary Smith.
1702.	June	20.	Daniel Root of Hartest	&	Ann Robinson.
	July	7.	Richard* Forster, clerk,	&	Eshter Ernseby.
	Oct.	2.	John Mays of Whepsted	&	Mary Gaut.
	Oct.	8.	Richard Clerke, of Barton	&	Anna Chinery.
	March	23.	Thomas Hawes, shepherd,	&	Ann Newman.
1703.	March	27.	John Pitches	&	Sarah Pung.
	Dec.	29.	Thomas King	&	Elizabeth Willingham.
	Jan.	2.	John Nichols	&	Mary Twite.
1704.	May	7.	John Rolfe	&	Mary Clerke.
	Oct.	10.	Edward Parker	&	Rachel Wyard.
	Jan.	3.	Isaac Garnham	&	Susanna Sharp.
1705.	May	10.	John Paman of Fornham	&	Elizabeth Ransome.
	Aug.	25.	William Ashman	&	Mary Lilly.

* Richard would seem to be a mistake in the original Register for Edward. See Burials and Sepulchral Inscriptions.—S. H. A. H.

	Sept.	27.	George Auburn	&	Elizabeth Web.
	Nov.	8.	Thomas Pit	&	Judeth Balls.
1707.	Aug.	4.	George Ship	&	Susan Pain.
	Sept.	9.	John Redging	&	Elizabeth Dising.
	Oct.	19.	James Spalding	&	Ann Bales.
	Oct.	23.	William Halls	&	Grace Smith.
1708.	Oct.	4.	Josuah Bunting	&	Elisabeth Hempsted.
1710.	July	23.	William Lait	&	Elisabeth Cornwall.
1711.			Mr. Sparrow	&	Widow Pans.
	Jan.	28.	Edmund Hempsted	&	Sarah Pung.
1712.	June	30.	Henry Cosens	&	Susan Pleasance.
	Sept.	11.	Mr. Thomas Smith, Rector of Rougham & Susan Wiseman.		
	Oct.	16.	Thomas Jackson	&	Elisabeth Reeve.
	Oct.	29.	Robert Pain	&	Francis Goldsmith.
1713.	Oct.	1.	Thomas Seaton	&	Susan Hempsted.
	Oct.	1.	Jeremy Moss	&	Sarah Maypoole.
1714.	April	6.	Mr. John Battely, clerk,	&	Mrs. Ann Sydey.
	July	20.	Jacob Turner	&	Elisabeth Maypoole.
	Sept.	30.	John Nunn	&	Elisabeth Gauden.
	Oct.	13.	Richard How	&	Elisabeth Barton.
	Oct.	13.	John Spicer	&	Elisabeth Owers.
1715.	July	21.	Jeremy Green	&	Mary Mortlock.
1716.	Oct.	16.	Samuel Prick	&	Prudence Manning.
	Feb.	26.	Stephen Cook	&	Widow Ling.
1717.	Sept.	15.	William Everadd	&	Lydia Willingham.
1718.	Sept.	30.	John Plympton	&	Margat Parker.
	Oct.	2.	Daniel Goodee	&	Mary Smith.
	Nov.	4.	Thomas Salisbury	&	Elisabeth Talbot.
	Nov.	26.	Henry Corbet	&	Margaret Middleditch.
	Feb.	10.	William Lias	&	Ann Ives.
	Feb.	11.	John Plail	&	Elisabeth Coe.
1719.	Oct.	8.	John Sparrow	&	Marial Pask.
1720.	Oct.	14.	Robert Smith	&	Avis Pung.
	Oct.	17.	John Oatly	&	Mary Lilly.
1722.	Oct.	23.	William Hempsted	&	Margat Goodee.

Jan. 7. Hugh Spencer & Mary Haward.
1723. May 28. James Woodcock of Harling in Norfolk & Mary Ward de Martin.
July 7. Thomas Steel & Hester Chinery.
Nov. 18. James Spalding & Elizabeth Avys, both of Troston.
1724. May 17. James Frost & Mary Battly.
June 20. Stephen Kerridge & Mary Sawbin.

1725.

Oct. 4. Richard Cuff of Cambridge, s., & Jane Helliot of Catlidge, Co. Cambridge, s.
Feb. 18. Thomas Pleasance of Risby, s., & Ann Bass of Horringer, s.

1726.

Sept. 13. Robert Parker of Sapiston s. & Martha Cooper of Horringer s.

1727.

Sept. 21. Isaac Lumly of Bury s. & Mary Elsden of this Parish s.
Oct. 18. Robert Hussleton of Bury w. & Sarah Goldsmith of this P. s. L.
Nov. 16. Abraham Kedington s. & Ann Ewen s. both of this P. L.
March 5. Francis Law s. & Elizabeth Spedding s. both of Newmarket. L.

1728.

Oct. 14. Thomas Frost s. & Mary Lias s. both of this P.

1729.

May 25. Thomas Cornwall s. of this P. & Priscilla Jackson s. of Whepsted.
June 19. Robert Kendal w. of Bury & Hannah Sargeant s. of this P.
Sept. 25. John Raye s. of Lawshall & Hannah Wiseman s. of this P. L.
Oct. 3. The Revd. Mr. Henry Craske s. of Reed & Mrs. Elizabeth Raye s. of Bury. L.
Oct. 23. John Last s. of Whepsted & Ann Holden s. of this P.
Oct. 27. Henry Bulbrook w. of Whepsted & Margaret Last s. of this P.
Dec. 12. John Sergeant w. & Alice Hollux w. both of this P.

1730.

Oct. 6. Henry How w. of Whepsted & Eliz: Ling s. of this P.
Feb. 17. William Frost s. & Ann Potter s. both of this P.

1731.

May 27. Benjamin Miller of Hargrave w. & Elizabeth Elmer of this P. w.

June 10. Peter Firman s. & Elizabeth Potter w. both of Westow. L.
Aug. 9. Robert Game of Whepsted s. & Sarah Adams of this P. s.
Oct. 5. John Levitt of Borely s. & Susannah How of this P. s.
Dec. 30. Thomas Jeffes s. & Dela: Ewin s. both of this P. L.

1732.

April 20. John Bolton s. & Elizabeth Cocksedge s. both of Bury. L.
May 29. William Daniel s. & Elizabeth Brook s. both of this P.

1733.

Oct. 15. Roger Liddyman s. & Sarah Adams w. both of this P.
Oct. 19. John Ottley w. & Mary Moss s. both of this P.
Dec. 21. Joseph Hammond of Bradfield Combust & Elizabeth Holden s. of this P. L.

1734.

May 28. John Hibble s. & Margaret Carter s. both of this P., with L.
Dec. 10. Mr. Robert Plampin of Shimpling s. & Mrs. Sarah Sidey of this P. s. L.

1735.

Oct. 1. John Brown s. & Mary Church s. both of this P.
Oct. 13. John Adkin of Gazely s. & Martha Parker of this P. w.
Oct. 23. Stephen Sparrow s. & Hannah Nash s. both of this P.
Oct. 30. Jeremiah Euson of Lawshall s. & Elizabeth Barton of this P. s.
Dec. 11. Lewis Mortlock s. & Ann Kedington s. both of this P. L.
Dec. 31. Robert Jacob s. & Mary Steel s. both of this P. L.

1736.

Oct. 1. John Woodruff of Bury St. Edmunds s. & Isabella Elsden of this P. s. L.
Jan. 6. John Bray s. & Ann Mortlock s. both of this P. L.
March 7. Thomas Huske s. & Alice Noel s. both of Newmarket. L.

1737.

Oct. 6. Stephen Ship of Risby s. & Hannah Smith s. of this P.
Oct. 9. William Bray of Flempton s. & Elizabeth Pettiver of this P. s. L.
Oct. 31. John Pausey of Somerton s. & Mary Jackson of this P. s.

1738.

Nov. 2. Thomas Fitch of Whepsted s. & Margaret Page of this P. s.
March 6. Joseph Goody s. & Elizabeth Lisset s. both of this P.

1739.

July 6. John Swan of Hessett s. & Elizabeth Daniel of this P. w. L.
Oct. 9. Castell Goodchild of Nowton s. & Susan Ewin of this P. s. L.
Feb. 1. John King s. & Mary Mortlock s. both of this P.
Feb. 16. Thomas Butler s. & Jane Ling s. both of this P.

1740.

Nov. 3. James Frost s. & Elizabeth Shaw s. both of this P.

1741.

Oct. 22. Stephen Leader s. & Mary Page s. both of this P.
Jan. 31. Joseph Negus of St. Mary's Parish in Bury St. Edmunds s. & Elizabeth Scot of this P. s. L.
March 1. Edward Roof [Rolf] s. & Mary Hows s. both of this P.

1742.

May 18. John Cook w. & Elizabeth Noble w. both of this P.
Oct. 7. George Avis s. & Grace Smith s. both of this P.
Oct. 19. Thomas Merton s. & Mary Howlet s. both of this P.

1743.

Sept. 1. The Rev. Mr. Thomas Smith of Pakenham s. & Mrs. Mary Ellis of Horningsheath s. L.
Sept. 30. John Bunton s. & Rebecca Gardiner s. both of this P. L.

1744.

Oct. 4. William Pear of Risby s. & Elizabeth Spicer of this P. s.

1745.

Sept. 8. Robert King of Beighton w. & Mary Wiseman of this P. s. L.
Nov. 10. Thomas Murton of this P. w. & Sarah Smith of Ickworth s. L.

1746.

Oct. 13. Thomas Frost s. & Elizabeth Brunning s. both of this P.

1747.

April 19. Robert Cooper s. & Susanna Jermen s. both of All Saints in Sudbury. L.

1748.

Dec. 25. Oliver Sparrow of Thorp s. & Mary Bedall of this P. s.

1749.

April 16. Samuel Dearsly of Owsden s. & Lydia Formin of this P. s. L.
July 14. Joseph Alderton of Welnetham w. & Ann King of this P.

Aug. 30. James Mirrels of Bury & Elizabeth Herrington of this P.
Jan. 8. Penson Sanders s. & Mary Day s. both of Ickworth. L.
Jan. 18. William Polly s. & Ann Sparrow s. both of this P.

1750.

June 7. Giles Frost s. & Mary Harvey s. both of this P.

1751.

April 8. James Finch s. & Katherine White s. both of this P. L.
Oct. 3. John Swan w. & Elizabeth Bunting s. both of this P.
Oct. 28. James Armstrong of Gasely s. & Sarah How of this P. s.

1752.

June 28. James Marchil s. & Mary Barton s. both of this P.
Oct. 30. Edmund Willingham s. & Sarah Wollage s. both of this P.

1753.

Feb. 26. Richard Smith of this P. s. & Susan Purchis of Saxham Parva s.
Feb. 27. Robert Norman s. & Mary Frost s. both of this P.
May 29. Thomas Bird s. & Elizabeth Frost s. both of this P.
June 12. William Beleman s. & Elizabeth Bass s. both of this P.
Oct. 18. John Nunn s. & Mary Whistly s. both of this P.
Oct. 23. John Tweed s. & Susan Sparrow s. both of this P.
Dec. 3. William Miller s. & Ann Cole s. both of this P.

1754.

Jan. 25. Samuel Brigg of Chevington s. & Susan Baker of this P.
Sept. 14. James Armstrong w. & Margaret Francis w. both of this P.
Dec. 26. Thomas Carrington of Gransden, Co. Hunt: s. & Mary Sparrow of this P. s. L.

1755.

July 29. James Haselwood s. & Sarah Polley s. both of this P.
Dec. 29. Richard Boyce w. & Elizabeth Underwood w. both of this P.

1756.

Oct. 11. Thomas Bedell s. & Martha Weeb s. both of this P.

1757.

May 31. Joseph Hammond jun. s. & Margaret Aylmer s. both of this P.

1758.

June 27. Thomas Lystor of Brockley w. & Elizabeth Catchpole of this P. s.
Oct. 24. Thomas Frost s. & Elizabeth Pattle s. both of this P.

Dec. 18. Thomas Richardson s. & Ann Attwell s. both of this P.

1759.

Feb. 27. John Smith w. & Sarah Holden s. both of this P.

1760.

April 22. William Alcock of Barrow s. & Elizabeth Frost s. of this P.
Nov. 24. Charles Browster of Gazely s. & Mary Frost s. of this P.

1761.

Oct. 22. William Miller w. & Susan Bunting s. both of this P.
Nov. 2. Joseph Underwood s. & Susan Pond s. both of this P.
Nov. 17. George Hilton s. of Nowton & Anne Went s. of this P.

1762.

Jan. 27. Thomas Cornell s. of this P. & Susannah Hague s. of Hengrave.
Sept. 5. William Plumb w. of Barrow & Isabelle Berthoud s. of this P.
Oct. 20. John Cooper s. & Mary Goldsmith s. both of this P.
Nov. 9. Thomas Frost w. of Whepsted & Sarah Ottewell s. of this P.
Nov. 22. William Hempsted w. & Mary Wilding s. both of this P.
Dec. 2. Job Malton w. & Susan Cooke s. both of this P.

1763.

Jan. 17. Richard Boyce w. & Susan Emerson s. both of this P.
May 9. John Rockel s. of this P. & Ann Whiting of Lidgate. L.
June 7. John Wright s. & Sarah Billman s. both of this P.
Oct. 11. Charles Rasbrook s. & Susan Lilly s. both of this P.
Nov. 27. William Bray s. & Sarah Rasbrook s. both of this P.

1764.

May 6. Christopher Rusbrook s. & Elizabeth Peach s. both of this P.
June 11. James Bailey s. of Whepsted & Isabella Spencer s. of this P.
Nov. 8. James How s. & Rebecka Gardiner s. both of this P.
Dec. 10. John Bray s. & Elizabeth Sparrow s. both of this P.

1765.

April 1. Stephen Crick s. & Sarah Crick s. both of this P.
July 26. Isaac Bray s. of Troston & Elizabeth Ottiwell s. of this P.
Oct. 11. Robert Tegon, clerk, s. & Dorothea Spark s. both of this P.
Nov. 7. Henry Cater s. & Elizabeth Mayhew s. both of this P.

1766.

Jan. 17. Thomas Holden s. & Mary Leader s. both of this P. L.

March 2. William Scott s. & Hannah Death s. both of this P.
July 17. James Rawlinson s. of St. Mary's, Bury, & Sarah Barker s. of this P.
Aug. 3. John Gardener s. & Sarah Maria Ranson s. both of this P.
Nov. 6. Joseph Bass s. of Gazely & Susan Deer s. of this P. L.

1767.

Oct. 12. John Adams w. & Mary Evered s. both of this P.
Oct. 27. Thomas Orridge s. & Ann Barrel s. both of this P.

1768.

March 27. Christopher Rosbrook sen. w. & Susan Cousins s. both of this P.
May 26. George Rogers, Rector, s. & Elizabeth Drew s. both of this P. L.
July 31. John Adkin s. of this P. & Elizabeth Lait w. of Chevington.
Oct. 14. Thomas Orridge w. & Mary Cornhill s. both of this P.

1769.

Jan. 12. John Frost s. & Sarah Haward s. both of this P.
Dec. 3. William Adams w. & Sarah Death s. both of this P.
Dec. 24. John Holden w. & Mary Sturton s. both of this P.

1770.

Nov. 15. William Frost w. & Sarah Cooper s. both of this P. L.

1771.

Sept. 22. Thomas Elsden s. & Hannah Everard both of this P. L.

1772.

Oct. 5. John Double s. of Wickambrook & Ann Scarfe s. of this P. L.
Oct. 13. James Otley s. & Hannah Copping s. both of this P.
Nov. 8. Samuel Holden s. of Whepsted & Mary Fitch s. of this P.

1773.

April 12. George Watson, clerk, of St. Mary's in Bury, & Sarah Drew s. of this P. L.
Dec. 12. William Candler s. & Mary Frost s. both of this P.
Dec. 27. William Frost s. of this P. & Sarah Baxter s. of Timworth.

1774.

Dec.* 5. Edmund Willingham s. of Hawsted & Mary Bunting s. of this P.

* As the entries are made at the time of the marriage, Dec. is an obvious slip of the pen. Probably it should be Jan.—S. H. A. H.

May 12. Edward Hibgame, clerk, of Long Stratton, Co. Norfolk, s. & Mary Smith s. of this P. L.
June 30. Andrew Pern, clerk, of Little Abingdon, Co. Cambridge, s. & Susan Smith s. of this P. L.
July 7. Thomas Orbell w. of Risby & Bridget Goodchild s. of this P. L.
July 14. James Scarlin s. of All Saints in Sudbury & Susan Drew s. of this P. L.
Aug. 2. William Polly s. & Mary Frost s. both of this P.
Aug. 29. George Challis w. & Abigail Adkin w. both of this P.

1775.

Jan. 24. John Warren s. & Susan Rasbrook w. both of this P.
Sept. 21. Charles Jackson s. of St. Mary's in Bury & Sarah Clarke s. of this P.

1776.

June 17. Thomas Scalf s. of St. Mary's in Bury & Alice Willingham s. of this P.
Sept. 15. Thomas Orridge w. of this P. & Ann Southgate of Wickham brook.
Oct. 10. Joseph Palfrey s. of Risby & Mary Fuller s. of this P. L.
Oct. 29. James Copsey s. & Ann How s. both of this P.
Nov. 11. Thomas Cater s. & Mary Sparrow s. both of this P.
Nov. 19. Thomas Frost w. & Frances Bryant s. both of this P.

1777.

June 3. William Ambrose s. & Elizabeth Bird s. both of this P.
Nov. 6. Henry Traice s. of St. Mary's in Bury & Mary Marshall s. of this P.

1778.

Jan. 18. Humphrey Betts s. of Nowton & Elizabeth Cater s. of this P.
Feb. 17. Samuel Burroughs s. of Stowmarket & Mary Drew s. of this P. L.
July 9. John Frost s. & Jemima Green s. both of this P.
July 12. William Bray w. & Susan Garrard s. both of this P.
Sept. 14. John Whymark w. & Mary Moore s. both of this P. L.
Sept. 14. Michael King s. & Catharine Finch s. both of this P.
Nov. 2. William Pierson w. & Alice Prick s. both of this P. L.

1779.

Aug. 9. William Cole w. & Ann Brown s. both of this P.
Oct. 18. John Stern s. & Mary Copping s. both of this P.

1780.

April 10. William Willingham s. & Elizabeth Layte s. both of this P.
April 10. Edmund Willingham s. & Alice Goodchild s. both of this P.

1781.

April 17. John Marshall s. of this P. & Sarah Waller s. of Hargrave.
Dec. 24. George Last s. & Rose Siderrey w. both of this P.
Dec. 31. William Meller s. of this P. & Elizabeth Gawsell of St. James' in Bury.

1782.

March 3. James Lyng s. of Reed & Phœbe Smith s. of this P.
Aug. 26. John Westrop of Brockly & Susanna Scarfe of this P. L.
Oct. 11. Thomas Copsey s. & Ann Rosbrook s. both of this P.
Oct. 11. Thomas Byford s. & Ann Bird s. both of this P.

1783.

Jan. 20. Daniel Wood s. of Flempton & Mary Lelia Scarfe s. of this P. L.
Feb. 3. William Layt s. & Mary Willingham s. both of this P.
Aug. 2. John Ranner s. of Hartest & Mary Pain of this P.
Nov. 4. Robert Goldsmith s. of Hargrave & Hannah Evered s. of this P.
Dec. 2. George Cater s. & Martha Beddel s. both of this P.
Dec. 7. Charles Seaman [Semes] s. of St. Mary's in Bury & Sarah Cater s. of this P.

1784.

Feb. 26. John Adkin s. of Ickworth & Elizabeth Smith s. of this P. L.
March 8. Anthony Crick s. of Ickworth & Elizabeth Prick s. of this P.
April 29. Charles Ward s. & Alice Calf both of this P.
July 13. James Norton s. & Sarah Adam w. both of this P.

1785.

May 22. John Harvey s. & Theophila Taylor w. of this P. L.

1786.

Feb. 12. John Bass s. of St. James' in Bury & Elizabeth Smith s. of this P.
Oct. 10. Richard Sparrow s. & Elizabeth Pawsey s. both of this P.
Dec. 26. Simon Seale s. & Mary Last s. both of this P.

1787.

April 10. John Death s. & Catharine Frost s. both of this P.
Oct. 11. Robert Subtle s. of Chevington & Delarivière Willingham s. of this P.

Dec. 25. James Reynolds s. & Margaret Daines s. both of this P.

1788.

Jan. 29. John King s. & Sarah Bray s. both of this P.
May 29. John Holden w. & Catharine Reeve of this P. L.
Dec. 4. William Robert Frost s. & Sarah Holden s. of this P. L.

1789.

June 5. John Marshall w. & Mary Humphrys s. both of this P. L.

1790.

April 12. Ambrose Seal w. & Sarah Frost w. both of this P.

1791.

Feb. 14. James Goodchild s. & Mary Eagle s. both of this P.
Feb. 27. John Elliss s. of Wooditton, Co. Cambridge, & Catharine Bird s. of this P. L.
May 16. John Cockle s. & Ann Rosbrook s. both of this P.
Oct. 17. George Root s. of this P. & Elizabeth Grice s. of Whepsted. L.
Dec. 17. William Emmet s. & Mary Hempsted s. both of this P. L.
Dec. 26. William Lilley s. & Hannah Griggs s. both of this P.

1792.

Jan. 5. Edward Hempsted s. & Frances Bull s. both of this P.
Jan. 17. William Richardson s. & Dorothy Reed s. both of this P.
Nov. 6. Thomas Tweed s. & Lucy Hilton s. both of this P.
Dec. 25. William Seal s. & Sarah Richardson s. both of this P.

1793.

Jan. 9. Joseph Prick w. & Sarah Cooper s. both of this P.
May 27. Stephen Brooks s. of this P. & Mary Peppen s. of St. James' in Bury. L. This marriage by desire of the parties was re-solemnized.* [It is entered again exactly as above under the following June 5.]
Oct. 11. John Warren w. & Susannah Scarff w. both of this P.
Oct. 17. Abraham Payne s. of Whepstead & Mary Daines s. of this P.
Oct. 21. Jonathan Biddle s. & Elizabeth Davy s. both of this P.

* This re-performance of the Marriage Service for some reason or other is said to be occasionally found in the Registers of the last century Notes and Queries, 9th Ser; iv. 9, 72.—S. H, A. H.

I

1794.

Nov. 4. John Goodrich w. & Rose Gardiner s. both of this P.

1795.

Jan. 26. William Last s. & Ann Molten s. both of this P.
Feb. 2. John Lanham s. of Hawsted & Elizabeth Sharpe s. of this P.
Feb. 10. Thomas Kempster s. of St. Mary's in Bury & Sarah Greenwood s. of this P.
May 12. William Norman s. & Elizabeth Bullard s. both of this P.
May 24. Samuel Mizen s. & Hannah Elsden s. both of this P.
June 16. Jonathan Flower s. of Market Downham, Co. Norfolk, & Mary Hearsine s. of this P. L.
Sept. 24. James Last s. & Ann Crack s. both of this P.
Oct. 17. Abraham Steed s. & Susan Scarff s. both of this P.

1796.

Oct. 13. Jonathan Green s. & Mary Beddle s. both of this P.
Oct. 31. Mark Hammond s. & Ann Cole s. both of this P.

1797.

Feb. 20. James Bradley w. & Sarah Clark s. both of this P.
May 1. William Frost w. & Bell Finch s. both of this P.
Nov. 1. Daniel Pask s. & Susan Ling s. both of this P.
Nov. 27. William Rosbrook s. & Mary Leech s. both of this P.

1798.

March 19. Robert Winch s. & Elizabeth Garrard s. both of this P.
July 23. John Brown s. & Ann Smith s. both of this P.
Sept. 19. John Reynolds s. & Clementina Double s. both of this P. L.
Oct. 10. William Abbott w. of Great Whelnetham & Mary Orridge s. of this P.
Oct. 22. Jonas Row s. & Rachael Bray s. both of this P.

1799.

Feb. 26. William Patten s. of Pedmarsh, Co. Essex, & Ann Coote w. of this P. L.
April 1. Thomas Gardiner s. & Frances Goodrich s. both of this P. L.
April 9. Samuel Hagreen s. & Ann Ambrose s. both of this P. L.
Aug. 18. Abraham Elsden w. & Mary Clark s. both of this P.

1800.

Jan. 6. James Bullas s. & Sarah Alvis s. both of this P.

1801.

Dec. 21. William Chanell s. & Elizabeth Rickwood s. both of this P.

1802.

April 22. Thomas Disney w. of St. Mary's in Bury & Ann Richardson s. of this P. L.

July 12. William King s. & Ann Ling s. both of this P.

Aug. 3. Thomas Burgess w. & Mary Steward s. both of this P.

Dec. 24. John Blackbourn w. & Ann Copsey s. both of this P.

1803.

Feb. 13. James Finter s. & Susan Frost s. both of this P.

May 30. James Wratham s. & Mary Spalding s. both of this P.

Dec. 13. Thomas Newman s. of Burrow-green & Susan Ramplin s. of this P.

Dec. 23. John Fenner s. & Ruth Cobbin w. both of this P.

1804.

Jan. 6. William Orridge s. & Mary Willingham s. both of this P.

May 5. James Salisbury jun. s. of Lawshall & Ann Spalding s. of this P. L.

June 12. William Collison s. & Mary Spark s. both of this P.

Dec. 2. Stephen Crick w. & Sarah Moyse w. both of this P. L.

Dec. 11. William Smith s. & Rose Ann Howe s. both of this P.

Dec. 16. Thomas Pentney s. & Alice Willingham s. both of this P.

1805.

Feb. 28. Robert Alves s. & Mary Parfrey s. both of this P.

April 4. Henry Hart s. & Elizabeth Tweed s. both of this P.

July 22. Thomas Atkin s. & Ann Double s. both of this P. L.

1806.

July 7. James Webb s. of Cavenham & Mary Walker s. of this P.

Nov. 10. John Buckle s. & Frances Bull s. both of this P.

Nov. 13. John Tricker w. & Sarah Sharpe s. both of this P.

1807.

Jan. 9. John Osborne s. & Susan Holden s. both of this P.

Feb. 5. James Boreham s. & Mary Copsey s. both of this P.

March 5. John Reeman s. of Lawshall & Ann Beales w. of this P. L.

March 14. Isaac Race s. & Sarah Willingham s. both of this P.
May 18. James Warren s. & Sarah Ling s. both of this P.
July 2. Edmund Houghton w. of St. Mary's in Bury & Harriet Moyse s. of this P.
Oct. 12. Abraham Rcoks s. & Matthew Copsey s. both of this P.
Nov. 9. Joseph Lofts s. & Mary King s. both of this P.

1808.

Nov. 23. Edward Willingham s. & Mary Brewster s. both of this P.
Dec. 25. John Death s. & Milla Harsom s. both of this P.

1809.

Nov. 23. Charles Double s. & Hannah Cater s. both of this P. L.
Dec. 24. William Rutter s. & Mary Cater s. both of this P.

1810.

May 20. Jonathan Marshall s. & Alice Howes s. both of this P.
Oct. 12. John Baker s. & Elizabeth Nunn s. both of this P.
Dec. 3. James Ramplin s. & Sophia Crack s. both of this P.

1811.

Feb. 18. James Abrey s. of All Saints, Icklingham, & Sarah Spark s. of this P.

1812.

Jan. 13. Robert Lyes s. & Hannah Elsden s. both of this P.
June 7. John Elliss w. & Elizabeth Sparrow w. both of this P.
Nov. 6. John Cater s. & Elizabeth Edwards s. both of this P.

1813.

March 16. John Greenwood s. & Mary Cater s. both of this P.
Dec. 20. William Frost s. & Susan Double s. both of this P.

1814.

Aug. 8. Thomas King s. & Martha Cater s. both of this P.
Sept. 8. John Mower s. & Elizabeth Double s. both of this P.
Nov. 3. William Root s. & Tabitha Copsey s. both of this P.
Nov. 7. William Cater s. & Sophia Middleditch s. both of this P.

1815.

Feb. 14. Charles Cooe s. & Elizabeth Bull s. both of this P.
March 6. William Last s. & Harriet Ebing s. both of this P.
Oct. 22. Samuel Earl s. & Charlotte Adkin s. both of this P.

Dec. 25. Louis Rosbrook w. & Rebecca Norman s. both of this P.

1816.

June 16. John Brown w. & Ann Ridnall w. both of this P.
Oct. 14. William Cook s. & Esther Saunders s. both of this P.
Oct. 16. John Sier s. of Risby & Frances Ling s. of this P. L.
Dec. 25. William Willingham w. & Sarah Thirgood s. both of this P.

1817.

March 11. William Lloyd s. & Susan Copsey s. both of this P.
May 1. John Copsey s. & Mary Cooke s. both of this P.
June 11. William Moyes s. & Lucy Pryke s. both of this P.
Aug. 22. Thomas Leonard w. & Mary Pettit s. both of this P.
Sept. 1. Benjamin Pryke w. & Sarah Steed s. both of this P.
Oct. 27. Henry Rudland w. & Sarah Crick w. both of this P.
Nov. 18. Simon Last s. & Mary Ling s. both of this P.

1818.

Jan. 12. Thomas Hazlewood s. of St. James' in Bury & Sarah Meller s. of Horsecroft. Witnesses, John Dearson Meller sen & jun. L.
April 2. William Palmer s. & Sarah King s. both of this P.
April 30. Barry Girling s. of Scarning, Co. Norfolk, & Susan Bidwell s. of this P. L.
Sept. 22. James Wallaker s. & Mary Lilly s. both of this P.
Oct. 22. Pooley Pearson s. of Shipdam, Co. Norfolk, & Mary Meller s. of this P. L.
Dec. 24. Philip King s. of Hargrave & Anne Mason s. of this P.

1819.

May 2. Abraham Cooper s. & Hannah Crack s. both of this P.
July 27. John Ellis s. & Mary Varer s. both of this P.
July 27. John Goldstone s. & Martha Ling s. both of this P.
Aug. 31. Robert Gooch s. & Mary Musk s. both of this P.

1820.

June 6. Abraham Steed s. & Sophia Wright s. both of this P.
Aug. 28. John Spalding w. & Ann Salisbury w. both of this P.
Oct. 26. James Fenton s. of Ingham & Mary Cater s. of this P.
Nov. 11. John Baker w. & Mary Adams s. both of this P.
Nov. 11. George Emmitt s. & Mary Baker s. both of this P.

Nov. 24. James Cater s. & Mary Gout s. both of this P.

1821.

Jan. 11. William Meeking s. of St. James' in Bury & Mary Anne Norman s. of this P.

March 29. Thomas Last w. of this P. & Sarah Adams s. of St. Mary's in Bury.

1822.

April 12. David Smith s. & Maria Lanham s. both of this P.

May 2. William Steel s. of St. Mary's in Bury & Frances Gardiner s. of this P. L.

May 2. William Edwards s. of Chevington & Mary Ann Gardiner s. of this P. L.

Nov. 28. John Adkin w. & Martha Cocksedge s. both of this P.

Nov. 30. George Musk s. & Jane Nelson s. both of this P.

1823.

Jan. 13. William King w. & Elizabeth Fitch s. both of this P.

Jan. 30. Joseph Baker s. of Thurston and Frances Double s. of this P.

Jan. 30. Isaac Willingham s. & Sophy Brown s. both of this P.

Feb. 11. William Wright s. of Audley End in the P. of Safron Walden & Maria Copsey s. of this P. L.

March 22. John Goldestone s. of Walsham, Co. Suffolk, & Mary Crack s. of this P.

June 17. Thomas Manning s. of Birdbrook, Co. Essex, & Mary Gallant s. of this P.

Aug. 14. William Pillans s. of East Dereham, Co. Norfolk, & Margaret Bidwell s. of this P. L.

Sept. 18. Henry Everard s. of St. Mary's in Bury & Lucy Gardiner s. of this P. L.

Oct. 12. William Adams s. of St. James in Bury & Hannah Lilly s. of this P.

Nov. 23. Thomas Pryke s. & Kezia Rayner s. both of this P.

Dec. 25. John Cornell s. of Chevington & Mary Ann Farrants s. of this P.

1824.

Feb. 16. John Rolfe s. of Walthamstow Co. Essex & Mary Winch s. of this P.

Feb. 24. James Elliss s. & Sarah Winter s. both of this P.

Nov. 28. Henry Taylor s. & Susan Gooding s. both of this P.

1825.

April 12. William Browning s. of this P. & Mary Stevens Goold s. of St. Cuthbert's in Thetford.
May 2. Samuel Mison s. & Sarah Herbert w. both of this P.
Sept. 13. Henry Cater s. & Rachael Rowe s. both of this P.
Sept. 19. Edward Folkes s. of Barton Parva, Co. Suffolk, & Mary Everett s. of this P.
Nov. 15. Edward Crack s. of this P. & Sarah Langham s. of Ickworth.
Nov. 18. Samuel Wilkin s. & Sarah Green w. both of this P.

1826.

Jan. 26. William Double s. of this P. & Louisa Spink w. of Tilbury, Co. Essex. L.
May 15. Philip Meadows s. & Anne Goodchild s. both of this P.
July 10. William Brame s. & Mary Ann Seeley s. both of this P.
Sept. 12. Robert Lawrance w. of St. Mary's in Reading & Bridget Gedge w. of this P. L.
Sept. 28. Elisha Barnes s. of this P. & Harriet Howe s. of Ickworth.
Oct. 26. John Mison s. of this P. & Frances Clarke s. of Ickworth.
Nov. 21. John Clarke s. of this P. & Susan Kemp s. of St. Mary's in Bury.

1827.

July 5. Charles Sterling s. & Susan Double s. both of this P.
July 26. Robert Catchpole s. of this P. & Sarah Crow of St. Mary's in Bury.
Sept. 5. Thomas Pratt s. of Belchamp Otten, Co. Essex, & Ann Sturgeon s. of this P. L.
Oct. 19. William Elsden s. & Rachael Cater w. both of this P.
Nov. 1. Joseph Mizon s. & Ann Cooke both of this P.

1828.

Jan. 20. John Moss s. & Elizabeth Adkins s. both cf this P.
Feb. 12. William Bullass s. & Harriot Cater s. both of this P.
April 1. John Wing s. & Mary Ann Last s. both of this P.
June 17. Robert Coe s. & Mary Cooper s. both of this P.
Sept. 18. Thomas Gardiner jun. s. & Mary Ann Everard s. both of this P. L.
Sept. 24. John Bull s. & Hannah Cockel s. both of this P.

Nov. 4. Richard Cockle s. & Susan Crack s. both of this P.
Nov. 11. Stephen Musk s. & Sarah Sharp s. both of this P.
Dec. 7. William Emmet s. & Mary Elsden s. both of this P.
Dec. 25. John Edwards s. & Sarah Green s. both of this P. L.

1829.

Jan. 23. John Smith of Dallingham, Co. Suffolk, & Elizabeth Payne of this P.
Feb. 13. John Elsden s. & Mary Pryke s. both of this P.
March 17. George Rose s. of this P. & Sarah Smith s. of St. James in Bury.
March 17. John Smith s. of St. James in Bury & Mary Ann Pearsons s. of this P.
June 6. William Gowson s. & Sarah Rawsbrook s. both of this P.
Aug. 27. George Brewster s. & Anne Maria Ambrose s. both of this P.
Oct. 19. Thomas Goodchild s. of this P. & Mary King s. of St. Mary's in Bury.

1830.

May 7. Isaac Race s. of this P. & Caroline Linge s. of St. Mary's in Thetford.
Aug. 5. Robert Thompson s. & Anne Boyce s. both of this P.
Aug. 10. William Eade w. & Jane Burgess s. both of this P.
Oct. 14. George Scarfe Double s. of this P. & Maria Everard s. of St. Mary's in Bury. L.
Dec. 26. William Wheeler s. of this P. & Frances Death s. of St. Mary's in Bury.

1831.

March 25. George Cooper s. & Sarah Tricker s. both of this P.
May 25. William Palmer s. & Sarah Boggis s. both of this P.
June 18. Robert Elsden s. & Mary Cater w. both of this P.
Nov. 8. William Pollard s. & Miriam Pearsons s. both of this P.

1832.

Sept. 29. Henry Rushbrook s. & Jane Crack s. both of this P.

1833.

May 27. Thomas Frederick Howe s. & Sophia Fenton s. both of this P.
June 17. Thcmas Fake s. & Mary Leech w. both of this P.
Oct. 5. Ezekiel Durrant s. & Charlotte Naylor s. both of this P.

Nov. 16. George Buckle s. & Sophia Baley s. both of this P.
Dec. 29. David Hammond s. & Elizabeth Harris s. both of this P.

1834.

Feb. 2. James Goodchild & Anne Batt both of this P.
March 18. John Bullass s. & Harriet Rutter w. both of this P. L.
April 27. James Vincent s. & Anne Double s. both of this P.
June 28. Charles Canham s. of Ixworth & Sarah Lilly s. of this P.
Aug. 3. George Crack s. & Elizabeth Bull s. both of this P.
Oct. 5. James Boreham s. & Lucy Ramplin s. both of this P.

1835.

Jan. 16. Robert Hammond s. & Eliza Crow s. both of this P.
Feb. 19. William Ambrose s. & Anne Bowers s. both of this P.
April 2. Joseph Child s. of St. Mary's in Bury & Elizabeth Bullock s. of this P.
May 15. Robert Petch w. & Harriet Tweed s. both of this P.
Dec. 25. Jarman Lewis s. & Sarah Wells s. both of this P.

1836.

Jan. 14. Thomas Catchpole w. & Sophia Hammond s. both of this P.
Jan. 28. Thomas Smith s. & Charlotte Bullass s. both of this P.
Sept. 26. Robert Johnson s. & Anne Mayhew s. both of this P.
Oct. 1. Robert Cook s. & Elizabeth Willingham s. both of this P.
Oct. 20. Edward Green s. & Jane Arbon s. both of this P.

1837.

Jan. 6. Thomas French s. & Nancy Tweed s. both of this P.
Feb. 14. John Green s. & Harriet Smith s. both of this P.
June 24. Robert Rooks s. & Mary Ann Baker s. both of this P.
Oct. 2. George son of William Cater & Ann Goodliffe.*
Dec. 25. Robert Challis w. of St. James', Bury & Lucy Varer w.

* With this entry begins a new Register book giving more information than the previous ones. I have put in some of that information but not quite all. From here to the end "of Horringer" is to be understood unless some other place is mentioned, "Labourer" is to be understood unless some other occupation is mentioned. The profession named on the bridegroom's side is his; that on the bride's side is her father's. "Single" is also to be understood unless it is stated otherwise.

1838.

Feb. 24. William son of Robert Spalding & Mary Coe.
June 5. Robert son of John Webb carpenter & Mary Ann dau: of George Farrants.
Nov. 3. John son of James Cross & Mary Ann dau: of Will: Willingham.
Nov. 8. Arthur John Gray of Great St. Andrew's Cambridge, carpenter & Elizabeth dau: of Robert Plum, gamekeeper.
Nov. 11. William son of William Makup & Eliza dau: of James Nunn.

1839.

Jan. 8. Robert son of Robert Kemp w. farmer & Charlotte Rosbrooke dau: of William Kemp w.
April 21. Joseph son of George Farrants blacksmith & Elizabeth dau: of John Winch.
May 30. William Gilbert son of Thomas Tuck clerk & Anne Elizabeth dau: of Edward Smyth gent.
Sept. 20. John son of Robert Bowers wheelwright & Elizabeth dau: of William Root carpenter.
Dec. 7. Thomas son of Thomas Wade & Sarah dau: of John Ridnall sawyer.

1840.

Feb. 20. William son of Thomas Gardiner farmer & Emily dau: of John Ramsey of Bury St. Edmunds tradesman.
March 16. Isaac son of James Boreham shoemaker & Mary Ann dau: of William Cage.
Oct. 1. Robert E. son of Robert Wright brickmaker & Elizabeth dau: of John Kemp farmer.
Nov. 14. Robert son of John Copsey & Sarah dau: of Isaac Root carpenter.
Dec. 24. William son of William Payne shoemaker & Mary dau: of Jeremiah Saunders shoemaker.

1841.

Jan. 12. William son of James Boreham & Mary Ann dau: of Robert Spalding.
March 30. John son of William Wright shoemaker & Martha dau: of John Hammond.
April 26. Elijah son of Robert Deacon brickmaker & Louisa dau: of Robert Lambert brickmaker.

May 8. James son of John Death w. & Rebecca Rosbrooke w. dau: of Thomas Norman woolcomber.

May 15. John son of Robert Gooch bricklayer & Caroline dau: of George Emmett.

June 19. Henry son of James Last of Saxham Parva & Mary Ann dau: of Edmund Willingham.

Sept. 18. James son of George Boreham of Whepstead & Mary dau: of William Cooke.

Oct. 16. William son of Simon Last & Mary Ann dau: of Edward Wyard.

Dec. 16. William son of Thomas Nunn & Suzan dau: of George Flack of Rede.

1842.

April 3. George son of James Cater & Mary Ann dau: of Simon Last.

1843.

March 24. James son of Robert Lambert of Bury St. Ed: gardener & Mary Ann dau: of John Leeks carpenter.

April 13. George son of Robert Brown servant & Susan Coe dau: cf Thomas Pearson horse dealer.

Oct. 13. Robert son of Robert Osborne of Wixoe & Charlotte dau: of William Shave.

Nov. 18. Samuel son of Jonas Rowe of Westley & Elizabeth Cook w. dau: of William Willingham.

1844.

Feb. 20. Thomas son of James Goodchild w. & Ann dau: of William Crack of Chedburgh.

March 3. John son of James Bullass w. & Susanna dau: of John Andrews of Rede.

July 27. Thomas son of Robert Wells shepherd & Mary Ann dau: of Thomas Nunn.

1845.

Feb. 20. William son of John Baker w. carpenter of Higham in the Parish of Gazely & Sarah dau: of William Partridge glazier.

April 29. William son of Robert Howard of Colchester solicitor & Elizabeth Mary dau: of William Bacon Wigson Esquire.

June 23. John son of Humphrey Baker w. & Martha Adkin w. dau: of Richard Cocksedge.

Dec. 25. Isaac son of James Ramplin & Susan dau : of George Ridgeon.

1846.

Jan. 29. Charles son of Thomas Smith w. farmer & Mary Ann dau: of William Steel, lawyer's clerk.

Feb. 28. Thomas son of William Orrage & Susan dau: of William Root carpenter.

April 4. John son of William Palmer of Westley & Hannah dau: of Abraham Orriss.

May 30. William son of John Copsey & Elizabeth dau: of Isaac Root carpenter.

June 6. George son of Robert Gooch & Harriet dau : of James Boreham.

Oct. 24. Jonathan son of Isaac Race & Emma dau : of Joseph Richardson.

Nov. 10. George son of George Goldsmith of Wyverstone gardener & Isabella Webb w. dau : of James Wylie gardener.

Nov. 19. William John Gardiner son of William Edwards wheelwright & Susanna dau : of John Winch farmer.

Dec. 25. James son of John Copsey & Elizabeth dau: of Robert Gooch bricklayer.

1847.

July 12. William son of Simon Last w. & Louisa Double w. dau : of Samuel Smith.

Aug. 20. Thomas son of Michael Crack & Eliza Humphrys w. dau: of John Eden hostler.

Sept. 14. William son of Samuel Fenton & Harriet dau: of William Root carpenter.

Nov. 23. Orbell son of John Maidwell of Hopton servant & Susan dau : of William Ray dealer.

Dec. 25. Henry son of Henry Cater & Sophia dau : of James Boreham.

1848.

Aug. 14. Benjamin son of Benjamin Bridge w. of Bury St. Ed : grocer & Rebecca dau : of John Goodliffe clerk.

Nov. 2. Thomas son of Abraham Arborn & Ann dau : of Thomas Nunn.

1849.

Feb. 10. George son of Joseph Richardson of Little Saxham & Susan dau : of Isaac Race.

Feb. 27. William son of John Simpkin & Catherine dau: of William John Charville, schoolmaster.

March 3. Simon son of Simon Last & Rachel dau: of William Elsden.

March 17. Henry John Arbon son of Edward Smith of Thetford, smith, & Maryann dau: of William Root carpenter.

July 8. Samuel son of William Bowers, of Chevington, shepherd, and Mary Ann dau: of Stephen Pask.

Oct. 29. George son of John Lydle, of Barrow, cordwainer, and Mary Ann dau: of William King, shepherd.

Dec. 1. Octavus son of Thomas Simpkin, of Wickhambrook, thatcher, & Eliza Boyes dau: of Robert Thompson, cordwainer.

1850.

Jan. 19. Henry son of John Copsey & Hannah dau: of Isaac Root, carpenter.

March 5. Joseph son of Richard Habergham, schoolmaster, & Emily Bennett w. dau: of Stephen Jaques, gardener.

April 19. John son of John Sexton servant & Sophia dau: of Edward Bullock of Beyton.

July 5. George son of William Pratt, of Exning, wheelwright & Caroline Tricker dau: of George Cooper, cattle dealer.

July 6. Charles son of John Mortlock, of Chevington, bricklayer, & Louisa dau: of Charles Levett, shepherd.

Aug. 3. William son of George Musk & Amelia dau: of Richard Cobbing.

Aug. 12. Thomas son of James Goodchild w. & Sarah Edwards w. dau: of John Green, schoolmaster.

BURIALS.

1558.	Nov.	22.	Margerie Plomer.
	Dec.	1.	Robert Maske.
	Dec.	4.	John Plomer.
	Jan.	12.	Edido the wyfe of William Page.
	Jan.	14.	Rose daughter of John Austin.
	March	1.	James Smith.
	March	4.	Robert Gylman.
	March	15.	John the sonne of John Wellam.
	March	24.	Alice the wyfe of John Wellam the yonger.
1559.	April	25.	John the sonne of John Lilly.
	Maie	3.	Edmond Sparow.
	June	4.	Thomas Blackman.
	Julie	9.	Thomas the sonne of Thomas Hill.
	Sept.	25.	Margaret the daughter of Robert Wellam.
	Oct.	6.	John Wellam th' elder.
	Jan.	30.	Ann the daughter of Mr. Jaslin.
1560.	April	4.	Frauncis Martin.
	Dec.	25.	Elizabeth Jehiue.
1561.	April	13.	Joane the daughter of John Wellom.
	Oct.	27.	Marie the daughter of Nicholas Cooke.
1562.	Oct.	31.	Elizabeth Rogers.
	Nov.	6.	Margaret the wyfe of John Lilly.
	Nov.	20.	John Prick.
1563.	Nov.	3.	John the sonne of Robert Wellam.
	Jan.	5.	John the sonne of John Sturgeon.
	Jan.	17.	Thomas Hil the blacksmith.
1564.	Oct.	13.	Edward Bardwel.
	Oct.	22.	John Wellam th' elder.
	Feb.	6.	Nicholas the sonne of William Austin.

1565.	Aug.	17.	Alice Wellam widowe.
	Sept.	22.	Margerie the wyfe of Richard Sillet.
	Dec.	5.	Elizabeth Drakelon.
	Jan.	13.	John the sonne of Thomas Brett.
	Jan.	31.	William Birde.
	March	12.	Robert Parker.
	March	19.	Margerie Case.
	March	23.	Roger Parker.
1566.	April	22.	William sonne of Robert Spalding.
	Sept.	27.	Richard Stapse.
	Oct.	20.	Edward the sonne of John Hande.
	Dec.	31.	Henrie the sonne of Roger Parker.
	Jan.	19.	Alice Bully widowe.
	Jan.	20.	John Hande.
	Jan.	24.	Alice the wyfe of John Goose.
	March	9.	Elenor Tupfeld widowe.
1567.	Maie	2.	Robert the sonne of William Lilly of Wichambrooke.
	Sept.	20.	Barbara Edmondes.
	Dec.	1.	John Steeven.
	Dec.	2.	Elizabeth Gylman.
	Feb.	10.	Marie the daughter of William Fynn.
1568.	Sept.	12.	Ann Godfrie widowe.
	Sept.	16.	William the sonne of Richard Cooper.
	Sept.	22.	William the sonne of John Goose.
	Oct.	16.	Jane the daughter of William Hawe.
	Oct.	28.	Reginold Fynn.
	Nov.	20.	Joan the daughter of William Lilly.
	Nov.	22.	Robert Carver.
	Jan.	12.	Katharine Allen.
	Jan.	13.	Margaret Fynn widowe.
1569.	June	12.	Margaret the wyfe of John Edmondes.
	Aug.	15.	John the sonne of John Bucknam.
	Sept.	1.	Margaret the wyfe of John Godfrie.
	Dec.	7.	Tomasin the daughter of John Bucknam.
	March	5.	John the sonne of John Mayhewe.

	March	12.	John the sonne of John Bucknam.
1570.	Aug.	8.	Ursula the daughter of William Man.
	Aug.	15.	Katharine the daughter of William Man.
	Nov.	17.	Marie Barret.
	Dec.	2.	John the sonne of John Edowes.
1571.	Oct.	3.	John Goose.
	Nov.	11.	Robert Nun.
1572.	Nov.	21.	Marie Redgrave.
1573.	Julie	29.	William Lilly.
1574.	April	5.	Philip Spalding.
	April	30.	William Fyshen.
	Maie	20.	John Lilly.
	Sept.	11.	Ann Tyndal daughter of Sir Ambrose Jermyn, Knight.
	Oct.	11.	Thomas Bannyard.
	Oct.	18.	John Asten.
1575.	Feb.	17.	Jane Fynn.
1576.	Maie	17.	Henrie Kobe.
	Jan.	3.	John Mahewe.
	Jan.	11.	Margerie Marten.
1577.	April	28.	Elizabeth Norman.
	Feb.	3.	Margaret Mahewe.
1578.	Maie	16.	Robert Page.
	Nov.	28.	John Waddelowe.
1579.	April	14.	Marie Hubbert.
	Maie	27.	Joane Barun.
	June	6.	Margaret Talmege.
	Dec.	28.	John Wellam.
	Jan.	13.	John Cooke.
1580.	Maie	3.	Thomas the sonne of Henrie Blagge esquire.
1581.	April	21.	Elizabeth Barret.
	Julie	15.	Elizabeth the wyfe of John Cooke.
	Julie	21.	Jane Gylman.
	Oct.	26.	John Harrison, clerke and Parson of this church.
	Dec.	26.	Joane Hadland.
	March	2.	Marie Mahewe.

	March	9.	William the sonne of John Mahewe.
	March	21.	Stephen the sonne of Stephen Bullen.
1582.	March	31.	Thomas Dearson.
	April	14.	Margeret the daughter of John Yonge.
1583.	Maie	16.	John the sonne of John Fishen.
	Maie	17.	Margaret Mahwe.
	Aug.	16.	Thomas Wellam.
	Sept.	29.	Alice the daughter of Thomas Brett.
	Jan.	10.	Agnes the wyfe of William Barret.
	March	3.	Nicholas Teuerson, laborer.
1584.	Nov.	22.	Agnes Worde, widowe.
1585.	Dec.	21.	Elizabeth Skinner, widowe.
	Dec.	21.	George the sonne of George Maio.
1586.	Dec.	11.	William Willingam.
	Jan.	28.	Alice the daughter of John Godfrie the yonger.
1587.	April	12.	John the sonne of William Fishen.
	Nov.	22.	Isabel the wyfe of John Buckenam, clerk.
1588.	April	14.	Ann Perrie.
	Maie	1.	Marie Rogers.
	Maie	11.	Robert Spalding.
	Maie	13.	Julian Rock.
	Julie	6.	Marie the daughter of John Godfrie the yonger.
	Aug.	7.	Thomas Chapman.
	Oct.	29.	Margaret Page, widowe.
1589.	Maie	22.	Robert Scot.
	June	21.	Hester the daughter of Henrie Blagge esquire.
	June	28.	William Barret, laborer.
	Dec.	2.	Margaret the wyfe of John Godfrie th' elder.
	Jan.	31.	Marie Scot.
	March	9.	Margaret the wyfe of William Fynn.
1590.	Dec.	28.	Margaret Barom.
	March	17.	Katharine Sillet.
1591.	Aug.	14.	Marie the daughter of William Page.
	Aug.	19.	Clement Lucas.
	March	22.	Agnes the wyfe of Thomas Corder.

K

1592.	Sept.	5.	John Turner, laborer.
	Sept.	23.	Thomas Frauncis, laborer.
	Oct.	5.	Clement } the children of Richard Sillet.
	Oct.	6.	Bridget } the children of Richard Sillet.
	Oct.	12.	Lettise the daughter of Thomas Scot.
	Oct.	14.	Agnes the wyfe of Edward Cock.
	Jan.	15.	Alice Gilman.
	Feb.	28.	Joane Gilman.
	March	19.	David Wignol.
1593.	Julie	28.	Agnes Dearson widowe.
	Julie	31.	Thomas Drakelon.
	Aug.	31.	Joane the wyfe of John Stanton.
	Jan.	25.	James Crick, laborer.
1594.	June	1.	Agnes the wyfe of Gregorie Burchenal.
	Julie	30.	Marie Newegate.
	Jan.	14.	John Mozer.
1595.	April	3.	George Maio, laborer.
	Maie	29.	Thomas Lucas esquire.
	Oct.	17.	John Buckenam, clerk.
	Oct.	26.	Richard the sonne of John Godfrie the yonger.
1596.	Dec.	25.	William the sonne of Robert Lilly.
1597.	Maie	13.	Joane the wyfe of Eustace Haward.
	Oct.	19.	William Dearson th' elder.
1598.	June	6.	Edmond Hasel.
	Nov.	12.	Alice Godfrie.
1599.	Maie	21.	Agnes Wignol.
	Aug.	4.	Joane the wyfe of Thomas Norman.
	Sept.	12.	William the sonne of Henrie Mahewe.
	Dec.	5.	Tomasin the wyfe of Robert Newegate.
1600.	May	9.	Alice the wyfe of William Emmyns.
	Nov.	28.	Alice the daughter of Isaac Trumble.
	Jan.	20.	John Stanton.
	March	11.	Richard Dearson.
1601.	April	15.	Richard Lillie.
	June	9.	Jeremie Goose.

	Sept.	11.	Susan Haward.
	Jan.	14.	Robert Wellom.
	Jan.	30.	Joane Drakloe.
	Feb.	26.	Daniel Gallant.
	March	5.	Katharine the wyfe of Edward Paine.
1602.	June	18.	Bridget the wyfe of Richard Sillet.
	Dec.	3.	Margaret Wellom, widowe.
	Jan.	18.	Dorothie the wyfe of Isaac Trumble.
	Feb.	8.	Tomasin the wyfe of Thomas Breat.
	March	7.	Thomas Moore.
1603.	June	5.	Robert the sonne of Robert Newegate.
	June	12.	Edward Sillet.
	Nov.	9.	Joane the wyfe of Thomas Garret.
	Jan.	15.	William Haule.
	Feb.	18.	Clement Lucas gent.
1604.	May	5.	Alise Haward.
	June	30.	John Godfrie.
	Oct.	22.	Elizabeth Spalding, widdowe.
	Nov.	6.	Rose Mahewe.
1605.	March	26.	Elizabeth Pannel.
	April	18.	James Sillet.
	Aug.	14.	Marie Sillet, widowe.
	Sept.	8.	John Gipse.
	Jan.	22.	Robert Hawle.
1606.	May	7.	Agnes Emyns.
	May	9.	Martha Steggel.
	Julie	2.	Christian Turner.
	Sept.	6.	Tomasin Foorde.
	Sept.	12.	Elizabeth Scot.
1607.	May	15.	Ann the wyfe of Robert Breat.
1608.	June	2.	Henrie Froste.
	Nov.	16.	William Baron.
	Feb.	19.	Robert Newegate.
	March	10.	Richard Cooper.
1609.	March	27.	Ann Stegol.

	Feb.	19.	Bridget Crick.
1610.	March	31.	John Emmins.
	May	7.	Valentine Short.
	May	8.	Edey Walker.
	May	11.	George Bucchenham.
	May	26.	Rose Langley.
	May	29.	John Gypse.
	Oct.	9.	Alise Goose.
	Nov.	26.	Agnes Goose.
	Dec.	16.	Alise Mahewe.
	Jan.	7.	William Bailie.
1611.	June	27.	William Amner.
	Julie	12.	Alise Haward.
	Nov.	13.	Joane Fynn.
	Nov.	30.	Harrie Blagge.
	Jan.	24.	Mary Haward.
1612.	June	3.	Robert Moore.
	Julie	1.	Martha Cutmare.
	Julie	4.	Audry Lilly.
	Julie	13.	Margaret Mahewe.
1613.	March	28.	Nicholas Friet.
	Aug.	3.	Margaret Francis.
	Dec.	10.	Eedie Gipse.
	Jan.	16.	Margaret Page.
	March	21.	Rebert Larner.
1614.	March	28.	Elizabeth Fuller.
	April	12.	Margaret Short.
	April	19.	Theodore Haward.
	Maie	21.	Barbara Fishon.
	Oct.	22.	Emme Cock.
	Oct.	25.	Judith Butler.
	Nov.	20.	[or 30]. Henry Wiard.
1615.	May	8.	Agnes Fishen.
	Sept.	3.	Edward Bulbrooke.
	Feb.	2.	Francys Vervy.

	Feb.	22.	Thomas Rogers, clerk.
	March	3.	Bridget Rogers.
	March	17.	Grace Deereson.
1616.	March	28.	Christian Wiard.
	April	17.	Hannah Scott.
	May	7.	John Hayward.
	Jan.	3.	Edward Payne.
	Feb.	28.	Anne Cutteris.
1617.	Jan.	10.	Anne Manning.
1618.	June	25.	Katherine Bret.
	Oct.	13.	Mary Lucas.
	Nov.	1.	Thomas Sharp.
	Dec.	8.	Robert Bret.
	March	10.	Elizabeth Bennet.
1619.	Feb.	29.	George Stegall.
	March	24.	Mary Ingold.
1620.	April	15.	Rose Church.
	June	3.	Alice Welham.
	Aug.	11.	William Godfry.
	Oct.	9.	Mary Larner.
	Oct.	10.	Joane Newgate.
	March	7.	Robert Carlile.
1621.	May	4.	Anne Baylie.
	Oct.	24.	John Goose.
	Nov.	10.	John Godfry, and Thomas Page.
	Nov.	18.	Anne Fiston.
	Feb.	1.	Bridget Covell.
	March	24.	Martha Handler.
1622.	March	29.	Mary Handler.
	July	22.	Frances Syllet.
	July	30.	Abigail Church.
	Aug.	1.	Robert Mayhew.
	Nov.	23.	Alice Hayward.
	Jan.	1.	William Fynne.
	Jan.	2.	Robert Newgate.

	Jan.	24.	Anne Walker.
	Feb.	15.	Margery Stanton.
	Feb.	23.	Elizabeth Cooper.
	March	22.	John Edhouse.
1623.	May	6.	Anne Sutton.
	June	26.	Richard Deareson.
	Dec.	11.	John Mason.
	Jan.	31.	Anne Goldsmith.
1624.	April	25.	Grace the daughter of William Bedell.
	June	22.	Katherine the wife of John Hayward.
	July	6.	William Page.
	Aug.	14.	Martha Blagge.
	Aug.	19.	Humphry Blagge.
	Dec.	31.	Agnes Bright.
1625.	March	25.	Martha the wife of John Gedge.
	May	2.	John Allen.
	June	10.	Thomas Covill.
	July	12.	Marie Lucas.
	Aug.	20.	Robert Spark.
	Aug.	13.	Elizabeth Stoneham.
	Sept.	4.	Elizabeth Wiard.
	Sept.	28.	Anne Cooper.
	Oct.	1.	William Cornish.
	Oct.	10.	Alice Goldsmith.
	March	7.	William Covell.
1626.	April	11.	William Gedge.
	April	20.	Margery Friet.
	May	10.	Mary Lucas.
	June	19.	Marie Godfry.
	July	9.	Stephen Godfry.
	Aug.	25.	Margaret Edhouse.
	Oct.	26.	Thomasin Bret.
	Nov.	14.	Anne Stavers.
	Dec.	23.	John Dizing.
	Jan.	17.	John Church.

	Feb.	3.	Margaret Richardson.
	March	9.	Marie Spinck.
	March	11.	John Chester.
	March	21.	Anne Godfry.
1627.	April	6.	William Toller.
	April	16.	Margaret Godfry.
	April	20.	Edward Paine.
	May	18.	Susan Tomson.
	June	3.	John Ingold.
	Nov.	4.	Alice Newgate.
	Feb.	9.	Marie Sillet.
	March	19.	Barbara Fiston.
1628.	April	16.	Joane Toller.
	April	24.	Anne Toller.
	July	5.	William Langham.
	July	14.	Lydia Lucas.
	Sept.	13.	Martha Fiston.
	Nov.	9.	Thomas Brett.
	Nov.	15.	Mary Ruggles.
1629.	June	9.	William Fysson.
	Feb.	9.	Marget Bucxnam.
1630.	June	2.	Robert Spinke.
	Aug.	26.	Joane Payne of [sic] Edward Payne.
	Oct.	9.	Edmund Blague.
	Nov.	30.	Lucie Chapman.
	Dec.	26.	An Maihewe.
	Feb.	13.	Thomas Wellham.
1631.	April	12.	Judith the wife of Henry Hayward.
	May	2.	Richard Gippes houshoulder.
	July	5.	Judith Godferie.
	June	21.	George Blague.
	Aug.	30.	Susan the wife of Josias Longe.
	Oct.	8.	Adrie the wife of Edward Sillet.
	Dec.	18.	Thomas Parker.
	Feb.	23.	Rose Sowter widowe.

	March	7.	Marie Sillet.
	March	9.	Alce Parker.
1632.	March	29.	Elizabeth Cooper.
	April	17.	Robert Godfrie.
	July	10.	Sara Godfrie.
	July	13.	Susan Wright.
	July	30.	Ann Towler.
	Aug.	10.	Holofernes Towler.
	Aug.	26.	Gilbert Towler.
	Nov.	8.	Edward Sillet junior.
	Nov.	20.	Alice Sparke.
	Jan.	5.	Edward Sillet senior.
	Jan.	8.	Marie Mudd.
	March	24.	Samuel the son of William Ruggles.
1633.	March	29.	Antony Hardy.
	April	4.	Henrie Wyard.
	May	25.	William Sawyer.
	Aug.	26.	John Warde.
	Dec.	12.	Thomas Clarke.
	Dec.	26.	Richard Sillet senior.
1634.	May	11.	Nicholas Buckenham, clark.
	Aug.	22.	Barbara Roulinsonne.
	Nov.	12.	Frances Bailie.
	Jan.	10.	Elisabeth Cotton.
	Jan.	15.	Alice Goody.
	March	24.	Thomas Stanton.
1635.	April	5.	Marie Spinke.
	June	24.	Thomas Chinnery.
	June	30.	John Titmus.
	July	1.	Margaret Spinke.
	July	11.	Alice Maihew.
	Oct.	19.	Elizabeth Steward.
1636.	April	25.	Sarah Bull.
	May	11.	Alice Churche.
	June	11.	Robert Mayhew.

	June	24.	Alice Hayward.
	July	16.	Robert Wellam.
	Aug.	1.	Phillip Newgate.
	Aug.	31.	Susan Mayhew.
	Sept.	2.	Sara Sparke.
	Nov.	30.	Richard Lyndall.
	Dec.	15.	Alice Godfry, widdowe.
	Feb.	21.	Rebecca Godfrie.
	Feb.	25.	William Heywarde.
1637.	Aug.	5.	Martha Brewster.
	Sept.	13.	Thomas Lucas.
	Sept.	29.	Marie Paine.
	Oct.	30.	Frances Nutman.
	Nov.	27.	Dorothy Sillet.
	Dec.	10.	Mary Talbot.
	Dec.	13.	Dorothy Sillet the elder.
	Jan.	12.	Anna Hall.
1638.	April	15.	Mary the daughter of Edward Godfry.
	April	16.	Robert Steward the elder.
	April	30.	Richard son of Robert & Margaret Goodrick.
	May	3.	Lettice Adames.
	July	14.	Jone Sharpe.
	July	23.	George Kerington.
	Sept.	5.	Anne Brewster.
	Oct.	21.	John Cooper.
	Oct.	30.	Gyles Hayward.
	March	5.	Henry Goldsmith.
1639.	June	22.	Elizabeth Cutteris.
	Sept.	28.	Clement Lucas.
	Oct.	4.	Martha Ruggles.
	Oct.	26.	Frances Baily.
	Jan.	13.	William Lucas.
	Jan.	21.	Margaret Godfrie.
1640.	May	14.	Isaac Trumble.
	May	24.	Frances Ewen.

	June	19.	Thomas Godfrie.
	Aug.	30.	Marable Parmen.
	Nov.	22.	Edward Finsham.
	Dec.	17.	Richard Couper.
	Jan.	12.	Francis Adams.
	Jan.	15.	Elizabeth English.
	Jan.	20.	William Clarke.
	Feb.	6.	Thomas Talbutt.
1641.	Sept.	30.	Elizabeth Ruggles.
	Oct.	11.	William Baylye.
	March	9.	William Manning.
1642.	May	14.	Susan Howton.
	June	4.	Josias Longe.
	June	8.	Sarah Wiffen.
	July	10.	Ambrose Goldsmith.
	July	25.	Richard Sillet.
	Sept.	15.	Edward Godfrie.
	Jan.	13.	John Hayward.
	March	5.	Grace Addams.
1643.	April	15.	Thomasin Sillet.
	April	22.	Martha Spinke.
	June	6.	Elizabeth Ruggles.
	Nov.	7.	Elizabeth Godfry.
	Nov.	21.	Robert Lilly.
1644.	July	16.	Henery Hayward.
	Sept.	24.	Robert Addams.
	Sept.	24.	Anne Towler.
1645.	June	7.	Barbara Turner.
	Jan.	30.	Em : Tailor.
1646.	May	16.	Robert Steward.
	Aug.	9.	Elizabeth Stanton.
	Nov.	13.	Frances Ewen.
1647.	June	8.	George Rowlison.
	Oct.	8.	Elizabeth Adames.
1653.	May	10.	Eleazar Goodrick.

	July	13.	John Cook.
	Dec.	21.	Margrit the wife of Robert Cooke.
	Feb.	25.	Jone Lendal, widowe.
	March	24.	The wife of John Grifing.
1657.	Aug.	28.	Andrew Wright.
	Sept.	4.	Thomas Wade.
1658.	Maye	31.	Robert Spinke.
	Dec.	21.	John Fisson.
1659.	July	15.	Thomas Godfrie.
1660.	May	17.	Edward Hayward.
	June	16.	Vincent Handler.
	July	12.	Widdow Ruggles.
	Aug.	28.	Widdow Wyard.
	Aug.	30.	Richard Cooke.
	Sept.	19.	Margaret Ford.
	Sept.	24.	Robert Goodrick, rector, sat.. : [?]
	Nov.	25.	Mary Cadman.
	Dec.	20.	Mary Fairy.
	Jan.	15.	Mary Womocke.
	Jan.	31.	The wife of John Steward.
	Feb.	3.	The widdow Clerke.
	March	20.	The wife of William Wiffin.
1661.	May	1.	Mr. Thomas Sache.
	May	22.	The widdow Margarett Toller.
	May	27.	Francis Taylor.
	June	17.	William Skinner.
	June	26.	William Hayward.
	Oct.	24.	Major Tho : Stanton.
	Nov.	6.	Ann the wife of Mr. Jaspar Blemel.
	Nov.	24.	Mr. William Covell.
	Dec.	8.	Margaret wife of James Wyard the yonger.
	Jan.	12.	Jane the wife of Mr. Valentine Gipps.
	Jan.	17.	George the son of Robert Kerrington.
	Jan.	27.	William Wiffin.
	Feb.	12.	Anne the daughter of William Gutteridge.

	Feb.	18.	Elizabeth daughter of Mr. Richard Gipps.
1662.	March	31.	Isaac son of John Smyth.
	May	19.	Joshua Wade.
	Aug.	29.	Timothy Oldman.
	Jan.	14.	Widow Ingall.
1663.	March	25.	Mary the wife of Robert Steward.
	March	29.	Thomas son of William Godfry.
	March	31.	Widow Godfry.
	April	8.	Elizabeth wife of Robert Booty.
	July	16.	Charles son of Gibson Lucas, Dr. in Divinity.
	Sept.	24.	James son of James Bland.
	Nov.	11.	Widow Houghton.
	Feb.	8.	Mr. Richard Gipps.
1664.	July	5.	Thomas Willson.
	July	11.	Thomas Manning.
	Oct.	15.	Henry the son of Henry & Joan: Godfrey.
1665.	April	29.	The widdow Freeth.
	June	4.	Clement the sonn of Gipson & Elisebeth Lukes.
	June	10.	Gipson the sonn of Gipson & Elisebeth Lukes.
	June	28.	Rebecka the dauter of John Stewerd.
	Aug.	26.	Ann the wife of Larrence Woomacke.
	Sept.	12.	The widdow Sage.
	Nov.	11.	Mrs. Mary Woomacke.
1666.	May	10.	Mary the dauter of Gipson Lukes.
	Aug.	11.	John Haywerd.
	Aug.	26.	The wife of Thomas Sillot.
	Dec.	3.	Elisebeth the dauter of William Ewen.
	Dec.	8.	Widdow Fiston.
	Jan.	23.	Ann the dauter of Robert Kerrington.
1667.	April	4.	Josias the sonn of Josias Right.
	April	24.	Thomas Garnner.
	May	22.	Widdow Bannack.
	June	6.	Robert Cook. Q.
	Dec.	18.	Robert the sonn of Thomas Sergant.
	Jan.	6.	The wife of Thomas Sergant.

	Jan.	18.	William the sonn of William Cater.
	March	17.	John Steward.
1668.	June	25.	The wife of Gipson Lukes.
	June	29.	The wife of John Cooper.
	July	6.	The wife of William Manning.
	July	23.	The wife of Hinry Godfry.
	Sept.	9.	Ritchard the sonn of William Covell.
	Nov.	28.	The widdow Godfry.
	Jan.	28.	Thomas Chinry.
1671.	April	16.	Edmund Hayward.
	May	8.	Widdow Elmes.
	May	21.	Widdow Chinery.
	May	29.	Anne the wife of Richard Sillett.
	Nov.	16.	Mary the wife of Thomas Wellham.
	Dec.	14.	Widdow Wiffin.
	March	13.	John Mantua.
1673.	March	31.	Elisabeth the daughter of William & Hannah Wiard.
	April	6.	Robert Goldsmith.
	May	30.	Henry Betts.
	June	1.	Rebecca the wife of Laurence Howard.
	Aug.	6.	Widdow Wiard.
	Aug.	22.	William the son of William & Mary Covell. Q.
	Nov.	18.	Widdow Steward.
	Dec.	31.	Henry Dearson.
1674.	May	1.	Judith the daughter of Mrs. Margarett Goodrick.
	May	12.	Anne Copping.
	Oct.	12.	Robert Booty.
	Jan.	25.	Anne the daughter of William & Elisabeth Ewen.
	March	8.	Margarett the wife of Mr. William Lucas.
1675.	April	7.	Elisabeth the daughter of John & Elisabeth Houghton of Westly.
	April	8.	Richard Rushworth.
	April	12.	Elisabeth the wife of John Noble.
	May	11.	Old Mrs. Gipps.
	July	17.	Abigail the daughter of Thomas & Mary Atkin.

	Sept.	21.	Mr. William Godfrey.
	Oct.	21.	Mr. Robert Kerrington, the son of Mr. George Kerrington.
	Nov.	23.	Old John Ewon.
	Dec.	4.	Elisabeth the wife of the same John Ewen.
	Jan.	20.	Joan the wife of Robert Steward.
	March	10.	William the son of Lawrence & Elizabeth Howard.
	March	22.	Thomas the son of William & Christian Cater.
1676.	June	9.	Robert Steward the younger.
	July	22.	William Guttridge.
	Oct.	30.	Luke Mahew the eldest, and William Manning.
	Dec.	13.	Timothy the son of Timothy Adamson.
	Jan.	6.	Elizabeth the daughter of William & Anne Lucas.
	Jan.	30.	Susannah the younger of the twin-daughters of John & Joan Hockly.
	.	.	Mary the eldest daughter of John & Joan Hockly.
1677.	May	18.	Lawrence the son of Lawrence & Elizabeth Howard.
	July	15.	Roger Houghton, father to Mr. John Houghton of Westly.
	July	27.	James the son of William & Elizabeth Ewen.
	Aug.	10.	Sherman the son of Mary Mantua.
	Aug.	31.	Elizabeth the wife of Robert Sparrow of Westly.
	Sept.	4.	Mary Mantua, aforesaid widdow.
	Sept.	17.	John Walker, late schoollmaster at Bury.
	Oct.	4.	John Crow, a servant of Mr. William Covell's.
	Nov.	24.	Christian the daughter of William & Anne Lucas.
	Jan.	8.	John, Elizabeth } children of John & Margarett Arnold.
	Feb.	1.	Mary the wife of John Robinson.
	Feb.	17.	Sarah the wife of James Ewen.
	March	11.	Old widdow Nelson, the mother of George Nelson.
1678.	April	13.	Old widdow Toller.
	May	6.	Joshua Sillett.
	June	12.	Grace the daughter of George & Mary Nelson.
	June	19.	Henry Godfrey.
	Oct.	16.	Natthaniell the son of Natthaniell & Anne Goodrick.
	Jan.	26.	Anne daughter of Nathaniell Goodrick.

	March	13.	Thomas Welham.
1679.	April	12.	John son of Francis & Frances Frost.
	May	26.	Abigail daughter of Lawrence & Anne Perkins.
	May	29.	Anthony Coast, late servant to Sir Richard Gipps.
	June	13.	Robert son of Robert & Anne Goldsmith.
	Sept.	2.	John Smith senior.
	Nov.	23.	Francis sonne of Francis & Jone Hockley.
	Jan.	20.	Thomas son of Thomas & Barbara Ford.
	Feb.	18.	James Ewen.
1680.	June	3.	Mr. Sylliard Gipps.
	Aug.	9.	Martha Hampeton.
	Sept.	30.	Robert Steward.
	Oct.	1.	William Prick.
	Oct.	7.	Robert Goldsmith, and Mary Ament.
	Dec.	30.	Christian Manning.
	Jan.	11.	Luke Mayhew the elder.
	Jan.	28.	Laurence Howard.
	Feb.	2.	William Frost.
1681.	May	4.	Margaret Wiffin.
	May	19.	Margarett Smith.
	May	30.	Daniel Clarke.
	May	31.	William Adams.
	June	7.	Mary Prick.
	July	24.	William Cater.
	Aug.	28.	John Cooper.
	Sept.	11.	Elizabeth Ling.
	Sept.	29.	Sir Richard Gipps.
	Oct.	4.	Mary Ford.
	Sept.	19.	The widdow Hayward.
	Nov.	24.	Thomas Sergeant.
	Dec.	10.	John Adamson of the Parish of St. Marie's in Bury.
	Jan.	20.	Henry Cozens.
	March	12.	Mr. Georg Gipps.
	March	18.	James Prick. [Prigg in the duplicate.]
1682.	March	29.	Dorothy Hayward.

	April	19.	William Smith.
	May	2.	The widdow Steward.
	July	29.	John Garner.
1683.	April	2.	Thomas son of Thomas Ford.
	April	8.	Robert Pack.
	April	23.	Elizabeth daughter of Timothy Adamson.
	May	8.	Susan Linge.
	Aug.	20.	Widow Cater.
	Aug.	19.	Thomas son of William Lucas.
	Sept.	10.	Josias Wright.
	Feb.	21.	Abraham Copping.
	Feb.	26.	Margaret Atkin.
	March	14.	Henry Potter.
1684.	May	5.	Widow Booty.
	May	31.	Mary Folkes.
	July	1.	Thomas Chinery.
	Nov.	8.	Samuel Parkin.
	Nov.	23.	Mary Parkin widow.
	Jan.	20.	Mary and Elizabeth, daughters of William & Anne Lucas.
	Feb.	18.	John Aimund.
	Jan.	21.	Lewis Mortlock.
	March	11.	William Goldsmith.
1685.	May	5.	Thomas Wiffen.
	Aug.	25.	Henery Sparke.
	Sept.	19.	Mary Smith.
	Oct.	25.	Ann Jervis.
1686.	Aug.	11.	Wife of Mr. Edward Parker.
	Dec.	11.	John Prick.
	Feb.	27.	John Matthews.
	March	1.	Frances Frost.
1687.	July	10.	Richard Sillet juniour.
	July	19.	Mary daughter of John Petchy.
	July	21.	Elizabeth wife of George Chadney.
	July	24.	Richard Sillet the elder.
1688.	April	2.	Widow Wiffen.

	June	17.	John Reeve.
	July	10.	Charles Lucas.
	July	30.	William Fissen.
	Aug.	25.	Robert Noble.
1689.	March	27.	Henery Houghton of Westly.
	June	6.	Henery Wyard.
	Nov.	12.	Widow Redgin.
	Nov.	26.	Edmund Rose.
	Feb.	5.	William Covell.
	March	12.	Mrs. Walker.
	March	21.	—— daughter of William Alderton.
1690.	Aug.	21.	Mary Herrington.
	Jan.	10.	Elizabeth Web.
	March	16.	John Howton of Westly.
1691.	April	11.	John Clerke.
	May	15.	Richard Covell.
	Aug.	29.	Gibson Lucas.
	Sept.	2.	Alice Covell.
	Jan.	30.	Sarah Edgely.
	Feb.	11.	Anthony Smith.
	Feb.	19.	Wife of Thomas Gardiner senior.
	March	13.	Mr. Edward Parker.
1692.	May	7.	Richard Edgely.
	May	22.	Mr. Brown of Norwich.
	May	22.	Widow Harvey.
	May	27.	Mary Cosens.
	July	9.	William Cosens.
	Sept.	2.	Mr. Nelson.
	Nov.	2.	Mrs. Covell.
1693.	May	18.	Elizabeth Farrar.
	June	17.	Hannah Wiseman.
	Sept.	3.	Goodman Crowch.
	Nov.	30.	Goodman Cadman.
	Dec.	14.	Mr. Thomas son of Mr. William Covell.
	March	11.	Widow Wellome.

1694.	May	21.	Widow Goldsmith.
	May	29.	Mr. John Covel, and Edmund Rose.
	May	31.	William Wyard.
	June	2.	Thomas Skinner.
	June	17.	Wife of William Alderton.
	July	7.	William Alderton.
	July	25.	Widow Smith.
	Aug.	4.	Alice Alderton.
	Feb.	5.	John Ling.
	Feb.	15.	Robert Talbot.
1695.	April	21.	Thomas Wix.
	Aug.	1.	Mary wife of Philip Parker, labourer.
	Aug.	10.	John Covel Kittle son of John Kittle, farmer.
	Aug.	16.	William Ewen, labourer.
	Sept.	7.	Susan daughter of John Clerke, labourer.
	Sept.	22.	Thomas son of Henery Cornwall, labourer.
	Nov.	7.	Jane daughter of Thomas Smith, clerke, and Eleanor.
	Dec.	29.	Susan Covel, widow.
	Feb.	4.	Mary Godfry, farmer's wife.
1696.	April	5.	Thomas son of John Lait, labourer.
	June	20.	Joseph son of Joseph Bunting, labourer.
	Oct.	7.	Thomas son of John Wiseman, woolcomber.
	Oct.	15.	Hannah Wyard, farmer's widow.
1697.	July	18.	William son of William Newport, labourer.
	Sept.	21.	Widow Prior, almswoman.
	Oct.	18.	Widow Frost, almswoman.
	Nov.	5.	Widow Prick, almswoman.
	Feb.	19.	Philip Higham of Kentford, labourer.
	March	6.	John Ernsby, labourer, near Thetford.
1698.	March	29.	Widow Willingham, wife of labourer.
	May	7.	Ann wife of Thomas Spensely of Bury, upholster.
	May	7.	Tabitha wife of James Wright, labourer.
	May	26.	Gipson Lucas, Dr Divinity, Professour of Divinity.
	Jan.	25.	A son of Thory & Mary Wix, woolcomber.
1699.	May	20.	Thomas son of John Wiseman, woolcomber.

	July	27.	Richard son of Richard Elsden, labourer.
	Aug.	27.	John son of John Bensted, labourer.
	Oct.	21.	Robert son of Robert Potter, labourer.
	Feb.	27.	Frances daughter of Henry Harvey, labourer.
	March	14.	Stephen son of Francis Foreman, labourer.
1700.	May	28.	Joseph son of Joseph Bunting, labourer.
	July	4.	Mrs. Ann Kerrington, gentlewoman.
	Nov.	29.	John Robinson.
1701.	April	5.	John son of William Cooper, labourer.
	May	19.	James Right, labourer.
	July	15.	Thomas Web, tailour.
	Sept.	25.	Ann Potter.
	Oct.	12.	Mary daughter of Edward Parker, labourer.
	Oct.	26.	Mrs. Howton, of Westly.
	Oct.	27.	Elizabeth daughter of Edward Parker, labourer.
	Nov.	2.	Rachel wife of John Lait, labourer.
	Nov.	18.	Sarah daughter of Edward Parker, labourer.
	Nov.	21.	John Lait, labourer.
	Feb.	26.	Thory [Theodore] Wix, clothier.
	March	19.	Jonathan son of John Clerke, labourer.
1702.	May	13.	Ann daughter of Henry & Elizabeth Cornwall, labourer.
	May	18.	Widow Pack of Ixworth.
	Sept.	10.	Thomas Chinery.
	Sept.	15.	Widow Parker.
	Oct.	11.	Isabella daughter of Richard Elsden, labourer.
	Oct.	16.	Widow Jarvis.
	Oct.	19.	John Goodrick.
	Jan.	5.	Ralf son of Ralf Adams, labourer.
1703.	May	16.	John Ewen.
	Aug.	30.	Robert son of John Petchy.
	Oct.	25.	Sarah wife of Edward Parker, labourer.
	Nov.	18.	Mary Rolfe.
	Dec.	29.	John Cooper, labourer.
	Jan.	31.	Frank son of James Frost, labourer.
	Feb.	14.	Elizabeth Paman.

March 12. George Gerald, labourer.
1704. May 1. Caleb Sillet.
Aug. 4. Widow Cosens.
Sept. 29. Edward Forster, clerke.
Oct. 30. John son of William Harrington, woolcomber, & Mary his wife.
Nov. 5. Margaret Pettiwood, widow.
Jan. 13. Edward Godfry, husbandman.
Jan. 18. Esther Gardiner.
Jan. 21. Thomas Sargant, labourer.
Jan. 27. John and Elizabeth, twins of Robert Potter, labourer.
1705. April 4. Ann daughter of Eshther Forster.
May 6. Sarah Sondcroft.
June 18. Goodman Mountague.
July 13. Ann Kittle.
Aug. 16. Luke Lilly.
Sept. 13. Widow Adams.
Oct. 6. Ann daughter of James Frost.
Oct. 23. Elizabeth wife of Thomas Goldsmith jun.
Feb. 26. Humphry son of Henry Cornwall.
1706. May 9. Eleanor wife of Thomas Smith.
May 16. Elizabeth daughter of John & Carr Brooke.
June 15. John son of Ralfe & Sarah Adams.
Sept. 6. Thomas Parker, and Martha wife of John Noble.
Jan. 6. Francis son of Francis & Else Shaw.
Jan. 15. John Lanseter, and Thomas son of Joseph Bunting.
Feb. 21. Edward Potter.
March 5. Thomas Chinery.
March 14. Richard Gardiner.
1707. April 6. Abraham Pain.
April 12. Mr William Covel.
April 19. Daniel son of Francis & Sarah Foreman.
April 29. John son of John & Mary Rolfe.
May 3. John son of James Frost.
May 4. Widow Ewen.

May 15. Ann Sparrow.
May 20. Mrs. Lilly.
Sept. 2. Widow Bass.
Sept. 8. Thomas Bass.
Sept. 10. Elizabeth Giblin.
Oct. 13. Margat Rolfe.
Dec. 1. Alice Adams.
Jan. 1. Elizabeth Spensely.
Jan. 18. Elisebeth wife of Charles Web elder.
Feb. 24. Judeth daughter of Henry How.
March 4. Judeth wife of Mr. Thomas Covel.
Feb. 11. Elisebeth wife of Henry Cornwell.
1708. April 10. Ann Fisson.
June 9. Simon Goldsmith.
July 1. Thomas Elms.
Sept. 23. Rebecca Spark.
Oct. 22. Elizabeth Rolfe.
Nov. 12. John How.
Nov. 13. Thomas Goldsmith.
Dec. 3. Isaac Bartel.
Dec. 28. Eleanor Manning.
Jan. 4. Anthony son of Henry Smith.
Feb. 9. Rebecca Edgely.
Feb. 16. Sarah How.
1709. April 12. Hannah daughter of Edward Parker.
May 1. Martha How.
May 4. Ann daughter of Mr. John Kittle.
May 13. Thomas Hempsted.
June 15. Georg Cadny.
Dec. 14. Samuel Bray, labourer.
Jan. 26. Alice Adam.
Feb. 13. Susanna Hempsted.
March 13. Robert Ling.
1710. April 3. Charles Web senior.
April 9. Hester Wright, widow.

	Sept.	27.	William Lucas.
	Jan.	27.	John Rolfe.
	Feb.	7.	Richard Gardiner.
	March	19.	William Adams.
1711.	May	3.	Francis Frost, labourer.
	May	30.	Ann Estling.
	July	29.	Mr. William Lilly.
	July	31.	Mary daughter of John Brook.
	Aug.	15.	William Brinkly.
	Sept.	23.	Mary wife of William Hempsted.
	Jan.	22.	Thomas Goldsmith.
	March	12.	Elisabeth Skinner.
1712.	May	19.	Margaret daughter of Michael King.
	June	2.	Joseph Bunting.
	Nov.	11.	Mary wife of James Mortlock.
	Nov.	16.	Samuel son of Robert & Ann Potter.
1713.	April	16.	James son of James & Ann Spalden.
	April	19.	James Hempsted.
	May	2.	William Rolfe. [Entered among the Baptisms.]
	June	3.	Edward son of Edward & Rachel Parker.
	Aug.	20.	Susan Brook.
	Oct.	9.	Mrs. Judeth Sharp, mother of Thomas Smith.
	Jan.	2.	Leah Manning.
1714.	April	6.	Widow Godfry of Risby.
	April	19.	John Clerk, labourer.
	May	29.	James Foreman.
	June	2.	Sarah Bray, and ——— Adams.
	June	3.	William Bunting.
	June	8.	Mrs. Godfry.
	June	18.	Elisabeth Goldsmith.
	Aug.	31.	Thomas Gardiner.
	Oct.	3.	Thomas Chinery, blacksmith.
	Feb.	18.	James Mortlock.
1715.	May	29.	John son of John & Ann Battely.
	June	13.	Ann wife of Mr. William Lucas.

July — Susan daughter of Miles [Michael] King.
July 21. Widow Bray.
Aug. 23. Mr. Thomas Covel.
Aug. 24. Alice daughter of Francis Shaw.
Nov. 17. Lady Gipps.
Dec. 20. Charles Brook, a child.
Fob. 6. John Smith.
1716. March 30. Widow Clerk.
April 11. Mr. Timothy Adamson, clerk.
July 2. Mary Newport.
Sept. 18. Mrs. Mary Adamson.
Oct. 20. Elisabeth daughter of Henry Cosens.
Oct. 24. Peter Firman.
Nov. 29. Mr. William Lucas, and Leah Jarvis.
Dec. 5. Mary Bunting.
March 12. Old John Rolf of Kentford.
1717. June 17. Rose Gerald.
Aug. 14. Hester Forster, widow.
Aug. 22. William Hempsted.
Sept. 8. Edmund Lemmon, a child.
Dec. 11. John Ewen.
Dec. 28. Mr. Howton of Westly.
Feb. 1. John son of Casaubon Howton.
1718. April 4. Widow Elisabeth Prick.
April 11. Paul son of Ralf Adams.
Aug. 3. Widow Talbot.
July 23. Elisabeth Howton.
Dec. 4. Mr. Thomas Spensely, clerk.
Jan. 10. Henry How.
Feb. 10. Thomas son of Henry Cosens.
1719. May 20. Thomas Ling.
May 31. Mary Pattle.
June 16. Susan wife of John Ong.
Aug. 16. Mary Mortlock.
Sept. 17. Hannah Prick, widow.

	Sept.	28.	William son of Ralf & Sarah Adams.
	Feb.	20.	Widow Smith.
1720.	April	14.	Mary daughter of Thomas & Mary Murton.
	May	9.	Elisabeth wife of Mr. John Kittle.
	June	18.	Widow Prick.
	Nov.	23.	Mrs. Margaret Blagge.
	Nov.	7.	George Freind.
	Jan.	6.	William Cooper.
	March	3.	John Sparrow.
1721.	April	3.	Thomas Rowly.
	May	25.	Hannah Ewen.
	July	12.	Mary wife of John Ong.
	Sept.	24.	Widow Cooper.
	Oct.	15.	Mary Cosens.
	Jan.	23.	Mary daughter of John & Elisabeth Spicer.
	March	9.	Mr. William Harrington.
1722.	June	3.	Susan Ship.
	July	22.	George Ship.
	Aug.	3.	Hannah wife of John Smith.
	Sept.	13.	Frances daughter of Thomas & Mary Murton.
	Dec.	22.	Widow Nelson.
1723.	Aug.	4.	Hugh son of Hugh & Mary Spencer.
	Aug.	28.	Margat Ewen.
	Sept.	12.	Edmund Hempson.
	Nov.	17.	Thomas Lait, an infant.
1724.	July	18.	Ann Jaggard.
	—	—	Wife of James Spark.
	Feb.	21.	Widow Chinery.
1725.	April	14.	The Reverend Mr. Thomas Smith, Rector of Horringer & Nowton.
	July	8.	James Mortlock.
	Aug.	3.	Thomas Crack.
	Sept.	1.	William Godfrey of Bury gent.
	March	18.	Thomas Jaggard.
1726.	July	5.	Mary Bowes.

	Oct.	15.	Henry Cosins jun.
	Nov.	30.	Robert Jarvis.
	Dec.	21.	Ann Beales.
	March	4.	Thomas How.
1727.	May	16.	Henry Cosins sen.
	June	25.	Ann daughter of Richard & Mary How.
	June	29.	Catharine Crack, widow.
	July	27.	Robert Fitch.
	Aug.	20.	Mary Bunting, widow.
	Aug.	21.	Mary wife of John Oatly.
	Aug.	26.	Margaret Arnold, widow.
	Sept.	17.	John Peachey.
	Sept.	30.	Elizabeth Gardiner of Fornham All Saints, widow.
	Oct.	4.	Ann Peachey, widow.
	Nov.	18.	Sarah Goldsmith.
	Nov.	25.	Thomas Jarvis.
	Dec.	5.	James Frost sen:.
	Dec.	25.	Mary wife of Isaac Lumly of Bury.
	Dec.	31.	Martha wife of William Cooper.
	Jan.	27.	Sarah Hempsted, widow.
	Feb.	14.	John & Thomas, twin children of John & Mary Symonds.
	Feb.	19.	James Spark.
	Feb.	25.	Mary Mayor.
	Feb.	28.	Ann Barton, widow.
	March	1.	Gabriel Hallux.
	March	6.	Rebecca Wymock.
1728.	April	10.	Robert Parker.
	April	28.	Susan Oatly.
	Aug.	1.	William Ewen.
	Sept.	3.	Daniel Foreman.
	Sept.	7.	William Emmet.
	Sept.	8.	Mr. Thomas Kedington.
	Oct.	1.	John Crack, infant. Received affidavit Oct. 11; not received within the time limited by the statute, of which I gave notice to Mr. Nelson, churchwarden.

	Oct.	2.	Ann wife of Abraham Kedington of Whepstead.
	Oct.	4.	John Noble.
	Oct.	5.	Abraham son of Abraham & Ann Kedington of Whepstead.
	Dec.	6.	John Sergeant.
	Jan.	20.	John Bray.
	Jan.	26.	Thomas Ling.
	Jan.	28.	Elizabeth Ling, widow.
	Feb.	14.	William Newport of Whepsted.
1729.	April	30.	Mary daughter of John & Mary Symonds.
	May	1.	Francis Frost.
	July	3.	Lydia wife of William Huggins of Mildenhall.
	July	12.	Ralph Adams.
	July	14.	Luke Jenkin.
	Aug.	26.	Hugh Spencer.
	Oct.	10.	Mary wife of Richard How.
	Nov.	13.	Herrington Ellis of Lavenham, infant.
	Jan.	1.	Thomas Goodchild of Great Saxham, infant.
	March	5.	Edward Parker.
1730.	April	5.	Sarah Lait, infant.
	April	21.	Elizabeth How, infant, and Hannah Kendal, infant.
	April	29.	Elizabeth Wells of Barningham, widow.
	May	10.	Joseph Elmer.
	Aug.	23.	George Oliver, infant.
	Aug.	27.	Francis How.
	Oct.	27.	Ann Wicks of Hartest.
	March	12.	John How, infant.
	March	16.	Alice Bensted, widow.
1731.	May	15.	Elizabeth Kettle of Thetford.
	May	29.	Richard Spencely of Dis.
	June	28.	Timothy Pond, infant.
	Aug.	26.	George How, infant.
	Sept.	2.	Thomas son of Thomas & Mary Frost.
	Oct.	28.	Stephen Cook.
	Dec.	10.	Thomas Pleasance, infant.
	Dec.	14.	Michael Howton, infant.

	Dec.	23.	Mrs. Mary Godfry of Bury, widow.
1732.	June	10.	John Gardiner.
	Aug.	3.	Elizabeth Daniel, infant.
	Oct.	5.	Mary Davers, infant.
1733.	May	18.	Robert Brook, infant.
	May	24.	John Byatt.
	May	31.	Potter Frost, infant.
	Sept.	20.	William Lait.
	Jan.	17.	George Nelson.
	Feb.	15.	Susan Daniel, infant.
1734.	June	19.	Robert Smith of Bury.
	June	28.	Frances Mortlack.
1735.	May	31.	Mary How, infant.
	July	11.	John Miller of Read.
	July	21.	Hannah How, infant.
	July	29.	Frances Frost, infant.
	July	30.	Casborne Houghton of Bardwell.
	Aug.	7.	Mary Davers, infant.
	Oct.	3.	Richard How of Whepsted.
	Oct.	12.	Mrs. Christian Kedington, widow.
	Oct.	13.	Robert Potter.
1736.	May	2.	Zacharias How of Hardwick, infant.
	Aug.	28.	John Sergeant.
	Sept.	23.	Samuel Pond, infant.
	Feb.	12.	Hannah wife of Stephen Sparrow.
	March	4.	Elizabeth, relict of the Rev. Mr. Smith, formerly Rector of this Parish.
1737.	April	2.	Rachel Parker, widow.
	May	13.	Sarah Cook, infant.
	Oct.	17.	Mrs. Witheford of Windsor.
	Oct.	25.	Elizabeth Gardiner, infant.
	Dec.	8.	John Brown, infant.
1738.	May	25.	John Ong.
	June	21.	Isabella wife of John Woodruff.
	Aug.	3.	Martin Holden, infant.

	Aug.	10.	Francis Shaw.
	Oct.	17.	Ann Potter, widow.
	Nov.	20.	Mary Davers, infant.
	Dec.	5.	Margaret wife of John Hibble.
	Feb.	3.	Sarah Willingham, infant.
1739.	April	10.	Susan wife of Richard Partridge of Fornham All Saints.
	May	8.	Jane Harvey of Westly, widow.
	Aug.	30.	Lewis Mortlock.
	Sept.	15.	Carolina wife of John Brook.
	Jan.	1.	Samuel Pond, infant.
	Jan.	28.	Hannah daughter of Joseph & Mary How of Hardwick.
1740.	May	19.	John Plumb, schoolmaster.
	June	19.	Elizabeth Miller of Hargrave, widow.
	Aug.	18.	John Frost.
	Sept.	4.	Elizabeth Houghton of Snailwell, Camb:
	Sept.	18.	Elizabeth Bowes, widow.
1741.	March	28.	Edward Ely, infant.
	April	22.	Elizabeth wife of John Pentney.
	May	10.	Jane Cook, infant.
	July	2.	Mary wife of Edmund Willingham.
	July	11.	Susannah Bigworth, widow.
	Aug.	17.	William Millington.
	Aug.	21.	Isabella wife of Richard Taylor.
	Sept.	20.	Ann Pond, infant.
	Oct.	7.	Alice Sergeant, widow.
	Oct.	30.	William Cooper.
	Dec.	1.	Timothy Pond, infant.
	Jan.	3.	Mary wife of John Cook.
1742.	April	3.	Charles, reputed child of Catharine Mortlock.
	May	19.	Francis Foreman.
	May	22.	Thomas Marshal.
	June	2.	Elizabeth Cosins.
	July	29.	Elizabeth Cobham, infant.
	Aug.	5.	Stephen Leader, infant.
1743.	March	29.	Isabella Davers, infant.

	May	19.	Robert Smith.
	July	23.	Richard Taylor.
	Aug.	12.	William Halls.
	Jan.	6.	Elizabeth Bass.
	Jan.	16.	Frances Merton.
	March	9.	Susan James, infant.
1744.	Aug.	16.	Thomas Elsden, infant.
	Nov.	9.	Martha Pond, infant.
	Dec.	27.	Mary Smith, infant.
	Jan.	25.	The widow Last.
1745.	April	29.	Joseph How.
	May	13.	Matthew Avis.
	May	27.	John Ewing.
	May	20.	Elizabeth Cater, infant.
	July	12.	Alice Secker, infant.
	Sept.	8.	Diana Secker, infant.
	Oct.	6.	Hanna wife of Richard Clarke.
	Oct.	8.	Abraham Kedington of Whepsted.
	Dec.	1.	Grace Cadney.
	Jan.	13.	Thomas Murton.
	Feb.	22.	Mary Harrington.
	March	3.	John Broke.
1746.	April	4.	Ann Mortlock.
	April	10.	Rowland Tayler.
	May	15.	Sarah Foreman.
	Aug.	15.	Hannah Wiseman.
	Jan.	11.	Grace Halls, widow.
	Feb.	13.	Thomas Gardener, senior.
	Feb.	17.	Joseph Betts of St. Mary's Parish, Bury.
1747.	June	9.	Matthew James of the Parish of Hesset.
	Sept.	20.	Mary Marchall of this Parish.
	Dec.	16.	John Smith, widower.
	Jan.	17.	Richard Clark of Bardwell.
	Feb.	5.	Mrs. Howton of Mildenhall.
	Feb.	12.	Elizabeth Howe, widow, aged 102.

	March	6.	Elizabeth Firmin.
1748.	April	5.	Elizabeth Hempsted.
	April	9.	Francis Cooper, an infant.
	May	7.	William Hempsted.
	June	5.	Grace daughter of John & Grace Avis.
	June	16.	Sarah daughter of William & Ann Frost.
	June	23.	Diana Lilly, widow, aged 92.
	Sept.	14.	Mary daughter of William & Ann Frost.
	Oct.	1.	Mary Otley.
	Oct.	13.	John Miller, an infant.
	Nov.	13.	John Pentney.
	Dec.	22.	Isaac son of Robert & Mary Jacob.
	Feb.	20.	Edmund Willingham.
1749.	May	16.	Frances Bigworth.
	Oct.	8.	Joseph son of William & Ann Gallant.
	Nov.	10.	Elizabeth daughter of John & Elizabeth Swan.
	Jan.	6.	Elizabeth Elsden.
	Feb.	10.	Thomas son of Thomas & Elizabeth Elsden.
	March	4.	Ann Frost.
	March	23.	Francis Gardiner of Hingrave.
1750.	March	29.	Steven Barker.
	Aug.	10.	John Otley.
	Sept.	28.	Valentine Munby Esq.
	Oct.	15.	Ann Spicer.
	Oct.	31.	Abigal wife of William Pache.
	Nov.	20.	Mary Turner, infant.
	Jan.	13.	Ann Howe.
	Jan.	15.	Elizabeth Swan, infant.
	Feb.	13.	Elizabeth wife of John Swan.
1751.	April	15.	Richard Elsden.
	May	13.	Sarah Mortlock.
	May	22.	Mary Avis, infant.
	June	18.	Mary Grove.
	Nov.	7.	Elizabeth Elsden.
	Dec.	4.	Alice Spencer.

1752.	Feb.	24.	James Norman.
	March	15.	Hannah Greenwood.
	March	8.	Elizabeth Wardin.
	May	14.	Thomas Harvey.
	May	29.	John Leader, infant.
	June	19.	Edmund Winney, infant.
	Aug.	8.	Hannah Greenwood.
	Sept.	23.	John Cater, infant.
1753.	Jan.	23.	Lea Jarvis.
	Feb.	11.	Edmund Frost.
	Feb.	15.	James Marchil, infant.
	Feb.	18.	Mary Cater, infant.
	May	4.	Mary Brown junior.
	May	17.	James Wyard.
	June	11.	Jane Cole.
	Sept.	21.	Elizabeth Cornwell.
	Nov.	19.	Elizabeth wife of Joshua Bunting.
	Nov.	22.	Margaret Hemsted, infant.
1754.	Jan.	6.	William Attlesy.
	Feb.	10.	Thomas Howe.
	July	6.	Elizabeth Bray, widow.
	Aug.	30.	Rachel Willingham.
	Sept.	17.	John James.
	Oct.	9.	Martha Abbot, infant.
	Oct.	17.	Mary Cousins.
	Nov.	17.	Martha James.
	Dec.	22.	Elizabeth Frost, widow.
1755.	Feb.	9.	James Marchil, infant.
	Feb.	22.	Elizabeth Swan.
	Feb.	23.	Edmund Prick.
	March	9.	William Miller, infant.
	April	27.	Humfrey Varoh, infant.
	May	16.	Margaret Hempstead, infant.
	May	28.	Ann Bunting.
	June	14.	Mabel wife of Mr. Boyce.

	June	26.	Frederick Varoh, infant.
	Aug.	21.	Charles Varoh, infant.
1756.	June	20.	Richard son of Richard & Martha Elsden of Tostick.
	July	31.	Jane daughter of Richard & Martha Elsden of Tostick.
	Aug.	6.	Susan wife of William Holden.
	June	30.	Giles Frost.
	Nov.	13.	William Smith, infant.
	Nov.	27.	Stephen Leader.
	Dec.	19.	Ann Smith.
1757.	Jan.	4.	Alice Shaw.
	Feb.	19.	William Lilly.
	March	20.	Mary infant daughter of Thomas & Mary Holden.
	March	25.	Elizabeth Hempstead.
	April	25.	Elizabeth Fermon, and Mary Payn.
	June	3.	William Pache.
	June	6.	Josuah Bunting.
	Sept.	27.	Samuel Pond.
	Nov.	8.	Mary Pond.
	Nov.	27.	Jonathan Ferman.
	Dec.	2.	Mary Ellis.
1758.	May	12.	Mary Sparrow.
	July	11.	Mary Willingham.
	Sept.	5.	Elizabeth Prick.
	Oct.	13.	William Deeks.
	Nov.	6.	William Hervy.
1759.	Jan.	22.	Mary Spencly of Bury St. Edmunds, widow.
	Jan.	24.	Richard Elsden.
	March	2.	Ann wife of William Miller.
	March	6.	Ann Miller, infant.
	May	2.	John Edwards of the Parish of Westly.
	May	18.	Elizabeth Cole of Bury St. Edmunds.
	June	28.	William Lyas.
	July	26.	Henery Page.
	Sept.	5.	Mary wife of John Sparrow.
	Sept.	18.	Margaret Leader.

1760. Jan. 26. Sarah Gardiner, widow.
Feb. 14. Charles Varo.
March 26. Susan Lilly, widow.
April 1. Sarah Lidiman, widow.
April 6. John Hempsted, infant.
May 25. Sarah Ablet, infant.
July 25. John Heble, infant.
Oct. 28. William son of William & Ann Frost.
Dec. 14. James Cater, singel man.
Dec. 24. Elizabeth Cook, widow.
Dec. 27. Mary Gee, singel woman.
1761. Jan. 29. Rebecca Gardener, widow.
March 10. Elizabeth wife of Joseph Hammond the elder.
June 30. Anne Pond, single woman.
July 5. Sarah Pond, widow.
July 19. Elizabeth wife of William Hempsted.
Aug. 30. Deborah daughter of William & Elizabeth Hempsted.
Oct. 2. Thomas son of John & Mary Brown.
Oct. 13. Elizabeth daughter of William & Elizabeth Hempsted.
Nov. 6. Benjamin son of Edward & Mary Rofe.
Nov. 14. Judith Keddington, single person.
Nov. 30. Robert Cook, infant.
Dec. 20. Sarah Sadler, a child.
1762. Feb. 6. Elizabeth daughter of Robert & Mary Jacob.
March 17. Joseph Cater, husbandman.
July 10. Rebecca daughter of John & Susan Rushbrook.
Aug. 16. Joseph Hammond the elder.
Sept. 18. Isaac, child of Elizabeth Jacob.
Oct. 24. Mary, wife of Thomas Frost.
Nov. 5. Mary Mortlock, widow, and Elizabeth, wife of Richard Boyce.
1763. Feb. 26. Mary Cater, child.
April 9. Susan Miller, infant.
May 17. Ann wife of John Miller.
June 24. Ann Ewin, widow,

M

	July	20.	Mary Cooper, infant.
	Oct.	15.	William James.
	Dec.	29.	Francis son of Mary Cater, widow.
1764.	Jan.	2.	A man found dead in the road, name unknown.
	Feb.	20.	Richard Elsden.
	March	23.	Thomas Allen.
	April	10.	John Sparks.
	March	28.	Alice Willingham.
	April	24.	Susan Allen.
	July	16.	Henry son of the widow Cater.
	Sept.	7.	John Firmin, single man of Brockly.
	Oct.	17.	Margarett wife of William Gault of Bury.
	Oct.	20.	Thomas Mortlock.
	Nov.	2.	Elizabeth Turner.
	Nov.	15.	William Bunting, infant.
	Dec.	28.	Elizabeth Cook, widow.
1765.	March	27.	Mary daughter of Francis & Mary Smith.
	May	9.	Elizabeth Layt, widow.
	May	20.	Ann Smith, widow.
	Dec.	12.	John Wiseman.
1766.	Jan.	7.	Ann wife of William Frost.
	Feb.	5.	Mary wife of Robert Potter.
	March	4.	Mary Margaret Elizabeth daughter of William Hempstead.
	April	17.	John son of Thomas & Martha Beddell.
	June	8.	Elizabeth Plesance.
	June	11.	Richard Boyce, and Gardiner son of James & Rebecca How.
	June	26.	William Everard, widower.
	July	3.	Robert James from Bury.
	July	20.	Charlotte Bray, infant.
	July	30.	Edmund son of James & Martha Spolden.
	Oct.	22.	Thomas Bird.
	Nov.	4.	Elizabeth Spicer.
	Nov.	13.	Mary wife of John Browne.
	Nov.	17.	Samuel son of James & Mary Marshall.
	Nov.	21.	Thomas Cornhill.

	Dec.	28.	Susan Cousins, widow.
1767.	Jan.	23.	John Dearson Miller.
	Jan.	15.	Ely, a servant of J. Cater's of Chevington, found dead in the snow.
	March	15.	Robert Potter.
	—	— .	Mary daughter of John & Mary Frost.
	March	25.	Margaret Spark.
	June	1.	Robert Carly.
	June	8.	Ann daughter of Robert & Sarah Frost.
	July (or Aug.)	2.	Ann Lyas, widow.
	Oct.	7.	Susan Rosbrook.
	Nov.	12.	James Sparke, infant.
1768.	Jan.	10.	Elizabeth wife of Thomas Elsden.
	Jan.	3.	Thomas Willingham, single man.
	Jan.	4.	John Lait, and Mary Cater, widow.
	Jan.	5.	Elizabeth Hempsted, widow.
	Feb.	13.	Joseph infant son of John Frost.
	Feb.	14.	Mary wife of Thomas Cadge.
	March	1.	Ann wife of Thomas Orridge.
	—	—	James infant son of James Spolden.
	April	2.	John Durrant.
	April	8.	Elizabeth Lyng.
	April	16.	Mary wife of John Durrant.
	May	1.	Ann wife of John Bray the elder.
	May	20.	Charles Rosbrook.
	May	27.	John infant son of Charles Rosbrook.
	June	5.	Edmund Payne.
	June	10.	John Cole.
	—	—	Elizabeth daughter of John Bray.
	June	30.	Edward son of William Hempsted.
	July	1.	Elizabeth daughter of Thomas Elsden.
	Aug.	28.	Martha wife of William Adams.
	—	—	Hannah daughter of Thomas & Elizabeth Frost.
1769.	June	20.	Alice wife of Benjamin Boolbrook.
	Sept.	20.	Mary Nicholls.

	Nov.	16.	Mary wife of Henry Boolbrook,
	&		Richard, reputed child of Sarah Death.
1770.	Feb.	1.	Rose daughter of James & Rebecca How.
	March	9.	Sarah daughter of James & Mary Marshall.
	March	10.	William son of Isaac & Mary Brookes.
	March	24.	Jane Elsden, widow.
	March	25.	Mary infant daughter of John & Mary Frost.
	April	30.	Ambrose son of James & Sarah Haslewood.
	July	28.	William Elsden.
	Aug.	22.	Mary daughter of Thomas & Elizabeth Frost.
	Oct.	10.	Thomas Frost infant son of John & Mary Frost.
	Nov.	22.	John & Thomas, twin sons of James & Sarah Crack.
1771.	Jan.	3.	Thomas Gardiner the younger.
	Jan.	27.	Michael Houghton.
	April	21.	Robert Jacob.
	April	25.	John son of Thomas & Elizabeth Frost.
	April	27.	Priscilla daughter of Priscilla Cornhill.
	April	25.	Priscilla Cornhill, widow.
	May	9.	Mary wife of John Whymark.
	Sept.	11.	Robert son of Robert & Elizabeth Mayhew.
	Sept.	24.	Mary Harvey, widow.
	Dec.	30.	Thomas Crack, single man.
1772.	Jan.	21.	Mary Otley, widow.
	Feb.	18.	John Spicer, widower.
	March	31.	William infant son of Robert & Mary Norman.
	April	7.	Joseph son of James & Sarah Haslewood.
	April	9.	William infant son of George & Sarah Challice.
	April	26.	Susan daughter of Thomas & Elizabeth Frost.
	May	15.	Ann infant daughter of John & Mary Cooper.
	June	2.	Ann daughter of Thomas & Ann Orridge.
	Dec.	16.	Edward Rolfe.
1773.	April	25.	Francis & William sons of Edward & Elizabeth Drew.
	May	27.	John King.
	Aug.	22.	Elizabeth wife of Joseph Gooday.
	Oct.	17.	Joseph Polley.

	Dec.	17.	Rose Ann daughter of James & Rebecca How.
	Dec.	24.	Thomas Gardiner the elder.
1774.	Jan.	6.	John Barton of the Parish of Chevington.
	Jan.	16.	Edward son of Edward & Elizabeth Drew.
	Feb.	3.	Sarah wife of George Challice.
	Feb.	6.	Stephen Barton.
	Feb.	10.	Martha wife of William Hempsted; and Mary Cocksedge.
	May	22.	Elizabeth [blank].
	May	28.	Andrew Fartier.
	Sept.	12.	Ann, child of Tamitha Wright & of William Hempsted the younger.
	Oct.	20.	Mary wife of Thomas Orridge.
	Nov.	4.	James Polly of Bradfield St. Clare.
	Nov.	13.	Elizabeth daughter of Robert & Elizabeth Hitchcock.
1775.	Feb.	10.	Grace daughter of Robert & Elizabeth Hitchcock.
	April	20.	Jonathan Brook.
	May	15.	Susan Edhouse.
	Aug.	11.	John Sparrow.
	Aug.	30.	Edward son of Rev. George & Elizabeth Rogers.
	Oct.	8.	Hannah Houghton, widow.
	Oct.	24.	Hannah wife of Thomas Frost the younger.
	Oct.	25.	Mary Jacob, widow.
	Nov.	20.	John Swan of the Parish of Hessett.
1776.	Jan.	1.	Robert son of Robert & Mary Norman.
	Jan.	2.	Robert Greenwood.
	Jan.	4.	Sarah daughter of Thomas & Elizabeth Frost.
	Jan.	28.	Susan Mortlock.
	March &	3.	Thomas son of John and Mary Frost, Mary wife of Ambrose Sale.
	March	7.	Sarah wife of William Bray.
	March	18.	Thomas son of Rev. George & Elizabeth Rogers.
	May	12.	Mary Bull infant.
	May	19.	Thomas son of William & Sarah Bray.
	June	16.	James son of Thomas & Mary Sparkes.
	June	19.	Joseph Gooday, widower.

	Oct.	20.	Jane daughter of John & Elizabeth Browne.
	Nov.	20.	Henry son of William & Sarah Adams.
	Nov.	23.	Thomas Willingham the elder.
1777.	Jan.	6.	Samuel son of William & Elizabeth Hempsted.
	Jan.	13.	James Spolding.
	May	15.	Richard infant son of Thomas & Mary Sparke.
	June	11.	Margaret wife of Joseph Hammond.
	July	10.	Thomas son of Thomas & Ann Orridge.
	Sept.	14.	Jeremiah Ashman, infant.
	Oct.	19.	Mary daughter of Edmund & Mary Willingham.
1778.	Jan.	18.	Frances child of Frances Frost.
	Jan.	29.	Susan wife of William Parsons.
	Feb.	1.	Ambrose Emerson, widower.
	Sept.	4.	John son of William Lilly.
	Nov.	23.	William Lilly.
1779.	Jan.	4.	Lewis son of Christopher & Elizabeth Rosbrook.
	Feb.	21.	Rose Gardiner, widow.
	March	1.	Elizabeth infant daughter of James & Sarah Hazlewood.
	April	3.	Mary Spencer, widow.
	April	11.	Elizabeth Cole.
	April	30.	Mary daughter of Samuel & Elizabeth Avis.
	May	7.	Mary child of Mary Norman.
	May	11.	Susan Bray, infant.
	May	12.	Sarah Brewster, infant.
	June	20.	—— —— of William & Mary Polley.
	July	2.	Mary daughter of William & Sarah Frost.
	July	8.	Edmund Payne.
	Sept.	28.	James son of John & Dillaravier Rolfe.
1780.	Jan.	23.	Ann Wiseman, widow.
	March	1.	Martha wife of William Ashley of Rockly in Norfolk.
	March	3.	William Adams.
	March	31.	William Miller child of Susan Bunting.
	June	30.	John son of Robert & Elizabeth Hitchcock.
	July	8.	Elizabeth Hitchcock.
	Aug.	7.	James Frost.

	Aug.	11.	William Swithin son of John & Ann Dubble.
	Aug.	13.	Maria Woodward, belonging to Bury.
	Aug.	19.	Robert Brooke.
	Sept.	5.	Elizabeth wife of William Billeman.
	Sept.	14.	Susan wife of Christopher Rosbrook senior.
	Nov.	1.	John son of John Holden.
1781.	Jan.	29.	Robert son of James & Ann Copsey.
	March	15.	William son of Robert Frost.
	July	13.	Robert Hitchcock.
	July	22.	Charles Brown.
	Aug.	5.	Christopher son of John Underwood.
	Sept.	10.	Elizabeth daughter of William Ambrose.
	Oct.	20.	A man, a stranger, supposed to have been a soldier.
	Oct.	25.	Robert Spalding.
1782.	Jan.	16.	Robert son of Rev. George & Elizabeth Rogers.
	Feb.	13.	Sarah wife of Edmund Willingham the elder.
	March	19.	Mary King, widow.
	March	21.	Ann Cooper of the Parish of Hessett.
	March	31.	Thomas son of William Frost.
	April	29.	Castell Goodchild.
	Oct.	26.	William son of William & Mary Pettit.
	Nov.	15.	Mary wife of James Marshall.
	Nov.	3.	Sarah daughter of John Browne.
1783.	Jan.	18.	John son of William & Mary Pettit.
	Feb.	6.	Martha wife of Richard Elsden.
	June	7.	William son of John Everall.
	June	8.	William son of William & Ann Lyng.
	Aug.	8.	William Bray.
	Aug.	18.	James son of Charles & Mary Cawston.
	Aug.	26.	Florida Stutton, widow.
	Sept.	20.	Ann wife of Thomas Orange.
	Oct.	30.	Edward son of Thomas & Ann Orange.
	Dec.	14.	William son of Thomas & Ann Byford.
1784.	Jan.	25.	William Frost.
	Feb.	25.	John Smith.

	March	19.	Mary Frost, widow.
	March	27.	Elizabeth daughter of George & Elizabeth Holden.
	April	3.	Henry Boolbrooke.
	April	4.	Margaret wife of Thomas Cadge.
	April	5.	Rebecca daughter of John & Sarah Avis.
	April	10.	George Scarfe son of John & Susan Westrop.
	April	12.	Susan daughter of Thomas & Mary Holden.
	April	14.	Ann daughter of Richard & Ann Adams.
	April	20.	William Billeman, widower.
	June	3.	Richard Smith.
	July	31.	Susan Goodchild, widow.
	Sept.	8.	Clementina Scarfe daughter of Daniel & Mary Lilia Wood of Flempton.
	Sept.	23.	Mary wife of John Holden.
	Oct.	3.	Sarah Merton, widow.
	Oct.	24.	John Bray.
	Nov.	16.	John Cooper.
	Nov.	25.	Mary Cooper.
1785.	March	29.	Richard Green.
	April	8.	James Spalding.
	April	20.	Mary Rolfe, widow.
	Aug.	2.	Esther Boreham, widow.
	Sept.	3.	William Alvis, infant.
	Sept.	24.	George Holden, infant.
	Oct.	2.	Frances Byford, infant.
	Dec.	10.	Thomas Elsden. Robert Wilden, infant.
1786.	Jan.	8.	Stephen Leeder, aged 83 years.
	Feb.	15.	George Smith.
	March	11.	Ann Cater, infant.
	June	11.	Ann daughter of William & Mary Polly.
	June	13.	Rebecca Howe, infant.
	June	28.	Thomas Frost aged 84.
	Aug.	8.	Jeremiah Rosbrook, a Pauper of the Parish of Rougham.
	Aug.	10.	William Alvis, infant.
	Sept	26.	David Hill.

1787. Jan. 12. Sarah Spalding, widow.
Feb. 20. Elizabeth wife of George Holden.
April 11. George Alvis, infant.
May 18. John Bunting.
June 3. Mary Rolfe, widow, aged 83.
July 1. Samuel Smith.
Aug. 5. Elizabeth Billerman, spinster.
Oct. 10. Mary Daines, infant.
1788. July 10. Sarah wife of John Brown.
Aug. 28. John Goldson, infant.
Oct. 7. Sarah wife, and Sarah daughter, of John Marshall.
1789. Jan. 18. Mary Leeder, widow.
Feb. 22. Hannah Brewster, infant.
Feb. 25. John Rowland, infant.
March 1. Delariviere Willingham.
March 4. Edmund Ward, infant.
May 29. Sarah daughter of Mary Nunn, infant.
July 21. Mary Mason, infant.
Aug. 18. Elizabeth wife of Ambrose Seal. William Death, infant.
Sept. 1. Elizabeth daughter of Thomas Mason.
Dec. 20. Frances Spalding, infant.
1790. Jan. 31. John Holden.
Feb. 7. Edward Willingham, infant.
Feb. 4. Sarah wife of Robin Frost.
Feb. 21. Mary wife of Edmund Willingham.
March 10. John & Mary Goldson, twins, infants
March 21. William Cater, aged 79.
July 5. Ann Lofts.
July 10. Alice Drew, infant.
Oct. 22. Rose wife of George Last.
Nov. 18. Thomas Swann.
1791. Jan. 25. Richard Butcher.
Feb. 10. Elizabeth Swann.
March 24. Susan wife of John Tweed.
April 11. Mary wife of John Marshall.

	April	12.	Simon infant son of Thomas Last.
	April	29.	Ann Oakley, spinster.
	May	9.	John Jaggard.
	May	18.	William Holden, widower, aged 78.
	June	13.	Mary wife of Charles Cawston, late Mary Bowers, spinster.
	July	17.	William Bannock, infant.
	Sept.	11.	John Sparke.
	Sept.	27.	John Billerman.
	Oct.	2.	Ann Alvis, infant.
	Oct.	12.	Theophila wife of John Harvey of Risby.
	Nov.	14.	Mary wife of Thomas Murton.
	Dec.	29.	Thomas Willingham.
1792.	April	30.	John Richardson, infant.
	June	29.	Sarah Cater, spinster.
	Oct.	28.	Susan wife of John Warren.
	Nov.	4.	Thomas Orridge.
1793.	Jan.	18.	Mary Goodchild, infant.
	Feb.	15.	Thomas Beddle.
	March	15.	John Ward, infant.
	June	26.	Catharine wife of George Knock.
	July	10.	William Seal, infant.
	Dec.	28.	Elizabeth Cater, widow.
1794.	March	20.	Mary Cooper, widow.
	July	1.	Hannah wife of Thomas Elsden.
	July	20.	Mary Marshall, infant.
	Dec.	1.	William Cole.
1795.	Jan.	22.	Thomas Elsden,
	&		Elizabeth wife of —— Bigsby of Felsham.
	March	15.	John Browne.
	May	22.	Elizabeth Ellis, infant.
	May	23.	Thomas Merton.
	May	24.	Mary Varer.
	June	4.	Jemima Butcher, infant.
	June	26.	George Alvis.
	July	4.	Mary Turner.

	July	22.	Sophia Ward, infant.
	Aug.	25.	Sarah Bull.
1796.	March	6.	Sarah wife of William Frost.
	March	10.	Mary Jaggard, widow.
	March	16.	Sarah wife of Ambrose Seale.
	April	26.	Sarah Spalden.
	May	19.	Sarah Bird.
	Sept.	11.	John Cooper.
	Sept.	15.	Mary Goodchild, infant.
1797.	Feb.	9.	Joseph Hammond, late of St. Mary's parish, St. Edmunds bury.
	July	29.	James Byford, infant.
1798.	April	15.	Elizabeth wife of Thomas Sharpe.
	April	22.	Susan wife of Benjamin Bullbrook.
	May	25.	John Tricker, infant.
	July	18.	Thomas Orridge.
	Aug.	9.	Stephen Brooks.
	Aug.	27.	Thomas Cater.
	Nov.	5.	John Bray.
	Nov.	8.	John Gardner, infant.
1799.	Jan.	21.	John Beales.
	Feb.	10.	William Nunn Spalding, infant.
	April	19.	Mary wife of John Elliss.
	April	28.	Elizabeth Elliss, infant. Samuel Last, infant.
	June	16.	Abraham Cobbin.
	June	30.	William Nunn.
	July	20.	William Twitchett.
	July	25.	John Crack.
	Oct.	6.	George Root, infant.
	Dec.	4.	Mary wife of James Crack.
1800.	Jan.	4.	John Double.
	June	21.	James Tweed.
	July	6.	Elizabeth wife of Richard Smith.
	Aug.	1.	William Tricker, infant.
	Aug.	11.	Ann Cole, widow.

	Sept.	30.	Louisa Lilly, infant.
	Dec.	4.	Mary wife of Robert Norman.
1801.	Jan.	9.	William Pearsons.
	May	3.	Sarah Crack.
	Aug.	13.	Robert Norman, widower.
	Sept.	1.	William Osborne, infant.
	Dec.	5.	Mary Norris, widow.
1802.	Feb.	16.	Benjamin Bullbrook, widower.
	April	2.	William Gardiner, infant.
	April	6.	John Adams.
	May	16.	Thomas Sharpe, widower.
	May	17.	Thomas Cater.
	June	1.	James Copsey.
	July	17.	William Hempsted.
	Aug.	29.	James Browne, infant.
	Sept.	5.	Mary Frost, widow, from Cotton.
	Sept.	20.	Edmund Willingham.
	Sept.	28.	Samuel Miseman, infant.
	Oct.	21.	William Bull.
	Oct.	27.	Hannah wife of Samuel Miseman.
	Nov.	17.	George Cook, infant.
	Dec.	1.	Thomas Richardson, infant.
1803.	May	21.	Bridget Callow, widow.
	Aug.	1.	Harriet Tricker, infant. John Steed, infant.
	Oct.	9.	Thomas Ridnell.
1804.	March	11.	Christian Catharine, wife of John Beales.
	April	12.	Mary infant daughter of George Lanham.
	June	13.	John Tweed.
	June	27.	James Pratt.
	Sept.	25.	James Hazelwood.
	Oct.	12.	Susannah Gooch, infant.
	Oct.	21.	Hannah Wiseman.
	Nov.	6.	Sarah wife of Stephen Crick.
	Dec.	10.	Thomas Death.
1805.	Jan.	4.	Susan Last.

	Jan.	8.	John Lilly, infant.
	Feb.	7.	John Gardiner.
	April	2.	Sarah Gardiner, infant.
	June	16.	Elizabeth wife of Henry Cater.
	July	25.	Mary wife of John Warren.
	Oct.	30.	Hannah Bullas, infant.
	Nov.	3.	Edward Bristow Blundell of Laytonstone, Co. Essex.
	Dec.	4.	Alice wife of Rev. Thomas Kerrich.
	Dec.	8.	William Goodchild, infant.
1806.	Jan.	1.	Elizabeth Frost, widow.
	Jan.	3.	Hannah wife of John Tricker.
	Jan.	5.	William Miller.
	March	10.	Harriett Tricker, infant.
	March	20.	Mary Hempsted, widow.
	May	25.	Mary Ann Double, infant.
	May	27.	Elizabeth Nunn, spinster.
	May	30.	Sarah wife of John Barrell.
	Aug.	14.	Thomas Howe.
	Dec.	18.	William Sparke.
	Dec.	30.	William Shinkfeild.
1807.	Feb.	11.	Elizabeth wife of Henry Hart.
	Feb.	22.	Sarah Merton, spinster.
	Sept.	22.	Ann Lilly, infant.
	Sept.	29.	Elizabeth wife of Samuel Alvis.
	Oct.	28.	Sarah Smith, widow.
	Dec.	22.	James Ramplin.
1808.	Jan.	4.	Tamar wife of Joseph Leech.
	Feb.	23.	Charles Shelver, infant.
1809.	March	28.	Ann wife of William Tunbridge.
	May	2.	John Hammond.
	May	10.	Susan Smith, widow.
	May	15.	Ambrose Seale.
	Nov.	30.	Robin Frost.
	Dec.	7.	James Lanham.
1810.	June	7.	Elizabeth Ridnell, spinster.

	Nov.	23.	Thomas Green, infant.
1811.	Jan.	27.	Ann wife of John Browne.
	Feb.	3.	Sarah Willingham, widow.
	Feb.	10.	Martha Beddle, widow.
	Sept.	6.	Thomas Ling.
	Nov.	27.	Mary wife of William Orridge of Nowton,
	&		James Warren, infant.
1812.	April	26.	Susan Miller, widow.
	May	18.	Edward Drew. George Sparke.
	June	25.	Mary Willingham, widow.
	Dec.	6.	Thomas Richardson.
	Dec.	14.	Elizabeth Butcher, widow.
	Dec.	20.	Maria Warren, infant.
1813.	April	30.	Martha Browne, spinster, 61 years.
	Nov.	2.	Martha wife of George Cater, 53 years.
	Nov.	14.	Elizabeth wife of Lewis Rosbrook, 36 years.
1814.	Jan.	9.	George son of John & Mary Greenwood, 11 weeks.
	March	20.	Mary wife of John Greenwood, 32 years.
	Jan.	18.	Revd. Thomas Kerrich, 28 years Rector of this Parish, 73 years.
	Jan.	18.	Joseph Leech of Bury, 84 years.
	Sept.	8.	John Nunn, 73 years.
	Sept.	22.	James Ramplin, infant.
	Oct.	6.	William Salisbury, 1 year.
	Oct.	7.	Mary Willingham, 2 years.
	Dec.	13.	Susan wife of Thomas Last, 55 years.
1815.	Jan.	17.	Thomas Ling, infant.
	Jan.	23.	James Goodchild, 52 years.
	Aug.	16.	Ann wife of William King, 36 years.
	Oct.	19.	Lucina Pryke, infant.
	Oct.	27.	Sarah Musk, 4 years.
	Nov.	8.	Thomas Rushbrooke, infant.
1816.	April	1.	Robert Drew of Bury, 8 years.
	April	18.	Eliza Gardiner of Bury, 2 years.
	June	4.	John Gardiner of Bury, 8 months.
	Aug.	29.	John Frost, 83 years.

	Sept.	12.	Thomas Byford of Little Saxham, 68 years.
	Oct.	27.	Elizabeth Adkin, 86 years.
	Nov.	28.	Stephen Crick, 76 years.
	Dec.	1.	Samuel Alvis, 73 years.
	Dec.	10.	Mary Death, infant.
	Dec.	29.	Margaret Chapman of Whepstead, 78 years.
1817.	March	17.	Elizabeth Willingham, 60 years.
	April	8.	Martha Susanna Scarling, infant.
	April	17.	Elizabeth Lilly, 42 years.
	April	20.	Mary Coe, infant.
	June	21.	Charles Myson, 20 years.
	Aug.	17.	Ann Richardson of Ickworth, 81 years.
	Sept.	22.	John Salisbury, 39 years.
	Oct.	1.	Mary wife of William King, 49 years.
	Nov.	1.	Frances Ling, infant.
	Dec.	16.	Elizabeth Baker, 41 years.
1818.	Jan.	11.	Peter Gedge, 59 years.
	March	26.	Sarah Norton, 72 years.
	April	5.	Sarah Crack, 76 years.
	Sept.	7.	Ann wife of Thomas Adkin, of Bury, 34 years.
	Sept.	14.	Maria Grimwood, infant.
	Oct.	10.	William Swithin Adkin, infant.
	Oct.	29.	William Musk, 12 years.
1819.	Jan.	6.	William Rosbrooke, infant.
	Feb.	23.	William Ambrose, 69 years.
	May	27.	Elizabeth Rosbrooke, 67 years.
	Aug.	8.	Elizabeth wife of John Adkin, 59 years.
	Oct.	7.	Charles Coe, 70 years.
	Nov.	14.	Mary Nunn, widow, 77 years.
	Nov.	25.	Elizabeth wife of John Brewster, 72 years.
	Dec.	19.	Mary Frost of Nowton, widow, 83 years.
	Dec.	26.	Edmund Willingham, infant.
1820.	Jan.	11.	William Moyse, 32 years.
	Jan.	24.	Rebecca Smith, 2 years.
	Feb.	21.	Susan Coe, infant.

	March	3.	Susan wife of James Everett, 56 years.
	March	6.	Mary wife of John Spalding.
	—	—	Jane daughter of John Spedding, of Bury St. Edmund's.
	June	11.	Nathaniel Adkin, 67 years.
	July	4.	Sarah Hazlewood, 82 years.
	July	16.	Mary Rolfe, 73 years.
	July	16.	Mary wife of Abraham Elsden, 43 years.
	Aug.	18.	Lucy Pryke, infant.
	Aug.	19.	Mary Burroughs, widow, 68 years.
	Oct.	31.	George Last, 80 years.
	Nov.	8.	Mary Hands of Bury St. Edmund's, 65 years.
	Dec.	8.	Elizabeth Ambrose, widow, 68 years.
1821.	April	25.	David Cooke, infant.
	May	1.	Elizabeth wife of John Simkin, 49 years.
	Nov.	9.	William Ling, 74 years.
	Nov.	10.	Sarah Alvis, 74 years.
1822.	Feb.	10.	Susan Warren, 76 years.
	June	2.	Thomas son of Thomas Atkin, 16 years.
	June	2.	John Rolfe, 74 years.
	Nov.	9.	Rebecca Howe, 82 years.
	Nov.	11.	Mary Ann Copsey, 17 weeks.
	Dec.	31.	John Gardiner of Bury St. Edmunds, 52 years.
1823.	Jan.	2.	John Brown, 81 years.
	Jan.	19.	Anne Copsey, 66 years.
	July	18.	Lucy Moyse, 29 years.
	Aug.	18.	Elizabeth Musk, 2½ months.
	Dec.	31.	John Warren, 70 years.
1824.	Jan.	9.	Elizabeth Farrants, 3 weeks.
	Jan.	22.	Mary Ann Wigson, of Horsecroft, 5 years.
	Feb.	6.	William Ambrose, 47 years.
	Feb.	25.	Elizabeth Copsey, 16 weeks.
	June	17.	Henry Cameron Cherry of Horringer Parsonage, 10 months.
	June	20.	Ann Lilly, 79 years.
	July	2.	Ann Death, 82 years.
	July	24.	Rachael Rowe, 49 years.

Aug. 24. Michael Sturgeon, 63 years.
Oct. 11. Sarah Rudland, 70 years.
Oct. 19. Elizabeth Scrivener commonly called Ling, 53 years.
Nov. 2. Thomas Wigson of Horsecroft, 1 day.
Nov. 4. James Bull, 72 years.
Dec. 18. Anne Gedge, 27 years.
1825. Feb. 10. Henry Cater of Fornham, 79 years.
May 19. Daniel Ellis, 4 months.
July 8. George Double, 50 years.
July 14. Maria Gostwick, 42 years.
Aug. 25. John Hazelwood, 60 years.
Oct. 3. Thomas Kerrich of Bury, 56 years.
Oct. 7. Elizabeth Ellis, 68 years.
Oct. 11. Christopher Rushbrook, 84 years.
Oct. 23. Thomas Cater, 77 years.
Nov. 24. James Scarlin, 87 years.
Dec. 5. Elizabeth Catchpole, 27 years.
Dec. 12. Harriet Lawrance, 33 years.
Dec. 15. John Gardiner, 16 years.
Dec. 27. Ann Double, 73 years.
Dec. 28. John Spalding, 77 years.
1826. Jan. 6. Sarah Wells of Horsecroft, 2 years.
Jan. 8. George Cater, 67 years.
Jan. 12. Thomas Rooks, 19 weeks.
Jan. 16. Eliza Double of Bury, 2 years.
Jan. 20. Abraham Rooks, 43 years.
Jan. 21. Henry Cooke Wigson of Horsecroft, 2 years & 4 months.
Jan. 29. Daniel Durrant, 11 years.
Jan. 31. Martha Rooks, 32 years.
Feb. 3. Henry Everard of Bury, 18 months.
Feb. 26. Jonas Rowe, 22 years.
March 12. James Durrant, 5 years.
March 16. John Michael Barwick of Bury, 8 months.
May 12. Mary Rutter, 38 years.
May 28. Henry Cater, 25 years.

June 12. Woodward Bidwell, 73 years.
July 9. Amy Dean, 32 years.
July 23. Keziah Pryke, 8 months.
Aug. 18. Robert Palmer, 8 months.
Aug. 20. Mary Meller of Horsecroft, 79 years.
Oct. 18. James Cater of Stansted, 37 years.
Nov. 2. George Sillett, 21 years.
Nov. 17. William Frost of Wickhambrook, 36 years.
Nov. 28. George Sillett, about 50 years.
Dec. 15. Jane Rhodes, daughter of John Rhodes Esq. of Halifax, Yorkshire, at Bury St. Edmunds, 17 years.
Dec. 19. Thomas Meadows, 3 weeks.
1827. Jan. 10. William Last, 34 years.
Jan. 16. Grace wife of John Marshall, 63 years.
March 15. Susan Coe, 70 years.
March 18. Abraham Elsden, 65 years.
April 2. Arthur Gostwick, 14 years.
May 3. Rebecca Rosbrooke, 13 months.
May 15. William Pond, 72 years.
May 15. Frances Miseman, 26 years.
June 11. James Goulding of Bury St. Edmunds, 2½ years.
June 13. Hannah Adams, 32 years.
Aug. 5. William Miseman, 2 months.
Sept. 30. John Gostwick, 1 year.
Dec. 31. Sophia Joiner, 37 years.
1828. Jan. 4. Sarah Mason, 77 years.
Jan. 7. Elizabeth Bull, 77 years.
Jan. 8. Samuel Brewster, 4 years.
March 9. John Brewster, 82 years.
May 22. Charles Ward, 70 years.
July 16. Elizabeth Ridnall, 21 weeks.
Sept. 9. William Smith, 51 years.
Oct. 24. Elizabeth Rosbroke, 88 years.
1829. Feb. 27. Daniel Clarke of Ickworth, 21 years.
March 29. Frances Rooks, 16 years.

	April	26.	Harriet Eade, 33 years.
	May	25.	Mary widow of Thomas Cater, 80 years.
	June	20.	Jane infant daughter of William & Harriot Eade.
	July	5.	Richard Adams, 91 years.
	Sept.	17.	Mary widow of Daniel Atkin, 66 years.
	Oct.	27.	Thomas son of Thomas & Mary Ann Gardener of Bury, 15 weeks.
	Nov.	25.	James Cook son of Joseph & Ann Miseman, 3 months.
1830.	Feb.	23.	William Bullass, 29 years.
	March	27.	Lewis Rosbrooke, 52 years.
	April	1.	Susan Ramplin of Bury St. Edmunds, 73 years.
	April	12.	Lavinia Partridge, 15 years.
	June	6.	Thomas Mason of Hargrave, 77 years.
	June	12.	Ann Wade, 50 years.
	Aug.	4.	Anne Cook, 7 months.
	Aug.	5.	William Double, 17 years.
	Aug.	10.	Elizabeth Wigson, of Horsecroft, 79 years.
	Aug.	25.	Phœbe King of Bury St. Edmunds, 26 years.
	Oct.	16.	Sarah Blois, 67 years.
	Oct.	21.	Robert Ebbens, 1 year & 8 months.
	Oct.	22.	Mark Harrison, 5 years.
	Oct.	31.	John Death, 66 years.
	Nov.	11.	Frederick Turnor Wigson of Horsecroft, 1 year & 4 months.
	Dec.	14.	Rachel Pond, 77 years.
	Dec.	17.	John Wing, 28 years.
1831.	Jan.	7.	James Evered of Great Saxham, 79 years.
	Feb.	25.	John Goldson, 65 years.
	March	14.	Susan Willingham, 1 year.
	April	16.	John Adkin, 74 years.
	May	2.	Anne Wade, 12 years.
	Aug.	23.	James Reynolds, 83 years.
	Sept.	7.	Elizabeth Coe, 50 years.
	Sept.	12.	Eliza Rosbrooke, 14 years.
	Dec.	8.	Sarah Gostwick, 3 years.
	Dec.	28.	Emma Root, 17 weeks.

1832. Jan. 9. Catharine Maria daughter of Revd. Edward and Mary Anna Penelope Gould, 2 months.
Feb. 26. John Marshall, 78 years.
March 5. James Rooks, 21 years.
May 8. Charles Tweed, 5 years.
June 3. Robert Cooper, 75 years.
June 7. Isaac Race, 47 years.
June 8. Joseph Baker, 8 years.
July 15. Anne Frost, 81 years.
Aug. 19. James Meadows, 10 days.
Oct. 2. Thomas Ling, 83 years.
Oct. 11. Thomas Ridnall, 14 years.
Nov. 4. Marianne Golden of Bury St. Edmunds, 3 years.
Nov. 16. George Goldsmith, 74 years.
1833. Jan. 16. Margaret Reynolds, 68 years.
Feb. 26. Elizabeth Pearsons, 59 years.
April 23. Septimus Seaber Wigson of Horsecroft, 15 weeks.
May 7. Thomas Tweed, 9 months.
May 12. Maria Musk, 6 months.
May 17. Alfred Pearson of Bury St. Edmunds, 9 months.
May 23. William Pollard, 23 years.
June 9. Abraham son of Sarah (widow of Isaac) Race, 11 years.
June 19. Ann, widow of William Ling, of Bury St. Edmunds, 82 years.
June 30. James son of Isaac Race, 12 years.
July 31. Lydia (Parsons) wife of Thomas Pryke of Westminster, 32 years.
July 31. William son of George & Sarah (Tricker) Cooper, 2 years.
Aug. 12. William Edwards, wheelwright, 62 years.
Nov. 4. Mary (Musk) wife of Robert Gooch of Bury St. Edmunds, 37 years.
Nov. 17. Stephen son of Robert & Mary (Musk) Gooch of Bury St. Edmunds, 7 weeks.
Nov. 19. Michael Crack, 53 years.
Nov. 26. Charles Rosbrooke, 53 years.

Dec. 15. Mary (Eagle) widow of James Goodchild, 67 years.
Dec. 23. Anne Bullass, 27 years.
1834. March 4. Deborah (Ling) wife of John Cockerill, 76 years.
March 28. Alice (Pryke) wife of William Pearson, 79 years.
March 29. John son of Abraham Cooper, 1 year & 8 months.
April 25. James son of Robert & Mary (Musk) Gooch of Bury, 3 years.
May 31. Elizabeth daughter of Matthew & Jane (Balls) Gostwick, 10 years.
Sept. 7. George son of Matthew & Marianne (Boggis) Mison, 15 weeks.
Sept. 25. Sophia (Last) wife of James Ramplin, 45 years.
Oct. 3. Ann (Elwood) wife of John Brown, late widow Ridnall, 76 years.
Oct. 15. Maria daughter of James & Sophia Ramplin, 12 years.
Oct. 21. Ann wife of —— Petch, 23 years.
Nov. 25. James Ramplin, 53 years.
Dec. 24. Ann (Rattler) Adams, widow, 84 years.
1835. Jan. 2. James Spalding, 43 years.
Jan. 21. Mary (Last) wife of Simon Sale, 75 years.
March 8. Susan Seapy, 70 years.
March 9. Thomas son of Thomas & Marianne (Everard) Gardiner of Bury, 3 months.
April 3. Alice daughter of Revd. Thomas Kerrich, late Rector of this Parish, of Bury, 61 years.
April 12. Sarah Anne dau: of Joseph & Anne (Cooke) Mison, 6 weeks.
April 29. Sarah Ann dau: of Charles & Elizabeth (Race) Collins, 9 months.
May 30. George son of George & Elizabeth (Bull) Crack, 17 days.
June 14. George son of William & Mary (Deeks) Ray, 19 weeks.
July 20. Mary Ann Crack, ill: dau: of Mary Ann (Crack) Cockerill, 9 years.
Aug. 9. Ann (Cooke) wife of Joseph Mison, 37 years.
Sept. 13. Harriet Gooch, spinster, 27 years.
Oct. 4. Robert son of Isaac & Mary Willingham of Bury, 16 months.
Nov. 8. Charles son of James Ramplin, 4 years.

Nov. 12. Robert James son of Robert & Anne (Boyce) Thompson, 18 months.
Nov. 13. Sophia dau: of James & Lucy (Ramplin) Boreham, 1 year.
Nov. 17. John Adkin, 91 years.
Dec. 6. Jane dau: of Ezekiel & Charlotte (Naylor) Durrant, 2 years.
Dec. 16. Susan dau: of Matthew & Mary Ann (Boggis) Mison, 1 week.
Dec. 20. Marianne wife of Matthew Mison, 31 years.
1836. Jan. 16. Catherine (Frost) Death, widow, 71 years.
Feb. 5. George son of Robert & Harriet (Tweed) Petch, 1 day.
Feb. 24. Mary dau: of Samuel & Sarah (Pearson) Mison, 23 years.
March 29. Jane dau: of Joseph & Ann (Cooke) Mison, 4 years.
April 8. Joseph son of Samuel & Sarah (Pearson) Mison, 32 years.
April 8. John son of J. & Eleanor Sergeant, 14 months.
April 27. John son of Samuel & Sarah (Pearson) Mison, 34 years.
June 26. Emma dau: of Joseph & Mary (Sillett) Mayhew, 15 months.
June 27. Eliza Edwards, 9 years.
July 14. Mary Ann dau: of William & Mary (Grimwood) Edwards, 17 years.
Aug. 16. Charles Tillett, 48 years.
Sept. 8. Ezekiel Durrant, 26 years.
Sept. 23. John son of late John & Louisa (Sturgeon) Barwick of Bury, 9 years.
Oct. 26. Jane (Crack) wife of Henry Rosbrooke, 26 years.
Nov. 22. Thomas Sharpe, 71 years.
1837. Jan. 11. Ann (Goodchild) wife of Philip Meadows, 38 years.
Jan. 24. Peggy (Drake) wife of Robert Ridnall, 36 years.
Jan. 26. Jane (Balls) wife of Matthew Gostwick of Westley, 45 years.
Feb. 7. David Varer, 44 years.
Feb. 9. Ezekiel son of Charlotte (Naylor) Durrant, widow, 18 months.
Feb. 23. Sarah widow of John Gardiner, 94 years.
Feb. 26. James son of Simon & Mary (Ling) Last, 6 years.
March 9. Robert son of Robert & late Peggy Ridnall, 17 years.
March 19. John Brown, 66 years.
April 1. Thomas Orgill, son of Susanna Partridge, 1 year.

	May	27.	John son of John & Marianne (Pearson) Smith, 2 years.
	July	10.	Ann daughter of Robert Ridnall, 16 years.
	July	18.	Susanna widow of Woodward Bidwell, 70 years.
1838.	March	8.	Thamar Cockrill of Bury, 8 years.
	April	6.	Maria Cockrill of Bury, 3 years.
	April	29.	Alfred Petch, 9 weeks.
	May	21.	Sarah Ann Simpkin, 11 months.
	July	5.	Alice dau: of Thomas & Mary (King) Goodchild, 5 months.
	Oct.	17.	Esther (Hustler) Death, 38 years.
	Nov.	5.	— dau: unbaptized of Richard & Susan Cockerill, 7 weeks.
1839.	Feb.	18.	Edmund Willingham, 60 years.
	Feb.	19.	Simon Last, 42 years.
	Feb.	21.	Robert Deacon, 47 years.
	Feb.	28.	Joseph Farrants, 74 years.
	March	4.	Elizabeth Thurlow, 62 years.
	April	20.	Sarah Catchpole of Whepstead, 13 years.
	April	21.	Sarah Charlotte Bullass, 17 months.
	April	28.	Joseph Rowe, 66 years.
	May	28.	John Pearsons, 75 years.
	June	17.	John Dearson Meller, 85 years.
	June	30.	James Race, 2 months.
	July	2.	Sarah Bullass, 57 years.
	Aug.	18.	George Brown, 3 years.
	Sept.	1.	Robert Cooke, 22 years.
	Sept.	30.	Anne Cooper, 75 years.
	Oct.	6.	Anne Spalding, 54 years.
	Nov.	1.	George Farrants, 6 weeks.
	Nov.	12.	Edward Musk, 14 days.
1840.	Jan.	27.	Susan Goodchild, 25 weeks.
	Feb.	2.	Thomas Copsey, 81 years.
	April	16.	Mary Anne Crack, of Bury St. Edmunds, 1 year.
	April	22.	Ann Gedge of Bury St. Edmunds, 70 years.
	May	1.	Susan Meller, 63 years.
	May	24.	Alice Ward, 86 years.
	May	29.	Alice Willingham, 84 years.

Aug. 14. Amy Palmer of Westley, 9 years.
Sept. 30. Mary Goodchild, 37 years.
Oct. 13. Edward Crack, 73 years.
Dec. 16. Mary Bullas, 21 years.
1841. Jan. 2. John Bannon, 11 months.
Jan. 20. Elizabeth King, 50 years.
Feb. 4. Elizabeth Bramwell of Bury St. Edmunds, 69 years.
Feb. 14. Edward Musk, 70 years.
Feb. 24. Ann Spalding, 1 year.
Feb. 28. Matthew Gostwick of Saxham Parva, 21 years.
Feb. 28. Sarah Farrants, 84 years.
March 7. Elizabeth Sale, 8 years.
March 7. Maria Sale, 18 months.
March 13. Thomas Gardiner of Bury St. Edmunds, 34 years.
March 18. John Spalding, 2 years.
May 12. Sarah Goodchild, 8 years.
June 11. Margaret Ann Byford, 9 months.
June 20. Harriet King of Bury St. Edmunds, 14 months.
Aug. 13. Sarah Gooch, 76 years.
Oct. 24. William Double, 56 years.
Oct. 31. Sarah Ann Pryke, 5 years.
Nov. 2. Esther Race, 18 months.
Nov. 5. Hannah Copsey of Bury St. Edmunds Union Poor House, 81 years.
Nov. 18. Elizabeth Meadows, 8 years.
Nov. 19. Susan Amelia Nunn, 4 years.
Nov. 27. Thomas Pryke, 7 years.
Dec. 20. George Crack of Bury St. Edmunds, 29 years.
Dec. 26. Harriet Bullass, 2 years.
Dec. 30. Thomas Grimwood Saunders, 3 years.
1842. March 25. William Cater, 18 years.
April 26. Harriet wife of John Bullass, 32 years.
May 13. Eliza Last, 4 months.
June 24. William Willingham of Bury St. Edmunds, 84 years.
July 7. Ann dau: (unbapt:) of George & Mary Cater, 6 weeks.

Aug. 20. John Dearson Meller of Bury St. Edmunds, 7 weeks.
Sept. 15. Thomas Gardiner, 75 years.
Sept. 25. Sarah Mison, 76 years.
Oct. 21. Sarah Sanders, 4 days.
Oct. 27. Matthew Gostwick of Saxham Parva, 61 years.
1843. Jan. 29. Robert Ridnall, 46 years.
March 26. Mary Anne Bullass, 11 years.
May 17. Edward Gooch, 82 years.
June 5. John Double, 70 years.
July 13. Mary Varo, 81 years.
July 25. Anne Byford of Ickworth, 82 years.
Aug. 27. John Parr, 64 years.
Sept. 5. Henry Crooks, 34 years.
Sept. 12. Hannah Double of Bury St. Edmunds, 59 years.
Sept. 20. Emily Boreham, 6 months.
Oct. 22. Charles Brown, 10 weeks.
Nov. 23. Mary Race, 29 years.
Dec. 28. Mary Anne Last, 27 years.
1844. Jan. 6. Frederick William Sturgeon, 20 weeks.
Jan. 21. John Gooch.
Jan. 22. John Edwards, Parish Clerk.
Feb. 20. William Levett, 8 months.
March 24. Ann Cooper, single woman, 74 years.
March 24. Edward Willingham, a deaf and dumb man, 47 years.
May 16. Sarah Last, 66 years.
May 19. Robert Gooch of Bury St. Edmunds, 46 years.
June 4. John Tricker, 78 years.
June 7. Anne Goodchild, 22 years.
June 20. Susan wife of Mr. James Scarling, 99 years.
June 26. Thomas Last, 84 years.
Aug. 19. Harriet dau : of William & Emily Gardiner, 6 months.
Sept. 5. Mary wife of John Baker, 69 years.
Sept. 28. Charles son of James & Lucy (Rampling) Boreham, 7 years.
Nov. 5. Charles Double of Buıy St. Edmunds, 66 years.
Nov. 24. James Boreham, 6 years.

Dec. 3. James Salisbury, 40 years.
Dec. 11. Charles son of William & Elizabeth Rowe of Bury, 10 weeks.
1845. Feb. 16. Henry Harroll son of Thomas & Sarah Wade, 4 years & 11 months.
Feb. 25. Thomas Goodchild, 10 months.
March 11. David son of Thomas & Lucy Tweed, 42 years.
March 20. Charlotte wife of Robert Kemp, late widow Rosbrooke, of Bury, 60 years.
April 13. Hannah wife of Abraham Cooper, 48 years.
April 20. Lucy Moyse Pryke, 17 years.
June 1. Ann dau: of Isaac & Mary Ann Boreham, 3 years.
June 15. Harriet dau: of James & Mary Boreham, 2 months.
July 17. Mary widow of William Edwards, 68 years.
Aug. 20. James Ellis, 86 years.
Sept. 17. Ann widow of Michael Sturgeon, 78 years.
Oct. 2. Samuel Mison, 82 years.
Oct. 15. Fanny Petch, 3½ years.
Dec. 25. Louisa Boreham, 2½ years.
1846. Jan. 22. Susan Gooch, 39 years.
Feb. 15. Thomas Evered, 54 years.
April 1. Alfred Evered alias Adams, 3 weeks.
May 1. Mary widow of Edward Musk, 79 years.
May 3. Simon Sale, 87 years.
May 28. Amy Tweed, 6 years.
June 25. Eliza dau: of William Willingham, 21 years.
July 19. Susan wife of William Nunn, 28 years.
Aug. 9. Catharine Offord dau: of Offord & Charlotte Edwards, of Bury, 7 months.
Aug. 15. James son of Stephen & Sophy Paske, 3 months.
Sept. 6. George son of William & Mary Boreham, 1 month.
Sept. 22. Thomas Wade, 66 years.
Sept. 27. Charles Cowper, 11 months.
Oct. 6. Abigail Sergeant, 7 months.
Oct. 9. Henry Metcalf, 3 years.

	Oct.	22.	Adelaide Jane Wigson of Horsecroft, 15 years.
	Oct.	29.	Walter son of George & Amelia Boreham, 11 months.
	Nov.	15.	Charlotte Rosbrooke, of Bury, 20 years.
	Nov.	19.	Josiah Sanders, 30 years.
	Dec.	10.	Mary Sharpe, widow, 82 years.
1847.	Jan.	29.	James McLean, 79 years.
	Jan.	30.	Caroline Scarling, 1 year.
	Feb.	14.	Susan wife of Thomas Orridge, 26 years.
	April	13.	James Palmer, 93 years.
	May	19.	Harry Swann, 4 months.
	June	17.	Frances widow of Thomas Gardiner, 78 years.
	June	26.	Sophia Boreham of Thingoe Union House, 9 years.
	July	8.	Mary Ann Swann, 4 years.
	Aug.	11.	Amos Nunn, 2 years.
	Aug.		Sophia Adams, 29 years.
	Aug.		Lilly Adams, 72 years.
	Oct.	5.	Frederick Cooper of Bury, 24 years.
	Nov.	3.	James Bullass, 80 years.
	Dec.	11.	Harry Musk, 14 months.
1848.	Jan.	17.	John Nunn of Whepstead, 58 years.
	April	24.	Hannah Avis of Horsecroft, 15 months.
	April	30.	Walter Boreham of Bury, 8 months.
	June	14.	Mary Ann Double of Bury, 72 years.
	June	22.	Charles Utting, 38 years.
	June	29.	Joseph Rowe, 15 months.
	June	30.	Emma Wigson of Horsecroft, 28 years.
	Aug.	15.	Elisabeth dau : of George & Susan Brown of Bury, 2 years.
	Oct.	22.	William Thurlow, 65 years.
	Oct.	26.	Susan Ambrose, 73 years.
	Dec.	31.	William Palmer, 88 years.
1849.	Jan.	11.	Anne Perkins, 83 years.
	Jan.	20.	Anne Bowers, 13 days.
	Feb.	1.	William Palmer of Westley, 57 years.
	Feb.	23.	Robert Rooks, 37 years.
	Feb.	27.	George Thomas Rolfe, 6 months.

	April	21.	Benjamin Pryke, 19 years.
	May	28.	Agnes Root, 13 years.
	June	3.	Thomas Rednell, of Bury St. Edmunds Union, 15 years.
	June	24.	James Ellis, 23 years.
	July	18.	Elizabeth Brown, infant.
	July	26.	Anne Sanders, 20 months.
	July	27.	George Boreham, 3 years.
	Aug.	13.	Elizabeth Farrants, 8 years.
	Aug.	22.	Caroline Elsden, 20 years.
	Aug.	22.	Joseph Farrants, 4 years.
	Nov.	28.	George Murking, 19 years.
	Dec.	31.	Martin Edwards, 3 years.
1850.	Jan.	2.	Elizabeth Double, 77 years.
	Feb.	17.	Hannah Palmer, 8 months.
	Feb.	22.	Mary Rutter of Chevington, 71 years.
	March	14.	Hannah King, 23 years.
	June	4.	Frederick Evered, 53 years.
	July	13.	Mary Pitt, 62 years.
	Aug.	4.	Mary Coe of Bury St. Edmunds, 67 years.
	Sept.	1.	Susan dau: of Stephen & Sophia Paske, 17 years.
	Sept.	1.	Henry son of Samuel & Mary Ann Bowers, 6 months.
	Oct.	19.	William Herbert Pratt, 2 weeks.

Appendix I.

CHURCH BRIEFS.

The following list of briefs from 1661 to 1699 is contained in the second volume of the Registers. A brief is defined in the N. E. D. as "a letter patent issued by the Sovereign as Head of the Church, licensing a collection in the churches throughout England for a specified object of charity; called also a church brief or King's letter."

A quotation is there given from Pepys' Diary:—

"1661. June 30. To church, where we observe the trade of briefs is come now up to so constant a course every Sunday that we resolve to give no more to them."

BRIEFS.

Horningshearth Magna. An accompt of such Breiffes as have been collected in the sayd parish since the yeare 1661, as ffolloweth.

		1661.	£	s.	d.
March	31.	Collected for a Burning at ffakenham in Norfolke ...		10 :	2½
Aprill	21.	Collected for the Repayring of Condover Church in Salop, the charge being to the value of 2750 pounds,		15 :	0
Aprill	28.	Collected for the Repayring of Ponfrett Church in Yorkeshire, the losse being to the value of 5000 pounds		18 :	6
Aprill	14.	Collected for a Burning att Ilmister in the County of Somersett, the losse being to the value of £20000;	1 :	10 :	0
May	5.	Collected for the Repayring of Scarborrow Church		15 :	10
May	12.	Collected for a Burning att East Hogborne in Berkshire		8 :	9

			£	s.	d.
May	17.	Collected for a Burning att Hedon in Yorksheire ...		9 :	9
May	26.	Collected for Milton Abbas in Dorsettsheire ...		8 :	9
June	23.	Collected for a Burning att Wapping in Middlesex, the losse being to the value of £1925, ...		5 :	11
July	21.	Collected for the Inhabitants of St. Bartholomews exchange and Bennett ffinch, London, ...		8 :	2
Aug.	11.	Collected for Watringbury in Kent		10 :	3
Sept.	22.	Collected for Ripon in Yorkesheire		16 :	0
Dec.	29.	Collected for the Burning att Oxford, the losse being to the value of £43601, ...	1 :	0 :	2
Jan.	5.	Collected for a Burning att Elmeley Castle in Worcestersheire, the losse being to the value of 4000 pounds,		5 :	7
Jan.	12.	Collected for a Burning att Chester for one Richard Dutton, the losse being to the value of £3500, ...		8 :	4
Feb.	16.	Collected for a Burning at South-Birlingham in ye County of Norfolk for Robert Newham and Edward Peak, ye losse being to ye value of £200, ...		5 :	8
		Collected for a Burning att Chertsey in the County of Surrey, the losse being to the value of 583 pounds, ...		8 :	9
		1662.			
March	30.	Collected for Henry Harrison, Mariner, for a losse att sea, being to the value of £7500, ...		13 :	6
April	6.	Collected for Pricilla ffeitier for a losse by ffyre for £450 the summe of		10 :	0
May	29.	Collected for the Towne of Bridgenoth in the County of Salop, losse by ffyre to the value of £60000,		15 :	6
June	15.	Collected for the Repayring the church of Bolingbrooke in the County of Lincolne, value of £2400,		7 :	4
July	6.	Collected for a Burning att Metheringham in the County of Lincolne, losse to the value of £4959, ...		9 :	6
Sept.	28.	Collected for Anne Walter of Redriffe in Surrey upon her losse att sea to the value of 1600 pounds, Paid to Constable.		7 :	0

			£	s.	d.
Nov.	9.	Collected for Phillip Capon of Torring in Sussex upon a Burning of his Malthouse etc to the value of £450, Pd to Constable.		6 :	7
Feb.	22.	Collected for the Parish Church in Gravesend to the value of £2528, ...		7 :	11
March	1.	Collected for Repayring the harbor of New-haven in Sussex to the value of £4000, ...		8 :	4
		1663.			
June	29.	Collected for a burning att Beckeve		5 ..	0
		Collected for a burning att Milton in Com: Cambridge		6 ..	0
Aug.	16.	Collected for a burning att ffordinbridge in Hamshire		7 ..	0
Oct.	11.	Collected for a burning at Tyverton in Devonshere ...		6 ..	6
Jan.	10.	Collected for a burning att Hexam in Northumberland		11 ..	3
Jan.	17.	Collected towards ye losse of William Sandwell sustained by sea		9 ..	2
Feb.	7.	Collected towards ye losse of John Jones sustayned by fyre		5 ..	0
Feb.	28.	Collected for a burning for John Norman of Southwell, Essex		5 ..	0
March	.	Collected for repayring Grymsby haven		7 ..	6
March	13.	Collected for repayring Harwich Church		7 ..	0
—	—	Collected for repayring Cromer Church and haven ...		9 ..	4
		1664.			
April	3.	Collected for a burning of ye blew bore in Houlbourne		7 ..	0
April	30.	Collected for Richard Clarke of Icklingham, Suffolk	1 ..	6 ..	0
June	5.	Collected for repayring Witham Church in Sussex ...		13 ..	3
July	10.	Collected for a burning of Tho: Burchett in Surry ...		6 ..	8
July	31.	Collected for Tinmouth Church in the Co. of Northumberland		5 ..	3
Aug.	13.	Collected then upon a Breife for Robert Ensdell for a losse of a shipp att sea		6 ..	4
Sept.	25.	Collected for a Burning at Grantham in Lincolnshire		8 ..	6
Jan.	1.	Collected for repayring Sandwich church		12 ..	0

			£	s.	d.
Jan.	8.	Collected for Edward Chorsham [?] of Grantham in Lincolnshire		6 ..	0
Feb.	12.	Collected for Lawrence Holder of Clacton in Essex		6 ..	7
Feb.	26.	Collected for Henery Lisle of Gisborne in Yorkshere		10 ..	6

1665.

			£	s.	d.
April	5.	Collected for repayring of Basing church in Southhamptonshere		7 ..	6
April	16.	Collected for a burning at Nether Wallop [?] ...		6 ..	4
April	21.	Collected for repayring of St. Maries church of Chester		10 ..	0
July	16.	Collected for John Chapman att Shadywell, Suffolk		15 ..	9
Aug.		Collected for ye releife of ye infected with ye sicknesse	1 ..	19 ..	1½
Sept.	6.	Collected for ye reliefe of the infected with the sicknesse	1 ..	14 ..	1
Sept.	24.	Collected for ye inhabitants of Noth church in Hertford		10 ..	0
		Also collected for the inhabitants of Shadwell in Essex		5 ..	0
Oct.	3.	Collected for ye releif of the infected with ye plague	1 ..	14 ..	6
Oct.	22.	Collected for ye inhabitants of Bidford in Warwickshire		4 ..	6
		Collected for Bramble stranger of Luton in Bedfordshire		2 ..	6
Nov.	8.	Collected for the releife of the infected with ye plague	1 ..	13 ..	4

1666.

			£	s.	d.
May	2.	Collected for ye releife of the infected with the plague	1 ..	3 ..	0
June	6.	Collected for the releife of the infected with the plague	1 ..	2 ..	9
Feb.	24.	Collected for ye repayiring of Clun church in Salop		11 ..	4

		1667.	£	s.	d.
June	23.	Collected for ye releife of ye inhabitants of Hinxton in Cambridgeshire		6 ..	8
July	7.	Collected for ye releif of John Osborn, Russia Merchant		4 ..	4½
		Collected for ye releif of ye inhabitants of Worksopp in Nottingamshire		4 ..	4½
		1668.			
May	31.	Collected for ye reliefe of Haverhill in Suffolk ...		17 ..	8½
Aug.	9.	Collected for ye reliefe of Loughborough in the County of Leicester		7 ..	10
Dec.	22.	Collected for ye reliefe of those captives under ye Turks dominion		9 ..	0
March	21.	Collected for ye redemption of captives under ye Turks, for loss at sea and by fire		12 ..	0
		1669.			
May	23.	Collected for ye reliefe of some distressed persons (impoverished by pirats) in ye Isle of Canon in Ireland		2 ..	0
Aug.	1.	Collected for a burning att Thetford in Norfolk ...		12 ..	3
		1670.			
July	3.	Collected for a burning at Samersham in Huntingtonshire		6 ..	6
July	10.	Collected for a burning in Beckles in Suffolk ...		6 ..	9
Sept.	11.	Collected for a burning at Collinend in Co. of Northampton		3 ..	9
Oct.	23.	Collected for ye redemption of captives ...		6 ..	7
		1671.			
April	2.	Collected for & towards ye redemption of captives out of Turkish slavery	3 ..	14 ..	10
July	23.	Coll: for a burning at Meer in Wilts.		9 ..	0
July	30.	Coll: for a burning in Isleam in Cambrigshire ...		13 ..	0
Oct.	15.	Coll: for & towards ye repairing of ye Parish Church of Waltham Abby in Essex		7 ..	6

o

			£	s.	d.
		1672.			
Jan.	12.	Coll: for a burning at great fford in Lincolnshire		5 ..	10
		1673.			
June ?	22.	Coll: towards ye repaire of ye parish church, chancell & parsonage house of little livermore in Co. of Suffolk		9 ..	4
		1674.			
July	4.	Coll: towards the loss by ffire at ffording-bridge in Hampshire		11 ..	10
Aug.	16.	Coll: towards the repaire of St. Katharine's Hospitall at London		6 ..	6
Nov.	15.	Coll: towards the loss by ffire at Litleton in Middlesex		3 ..	1
March	21.	Coll: for the ffire at ffording-bridge in Co. of Hampshire		11 ..	11½
		1675.			
May	9.	Coll: towards the ffire at Nether Wallop in Hampshire		5 ..	6
May	30.	Coll: towards the repaire of the church at Benenden in Co. of Kent		4 ..	9
July	4.	Coll: towards the two ffires in Redburne in Co. of Hertford		2 ..	7
Sept.	19.	Coll: then towards the loss of the Towne of Watton in Co. of Norfolk by ffire		5 ..	8
		1676.			
April	16.	Collected then for Newent church		4 ..	10
May	14.	Coll: in our Parish for the rebuilding of the church of Oswestree in Shropshire		4 ..	0
May	28.	Coll: towards Anthony Barretts loss by ffire at Dalham		7 ..	0
July	16.	Coll: towards the releif of Northampton ...	1 ..	11 ..	3
		1678.			
June	9.	Coll: towards ye relief of William Rushley of Rickmersworth		3 ..	10

			£	s.	d.
		Coll: towards ye relief of the Towne of Wem in Co. of Salop		6	10
		Coll: towards ye losse of Josiah Buxbanck of Harlington in Middlesex		5	1

1679.

			£	s.	d.
Aug.	3.	Coll: towards ye losse of ye widdow Grime of Horsham St. Faith, Norfolk, ...		10	6
Aug.	24.	Coll: for ye rebuilding of ye church of Windlesham in Surrey		8	10
Sept.	7.	Coll: towards ye losse of Thomas Osborne of Dover		4	4
Nov.	23.	Coll: towards ye losse of William Browne and others of ye Towne of Lurgishull in Co. of Wilts		8	0

1680.

			£	s.	d.
March	28.	Coll: towards ye losse of William Flint and others of ye Towne of Weedon Beck in Co. of Northampton		4	7
July	11.	Coll: then towards ye losse of ye inhabitants of Dearham in ye Co. of Norfolk	1	0	5
Oct.	31.	Coll: towards ye redemption of ye Captives at Algiers	1	7	9
Feb.	6.	Coll: towards ye losse of Henry Wastle, Thomas King and others of ye Town of Duxford in Co. of Camb:		5	3

1682.

			£	s.	d.
Sept.	17.	Coll: for the breife for Caister		6	2
Nov.	26.	Coll: towards the loss of Thomas Nichalls of London		4	10
Jan.	21.	Coll: for the breife for New Windsor		8	1

1683.

			£	s.	d.
May	20.	Coll: for the breif for Ensham in Oxfordshire ...		4	4
June	24.	Coll: for the breif for Stooke		4	0

			£	s.	d.
July	15.	Coll: for the breife for Preston Candever in Southampton		8 ..	6
Oct.	28.	Coll: for Channel row in London		6 ..	10
Jan.	6.	Coll: for Bassingborn in Cambridgeshire... ...		8 ..	6
		1684.			
April	20.	Coll: for Wapping in London		17 ..	1
June	15.	Coll: for Bradninch in Devon ...		7 ..	2
July	13.	Coll: for Warsop in Nottinghamshire		8 ..	2
Jan.	11.	Coll: for Saresden in Oxfordshire ...		5 ..	2
Jan.	19.	Collected for Ely		6 ..	9
		1685.			
July	19.	Coll: for the Village of Kirksanton and Haverigge		8 ..	0
Sept.	6.	For Alsriston in Sussex ...		4 ..	10
Oct.	4.	For Stanton in Suffolke			
Oct.	11.	For John Pyle, clerke of Stody in Norfolke		14 ..	6
Nov.	22.	For Beamister in Dorsetshire		9 ..	3
Jan.	10.	Coll: for Bullfoid in Wilts ...		7 ..	6½
		1689.			
Nov.	12.	Collected for the Irish Protestants ...	4 ..	4 ..	0
		1691.			
June		Collected for Stafford ...		2 ..	0
Oct.	2.	For St. Ives		7 ..	0
		1693.			
Aug.	6.	For redemption of slaves ...	1 ..	10 ..	0
Nov.	5.	For Churchill ...		6 ..	8
Dec.	3.	For Dennis Gunton		4 ..	11
Dec.	17.	For Wooller in Northumberland ...		5 ..	1
		1694.			
Sept.	2.	For Yalding in Kent		5 ..	6
Sept.	14.	For the French Protestants	2 ..	0 ..	0
Sept.	30.	Coll: for St. Briget's church in Chester ...		2 ..	6
Jan.	13.	Collected for Yorke		8 ..	5

			£	s.	d.
		1695.			
June	22.	Collected for Netherhaven ...		7 ..	6
		For Gillingham in Dorsetshire		8 ..	5
May	26.	Coll: for Grandcester in Cambridgeshire		5 ..	0
June	9.	Coll: for Trinity Church in Kingston upon hull ...		3 ..	0
Nov.	17.	Coll: for Mr. Joseph Peters		5 ..	6
		1696.			
		Coll: for Mr. Morley in Mildenhall		6 ..	3
		Coll: for the church of Westhatton in Lincolnshire		5 ..	9
		1697.			
		Collected for Litchfeild		6 ..	10
		Collected for Wolverhampton		10 ..	0
		1698.			
		Collected for Richard Uriel		3 ..	9
Jan.	2.	Collected for Newberry		4 ..	4
Feb.	9.	Collected for Soham in Cambridgeshire		3 ..	11
March	6.	Collected for Derby Court		5 ..	8
April	3.	Collected for Minehead		6 ..	0
April	17.	Collected for Lancaster		4 ..	9
May	8.	Collected for Drury lane		5 ..	2
		1699.			
April	10.	Collected for the Vaudois in Piedmont	3 ..	8 ..	5½

Appendix II.

Monumental Inscriptions within Horringer Church.

Nos. 1, 2, are flat stones in the Chancel; Nos. 3, 4, 5, 6, 7, 8, are flat stones in the Vestry; Nos. 9, 10, 11, 12, are on the West wall of the North aisle; No. 13 is in the Tower; Nos. 14, 15, 16, 17, 18, are in the South Chapel. Originally Nos. 1 to 12 were all in the Chancel, and No. 13 on the West gallery.

1. Here lie the remains of Peter Gedge who died Jan. 7, 1818, aged 59 years.
   A tablet to his memory is erected in St. Mary's Church, Bury.
   The man of benevolence, integrity, and Christian piety.
   Also of Ann his wife who died April 16, 1840, aged 70 years.
   Ann daughter of the above died Dec. 14, 1824, aged 27, and was buried in the churchyard.

2. *The upper part of this stone is concealed by the choir seats. All that can now be read is as follows:*
   said Christian Lucas. This stone was laid by Mr. John Lurkin and Mr. Thomas Roper, the executors of Mrs. Sach.

3. Here lyeth the body of William Lucas Esquire who departed this life Jan. 1639.
   Here lyeth the body of Elizabeth Lucas wife of Dr. Lucas, who dyed June 24, 1668.
   Hic jacet Dr. Lucas qui obiit May 24, 1698, ætat: 83.

4. Here lyeth the body of Ann the wife of Mr. Abraham Kedington and eldest daughter of Mr. John Ewin of this Parish who departed this life Sept. 30 anno dommini 1728, ætatis 27.
   Also Abraham their son who died an infant.

5. H. S. E. Edvardus Foster A.M. Ecclesiæ Badeliensis Pastor per annos xiv, fidelis, pius et indefessus, qui studiis assiduis & exinde morbis exhaustus gregi æquue ac amicis flebilis omnibusque desideratus, obiit (heu præmature) v Kal. Oct. anno salutis MDCCIV, ætatis xxxvii. Uxor moerens posuit.

Here lyeth also the body of Mrs. Ann Foster, daughter of Mr. Edward Foster and Hester his wife, who dyed April 1, 1705, being fifteen weekes old.

6. Underneath this stone are interred the remains of Henry Cameron Cherry, son of the Revd. Henry Curtis Cherry M.A. curate of this parish and Anne Alicia his wife. Born Aug. 13, 1823. Died June 11, 1824.

7. Catharine Maria daughter of the Revd. Edward Gould and Mary Ann Penelope his wife. Died Jan. 5, 1832, aged 2 months.

8. *This inscription is on a small brass let into the stone.*

Here lyeth the body of Mary Lucas the eldest daughter of William Lucas of Horscroft in Horninger esquier, which departed this life Oct. 13, A.D. 1618.

9. To the Memory of Woodward Bidwell Esq. who died June 6, 1826, in the 74th year of his age.

Also of Susanna his wife, daughter of the late Gregory Sparke Esq. of Risby in this County, who died July 11, 1837, in the 70th year of her age.

Their mortal remains are deposited at the north side of this church.

Blessed are the pure in heart, for they shall see God.

The memory of the just is blessed.

This tablet is erected by an affectionate friend and near relation as a grateful memorial of their virtues and of the constant proofs of their kindness and friendship experienced for many years.

10. Valentine Munbee Esq. departed this life Sept. 24, 1750, aged 55 years. He was a person of great good sense, learning, knowledge and integrity, qualities which made him beloved and esteemed when alive, and bewailed when dead, by those who were always dear to him, his family and his friends.

Mr. Gage thus describes the arms: Azure fretty Or, on a canton gules, a cross formè Argent.

11. Here lyeth the body of Dame Elizabeth Gipps relict of Sir Richard Gipps of Horrenger. She departed this life Nov. 11, 1715, in the 67 year of her age.

On a lozenge-shaped shield are the arms of Gipps impaling Poley.

12. Here lyeth the body of Sir Richard Gipps of Little Horninger in the County of Suffolk Knight, who marryed Elizabeth the eldest daughter of Sir Edmund Polly of Badly of the same County Knight, who dyed Sept. 28, A.D. 1681, in ye 36 yeare of his age.

This stone has two shields, one of which has the arms of Gipps, and the other has Gipps impaling Poley.

13. To Arthur John Brooke Esq. by whom this church was completely repaired and beautified; the pulpit, desk, pews and gallery erected; the East window framed with coloured glass; the bells, with the addition of a new one, recast; and the clock presented; the inhabitants of Horningsheath (his native village) inscribe this tablet as a memorial of his munificence. MDCCCXVIII.

14. Sacred to the memory of Elizabeth relict of William Wigson Esq. of Colchester, Essex, who died Aug. 2, 1830, aged 79 years.

15. Sacred to the memory of Adelaide Jane, youngest daughter of William Bacon Wigson and of Mary Ann his wife, who died Oct. 15, 1846, aged 15 years.
Also of Emma their second daughter, who died June 23, 1848, aged 27 years.

16. Mary Ann Wigson. Born Feb. 4, 1819. Died Jan. 14, 1824.
Thomas Wigson an infant, died Nov. 1, 1824.
Henry Cooke Wigson, died Jan. 17, 1826, aged 2 years, 4 months.
Frederic Turnor Wigson. Born July 3, 1829. Died Nov. 7, 1830.
Septimus Seaber Wigson. Born Jan. 1. 1833. Died April 20, 1833.

17. William Bacon Wigston. Born Jan. 30, 1787. Died Feb. 7, 1872.
Mary Ann Wigston. Born Oct. 16, 1793. Died Aug. 28, 1879.

18. D O M S Surgite, mortui. In te, Domine, speravi, non confundar in æternum.
Hic jacet corpus Johannis Cooke generosi, qui obiit Julii 12, anno salutis 1653, ætatis suæ 72.
Et corpus Thomæ Covel generosi, qui obiit Aug. 20, A.D. 1715, ætatis suæ 81.

Et corpus Judithæ uxoris Thomæ Covel generosi, quæ filia erat Ambrosii Blagg armigeri, et obiit March 1 anno MDCCVII, ætatis suæ 87.

Et corpus Margaretæ Blagg filiæ etiam dicti Ambrosi, quæ obiit—anno—ætatis suæ. In spe beatæ Resurrectionis ad æternam gloriam.

Mr. Gage in his History of Thingoe Hundred, 1838, mentions the following which I cannot see now.

1. Here lieth Christian Sach, the late wife of Thomas Sach, gent. of Great Horringer, who was formerly the wife of William Lucas Esq., who died in Sept. A.D. 1666, aged 79 years.

2. Hic jacet Lucy Chapman, ætatis 21 annorum, nuper uxor Henrici Chapman, generosi, nupt: filia Gulielmi Lucas, armigeri. Quæ dum vixit bona fuit mulier testis est populus; melior filia testes sunt parentes; optima uxor testis maritus: pietate nullæ secunda testis est Deus.

   This soul too rich a prize for mortal race,
   Endew'd with nature and the gifts of grace,
   Once view'd this world, and then in much disdain
   Left this void earth and now in glory reigne.

Arms of Chapman impaling Lucas.

3. Here lieth buried the body of Thomas Stanton Esq. of Mildenhall in the County of Suffolk, who died Aug. 20, 1661, aged 61.

He also says there were stones with the following names on them, which I cannot now see:

Revd. Thomas Smith, Rector of Horringer, who died April 12, 1724, aged 68 years;

Elizabeth his second wife who died Feb. 26, 1736/7, aged 75.

Thomas Keddington Esq. who died Sept. 6, 1728, aged 57 years,

Christian his wife who died Oct. 10, 1735, aged 65 years,

Abraham their son who died Oct. 5, 1745, aged 43 years;

Ann Mortlock their daughter who died March 9, 1746, aged 51 years;

Judy Keddington who died Nov. 1761, aged 57.

Stephen Brooks, gent., who died Aug. 4, 1798, aged 32.

APPENDIX III.

MONUMENTAL INSCRIPTIONS IN HORRINGER CHURCHYARD.

Nos. 1 to 33 inclusive are in the triangular space between the two paths leading up to the Chancel door and South porch respectively.

Nos. 34, 35, 36, 37, lie flat at the East end of the South chapel.

Nos. 38 to 79 are on the South side of the Church between the path leading to the chancel door and the East hedge.

Nos. 80 to 96 are on the South side of the Church between the path leading to the South porch and the West hedge.

Nos. 97 to 119 are under the tower.

Nos. 120 to 220 are on the North side of the Church.

I have left out the words "Here lies" or "In memory of," and have sometimes put [died] instead of its longer equivalent. With such exceptions the inscriptions are given exactly. Occasionally differences will be found between the tombstones and the Register, both as to the age of the person buried and as to the year of burial. Owing to the foolish and exaggerated use of thin strokes by stonecutters, the difference between 1 and 4 is sometimes very soon annihilated.

1. Richard ye son of Richard and Martha Elsden, who died June 23, 1756, aged 4 years.

Also Jane their daughter died July 26, 1756, aged 16 months.

The great Jehovah full of love
An angel bright did send,
To snatch away these spotless doves
To joys that have no end.

2. Martha Elsden who died Feb. 1. 1783 aged 56 years.

3. Isabella wife of John Woodruffe who died June 18, 1738, aged 32 years.

Short was my time, the longer is my rest;
God called me hence because he thought it best;
Therefore dear friends lament for me no more;
I am not lost, but gone awhile before.

4. Elizabeth Elsden who died Jan. 3. 1749, aged 53 years.

Affliction sore long time I bore,
Physicians all in vain,
Till God did please to give me ease,
And rid me of my pain.

5. Mrs. Elizabeth Houghton, daughter of Mr. John Houghton of Westley, died July 1718 aged . . years.

6. Thomas Mitchell died May 29, 1880, aged 55 years.

Thy will be done. Mat. vi. 10.

Also Elizabeth his widow, died Sept. 28, 1889, aged 65 years.

Resting in hope.

7. William Plum who died Feb. 12, 1864, aged 67 years.

Gracious is the Lord and righteous, yea our God is merciful. Psalm 116, 5.

Also Mary his wife, who died Dec. 27, 1870, aged 75 years.

The weary are at rest.

8. M. S. Reverendi viri Timothei Adamson et Mariæ uxoris ejus. Obiërunt, ille 8 die Aprilis, illa 15 Septembris, anno 1716.

Ille natus annos 79, illa 76.

Hic etiam jacent tres eorumdem filii.

Abi, viator, et disce mori.

Prope ab hoc tumulo sepulti sunt Johannes Walker generosus et Maria uxor ejus.

I give Mr. Gage's description of the shield on this stone: Three crosslets fitchée, a mullet, Adamson, impaling a cross flory between three trefoils slipped.

9. John Dearson Meller who died June 13, 1839, aged 85 years.

Mary, wife of John Dearson Meller, who died Aug. 15, 1826, aged 79 years.

10. John Dearson Meller who died Jan. 14, 1767, aged 48 years.
Ann his wife died May 26, 1763, aged 36 years.
Also of John Dearson their son who died in his infancy in 1748.
Also Mrs. Mary Nickhols their aunt, who died in the year 1769 aged 72 years.

11. Stephen Crick who [died] Nov. 25, 1816, aged 73 years.

Hark from the tomb what doleful sound!
My ears attend the cry;
Ye living men, come view the ground
Where you will shortly lie.

Sarah Rudland died Oct. 5, 1824, aged 70 years.

12. Sarah wife of Stephen Crick, who died Nov. 1. 1804, aged 77 years.
That ye be not slothful, but followers of them who through faith and patience inherit the promises. Hebr. vi. 12.

13. Elizabeth the daughter of John Kettle sen. who died May 14, 1731, ætatis 32.

14. John Kettle who died March 18, 1729, ætatis 63 [?].

15. Hic jacet corpus Gulielmi Covel generosi, qui obiit xxi Novemb: anno 1661.
Et Gulielmus Covel generosus, filius ejus, ætat: lxxix, qui obiit ix die April, 1707.

16. John Dearson Meller of Bury St. Edmunds, who died May 22, 1863, aged 76 years.

In the day of Judgment, Good Lord deliver us.

Sarah, widow of John Dearson Meller, born Dec. 11. 1809, departed March 3, 1876.
O ye spirits and souls of the righteous, bless ye the Lord, praise him and magnify him for ever.
Also of John Dearson son of John Dearson and Sarah Meller, who died Aug. 1842, aged 7 weeks.

17. Susannah Meller who died April 25, 1840, aged 62 years.

18. Here lyeth the body of Thor: Wickes, who dyed 14 Feb. 1701, aged 32 years.

The peaceful grave my bons shall keep
Untell that glorious day,
I shall awake from my long sleep,
And leave this bed of clay.

19. Mary the wife of John Whymark, who died May 5, 1771, aged 31 years.

20. Here lyeth the body of John Arnsbey,* who married Hester daughter of Josias Wright, who dyed 4 March, 1697, aged 39 years.

21. Edward Rutherford who fell asleep in Jesus, March 12, 1883, aged 32.

Now is the spirit with the Lord,
And soon the mouldering frame
Shall put on immortality,
And rise in Jesu's name.

22. Here lieth the body of Ann Barton, widow, who died 26 Feb. 1727/8, aged 75 years.

23. Margaret Gault daughter of John and Anne Ewin. She died Oct. 8, 1764, aged 35 years.

24. John Ewin who died May 25, 1745, aged 76 years. Also 2 sons and 2 daughters.

25. Ann wife of John Ewin sen., who died June 21, 1763, aged 88 years.
Also John son of John Ewin jun. died Dec. 9. 1717, aged 18.

26. Here lyeth ye body of Margreat Ewin wife of John Ewin, who departed Aug. 26, 1723, aged 85 years.

27. Here lyeth the body of John Ewin who [died] May 14, 1703, aged 69 years.

28. Hannah the daughter of John Ewin, died May 23, 1721, aged 17 years.

All you who . . . . . . do see,
Take care how you all times prepared be.
You see how sudingly death called mee,
So sudingly may he summuns ye:
Your life's uncerten for you know not when,
You are hear to day and tomorrow gone.

* Ernesby in the Registers.

29. William Ewin who died 29 July anno domini 1728, aged 21 years.

O thinke on heaven and on God's mercy call,
In early years God gave to me my fall.

30. David Hill who died Sept. 23, 1786, aged 48 years.

31. Theophyla Harvey who died Oct. 7, 1791, aged 51 years.

32. William Godfrey late of Bury St. Edmunds gent, who departed this life Aug. 29, 1725, aged 61 years.

As likewise of Mary his wife, who died Dec. 23, 1731, aged 73 years.

33. Edward Drew who died May 12, 1812, aged 68 years.

34. William son of Isaac & Mary Brook, who died March 7, 1770 aged 1 month.

35. Castle Goodchild who died April 21, 1782, aged 61 years.

36. In memory of three children of Edward Drew jun. & Elizabeth his wife.

Francis died April 11, 1773, aged 10 days. William died April 16, 1773, aged 12 days. Edward died Jan. 17, 1774, aged 9 months, 13 days.

37. Susan the wife of Castle Goodchild, who died July 26, 1784, aged 73 years.

38. Elizabeth wife of John Adkin, who died Aug. 4, 1819, in the 60th year of her age.

39. John Adkin, who died April 12, 1831, aged 74 years.

A loving husband, father dear,
Such was he who's buried here;
We hope his soul is gone to rest,
In Christ alone we can be blest.

40. Thomas Sargant dyed Jan. 20, 1704, aged 46 years.

41. Margareta wife of John Hibble, who died Dec. 2, 1739, aged 31 years.

42. Elizabeth wife of Joshua Bunting who died Nov. 15, 1753 aged 67 years.

A long affliction did my life attend,
But time with patience brought it to an end,
And laid me in this bed of clay
Untill the joyfull Resurrection day.

43. Joshua Bunting who died June 3, 1757 in ye 80th year of his age.

As time and hours pass away,
So doth ye life of man decay;
Weep not for me, my glass is run,
It is the Lord, His will be done.

44. Elijah Pryke. Born Jan. 10, 1831. Died July 5, 1860.

The dearest friends on earth must part,
And bid adieu to all;
Happy are those that are prepared
To meet that solemn call.

45. Benjamin son of Thomas & Kezia Pryke. Died April 18, 1849, aged 20 years.
Kezia wife of Thomas Pryke. Died Feb. 18, 1852, aged 50 years.

Put your trust in God, for he will never forsake you.

46. Thomas Pryke, who died Jan. 30, 1879, aged 81 years.

In thee, O Lord, have I put my trust.

47. Sarah wife of Thomas Pryke, who died Sept. 25, 1868, aged 57 years.
I heard a voice from heaven saying unto me, write, From henceforth blessed are the dead which die in the Lord; even so saith the Spirit; for they rest from their labours.

48. Thomas Willingham sen., who died in 1776 aged 88 years.
Also Alice his wife, who died April 4, 1764, aged 69 years.

49. William Newport, who died Feb. 7, 1728 aged .3 [?] years.
Ann* Newport died June 25, 1716, aged 66 years.

50. William Pond, who died May 10, 1827, aged 72 years.
Rachael his wife, who died Dec. 9, 1830, aged 77 years.

51. William Moyse who died Jan. 5, 1820, aged 35 years.

Think, living men, how frail is man!
How few his days, how short his span!
Who can secure their vital breath
Against the bold demands of death?

52. Lewes Mortlock, who died Aug. 27, 1739, aged 40 years.

53. Ann the wife of Thomas Atkin, who died Sept. 1818, aged 35 years.

54. Elizabeth wife of Joseph Hammond sen. of Horningsheath, who died March 7, 1761, aged 70 years.

As days and hours do pass away,
So doth the life of man decay.

* Called Mary in the Registers. Ed.

55. John Double, who died Dec. 30, 1799, aged 55 years.
Ann his wife, who died Dec. 21, 1825, aged 73 years.

O cruel death, that would not spare
A loving husband and a tender father dear;
This world he have left and us behind,
Our guide to lament and friends to find.

56. William Swithin Double, son of John & Ann Double, who died Aug. 8, 1780, aged 1 [or 4] years.

57. George Scarff Westrup, son of John and Susanna Westrup, who [died] May 7, 1784, aged 6 months.

58. Mary Ann daughter of George and M. A. Double, who died May 22, 1806, aged 23 weeks.

59. George Scarffe Double who died July 5, 1825, aged 50 years.

The best of husbands the grave incloses here,
A tender father to his children dear;
Great was our loss for his eternal gain,
But hope in Heaven we shall meet again.

Also Mary-Ann wife of the above George Scarffe Double, who died June 9, 1848, in the 72 year of her age.

60. William Nayler the son of George Scarffe and Mary Ann Double, who died Aug. 1. 1830, aged 17 years.

Our life hangs by a single thread,
Which soon is cut and we are dead;
Then boast not, reader, of thy might,
Alive at morn and dead at night.

61. John Beales who [died] Jan. 18, 1799, aged 80 years.
Deaf and dumb from his infancy.

62. Christian the wife of John Beales of Horningsheath, who died March 5, 1804, aged 57 years.

While sorrow weeps o'er Virtue's sacred dust,
Our tears become us and our grief is just:
Such were the tears he shed who grateful pays
This last sad tribute of his love and praise,

Who mourns the best of wives and friends combin'd;
Mourns her, not murmurs, sighs but not despairs,
Feels as a man, but as a Christian bears.

63. William Edwards, who died Aug. 6, 1833, aged 62 years. He was wheelwright of this parish 33 years.
Mary his wife, who died July 13, 1845, aged 68 years.

64. Thomas French, who [died] Sept. 28, 1853, aged 41 years.

Our life hangs by a slender thread,
And soon is cut and we are dead;
Then boast not, reader, of thy might,
Alive at morn and dead at night.

65. Thomas Tweed, who died May 13, 1852, aged 85 years.

Afflictions sore long time I bore,
Physicians were in vain,
Till God did please to give me ease,
And free'd me of my pain.

66. John Pearsons, who died May 22, 1839, aged 74 years.
Also John Smith, son of John and Mary Ann Smith, who died May 22, 1837, aged 2 years.

67. Elizabeth the wife of John Pearsons, who died Feb. 13, 1833, aged 62 years.

Thou art gone to the grave, we no longer behold thee,
Nor tread the rough path of the world by thy side;
But the wide arms of mercy are spread to enfold thee,
And sinners may hope since the Saviour has died.

Thou art gone to the grave, but we're wrong to deplore thee,
When God was thy ransom, thy guardian, thy guide;
He gave thee and took thee and soon will restore thee,
Where death has no sting since the Saviour has died.

68. Thomas the son of John and Elizabeth Pearsons, who died Oct. 10, 1831, in the 20th year of his age.

Say, sprightly youth, dost thou on life presume?
Observe the date and tremble at this tomb;
To health nor strength nor youthful vigour trust;
Behold here death has laid them in the dust.

P

69. George Tweed, who died Sept. 14, 1877, aged 76 years.

On Jordan's stormy banks I stand,
And cast a wistful eye
To Canaan's fair and happy land,
Where my possessions lie.

Sarah the beloved wife of George Tweed, whodiedMarch 2, 1872, aged 71 years.

Why should our tears in sorrow flow
When God recalls his own,
And bids them leave a world of woe
For an immortal crown?

70. Susan dearly beloved wife of Joseph Alston Murton, who died April 6, 1865, aged 30 years.

Also of Henry, eldest and well beloved son of the above, who died April 13, 1865, aged 13 months.

Also of Charles Willie, son of J. A. and Susan Murton, who died Dec. 26, 1865, aged 9 months.

71. Edith the beloved wife of Charles Bilson, who entered into rest Sept. 19, 1878, in the 55th year of her age.

Also Matilda beloved daughter of the above, who fell asleep Nov. 13, 1877, in the 25th year of her age.

Our loved ones are absent from the body but at home with the Lord.

Write, Blessed are the dead, etc.

72. Joseph Bridgman, who died June 6, 1863, aged 70 years.

Also Charles son of the above, died in America Aug. 4, 1863, aged 36 years.

73. Rebecca Copping, who died July 5, 1869, aged 73 years.

For 43 years a faithful servant and beloved friend in the Bristol family at Ickworth.

74. Abraham Elsden, who died June 29, 1864, aged 25 years.

In the midst of life we are in death. Of whom may we seek for succour but of thee, O Lord.

75. John Elsden, who died Oct. 2, 1871, aged 68 years.

For me to live is Christ, but to die is gain. Thy will be done.

76. R. Cook died Aug. 26, 1839, aged 22 years.

77. Edward Musk, who died Feb. 9, 1841, aged 70 years.

An aged Christian slumbers here,
Whose faith was strong, his love sincere;
Content he passed life's little span
In fearing God and serving man.

Also Mary-Ann his wife, who died April 26, 1846, aged 79 years.

78. William Frost, who died Nov. 10, 1826, aged 36 years.

79. John Brewster, who died March 1828, aged 82 years.
Also Elizabeth his wife, who died Nov. 1819, aged 72 years.

80. William Last, who died Jan. 2, 1827, aged 32 years.

His cheerful mind & vigorous frame
Evinc'd no symptoms of decay;
His foundering heart too large became,
And Heaven beckon'd him away;
A widow's grief and parents love
Resigned with faith to Him above.

81. James Evered, who died Jan. 2, 1831, aged 79 years.
Susan wife of James Evered, who died Feb. 28, 1820, aged 56 years.

82. Thomas Wade, who died Sept. 17, 1846, aged 66 years.
Ann his wife, who died June 6, 1830, aged 50 years.
Also Ann their daughter, who died April 26, 1831, aged 12 years.
Likewise Henry Harrold Wade, son of Thomas & Sarah Wade, who died Feb. 10, 1844, aged 4 years.

83. Elizabeth the wife of Henry Cater, who died June 14, 1805 aged 62 years.
Also Henry Cater, who died Feb. 5, 1825, aged 79 years.

84.* [Michael Houghton] who died Jan. 21, 1771, aged 67 years.
[Hannah Houghton] who died Oct. 1, 1775, aged 73 years.

Afflictions sore long time we bore,
Physicians were in vain,
Till God did please to give us ease,
And rid us of our pain.

* The upper part of this stone is gone. What is printed within brackets I have supplied from the Register of Burials.

85. Sarah Wilkin, who died Jan. 10, 1861, aged 81 years.
Our Lord Jesus Christ who died for us, that whether we wake or sleep we should live together with him.

86. Edward Godfrey of Risby, dyed Jan. 10 1705, aged 82 years.

87. Jane Harvey widow, who died May 8, 1739, aged 82 years.
Also Thomas Harvey her son, died May 12, 17[52], in ye 54th year of his age, after having serv'd ye Rt Hon. John, Earl of Bristol, upwards of 45 years.

88. Here lies waiting for the resurrection of the flesh the body of Mary Ann Kemp who [died] Oct. 22, 1858. Her distressed relatives placed this tomb as a monument of their sorrow and of their hope.
Here lies waiting for the resurrection of the flesh the body of John Kemp who [died] Oct. 26, 1867, aged 74.

89. Elizabeth daughter of Robert & Mary Jacob, who died Feb. 3, 1762, aged 20 years.
(Here follow 4 lines which are illegible.)

90. Here lyeth the body of Mary wife of John Rolph sen, who died Nov. 16, 1703, aged 62 years.

91. John Langham who died June 30, 1854, aged 88 years.
Also Elizabeth his wife, who died June 29, 1855, aged 92 years.
To this end Christ both died and rose and revived, that he might be Lord both of the dead and living. Rom. xiv. 9.

92. Thomas Sharpe, who died May 12, 1802, aged 64 years.
Elizabeth the wife of Thomas Sharpe, who died April 10, 1798, aged 63 years.

93. William Parsons, who died Jan. 2, 1801, aged 72 years.

This silent grave my dust contains,
My soul releas'd from mortal chains;
My weeping friends, prepare to come,
That heaven may be our lasting home.

Alice his wife, who died March 22, 1834, aged 79 years.

A loving wife, a tender mother dear,
A faithful friend, lies buried here;
We hope her soul is gone to rest,
In Jesus Christ we all are blest.

94. Richard Boyse, who died June 9, 1766, aged 72 years.

Dear wife, forbear to mourn or weep
Till I have taken my heavenly sleep;
And when the blisfull day appear,
I hope in Heaven to meet you their.

95. Margett Pettywood widdo, died Nov. 3, 1704, aged 80 yeares.

As you walk on earth so once did I;
Death call'd me hence and here I lye;
And must remain ontell ye Judgment day
The trumpet sound and call me hence away.

96. William the son of Robert and Sarah Frost, who died March 11, 1781, aged 18 years.

Decreed by God in mercy to mankind
Our troubles are to this short life confined;
While weakness, pain, disease and sorrow have
Their general quietus in the grave.
The living never should the dead lament;
Death is our reward and not our punishment.

97.* Sacred to the memory of the Revd. Mr. Thomas Spenceley, who died Dec. 2, anno ætatis 27, salutis 1718.

Mrs. Mary Spenceley, relict of the Revd. Mr. Thomas Spenceley, who died Jan. 16, 1759.

Also Mary Spenceley, daughter of the Rev. Thomas Spenceley & Mary his wife, who died May 3, 1796, aged 81 years.

Sacred to the memory of Benjamin Hands, late Captain in the Leicestershire Militia, who died April 9, 1817, in the 55th year of his age, and was buried at Enniscorthy in Ireland.

Sacred to the memory of Mary Hands, widow of Benjamin Hands, late Captain in the Leicestershire Militia, and second daughter of Thomas Moyle Esq., late of H . . . . in the County of Norfolk, [who died Nov. 1820] aged [65] years.

*No. 97 is a large altar-shaped stone. What is printed within brackets is supplied from the Registers. Nos. 98, 99, 100, 101, are not now in their proper position, but have been used to support No. 97. S.H.A.H.

98. Here lyeth ye body of Mr. Richard Sillet ye elder who departed this life July 24 anno domini 1687 in ye 60th yeare of his age.

99. Here lyeth ye body of Anne ye wife of Richard Sillet ye elder who departed this life May 29, anno domini 1671.

100. Here lyeth ye body of Richard Sillet ye younger and son of Richard, Marster of Arts, who departed this life July 10, anno domini 1687, aged 34 yeares.

101. [This is quite illegible.]

102. John Gardiner died Feb. 2, 1805, aged 72 years.
Sarah Gardiner died Feb. 15, 1837, aged 94 years.

103. Thomas Gardiner obiit Sept. 8, 1842, ætatis 75.
Frances wife of Thomas Gardiner obiit June 10 1847, ætatis 77.

104. John son of William and Mary Gardiner, who died Nov. 5, 1798, aged 2 months.

105. Rebecca Howe, who died Nov. 3, 1822, aged 82 years.

106. Thomas Howe, who died Aug. 11, 1806, aged 29 years.

107. Anna the wife of Richard Clark, who died Oct. 1. 1745, aged 67 years.

108. George Nelson, who dyed Aug. 31, 1692.
Also ye bodys of George & Grace, son & daughter to George Nelson.

109. Mary the wife of Mr. George Nelson, who [died] Dec. 19, 1722, aged 81 years.

110. M. S. 1779. H. S. 1729.
[*The headstone belonging to this foot stone is gone. I gather from the Register of Burials that these are the initials of Mary Spencer and Hugh Spencer.*]

111. John Barton, who died Jan. 3, 1774, aged 86 years.
Also Stephen Barton, who died Feb. 3, 1774, aged 81 years.

Though we did live old age to see,
You in your youths may follow we;
And when the blessful day appear,
I hope in heaven to meet you there.

112. John Frost, who died Aug. 17, 1740, aged 34 years.
But he knoweth the way that I take; when he hath tried me I shall come forth as gold. Job. xxiii. 10.

113. Francis Frost, who died April 28, 1729, aged 29 years.
O think on heaven & on God's mercy call,
In early years God gave to me my fall.

114. Ann Frost widow, who died March 3, 1749, aged 82 years.
Here, reader, thy days are but few,
They pass like the morning dew;
Though I did live old age to see,
Thou in thy youth may follow me.

115. Hannah wife of Thomas Frost, who died Oct. 20, 1775, aged 32 years.

116. Thomas Byford, who died Sept. 7, 1815, aged 58 years.
Ann his widow, who died July 20, 1843, aged 82 years.
Also Margaret Ann, daughter of James & Susan Byford, who died June 6, 1841, aged 9 months.

117. Thomas Evered, who died Feb. 11, 1846, aged 54 years.
In one brief moment I was call'd away,
And this to thee may be thy final day.
Frederick Evered, who died June 1, 1850, aged 53 years.
In an instant I sunk neath the shadows of death,
And eternity round me arose;
O reader, remember that life is a breath,
And a breath may bring thine to a close.

118. Thomas Murton, who died May 21, 1795, aged 80 years.
Mary wife of Thomas Murton, who died Nov. 9, 1791, aged 80 years.
The last enemy that shall be destroyed is death.

119. Thomas Murton, who died Jan. 13. 1745/6, aged 63 years.
The world is nothing, but Heaven's all,
The lower half of this stone is broken off and gone.

120. Robert Potter, who died March 11, 1767, aged 65 years.
Mary the wife of Robert Potter, who died Feb. 2, 1766 aged 67 years.

Farewell, vain world, I've had enough of thee,
And now am careless what thou sayth of me;
Thy smiles I court not, nor thy frowns I fear,
My cares are past, my heart lyes quiet here:
What faults you've seen in me take care to shun,
And look at home, enough there's to be done.

121. Thomas Sharpe who [died] Nov. 17, 1836, aged 71 years.
Also Mary his wife, died Dec. 6, 1846, aged 82 years.

122. William Cater, who died Dec. 26, 1860, aged 70 years.
Also Sophia Cater his wife, who died Aug. 4, 1861, aged 70 years.

Within this silent tomb lie buried
The kindest parents to their children dear;
Great was our loss for their eternal gain,
But hope in Heaven that we shall meet again.

123. William Lilly, who died Nov. 23, 1859, aged 89.
Also Hannah his wife, who died Feb. 15, 1854, aged 86.
And Hannah their daughter, wife of William Adams, who died July 9, 1827, aged 32.

Thy will, O Lord, be done.

124. Mary the beloved wife of William Spalding, who died March 8, 1885 in her 66th year.

I was in pain and sore oppressed,
Which wore my strength away,
And made me long for heavenly rest,
Which never can decay.
There is rest in Heaven.

Also William her husband, who [died] April 5, 1899 aged 82 years.

His end was peace.

125. Walter son of William and Mary Spalding, who died Feb. 21 1881, in his 32nd year.

I've bid the world a glad farewell,
I've done with suffering now;
And never more one passing grief
Shall shade my peaceful brow.

126. Mary the wife of John Spalding, who died March 1, 1820, aged 72 years. Also John Spalding died Dec. 24, 1825 aged 77 years.

127. Sarah daughter of Robert and Elizabeth Catchpole, who died April 15, 1839, in the 14th year of her age.

Grieve not for me, my parents dear,
Nor yet be over sad;
The fewer years I lived on earth,
The less the faults I had.

The shorter stay I made on earth,
The longer is my rest;
God took me away in early life,
Because he thought it best.

128.* John Sturgeon, who died Sept. 28, 1857, aged 56 years. Also Elizabeth his wife, who died March 14, 1893, aged 88 years.

129.* Frederick William twin son of John & Elizabeth Sturgeon, who died Jan. 2, 1844, aged 5 months.

130.* Michael Sturgeon, who died Aug. 19, 1824, aged 65 years. Also Ann his wife who died Sept. 12, 1845, aged 76 years.

131.* In memory of two sons of John and Louisa Barwick. John Michael died March 8, 1826, aged 2 years: John died Sept. 16. 1836, aged 9 years.

Secure tho' early laid in this their last retreat,
Unheeded o'er their silent dust the storms of life shall beat.

132.* Jane only child of the late John Rhodes Esq. and of Hannah his wife of Savile house near Halifax. Deservedly beloved, deeply and tenderly regretted, she departed this life Dec. 8, 1826, aged 17 years.

As for man his days are as grass; as a flower of the field so he flourisheth; for the wind passeth over it and it is gone. But thanks be to God who hath brought life and immortality to light through the Gospel.

The graves in this inclosure* are those of sisters' children.

Lasting will be the remembrance of their virtues, consoling is the hope of their reward.

133.* Jane Spedding, whose remains are deposited under this stone, the affectionate, beloved and only daughter of John Spedding of Mirehouse in the Co. of Cumberland, Esq. She died at Bury April 3, 1820, aged 17 years.

In the midst of life we are in death; of whom may we seek for succour but of Thee, O Lord.

* Nos. 128, 129, 130, 131, are in the same enclosure with a padlock! Nos. 132 and 133 are together in another enclosure. S.H.A.H.

134. John Gardiner, who died Dec. 27, 1822, in the 52nd year of his age.

Praises on tombs are trifles vainly spent;
A man's good life is his best monument.

135. John Gardiner who died Dec. 12, 1825, aged 16 years.

136. Thomas Gardiner died March 8, 1841, aged 33 years.
Also two children who died infants.

137. The Revd. Thomas Kerrich, Rector of this Parish 32 years, who died Jan. 10, 1814, aged 76 years.
And Alice his wife who died Nov. 29, 1805.
Also Thomas their son who died Sept. 29, 1825, aged 56 years.
And Alice their daughter who died March 30, 1835, aged 61 years.

138. Mary Burroughs, who [died] Aug. 15, 1820, aged 67 years.

139. Elizabeth widow of George Bramwell Esq. of London, died Jan. 27, 1841, æt. 69.

140. Woodward Bidwell died June 6, 1826, aged 74 years.
Susannah his widow, third daughter of Gregory Wood Sparke of Risby, died July 11, 1837, aged 70 years.

141. Woodward Bidwell of this parish, who died June 23, 1855, aged 60 years.

142. James Bidwell: born April 7, 1790, died Aug. 20, 1865.

143. Ann daughter of Peter and Ann Gedge died Dec. 14, 1824, aged 27 years.
Cut down like the flower of the field she will rise again in a brighter day.

144. Sarah wife of Thomas Rowe, who died Feb. 11, 1868, aged 65 years.
Thomas Rowe who died Feb. 23, 1863, aged 61 years.
My hope hath been in Thee, O Lord; I have said, Thou art my God.

145. Elizabeth wife of Benjamin Pryke, who died Feb. 13, 1857, aged 78 years.

An angel saint lies here in peace,
For here the storms of life all cease;
Her lot was not through life to glide,
Her faith and patience long were tried;
Wave after wave secure she passed,
And rose in triumph o'er the last.

146. George Frederick Morgan, who died Nov. 11, 1886, aged 21 years.

Day by day the voice saith, Come,
Enter thine eternal home;
Asking not if we can spare
This dear soul it summons there.

Also Sergeant Charles Albert Morgan, K.O.S. Borderers, died June 20, 1889, aged 33 years.

Had he asked us, well we know
We should cry, O spare this blow!
Yes, with streaming tears should pray,
Lord we love them, let them stay.

147. William Morgan who died June 19, 1883, aged 57 years.

Therefore be ye also ready; for in such an hour as ye think not the Son of Man cometh.

148. Edward Drake who died Nov. 18, 1861, aged 61 years.

Affliction sore long time I bore,
Physicians were in vain,
Till God was pleased to give me ease,
And free'd me from my pain.

149. Elizabeth Mary, relict of Edward Drake, who [died] Dec. 4, 1886, aged 72 years.

Did ever mourner plead with Thee,
And Thou refuse that mourner's plea?
Does not the word still fixed remain,
That none shall seek thy face in vain?

150. James Thomas youngest son of Edward and Elizabeth Mary Drake, who [died] Nov. 8, 1887, aged 39 years.

God who in his strict decrees
Remembers mercy still,
Can in a moment, if he please,
Our hearts with comfort fill.

151. George Palmer who died June 10, 1872, aged 89 years.

152. Isaac Cater who died Sept. 2, 1827, aged 84 years.

153. James Scarlin who died Nov. 5, 1825, aged 87 years.
Susan wife of James Scarlin, who died June 14, 1844, aged 98 years.
She thought the world was like herself sincere.

154. William Sale died Jan. 5, 1861, aged 50 years.
Blessed are the dead which die in the Lord.
Ann Sale died Sept. 29, 1888, aged 79 years.
Surely he hath borne our griefs.

155. William Double who died Oct. 19, 1841, aged 56 years.

156. George Farrants, born Nov. 18, 1794, died July 29, 1865.
Also Mary his beloved wife, born May 8, 1791, died July 2, 1857.

157. John Farrants born Aug. 19, 1851, died Dec. 29, 1875, in his 25th year.
Affliction sore long time I bore,
Physicians were in vain,
Till Christ was pleased to give me ease,
And rid me of my pain.

158. Samuel Rowe who died Oct. 5, 1878 aged 67 years.
In the solemn hour of dying,
In the awful judgment day,
May our souls on Thee relying
Find Thee still our hope and stay.

159. James Rowe who died June 30, 1881, aged 41 years.
Watch therefore, for ye know not the hour your Lord doth come.
Our days are like the grass,
Or like the morning flower;
If one short blast sweep o'er the field,
We perish in an hour.

160. John Richards who [died] April 5, 1890, aged 52 years.
Come unto Me all ye that labour and are heavy laden, and I will give you rest.
Also Harriet his wife, died Feb. 9, 1892, aged 58 years.
Thy will be done.

161. Susan Amelia daughter of William J. and Sally Nunn, who died Dec. 19, 1841, in the 4 year of her age. Belov'd.

162. James Death who died March 4, 1867, aged 70 years.
Also Esther his wife, who died Oct. 15, 1838, aged 38 years.
And Rebecca his second wife, who died Dec. 31, 1865, aged 72 years.

163. Sarah Christiana wife of Samuel Mison, who died March 12, 1852, aged 65 years.
We saw her on her deathbed, and marked how the gloom of the opening grave was scattered by a hope full of immortality.

164. Joseph Mison who died April 5, 1836, aged 33 years.
Ann his wife who died Aug. 4, 1836, aged 38 years.

This earth is nothing, heaven is all;
Death hath not hurt us by our fall;
Tell all our weeping friends so dear,
We are not lost but sleeping here.

Also four of their children who died infants.

165. James Scarlin who died May 25, 1854 aged 85 years.
Martha relict of James Scarlin, who died May 11, 1859, aged 80 years.

166. James Henry son of James Matthew and Elizabeth Scarlin, who died Sept. 13, 1859, aged 22 years.

167. Caroline daughter of James Matthew and Caroline Scarlin, who died Jan. 30, 1847, aged 3 months.

168. William Cockrill who died Feb. 12, 1855, aged [74] years.
Also Thamar his wife, died Feb. 16, 1874, in her 78th year. R. I. P.
Maria daughter of William and Thamar Cockrill, died April 3, 1838, aged 3 years.
Nathaniel son of William and Thamar Cockrill died March 18, 1859 aged 21 years. May he rest in peace.
Thamar daughter of William and Thamar Cockrill died March 3, 1838, aged 8 years.

169. Harriot the wife of William Eade, who died April 20, 1829, aged 33 years.
Also Jane their daughter who died in her infancy.

170. Emily wife of Henry Cater, died Dec. 12, 1863, aged 51 years.
Blessed are the dead which die in the Lord from henceforth, yea, saith the Spirit, that they may rest from their labours, and their works do follow them.

171. Phœbe Pryke died July 1, 1897, aged 76 years.
Also James Pryke her husband, died Nov. 20, 1888, aged 74 years, interred in Chedburgh churchyard.
Also Emma Pryke their daughter, died May 30, 1886, aged 20 years.
The Lord gave and the Lord hath taken away; blessed be the name of the Lord.

172. Susan Rampling who died Oct. 10, 1894, aged 69 years.
Her end was peace.

173. Elizabeth Brown who died April 22, 1886, aged 35 years.
Our life is but a fading dawn,
Its glorious noon how quickly past;
Lead us, O Christ, when all is gone
Safe home at last.
With Christ, which is far better.

174. Elizabeth the beloved wife of Robert Baker, who died May 24, 1879, aged 65 years.
Blessed are the pure in heart, for they shall see God.
Also the above Robert Baker died Nov. 9, 1888, aged 70 years.
Also in loving remembrance of two beloved children of Robert and Elizabeth Baker: Elizabeth died April 27, 1874, aged 23 years: Leonard George died Dec. 24, 1875, aged 22 years.
God shall wipe all tears from their eyes, and there shall be no more death neither sorrow nor crying, neither shall there be any more pain.

175. Thomas Goodchild who died Oct. 21, 1876, aged 73 years.
The Lord gave and the Lord hath taken away; blessed be the name of the Lord.

176. Amy the beloved wife of Thomas Parker, who died Feb. 18, 1877, aged 76 years.
Yea, though I walk through the valley of the shadow of death I will fear no evil, for thou art with me.

177. Jemima wife of John Thompson, who died March 20, 1886 aged 85 years.
Sweet is the thought—time flies apace,
This earth is not our resting place;
And sweet the promise of the Lord
To all who love his name and word.

178. Fanny widow of the late John Simkin of this parish, who died June 22, 1886, aged 84 years.
Come unto Me all ye that labour and are heavy laden, and I will give you rest.

179. Robert Wells who died Dec. 12, 1857, aged 64 years.
Also Sarah Wells his wife, who died Feb. 10, 1880, in her 88th year.

180. Alfred Musk who died Feb. 10, 1890, aged 26 years.

Weep not for me, my parents dear,
I am not dead but sleeping here;
I was not loved by you alone,
My Saviour called, and I am gone.

His end was peace.

181. Susan Garwood who died Jan. 27, 1885, aged 55 years.
In the hour of death and in the day of judgment, good Lord, deliver us.
This stone is erected by her loving son Obadiah.

182. Charlotte Marian Gay. Passed away Aug. 8, 1887.

183. Alice Maude infant daughter of Charles Edward and Alice Barnes. Born Dec. 3, 1885, died March 10, 1886.

Of such is the kingdom of Heaven.

184. Harriet Rowe who died Sept. 27, 1894, aged 52 years.
Not dead but gone before.

Without a sigh her fetters broke,
We scarce could say, She's gone,
Before her ransomed spirit took
Its mansion round the throne.

185. Arthur George Girling, aged 23 years, died May 13, 1886.

186. Henry Byford who died Oct. 25, 1888, aged 21 years.

Thy will be done.

187. George Fryer who died Jan. 13, 1898, aged 39 years.

Lord, thy purpose we cannot see;
All is well that's done by thee.

188. John Langham who died Jan. 22, 1882, aged 69 years.

Return unto thy rest, O my soul.

Also Mary his wife who died Nov. 8, 1889, in her 85th year.
In death lamented as in life beloved.

189. James Byford who died Jan. 23, 1888, aged 83 years.
Susannah wife of James Byford, who died Aug. 8, 1876 aged 75 years.
Thy will be done.

190. John Sargent who died Oct. 26, 1877, aged 73 years.
Also Charlotte his wife, who died May 22, 1883, aged 78 years.

191. Elizabeth Bowers who died July 9, 1895, aged 79 years.
I know that my Redeemer liveth. For ever with the Lord.

192. Matilda Leech who died May 23, 1896, aged 76 years.
Hope; though thy dear ones round thee die,
Behold with faith's illumined eye
Their blissful home beyond the sky;
Abound in Hope.
Also Ellen her daughter, who died May 23, 1876, aged 21 years.

193. Hannah Wallace who died Sept. 5, 1884, aged 69 years.
Thy will be done.

194. Emma the beloved wife of John Eley, who [died] April 10, 1884, aged 60 years.
Her end was peace.

195. James Matthew Scarlin died Dec. 14, 1890, aged 80 years.
Eliza Ann Scarlin died July 6, 1893, aged 57 years.
Caroline Scarlin died June 2, 1884, aged 68 years.
Agnes Mary Scarlin died Feb. 15, 1873, aged 17 years.
Mary Octavia Scarlin died Sept. 16, 1873, aged 16 years. R.I.P.

196. Gwennie dearly loved daughter of Samuel and Carrie Cook. Born Jan. 5, 1895. Died Jan. 26, 1896.
Lost awhile our treasured love,
Gain'd for ever safe above.

197. Charles Sale who died May 18, 1888, aged 4 years & 2 months.
Suffer little children to come unto Me.

198. William Foster who died Oct. 24, 1868, aged 57 years.
In the hour of death and in the day of Judgment, Good Lord, deliver us.

199. George Thomas son of George and Jane Rolfe, who died Dec. 1. 1871, aged 21 years.
Them also which sleep in Jesus will God bring with him.

200. Percy Michael Edwards. Born July 6, 1879. Died Nov. 8, 1893. R.I.P.

201. Edward Crack. Born April 18, 1837. Died July 31, 1897.
Be ye therefore ready also; for the Son of Man cometh at an hour when ye think not.

202. Edward Crack who died May 14, 1875, aged 79 years.
In the midst of life we are in death.

203. John Thompson who died Oct. 24, 1873, aged 73 years.

To Jesus go, if happiness you crave,
The joy he gives endures beyond the grave;
Then thoughts of dying will not give you pain,
Secure in Him to die will be your gain.

204. George Cater who died Sept. 21, 1871, aged 56 years.
The Lord gave and the Lord hath taken away; blessed be the name of the Lord.

205. John Green who died Oct. 23, 1871, aged 57 years.
In the midst of life we are in death.

206. John Henry youngest son of John and Harriet Green and late of the Royal Artillery, who after a service of 12 years in India died April 20, 1875, aged 29 years.

207. William Edwards who died May 12, 1865, aged 67 years.
Also Mary Ann his wife who died Jan. 20, 1886, aged 83 years.
Mary Ann Edwards died March 6, 1865, aged 29 years.
Edward Edwards died March 8, 1890, aged 52 years.

208. William Jones who died at the Shrubbery, Horringer, July 17, 1865, aged 69 years.
In the midst of life we are in death.

209. General Sir James Simpson, G.C.B., Colonel 29th Regiment, who departed this life April 18, 1868, after a service of nearly 60 years, aged 76.

Q

210. John Cornell died Nov. 3, 1887, aged 90 years.
Also Mary Ann his wife died Oct. 13, 1871, aged 81 years.
Emily their daughter died Feb. 18, 1875, aged 48 years.
And what I say I say unto you all, Watch.

211. John Fowler Dove of the Hopleys in this parish. Born Oct. 20, 1787, Died Oct. 17, 1866.
This monument is erected by his sorrowing widow Elizabeth, who died July 12, 1876, aged 88

212. Mary Ann Last who died July 28, 1881, aged 38 years.

Go home, my friends, and shed no tears,
I must be here till Christ appears;
Long was my pain, short was my rest,
Christ took me when he thought it best.

Her end was peace.
This stone is erected in affectionate remembrance by her late fellow servants at Nevill Holt.

213. General Sir Charles Ellice, G.C.B. Born May 10, 1823. Died Nov. 12 1888.

214. James Boreham. Born June 4, 1810. Died April 2, 1898.
Also Mary Boreham. Born May 5, 1819. Died March 30, 1898.
God shall wipe away all tears from their eyes, and there shall be no more death neither sorrow nor crying, neither shall there be any more pain, for the former things are passed away.

215. Jane Rolfe who [died] July 6, 1891, aged 73 years.
Come unto me, ye weary, and I will give you rest.

Christ will gather in his own
To the place where he is gone;
Where their heart and treasure lie,
Where our life is hid on high.

Also George Farrants Rolfe her husband, who died Dec. 18, 1898, aged 85 years.

216. Mary Ann Hunt who died July 13, 1894, aged 79 years.
With Christ, which is far better.

217. Mary Cater who died April 27, 1884, in the 94th year of her age.
Her end was peace.

218. Rebecca Rolfe who died April 17, 1887, aged 60 years.
Sarah Rolfe who died Sept. 24, 1888, aged 71 years.
Mary Ann Foster their sister, widow of William Foster, who died March 31, 1890, aged 78 years.
Be thou faith-ful unto death, and I will give thee a crown of life.

219.* In loving memory of George Brown who died March 21, 1870, aged 57 years.
Also of Susan Brown his widow, who died Oct. 30, 1898, aged 72 years.
In the midst of life we are in death.

220* George Garwood died July 4, 1898, aged 58 years.
Also Caroline his daughter who died Dec. 22, 1898 aged 33 years.

Just as I am without one plea
But that thy blood was shed for me,
And that thou bidst me come to thee,
O Lamb of God, I come.

* These 2 stones, 219 and 220, were put up after I had copied the inscriptions on all the others and just at the moment of sending these sheets to the printer. Otherwise their numbers according to their position would have been 171 and 191 respectively.

APPENDIX IV.

CHURCH RATES—1693, 1699.

The parish chest in Horringer Church not only contains no medieval accounts, but is also very poorly furnished with those records, rates, and accounts of the last two centuries which most parishes possess, and which often throw much light upon what was done and how and when.

There is a volume containing only the barest summary of what was received and what spent every year by the Churchwardens from 1723 to 1842. This volume contains the signatures of those who were present at each annual Easter vestry during that time, and the names of the churchwardens who were then appointed. Two questmen were also appointed at each Easter vestry as well as two churchwardens. No questmen seem to have been appointed after 1765. Questmen are in some parishes called sidesmen. Other parish books have I presume got into private hands, and either wrongfully remain there or have been lost.

There are two pieces of parchment, both imperfect, containing portions of rates made in 1693 and 1699 respectively. These I print here. The later one is the least imperfect. The original manuscript gives in parallel columns what each man's rate is at a farthing in the pound and what he actually has to pay when that rate is multiplied by 5 or 20 as the case may be. I have omitted the former column, which of course in the one rate is one-fifth and in the other rate is one-twentieth of the column which I have given. In the heading to the rate "doubled" means multiplied. Lady Gipps who heads the list pays for Little Horringer Hall. She was the widow of Sir Richard Gipps. John Ewen who comes next pays for Great Horringer Hall, which then belonged to the Jermyns of Rushbrook, whose tenant he was. The Lucas family pay for Horsecroft, which they then owned. What the college was for which they pay I know not. It was probably some medieval religious house which had been abolished at the Reformation, and it may be the College Farm in the Horringer of to-day.

Horringshearth. August 31. 1693. A rate made there by Mr. Thomas Covell and William Harrington, Churchwardens, with the assistance and approbation of the rest of the Inhabitants of Horringshearth aforesaid at a farthing in the pound for every man's estate, and the rate to be doubled five times for reimburseing the moneys by them expended.

	s.	d.
The Lady Gipps for parte of Little Horringshearth	3	9
The same for the remainder late in the use of Parker	15	0
John Ewen for the Hall farme	10	10
William Wyard for Newhaugh closses & feild land		10
The same for land late Josias Wrights		$7\frac{1}{2}$
The same for Bury land		5
The same for Bury towne land late James Wyard		$7\frac{1}{2}$
James Wyard jun. for Buxhall late Will: Wyard		$3\frac{3}{4}$
John Wiseman for William Wyard	2	1
James Wyard sen.	1	$10\frac{1}{2}$
The same for Hosteler yard		$6\frac{1}{4}$
William Lucas Esq. for Horsecroft house, Wallnutt tree pightell, little Bunton's maple, Ladymans close, Dovehouse closse, Watts grove and great Bunton's maple	2	1
The same for lands late John Godfrey		10
The same for 3 closses & ye long closse late Widow Whites	2	1
The same for Richard Hernsbyes		$8\frac{3}{4}$
The same for Hopley meadow late Robert Custone		$6\frac{1}{4}$
Phillip Parker for Capt: Lucas Dayre farm	2	$7\frac{1}{4}$
The same for the Deane land	1	$0\frac{1}{2}$
Thomas Smith of Bury for Wrights closse & mead	2	1
Edward Parker late Richard Edgley		$6\frac{1}{4}$
Dr. Lucas for the Colledge	3	$1\frac{1}{2}$
The same for Whitshall wood	1	$0\frac{1}{2}$
The same for little Hopley		$2\frac{1}{2}$
The same for the remainder of great Hopley	1	$5\frac{1}{2}$
Margarite White of Bury for Dr. Lucas Lynckes	2	1
The same for ye Stubb wood between Whitshall & ye Parke... ...		10
John Crouch for Dr. Lucas at the Road		$6\frac{1}{4}$

Edmond Hallock for Dr. Lucas late Kedmore	1	8
The same for Stubbings		10
Mrs. Mary Nelson for Dr. Lucas next ye parsonage	1	10½
The same for Mrs. Goodricks		8¾
The same for the Widow Welhams		10
The same for William Lilly late Will: Wyard		6¼
Thomas Goldsmith jun for Mrs. Nelsons		3¾

The remainder is torn off.

Horninger. Com: Suff: 1699. A rate there made Aug. 18, 1699, by Thomas Covell gen: and John Wiseman, churchwardens, with the assistance and approbation of the rest of the inhabitants of Horninger aforesaid at a farthing in the pound for every man's estate, and the rate to be doubled twenty times, for reimburseing the money by them expended, as followeth:

	£	s.	d.
John Rolfe for the Lady Gipps	3	15	0
John Ewen for the Hall farme	2	3	4
James Wyard sen:		7	6
The same for Hosteler yard		2	1
Capt: William Lucas Esq. for Horsecroft house, Wallnut tree pightell, Ladymans closse, Dovehouse closse, little Buntons maple and Sparrow land		7	11
The same for the three wood closses		7	6
The same for Whitsall wood late Dr. Lucas		4	2
The same for the remaynder of greate Hopley		5	10
John Herne for Capt: Lucas Daire farme		5	10
The same for Wrights closse & ye mead late in Smiths use		8	4
Thomas Chinnery for Watts grove & greate Buntons maple		3	9
The same for Mr. Adamsons late Capt: Lucas		2	11
The same for Mr. Adamsons at Horscroft...		3	9
The same for Thomas Dearsons land			10
The same for two peeces of feild land belonging to ye Daire			10
The same for land late in Godfreys use			10
John Lyng for Capt. Lucas late in Parker's use		2	1

Thomas Wiseman for Capt. Lucas Colledge late Dr. Lucas		12	6
The same for feild land late William Wyard		1	3
Francis Frost for the house at the Roade		2	6
The same for little Hopley			10
Thomas Ford for the long closse late Dr. Lucas			10
John Crouch of Bury for Capt. Lucas L. pickle.		8	4
The same for the Stubb wodes next the parke		3	4
William Hempsted for Mr. Woodruffe late Capt. Lucas		2	11
Henry Cornell for Thomas Wiseman late Dr. Lucas		6	8
The same for Stebbings late Dr. Lucas		3	4
John Wiseman for Capt. Lucas next the Parsonage		7	6
Mrs. Mary Nelson for Mr. Goodricke		2	11
The same for Widow Welham		3	4
The same for William Lilly late William Wyard		2	1
The same for land late Thomas Chinnerys		2	1
Thomas Goldsmith jun : for Mrs. Nelsons		1	3
William Covell gen. for his owne Pakenham & Lord Jermins lands ...	1	15	5
Thomas Covell gen. for lands in his hands	1	14	7
William Wyard for his farme		11	8
The same for Bury Towne land		4	2
John Laite for the gravill pitt		2	1
Thomas Goldsmith sen. for Mr. Thomas Covells		1	8
Mr. John Kittle, Mrs. Frost for Mr. Robert Kedingtons ...		6	3

The rest is torn off.

APPENDIX V.

PERAMBULATION OF HORRINGER.

This account of the bounds of Horringer is written in pencil in a note book which is in the parish chest. Apparently it was scribbled as the perambulation was going on. The date of it would appear to be early in this present century. The churchwardens' accounts show that there was a perambulation of the parish made in 1821. Possibly it was scribbled then. I presume that the starting point "the 1st plantation in the park" is the grove that lies across the footpath that leads from Horringer gate to Ickworth Lodge, half way between the two. From thence they proceeded across the present cricket ground, which seems to be partly in Ickworth and partly in Horringer. The pond and (I think) the marked tree near the cricket ground are still there. The pestle that they came to soon afterwards must be what is now a wood called Pestle wood. Bayard's meadow, reached soon afterwards, deserves a word of explanation.

In an old Ickworth parish rate-book of the last century I have noticed that that part of the stream which flows near Bayard's meadow is called Bayard's water. Bayard was an old English word meaning originally a bay horse, afterwards any horse. Bayard's water must mean the horses' watering place. And as the high road from Bury to Chevington passed by this spot, and the blacksmith's shop formerly stood here, it is easy to see the possibility of the suitability of the name.*

Lady Gipps' road must be a road leading to Little Horringer Hall. I have not exactly identified the acre called Gospel acre, nor do I know why the Gospel was read there. There are several Gospel oaks in the country, which were mark or boundary oaks where the Gospel was read at perambulations. In Walker's "Sufferings of the Clergy" we read that Mr. Bond, Vicar of Debenham, was sequestred in or

*Bayswater in London is believed to be a corruption of Bayard's water. Notes & Queries, Ser. viii. Vol. 12. Ser. ix. Vol. 1.

about 1644 "for observing the orders and rules of the Church, reading part of a Gospel at the cross in a perambulation," etc. p. 209.

Foaming Sea is still so called, being where the brook goes under the road (Poulter's Lane) between Horringer and Chedburgh. That brook afterwards enters Ickworth park and flows through it, coming out of it near Bayard's meadow, and flowing on to Bury.

Starting mark an oak in the 1st plantation in the park H, bear N.W., mark a tree opposite the pond, the pond on the right, mark a post in the park pales, cross the ley to a style, mark a tree, turn to the right, cross the pestle to a pollard, last but one marked, turn west down the pestle to Bayards meadow, mark a tree, thro the hedge into the meadow, point to the brook, mark an oak tree, leave 2 trees on the left, thro' the hedge into the open field, brook on the left by the road half way up 16A, mark in the ground on the right hand, turn down to Westley bottom, cross mark in the ground at the bottom, turn to the right sharp, mark in the ground to the right of the cross road, cross the bottom, take in all the Westley bottom to the top of Chalk hill, ground mark, turn to the right upon the ridge, at the end turn to left 4 rod, turn to the right 10 rod, turn to the right up the hill, mark on the mear, turn to the right at the end at Westly road, to a mark on the mear at the cross roads, turn to the right, turn to the right at the road to Saxham to a white post, mark in the ground, cross the bottom to Gosple acre, mark in the ground, up to Lady Gipps road, read the Gospel, mark in the ground 2 rod beyond B [Bury] bounds, turn to the right up the land, towards the mill, to the road to Horringer hall, turn to right 4 rod, mark, turn to the left down the meres, mark close to Bury road above the stone, 4 rodd, down to the stone, thro the hedge cross Nunns 20 acres up to Bury post on the road to Hargate [Hardwick] heath, leave the post on the right 12 rod, mark on the right of the road, half the road in B., down to cross road, turn to the right towards Horsecroft to the stone, turn to the left, cross the land, mark in the ground 6 rod to the right of Bury stone, turn to the right, leave the hedge on the left, over stile, mark a tree in Millers field, thro 3 of Millers field, turn to the right down the lane to the stile on the left, over the stile to a stile to J. Nunns, mark a tree, cross the park to J. Nunns house, pass between the house and backhouse close to the dwelling house thro a gate into the rack yard between the house and the stable, leave the barns on the left, take in a cart lodge, over the hedge into a pasture, mark a tree at the end of a ditch, leave the pond on the left, mark a syccamine, into the road, cross Gags Green, mark a timber oak, cross the road, mark in the ground, over hedge into a field J. Nun, mark a tree ash, mark an oak at the [sic] of a plantation, go at the head of Horsecroft lands, take in Hawsted grove, cross the drift to Hawsted place, mark a sycamine, into a triangle peice, turn to left over a stile beside the Whepstead road, mark a tree, over into the road, under the hedge to an oak tree the corner of a plantation, cross the road under the hedge on the right, turn the corner into the lane to a post, over the left into Whymark field, mark an ash, leave the pond on the left, lane on the right, cross at a stile, ground mark in the lane, down the lane to a gate into a field, mark a pollard 4 rod from the gate, leave the wood to the right, mark a tree, into the wood, cross the wood to a [?], go by the head of the land to foaming sea, marked a maple up the road, turn into the grove at a marked post, cross into the glade up it, into the park thro the great gate to a timber marked, turn to the left to the brick kiln, leave the brick kiln on the left, marked a tree near the corner of the park pales, cross [to] the marked tree from whence we began.

Appendix VI.

The Rectors of Horringer.

Mr. Gage in his History of Thingoe Hundred gives a list of the Rectors of Great and Little Horringer. But finding some errors in his list I have had a fresh one made out from the Institution books in the Diocesan Registry at Norwich. All the Rectors of both Horringers before 1550 were presented by the Abbot of Bury, excepting James Hert in 1484.

Of the pre-Reformation rectors there is not much to be said. In many cases their names show some village with which they had some family or personal connection. Barton, Battisford, Elmswell, are villages in Suffolk; Tottington, Drayton, Saham Toney, Lexham, are in Norfolk; Lowthorpe is in Yorkshire. The only name among the early ones which is from a trade and not from a place is that of Richard le Sauser in 1305. I know not what trade that may be unless it is a bit of careless writing for Chaucer, which is thought to represent the Norman-French word for shoemaker. The grandfather of Chaucer the poet is believed to have been a Robert Chaucer of Ipswich, whose widow married a probable cousin, Richard Chaucer. (Dict: Nat: Biog:)

Short accounts of some of the Rectors will be found in the Biographical Notes at the end of this volume.

The title "apostolicus" applied to John of Lexham in 1374 is believed to imply that he had been on a mission of some kind to Rome.

Those of whom it is said "primam habens tonsuram clericalem" are called "shavelings" by Blomefield, having as yet only been admitted to the first tonsure.

The dates 1535 and 1548 are both given as the date of the union of the two Horringers. Probably the first date is that of a temporary union, and the latter date is that of a permanent one. The site of Little Horringer Church is known, and I presume that its foundations are still in the ground, and its dead still lie where they were.

In 1836 the Archdeaconry of Sudbury was transferred from the diocese of Norwich to that of Ely. After the death of Mr. Hasted in 1852 the parishes of Horringer and Ickworth were united.

RECTORS OF LITTLE HORRINGER.

8 Ides Oct. 1305.	Magister Ricardus, dictus le Sauser, acolitus.
6 Ides Nov. 1317.	Robertus de Louthorp, subdiaconus.
10 Kal: March 1331.	Willelmus de Draghtone, subdiaconus.
9 Jan. 1373/4.	Johannes de Lexham, apostolicus.
12 Jan. 1376/7.	Magister Johannes Brumpton de Elmeswell, primam habens tonsuram clericalem.
22 Feb. 1387/8.	Andreas Bomond, presbyter, (on resignation of Brumpton).
Penult: Feb. 1387/8.	Johannes Goldyng, presbyter.
11 May 1433.	Johannes Maggard, presbyter.
6 Feb. 1433/4.	Johannes Kyng, presbyter.
27 July. 1436.	Thomas Umfray, presbyter, (on resignation of Kyng).
19 Dec. 1436.	Edmundus Qwysson, (on resignation of Umfray).
28 March, 1441.	Thomas Hermer, (exchanged with Aldborough, on resignation of Qwysson).
17 Nov. 1446.	Bernardus Kele, presbyter, (on resignation of Hermer).
15 Jan. 1455/6.	Thomas Grene, presbyter, (on resignation of Kele).
31 May. 1462.	Thomas Cook, capellanus, (on resignation of Grene).
7 Aug. 1467.	Averedus Masse, presbyter, (on resignation of Cook).
5 May 1472.	Edmundus Boland, presbyter.
2 Dec. 1484.	Jacobus Hert. Presented by the Bishop.
27 June 1494.	Robertus Faunderoy, in jure Baccal: presbyter.
1 Aug. 1506.	Philipus Adeson.
8 Oct. 1510.	Arthurus Leftwich.

8 Feb. 1514/5.	Robertus Bataile.
1 April 1518.	Rogerus Fynds, in decretis Baccalaureus, (on resignation of Bataile).
18 April 1519.	Willelmus Brereton, (on resignation of Roger Feneaux).
5 Jan. 1524/5.	Thomas Lewen, capellanus, (on death of Brereton).
On Nov. 20, 1535,	Thomas Lewen resigned Little Horringer and it was united to Great Horringer for the life of its then Rector, John Griffith alias Getto.

RECTORS OF GREAT HORRINGER.

Kal: May, 1300.	Johannes de Barton.
Circa 1326.	Thomas de Totyngton.
Kal: Oct: 1333.	Johannes Wyth de Draughton, acolitus.
14 June 1349.	Magister Johannes de Batesford, primam habens tonsuram clericalem.
4 Jan. 1357/8.	Ricardus Gegh de Saham Tony, primam habens tonsuram clericalem.
26 Sept. 1393.	Magister Nicholas Hethe, acolitus.
25 July 1394.	Johannes Gillyng, canonicus ecclesiæ collegiatæ Sancti Audr: in Aukland, et prebendarius prebendæ de Morley in eadem villa. (An exchange on resignation of Hethe.)
19 Jan. 1421/2.	Magister Henricus Burghwasch, presbyter, (on resignation of Gilling).
22 Sept. 1425.	Roger Philpot, (on resignation of Burghwasch, an exchange with Cogeshall).
28 Nov. 1425.	Robertus Potter, (on resignation of Philpot, an exchange with Bergh cum Apton capella).
13 July 1440.	Willielmus Cote, LLB, (on death of Potter).
28 Oct. 1448.	Dominus Thomas Coote, presbyter, (on resignation of William Coote).
21 May 1504.	Dominus Willelmus Tomlin, prior Domus Sancti Johannis Evang: in Cantabrig:, (on resignation of Thomas Coote).
5 May 1520.	Thomas Reve alias Noille, (on resignation of Tomlin).

1 Sept. 1528.	Johannes Griffith, capellanus, (on resignation of Reve alias Newell.

RECTORS OF GREAT AND LITTLE HORRINGER.

2 April 1558.	Johannes Harrison, presbyter, on death of John Griffith alias Getto. Presented by Ambrose Jermyn.
23 Nov. 1581.	Thomas Clerk,* clericus, on death of Harrison. Presented by Thomas Sackville, Lord Buckhurst, by grant from Thomas, Lord Paget, patron.
10 Dec. 1581.	Thomas Rogers, clericus, on death of last incumbent. Presented by Queen Elizabeth.
13 March. 1615/6.	William Bedell, S.T.B., on death of Rogers. Presented by Sir Thomas Jermyn.
— — 1629.	Robert Goodrick.†
24 July 1662.	Laurence Womack, S.T.P. Presented by Sir Thomas Jermyn.
19 June 1683.	Thomas Smyth, on resignation of Womack. Presented by Robert Sharpe, patron for this turn.
19 June 1725.	John Symonds A.M., on death of Smyth. Presented by Sir Jermyn Davers.
24 Feb. 1758.	John French, on death of Dr. Symonds. Presented by Sir Robert Davers.
3 Feb. 1767.	George Rogers B.A. on death of Mr. French. Presented by Sir Charles Davers.
14 May. 1784.	Thomas Kerrich L.L.B. on Mr. Rogers' cession. Presented by Sir Charles Davers.
20 April. 1814.	Henry Hasted M.A. on death of Mr. Kerrich. Presented by Fred: Will: Earl of Bristol.

* I strongly suspect that this Thomas Clerk had no real existence, but is the same man as Thomas Rogers, clerk, who is next in the list. He may have been instituted twice over in consequence of some doubt as to who was patron.

† Mr. Fred. Johnson, who has made these lists for me, tells me that Goodrick's institution is not in the books at Norwich, but that he has supplied his name from the Institution books at the Record Office in London. Goodrick was buried in Sept., 1660, so that the living seems to have been vacant for nearly 2 years.

24 Dec. 1852.	Arthur Charles Hervey, on death of Mr. Hasted. Presented by himself as patron for the turn.
1869.	Richard Burgess, on the resignation of Lord Arthur Hervey. Presented by the Crown.
1881.	Arthur Linzee Chatterton Heigham, on the death of Dr. Burgess. Presented by the Marquis of Bristol.
1883.	James Giddens, on the resignation of Mr. Heigham. Presented by the Marquis of Bristol.

Appendix VII.

Poll Tax Payers of 1381.

In the year 1380 Parliament determined to obtain funds by means of a poll tax. Three groats or twelve pence were to be paid for every lay person male and female of 15 years and upwards, beggars only excepted. Each township had to find as many shillings as it contained residents over 15 years of age. But within certain limits the rich were to pay more than the poor. The limits were that no one should pay more than 60 groats nor less than one groat for himself and his wife. This tax was very unpopular and caused a rising of the peasantry. An account of this rising so far as it affected the East of England has lately been written by Mr. Edgar Powell, and in an appendix he has given lists of those who paid the tax in about 50 Suffolk villages. From this book I take the names of those who paid in Great and Little Horringer. It gives us the names of all the people in the two parishes just 200 years before the Registers begin. From it we see that there was no resident gentleman, the lord of both manors being the Abbot of Bury. There is one farmer, one draper, two carpenters, and the rest are labourers and serfs. It is possible that there may have been some who somehow avoided payment, and so are not in this list. In Great Horringer there were 53 persons of 15 years and upwards, and so they paid 53 shillings between them; in Little Horringer there were 21, and so they paid 21 shillings. In the original Poll tax document Hornyngesherth is the form which the name takes.*

* The Rising in East Anglia in 1381, by Edgar Powell, 1896. I have taken my description of the Poll tax from this work. Mr. Powell's lists are made out from the original documents in the Public Record Office in London.

GREAT HORRINGER.

	s.	d.
Robertus Gobet, draper, Alicia uxor ejus	3	0
Michael Goss, carpenter, Alicia uxor ejus	2	4
Robertus Prest, carpenter ...	1	0

LABORATORES.

	s.	d.
Johannes Dane Alicia uxor ejus	2	0
Johannes Brycete Johanna uxor ejus	2	0
Galfridus Wepstede Agneta uxor ejus	2	0
Johannes Bare Isabella uxor ejus	2	4
Thomas Coupere Margeria uxor ejus	2	0
Symon Jent ...	1	0
Benedictus Knyth Johanna uxor ejus	2	0
Willelmus Brend Johanna uxor ejus	2	0
Johannes Busschop Cristina mater ejus	2	4
Alanus Noble Katerina uxor ejus	2	8
Nicholaus Gandawe Johanna uxor ejus	2	0

SERVIENTES.

	s.	d.
Johannes Alysawe ...		8
Johanna Fyssche ...		8
Robertus Boyler ...		8
Adam Godefrey Katerina uxor ejus	2	0
Edmundus Kynch ...	1	0
Johannes Godefrey ...		8
Johannes Ryngedale ...		8
Robertus Asscheman ...	1	0
Thomas Brend ...	1	0
Willelmus Godefrey ...	1	0
Ricardus Goos ...	1	0
Johannes Newhawe ...		8
Matilda Lewote ...	1	0
Margeria Lewote ...	1	0
Thomas Rose ...	1	0
Agneta Rungeton ...	1	0
Johannes Clerk ...	1	0
Thomas Blok Agneta uxor ejus	2	0
Willelmus Driwer Johanna uxor ejus	2	0
Johannes Pypere ...	1	0
Thomas Clenewalle ...	1	0
Johannes Pyc Margeria uxor ejus	2	0
Robertus Godefrey ...	1	0

Summa nonimum LIII.

Summa denariorum LIII s.

LITTLE HORRINGER.

AGRICOLA.

	s.	d.
Johannes Lacford	2	0
Emma uxor ejus	2	0

LABORATORES.

		s.	d.
Rosia le Smyth	...	1	0
Alicia Hermer	...	1	0
Emma Hermer	...		6
Johannes Goldynge	...	1	0
Sabina uxor ejus	...	1	0
Emma Goldynge	...	1	4
Thomas Pulrose	...		4
Alicia uxor ejus	...		4
Johannes Aubry	...	1	0
Emma Dun	...		8

SERVIENTES.

		s.	d.
Robertus Hermer	...	1	0
Rosia uxor ejus	...	1	0
Thomas Lacford	...	1	0
Caterina uxor ejus	...	1	0
Johannes Goldynge jun	...	1	0
Matilda Goldynge	...	1	0
Rogerus Gardiner	...	1	0
Johannes Rudham	...	1	0
Margeria uxor ejus	...	1	0

Summa personarum XXI.

Summa denariorum XXI s.

APPENDIX VIII.

DOMESDAY BOOK.

Having in the last Appendix gone back 200 years before the Registers begin and shown how the population of Horringer was made up in 1381, I must go back another 300 years from then and show how it was made up in 1081 or thereabouts. Apparently at that time it had not yet been divided into two parishes, though it was so not long afterwards. This is what Domesday book says of it. The first of the two following paragraphs shows the land in Horringer held under the Abbot of Bury; the second shows the land held under Richard son of Earl Gislebert.

1. At Horningsworda St. Edmund held in King Edward's time 4 carrucates of land as a manor. There were always 3 villani, and 15 bordarii: always 4 plough teams in demesne, and always 5 plough teams belonging to the men: always 7 servi, and 3 acres of meadow; wood for 5 hogs: and now 5 rouncies, and now 14 beasts, and 30 hogs and 45 sheep; and 15 socmen with a carucate of land and a bordarius; always 4 plough teams. These men are under the Saint [Abbey] by sac and soc and all that is customary, and they could not give or sell the land without the Abbot's licence. A church with 6 acres of free land. Then this manor was worth 6 pounds, now 8. It is 9 quarentenes long and 8 broad; and pays 20 pence in gelt. Others have holdings there.
2. In Horningeserda a socman under Wisgar with 20 acres and 2 bordarii. Always 1 plough team, and worth 4 shillings.

In these two paragraphs I have mainly used the translation made by Lord John Hervey for his privately printed Suffolk Domesday. A few Latin terms I have left untranslated. Possibly the two paragraphs foreshadow the two Horringers.

In the first paragraph we seem to see a population of 3 villani (servile tenants), and 15 bordarii (cottagers), and 7 servi (bondsmen or serfs) as being there in the time of King Edward the Confessor, A.D. 1042 to 1066: and in 1086 when the Domesday survey was made 15 socmen are mentioned and (apparently) 15 bordarii.

In the second paragraph we see a socman and 2 bordarii.

Rouncies are ponies. A quarentene is a furlong. A carucate is the variable amount of land that may be tilled by one plough.

APPENDIX IX.

SUBSCRIBERS TO THE SUFFOLK SHIP.

A general meeting of the County of Suffolk was called by the High Sheriff and held at Stowmarket on Aug. 5, 1782, at which it was resolved "*That the County of Suffolk sensible of the inferiority of the naval force of Great Britain compared with that of other European powers with whom we are at war, do undertake by voluntary subscriptions to build a man of war of 74 guns for the service of the public.*" This plan was taken up with great warmth. Over £4000 was promised in the room, Lord Bristol (Bishop of Derry) heading the list with £1000. A committee was appointed to receive subscriptions, and £19,766 was promised. Nearly all this came from the County, but there were a few subscriptions from outside. Among these was £600 from the clergy of the diocese of Derry. It is evident that the Bishop of Derry had taken up the idea warmly, which had been first proposed by his brother-in-law Sir Charles Davers. The Rev. Dr. Young writing to his brother Arthur at Bradfield says, *When your silly Suffolk scheme of building a ship was first mentioned to Lord Keppel, he said, If they could find him seamen he should be obliged to them, for he had ten more ships ready if he had seamen to put into them. . . . . If your Suffolk gentry would take care of their own duty and suppress the smuggling on their coast, it would be well.* (*Autobiog: of A. Young, p. 108.*) Lord Keppel, however, appears to have promised £300. The scheme was attacked in the "Bury Post" by some very long letters from Mr. Capel Lofft of Troston, while Mr. Arthur Young wrote to defend it. Lord North is said to have approved of it, while Mr. Fox condemned it as illegal. Peace being soon afterwards declared the scheme came to nothing.

The promised subscriptions were printed by parishes. From a copy in the Library of the Suffolk Archæological Institute at Bury I take the subscriptions that were promised from Ickworth and Horringer. Dr. Knowles who was then Rector of Ickworth promised ten guineas, which comes under Chedburgh.

HORRINGER.

		£	s.	d.
Rev. George Rogers	...	10	10	0
Mr. William Brookes	...	5	5	0
— D. Miller	...	1	1	0
— Isaac Brookes	...	9	0	0
— Robert Frost	...		10	6
— Drew sen.	...	5	5	0
— Thomas Elsden	...	1	11	6
— Edward Drew jun.	...	5	5	0
Mrs. Scarfe	...	1	1	0
— Dubble	...	1	1	0
Miss Chaplyn	...	2	12	6
— Crick	...	1	11	6
Rev. Thomas Kerrich	...	5	5	0
Mrs. Goodchild	...	5	5	0
— Evered	...	5	0	0
Mr. John Elden	...	1	1	0
Mr. Edward Nunn	...	5	5	0
Mr. William Seaber	...	10	10	0
		77	0	0

ICKWORTH.

		£	s.	d.
Hon. Col. Hervey	...	100	0	0
Lord Bristol's Servants.				
Mr. Chevalier	...	1	1	0
— Button	...	2	2	0
— Berwick	...	2	2	0
— Vincent	...	2	2	0
— Frost	...	2	2	0
— Simon	...	1	1	0
— Humphries		1	1	0
Mad: Chanson		1	1	0
Mrs. Button			10	6
— Finney			10	6
— Franks			10	6
— Chevalier			10	6
— Grayham			10	6
Servants-hall		4	17	6
Sundries	...		15	0
		120	17	0

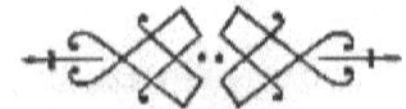

Appendix X.

Horringer Voters.

In 1727 there was a Parliamentary election for the County of Suffolk. There were three candidates for the two seats, and the result was thus: Sir Jermyn Davers 3077. Sir William Barker 2963. John Holt Esq. 2365.

This is how the Horringer voters voted:

James Wyard ...	B.	D.	Thomas Gardiner ...	B.	D.
John Wiseman ...	B.	D.	George Nelson ...	B.	D.
John Deerson ...	B.	D.	John Ong ...	B.	D.
Thomas Kerrington ...		D.	William Haws ...	B.	D.

In the election for the County in 1790 the candidates were Sir John Rous 2761, Sir Thomas Charles Bunbury 3049, and Sir Gerard William Vanneck 2080. These were the voters from Horringer:

Richard Ablett ...		B.	V.	John Gardiner ...			V.
Isaac Brooks ...		B.		John Green ...			V.
William Brooks ...		B.	V.	Rev. Thomas Kerrich ...			V.
John Cook ...	R.	B.		Edmund Nunn ...	R.	B.	
Stephen Crick ...		B.	V.	John D. Miller ...		B.	V.

In the first list James Wyard resided at Great Whelnetham; in the second list William Brooks resided at Felsham, John Cook at Mildenhall, and John D. Miller at Horsecroft.

In the County election of 1830 the candidates were Sir Henry Edward Bunbury 1097, Charles Tyrell 1064, Sir Thomas Gooch 627. The Poll-book has no voters from Horringer, which I don't at all understand.

In 1835 the candidates were Henry Wilson of Stowlangtoft 1723, Robert Rushbrook 1655, Hart Logan of Melford 1509, John Turnor Hales of Herringswell 1350. The Horringer voters were thus:

Arthur Brook ...	R.	L.	John Deerson Miller ...	R.	L.
John Fowler Dove ...	R.	L.	Elias Sturley Nunn ...	R.	L.
John Kemp ...	R.	L.	James Scarlin ...	W.	H.
William Lilly ...	R.	L.	William Bacon Wigson ...	W.	H.

Mr. E. S. Nunn resided at Bury.

Appendix XI.

THE CURATES OF HORRINGER.

Horringer is a pleasantly situated village, with some advantages and attractions and only two miles from Bury St. Edmunds, and therefore has not suffered so much in the past from non-resident rectors as many parishes have. Consequently the number of curates that have been here is comparatively small. I take the following list which is more or less complete from the Registers, where they appear either as fathers of children brought to be baptized, or as officiating, or as signing their names at the foot of a page. In many cases I cannot say much beyond giving their college and the date of their B.A. degree. I give the dates of their being here so far as I can.

UNDER DR. WOMACK.

Dr. Womack was rector from 1662 to 1683. I imagine from baptisms and burials of members of his family that he was a resident rector, but being an archdeacon he may have required the services of a curate.

JOHN HARRIS in 1672. Signs a page in the Registers as Curate. Probably of Caius Coll: B.A. 1662.

HENRY GRAY in 1674. He was probably of Clare Coll: Cambridge, B.A. 1666.

UNDER DR. SYMONDS.

Dr. Symonds who was rector from 1725 to 1758 was resident till about 1741, but not afterwards.

BERNARD MILLS in 1743. He was a native of Bury, fellow of Trin: Coll: Cambridge, B.A. 1736, D.D. 1758. From 1745 to 1757 he was reader, from 1757 to 1766 he was lecturer, at St. Mary's Church, Bury. He was appointed to Wordwell in 1750. He was also Rector of Hitcham, where he died in 1787 aged 72 years, and was buried at St. James', Bury. His portrait by Ralph was engraved by Singleton.

STUART GUNNING in 1745. He was fellow of St. John's Coll: Cambridge B.A. 1741. He was afterwards Rector of Ufford in Northamptonshire, a college living, and died in 1774.

ABBOT UPCHER in 1746. He was of St. Catharine's Coll: Cambridge, B.A. 1745. Mr. Tymms in his account of St. Mary's Charities mentions one left by him. He is there described as "of Sudbury."

ROGER STURGEON in 1747. He was son of Robert Sturgeon, carpenter, of Bury St. Edmunds; educated at Bury Grammar School and Caius Coll: Cambridge, B.A. 1740; Vicar of Waterbeach 1749-1759. His other preferments and two marriages are given in Venn's Biog: Hist: of Caius Coll: He died in 1759, and was buried at St. Edward's, Cambridge.

WILLIAM TONG, 1748 to 1757. He was of St. John's Coll: Cambridge, B.A. 1747. He had two daughters baptized here, in 1756, 1757.

UNDER MR. FRENCH.

Mr. French was rector from 1758 to 1767, and I think was entirely non-resident, though not far off.

JOHN CULLUM takes a wedding in 1758 and 1759 and writes Curate after his signature, but I am not certain that he was Curate of Horringer. He was born at Hawstead, educated at Bury Grammar School and St. Catharine's Coll: Cambridge, B.A. 1756, became Rector of Hawstead in 1762, Vicar of Great Thurlow in 1774, succeeded his father, Sir John, as sixth baronet in 1774, and died in 1785 aged 52. He was a scholar and antiquarian and wrote a history of Hawstead.

ROBERT LEMAN puts Curate after his signature in 1758, but he too may have been a curate in the neighbourhood. He was of Caius Coll: Cambridge, B.A. 1756, D.D. 1778. He was Rector of Pakefield, inherited Wingfield Castle from the Catelyns, and died in 1779.

ROBERT JEGON from 1762 to 1765. He was of Jesus Coll: Cambridge, B.A. 1761.

GEORGE ROGERS from Nov. 1765 to Feb. 1767, when he became Rector. (See Biog: Notes.)

UNDER MR. HASTED.

Mr. Hasted was rector from 1814 to 1852. His non-residence was of a very mild kind, as he lived at Bury St. Edmunds, and preached and ministered and was well known here.

GEORGE JOHN SKEELES, 1815 to 1819. He was the only son of Preb: Skeeles of Peterborough: was at Rugby School and Christ's Coll: Cambridge; Bell scholar 1810, B.A. 1813. He was appointed Rector of Kirkby Underwood, Co. Lincoln, in 1831, Vicar of Cranwell in 1833, and I think died not long afterwards.

HODGSON RICHARD SHEPHERD, 1820 to 1822. He was son of Rev. Henry Shepherd, a Chaplain at Calcutta, and grandson of Richard Shepherd, Rector of Wetherden and Archdeacon of Bedford. He matriculated at St. Alban's Hall, Oxford, in 1819, aged 21 years, served with 24th Dragoons in India, Chaplain H.E.I.C.S. at Dacca 1823, died 1866.

HENRY CURTIS CHERRY, 1822 to 1826. He was of Clare Coll: Cambridge, B.A. 1821; appointed Rector of Burghfield in 1827, and Vicar of Beenham Vallence in 1840, which livings, both in Berkshire, he held together. He had three children baptized here. He published in 1844 a volume called "Illustrations of the Saints' Days and Festivals."

GEORGE HUGHES, 1827 to 1829. I think he was of Christchurch Coll: Oxford, and died in 1830, aged 43 years.

EDWARD GOULD, 1830 to 1836. He was the son of Colonel William Gould of Bury St. Edmunds, and was educated at Christ's Coll: Cambridge, B.A. 1822. In 1836 he was appointed Rector of Sproughton and died in 1849. He had three daughters baptized here. He married Mary Anna Penelope Heigham, who was the daughter of Rev. Henry Heigham, of Hunston Hall, by his wife Elizabeth, a daughter of Captain Thomas Symonds. (See Symonds in Biog: Notes.)

HENRY THOMAS COOPER HINE, 1836-37. Of C. C. Coll: Camb: B.A. 1833. Reader at St. James' from 1839 to 1845, when appointed to a living in Lincolnshire. His father was a linen draper in Abbeygate St., Bury.

WILLIAM HALL, 1837 to 1844. Also Rector of Tuddenham from 1829 to 1852. Rector of Little Saxham from 1852 to 1885. He was land steward of the Ickworth estate for many years till 1859. He died in Jan. 1885 and was buried at or near Brighton, from whence he had come.

ARTHUR CHARLES HERVEY, 1844 to 1852, when he became rector. (See Biog: Notes.)

THOMAS MURRAY COOKESLEY, 1850-1851. He was at Eton and Oriel Coll; Oxford, B.A. 1833. From 1866 till his death in 1877 he was Rector of Broughton, Northants. His elder brother, William Gifford Cookesley, was assistant master at Eton from 1830 to 1854.

FORSTER GEORGE SIMPSON, 1851 to 1860. He came here shortly before Mr. Hasted's death, and remained with Lord Arthur Hervey. He was the son of Richard Simpson of Norwood; was of St. Edmund's Hall, Oxford, B.A. 1843. From 1860 to 1866 he was Rector of Shotley in Suffolk. In 1871 he was appointed Rector of Sidestrand, near Cromer, where he died in 1892 aged 73 years. He published in 1852 a volume called "Lectures on the typical character of the Jewish Tabernacle."

UNDER LORD ARTHUR HERVEY.

Lord Arthur Hervey was rector from 1852 to 1869, and during his time there was generally a curate residing at the old Horringer Rectory.

After Mr. Simpson left there came Rev. Henry S. Mott, 1860 to 1863; Rev. Simeon Dowell Brownjohn 1864 to 1870.

And there I will stop.

APPENDIX XII.

CHRISTIAN NAMES.

The total number of Baptisms in this volume is 3422, which are thus distributed:—

	Boys.	Girls.	Total.
1558 to 1650 ...	406	375	781
1651 to 1750 ...	454	430	884
1751 to 1850 ..	887	870	1757
Total ...	1747	1675	3422

I give in this Appendix a list of the Christian names given to those 3422 children, with the number of times that each name occurs in each of the three periods of 100 years. I have taken no count of second and third names given to children. That custom has sprung up within this present century. It will be seen that in each period John has an easy majority amongst the boys, whilst Elizabeth and Mary stand highest among the girls. In a few cases, *e.g.*, Mary Ann, Anna Maria, where the second name seems to be almost a part of the first, I have put down the two together in the list as though they were one.

The name Jermyn as a Christian name was of course given either as a compliment or by reason of relationship to the Jermyns of Rushbrook, who were Lords of the Manor of Great Horringer from the time of the dissolution of the abbeys to about 1700. The name Henrietta Maria may come from the same source, Henry Jermyn, Earl of St. Albans, being supposed to be married to Henrietta Maria, the widow of Charles I.

It has occurred to me that possibly the name Sherman may come from the same source. This name was given in 1658 to a son of John Manteau, or Mantua, as it is sometimes written. I take it that he was a foreigner, possibly brought over to England by the Earl of St. Albans, or a retainer of Queen Henrietta's, and settled in a house at Horringer belonging to the Jermyns. And then wishing to call his son after his patron, and being told by the clergyman, Name this child, he replied with his foreign accent, Sherman (for Jermyn), and was misunderstood by the clergyman, and so a new christian name arose out of a misunderstanding or mispronounciation.

I will give another instance of the accidental creation of a new name. There is in Ickworth Park a small wood called "Downter's Wood." When it was being planted in or about 1820 the then Earl of Bristol used constantly to be going to look at it, and when his children were asked where he was they used to say, "He is gone down to the wood." And so gradually and imperceptibly the wood got to be called "Downter's Wood," and so it is called to-day.

The name Delariviere will be found several times in the following list, and this name also is owing to the connection between Horringer and the owners of Rushbrook. Thomas, Lord Jermyn, who died in 1703, left no son but five daughters. One of these daughters was Delariviere, who married Sir Symonds D'ewes, grandson of the better known Sir Symonds. She had a sister Merelina, who married in 1691 Sir Thomas Spring of Pakenham. They had a daughter Delariviere, and the name was kept up in the family for several generations.* From this time it constantly appears in the Horringer Registers. The first there to have it was a daughter of John Ewen baptized in 1705. John Ewen was a substantial farmer who occupied Great Horringer Hall, and so was a tenant of the owner of Rushbrook. The next in Horringer to receive the name, 1732, was a daughter of Mr. Symonds, the Rector of Horringer, and she got it owing to her mother being a sister of Delariviere Spring. And then during the following hundred years it appears in the families of Bunting, Brown, Willingham, and Orridge. I do not know whether anyone living to-day bears it, but as a boy I

* Delariviere was also one of the names of Mrs. Mary Manley, authoress of the New Atalantis, who was born in or about 1672. She also wrote a poem which so pleased John, Lord Bristol, that he said he would as soon think of mending the Magnificat as of mending it. Letter 529. The poem is printed at the end of his Diary.

recollect a Delariviere (or Dilly as we called her) Willingham, and I see in the Register that a Delariviere Willingham was buried in 1876 aged 95. Another life of equal length joined on to hers would carry one back to the original Delariviere Jermyn.

The name Merri-woe given to a girl in 1589 may have some reference to the state of affairs at the time, either political or religious. It was the year following the defeat of the Spanish Armada, and a time also of religious changes.

In two cases Matthew is a woman's name. (Marr: 1807. Bapt: 1798. 1803. 1809.)

This list does not include all the names in the Registers, but only those entered as being given at Baptism. There are others which occur as parents' names and in the Register of Burials and Marriages.

Column A is from 1558 to 1650, Column B is from 1651 to 1750, Column C is from 1751 to 1850.

BOYS' NAMES.

	A	B	C	Total		A	B	C	Total
Abel ...		1		1	Edward ...	23	9	17	49
Abraham ...		2	10	12	Elias ...			1	1
Alexander ...			1	1	Elijah ...			2	2
Alfred ...			3	3	Epinetus ...	1			1
Ambrose ...	2	2	2	6	Ernest ...			1	1
Amos ...			3	3	Esau ...			1	1
Antony ...	1	3	1	5	Ezekiel ...			1	1
Arthur ...			7	7	Ezra ...			1	1
Augustus ...			1	1					
					Francis ...	8	10	6	24
Bacchavil ...	1			1	Frank ...		1		1
Benjamin ...	1		5	6	Frederick ...	2	1	17	20
Benninfield ...	1			1					
Byron ...			1	1	Gabriel ...		1		1
					Gardiner ...			2	2
Caleb ...	1			1	George ...	6	10	68	84
Charles ...		8	25	33	Gibson ...	2	1		3
Christopher ...	2	1	2	5	Gilbert ...	1			1
Clement ...	2	2		4	Giles ...	1		1	2
Daniel ...		2	4	6	Harold ...			1	1
David ...			5	5	Harrison ...			1	1
					Harry ...	3		3	6
Edmund ...	8	8	16	32	Harvey ...	1			1

	A	B	C	Total
Henry ...	19	12	42	73
Hercules ...			1	1
Holofernes ...	1	1		2
Hugh ...		3		3
Humfrey ...	1		1	2
Isaac ...		3	8	11
Jacob ...	1			1
James ...	11	22	97	130
Jasper ...	1			1
Jeffery ...	1			1
Jeremiah ...			4	4
Jeremy ...	2			2
Jermyn ...	1	2	1	4
John ...	90	94	140	324
Johnson ...			2	2
Jonas ...			1	1
Jonathan ...	1	2	5	8
Joseph ...	2	8	22	32
Joshua ...	2		3	5
Josiah (s) ...	3	2	1	6
Kenelm ...			1	1
Lawrence ...	2	2		4
Leonard ...		1		1
Lewis ...		2	3	5
Lionel ...			1	1
Luke ...	1			1
Lyas ...			1	1
Lyon ...	1			1
Mark ...	1		1	2
Martin ...		1	2	3
Matthew ...		1	2	3
Melmoth ...			1	1
Micah ...			1	1
Michael ...		3	2	5
Mountjoy ...		1		1
Nathanael ...	1	1	1	3
Nicholas ...	3	1		4
Obadiah ...			1	1
Oliver ...		1		1
Paul ...		2		2
Peter ...			2	2
Philip ...	1	2		3
Potter ...		1		1
Rainold ...	1			1
Ralph ...	1	2		3
Randal ...		1		1
Richard ...	22	17	9	48
Robert ...	37	31	50	118
Robin ...			1	1
Roger ...	2	1		3
Sache ...		1		1
Samuel ...	2	15	14	31
Sebastian ...	1			1
Septimus ...			1	1
Sherman ...		1		1
Simeon ...			1	1
Simon ...	2		3	5
Stephen ...	2	5	5	12
Sulyard ...		1		1
Sydney ...			1	1
Theodore / Thory ...	1	1		2
Thomas ...	59	80	86	225
Timothy ...		3		3
Valentine ...		1	2	3
Vincent ...	2	1		3
Walter ...		1	4	5
William ...	62	57	147	266
Zachariah ...		1		1
Total ...	407	450	880	1737

GIRLS' NAMES.

	A	B	C	Total
Abigail ...	2	3	1	6
Ada ...			1	1
Adelaide ...			1	1
Adrian ...	1			1
Agnes ...	11		1	12
Alice ...	18	5	12	35
Almond ...			1	1
Alse ...	2	1		3
Amelia ...			2	2
Amy ...	3	1	8	12
Anable ...	1			1
Ann ...	40	46	65	151
Anna Maria ...		1	6	7
Arabella ...			2	2
Audrie ...	3			3
Barbara ...	4	1		5
Bet ...			1	1
Betsy ...			3	3
Betty ...		1	6	7
Bridget ...	17	2		19
Caroline ...			9	9
Charlotte ...		1	7	8
Christian ...	4	8		12
Diana ...		1		1
Deborah ...	1		1	2
Delariviere ...		3	6	9
Dorcas ...	1			1
Dorothy ...	8			8
Edith ...			1	1
Eedie ...	3			3
Eleanor ...		1		1
Eliza ...			28	28
Elizabeth ...	57	87	100	244
Ellen ...	1	1	3	5
Ellis ...			1	1
Else ...		4		4
Emily ...			11	11
Emma ...			19	19
Esther ...	2	4	5	11

	A	B	C	Total
Etheldred (see Audrie) ...				
Fanny ...			6	6
Frances ...	12	9	11	32
Frederica ...			1	1
Georgina ...			3	3
Grace ...	2	3	1	6
Gricyll ...		1		1
Hannah ...	2	17	18	37
Harriet ...			28	28
Helen ...			1	1
Henrietta ...		1		1
Henrietta Maria		1		1
Hester (see Esther) ...				
Isabel (la) ...	2	6	1	9
Jane ...	6	4	20	30
Jemima ...			1	1
Joan ...	13			13
Judith ...	3	1		4
Katherine ...	6	10	5	21
Keziah ...			2	2
Kitty ...			1	1
Leah ...	1	1		2
Lehabin ...			1	1
Lettes ...	1			1
Liddy ...			1	1
Louisa ...			9	9
Lucinda ...			2	2
Lucina ...			1	1
Lucy ...	1		17	18
Lydia ...	3		3	6
Margaret / Marget ...	37	12	4	53
Maria ...			26	26

		A	B	C	Total
Marian	...		1		1
Martha	...	12	6	22	40
Mary	...	46	100	112	258
Mary Ann	...			65	65
Matilda	...			1	1
Merriwoe	...	1			1
Milla	...			1	1
Nancy	...			2	2
Penelope	...	1		1	2
Philip	...		1		1
Phœbe	...			4	4
Priscilla	...		1		1
Prudence	...	1			1
Rachel	...		7	6	13
Rebecka	...	3	5	12	20
Rhoda	...			1	1
Rose	...	8	4	5	17
Sally	...			1	1
Sarah	...	11	30	84	125
Sicely	...	1			1
Sophia	...			15	15
Sophy	...			3	3
Susan (na)	...	22	34	68	124
Tabitha	...			1	1
Tammy	...			1	1
Theodosia	...			1	1
Ursula	...	1			1
Winnifred	...			1	1
Total	...	375	426	871	1672

BIOGRAPHICAL NOTES.

Some of these notes are much longer than I originally meant them to be, but it is sometimes difficult to confine oneself to the half a dozen dates and half a dozen abbreviated words which usually constitute a biographical note. But whilst longer they are not nearly so numerous as I meant them to be. I should have liked to have identified many more persons than I have done, but time did not allow of it.

I have not given authorities for every statement that I have made, and so I will set down here a list of works to which I am chiefly indebted. There are other authorities for statements which I have mentioned in the notes themselves.

Allibone's Dict: of Authors. 3 vols. 1877.
Blomefield & Parkin's History of Norfolk. 11 vols. 1805-1810.
Bristol, Earl of, Letters of John Hervey. 3 vols. 1894.
Do. Diary of Do. 1 vol. 1894.
The Burian, vol. v., containing admissions to the Bury Grammar School from 1730. 1899.
Burke's Extinct Baronetcies. 1844.
Bury Post. Vol. 1. 1782 to 1785.
Bury St. Edmunds and Environs, Concise description of, 1827.
Bury St. Edmunds, Tymm's History of St. Mary's Church, 1854.
Bury St. Edmunds, Beckford Bevan's Brief Records of St. James' Church, p.p. 1878.
Clergy List for 1842.
Dictionary of National Biography. 61 vols. with more to come.
Doyle's English Army Lists, 1661-1694. 3 vols. 1892-96.
English Catalogue of Books, 1835 to 1863, by Sampson Low.
Gage's History of Thingoe Hundred. 1838.
Graduati Cantabrigienses. 1659 to 1824.
Do. Do. 1800 to 1872.
Foster's Alumni Oxonienses, 1500 to 1886. 8 vols.
Foster's Index Ecclesiasticus, 1800 to 1840.
Foster's London Marriage Licences, 1521 to 1869.

Ickworth Parish Registers, 1566 to 1890. 1894.
Index to Obituary Notices in the Gent: Mag: 1731 to 1780. 1891.
Jermyn MSS, Suffolk Families, 23 quarto vols., in library of the Suffolk Archæol: Institute.
Jermyn MSS, 1 folio vol., in my library.
Page's Supplement to the Suffolk Traveller. 1844.
School Lists of Eton, Merchant Taylors, Rugby and Westminster.
Suffolk Archæolog: Institute, Proceedings of, 1848-1897. 9 vols.
Venn's Biographical History of Caius College, Cambridge. 2 vols. 1897-8.
Visitations of Suffolk, 1561, 1577, 1612, edited by Metcalfe. 1882.
Visitation of Suffolk, 1561, with additions by Dr. Howard. 2 vols. 1866.

I give a list of natives and residents of Horringer and of those closely connected with them, of whom a memoir will be found in the Dictionary of National Biography.

Battcley, John
— Nicholas
Bedell, William
Blagge, Margaret (Godolphin)
— Robert
Burgess, Richard
Covell, John
Cullum, Sir John
Gedge, Sydney
Gipps, Sir Richard
Goodrich, Richard
Hervey, Arthur C.
— Eliz: C. (Devonshire)
— Frederick (Bristol)
Rogers, Thomas
Simpson, Gen. Sir James
Symonds, John
— Sir Thomas
— Sir William
Womack, Lawrence?

REV. TIMOTHY ADAMSON and Mary his wife were both buried here in 1716, and it would appear that they had been living here for about 40 years previously. Whether he was curate here or not I can't say. In 1701 he seems to have been rector of Wordwell. He was of Jesus College, Cambridge, and took his M.A. degree in 1662. From the arms on his tombstone in the churchyard, No. 8, he would appear to be one of the Adamsons of Wereham or Wireham in Norfolk. (See Blomfield's Hist: of Norfolk, vii. 507.) Mr. James Oakes, who died in 1829 aged 87, married one of the Adamsons of Wereham, and these same arms are impaled on his monument in St. Mary's Church at Bury. The above Mary must have been Timothy's second wife, as in January, 1667, he obtained a license to marry Martha Feltham, widow. They are both described as being of Bury St. Edmunds, his age about 27, and the marriage to take place at Westley, Hessett or St. Mary's in Bury. (Foster's London Marriage Licenses.)

REV. JOSEPH ALEXANDER.—The index to the Baptisms show three children of Joseph Alexander baptized respectively in 1693, 1695, 1702. These children are also entered in the Ickworth Registers, from which the blank in 1702 may be filled up with the name Marget. Their father was Rector of Ickworth from 1692 to his death in 1719. Ickworth parsonage house was in a bad state of repair and uninhabitable when Mr. Alexander came there; he rebuilt it at a cost of over £140, and a few years afterwards, in or about 1702, it was accidentally burnt down. In 1712 the parishes of Ickworth and Chedburgh were united, Mr. Alexander was exempted by the Bishop from rebuilding Ickworth parsonage house, and such materials of it as had survived the fire were used for the repair of Chedburgh parsonage house. Parsonage house and parson are now gone from Ickworth, and only Parson's pond is left.

All this accounts for Mr. Alexander living for a time at Horringer. I imagine him to have been a Bury man, as I have seen the name in the Registers of St. James' Parish.

The Parsonage house at Ickworth has been gone just 200 years, but a barn or out-house of some sort belonging to it was left standing, and an old man now living (1899) tells me that when he was a boy an old man told him that he recollected seeing it.

Mr. Alexander was married in Whepstead Church in May, 1691, to Frances daughter of John Frost of Duffin hall. The Frosts owned Duveton or Duffin hall in the parish of Whepstead for about 150 years, viz., from the reign of Edward VI to 1702, when they sold it to John, Lord Bristol.

BARBER.—I cannot say much about this family excepting that there were two members of it residing here in the reign of James I, and that by more than one marriage they were connected with the Jermyns of Rushbrook and the Blagges of Little Horringer. The following pedigree, which I make out from the Jermyn MSS belonging to the Suffolk Archæological Institute, from Gage's Thingoe Hundred and from other sources, will show these marriages.

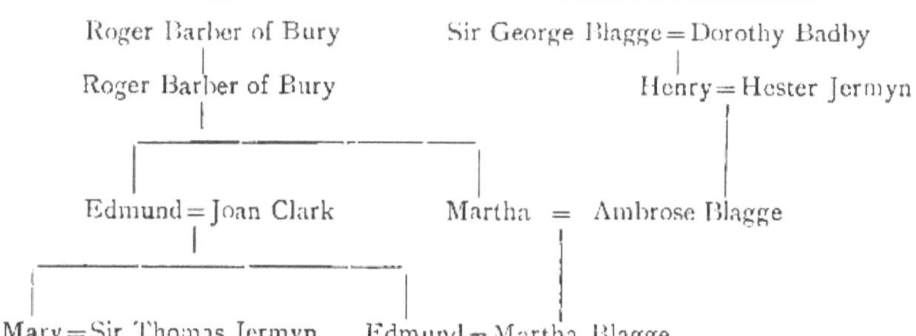

I imagine that the eldest Edmund in the above pedigree is he who had one child baptized in Horringer Church, viz., Sarah in 1612, but I am not quite certain about it. The Jermyn MSS give him ten children, but no Sarah among them. Sir Thomas Jermyn, the constant friend and patron of Bishop Bedell, seems to have married one of them. Another, John, went to Virginia. Another, Matthew, was killed in the Civil War. Another, the second Edmund, who married his first cousin Martha Blagge, was a Poor Knight of Windsor. Another, Ann, married Frederick Cornwallis.

Nicholas Barber was married here in 1617 to Mary Birle, and had three children baptized here between 1620 and 1625. Where his place is in the above pedigree is not clear. Possibly he was a son or nephew of the first Edmund, or he may have been a much younger brother. He seems to have left Horringer in 1624 or 1625, and gone to Chevington, as he had a son baptized there in 1625, and his wife Mary was buried there in 1626. I can say no more about him except that Mary his daughter seems to have married William Bedell, the eldest son of the Bishop, (see Bedell), and that a Nicholas Barber who may have been his son was married at Whepstead in 1662 to Martha Trowle.

Edmund and Nicholas, neither of whom were buried here, do not seem to have been living here at the same time, but one succeeded the other, and so they may have successively occupied the same house. Where that house was I cannot say, but possibly it was the house which 130 years afterwards was occupied by Frederick Hervey, who was afterwards Bishop of Derry. (See Hervey.)

SAMUEL BATTELEY.—During the time of the Civil War and the Commonwealth there was an apothecary at Bury St. Edmunds, named Nicholas Batteley, bringing his children to the font in St. James' Church. Having had the kind permission of the Rev. George Hodges to search the registers of that parish I have found John 1646, Nicholas 1648, Thomas 1655, William 1659, Henry 1661. Of these John and Nicholas were sufficiently distinguished to find a place in the Dictionary of National Biography.* Both were clergymen and antiquarian authors. John became Archdeacon of Canterbury, where he was buried in 1708; and Nicholas, after being Rector of Nowton from 1680 to 1685, became Rector of Beakesbourne in Kent, and died in 1704. I imagine that there was another brother, Samuel, though I cannot find him in the Register of Baptisms in St. James Church. But as the times were troublous it is perfectly possible that he may have been forgotten to be entered. A sister, Mary, buried in 1654, certainly was forgotten, and it will be seen that there is a long interval after Nicholas, during which he may have been born. At any rate, whoever's son he was, he was born at about this time. In 1682 he was married to Mary Bright in Nowton Church, where his brother Nicholas was then Rector; in the course of the next 14 years he had five children christened at St. James'; he was churchwarden of that parish in 1686; on Jan. 1, 1697, his wife was buried; a year or two afterwards he married again, had a son Nicholas baptized at St. James' in 1699, and then seems to have come and settled in Horringer. He had a son Samuel baptized there in Feb. 1701/2. Under July 15, 1714, Lord Bristol records in his diary, "*My good friend and honest neighbour Mr. Samuel Battely dyed at his house in Horringer.*" I have not been able to make out where that house was. In January, 1712, Mr. Joseph Weld, Recorder of Bury and its representative in Parliament, died suddenly. Lord Bristol's eldest son, Carr Hervey, for whom the seat was hoped, was abroad on a long tour, and so Mr. Samuel Batteley was chosen to fill the vacancy. Lord Bristol wrote him a letter of congratulation, and wrote to his son Carr at Venice, saying, "*Serjeant Weld dyed suddenly of an apoplexy last week, so that Bury is unprovided of a Recorder and a Burgess. Mr. Turnor solicits to supply ye former vacancy, and I believe Mr. Battelly will accept ye latter as your trustee till your return, which he has already kindly signified to be his only purpose in medling with it.*"

* This Dictionary gives the year of their births as respectively 1647 and 1650, which is not quite correct according to the Registers. It also states that Nicholas was Rector of Newton, which should be Nowton. I will take this opportunity of correcting a mistake of my own. In the Notes to the Contents of Vol. 3 of Lord Bristol's Letterbooks the Rev. Mr. Battely to whom Letter 853 is written is said to be Nicholas, Rector of Nowton. It is not him, but his nephew (or son) John, who lived for a time at Horringer and held several livings in the neighbourhood.

(Letters 374. 375.) Three months afterwards Mr. Battely was seriously ill in London, and his death was expected every minute, and the question of a successor to him had to be considered. (Letters 384. 386. 387.) However he lived on till 1714. His Parliamentary life was a very short one, as there was a general election in Sept. 1713, when Carr Hervey was chosen in his place, though he had not yet got back from his travels. Mr. Batteley though dying in Horringer was carried to Bury for burial. The Register of St. James records that on July 28, 1714, was buried Mr. Alderman Batteley.

REV. JOHN BATTELEY.—In 1714, about three months before the death of Samuel Batteley, the Horringer Registers record the marriage of John Batteley and Ann Sydey. I imagine that this John was the son of the above Samuel, though curiously just as I could not find Samuel amongst the other children of Nicholas in the Registers of St. James at Bury, so also I cannot find there this John amongst the other children of Samuel. He was a scholar of Trin: Coll: Cambridge, taking his B.A. degree in 1708. He was Rector of Troston from 1714 to 1724; Timworth 1717 to 1741; Ingham 1727 to 1741; Wordwell 1736 to 1741. He was presented to this last living by Lord Bristol. From 1726 to 1741 he was preacher or lecturer at St. Mary's, Bury St. Edmunds. He must have been residing at Horringer from 1714 to 1727, as between those dates he had nine children baptized there, viz., John, Samuel, Ann, Katherine, John, Charles, Elizabeth, Nicholas, William. The first of these died in infancy.

I don't know that he ever published anything, but in 1726 he sent Lord Bristol the manuscript of some theological work of his, which was probably intended for publication. It was acknowledged in a characteristic letter. Letter 853.

Soon afterwards Lord Bristol wrote to the Bishop of Lincoln, asking that a small prebend likely soon to become vacant might be bestowed upon "my neighbour and friend" Mr. Batteley. In a postscript he says, "*Mr. Batteley is nephew to the late Archdeacon of Canterbury, and for whose learning and exemplary life and conversation I will stand answerable to your Lordship and the whole world.*" *Letter 859.*

John Batteley died at Bury in 1741. Mr. Tymms in his account of St. Mary's Church quotes the Register of that parish as recording that "*he preached att both parishes forenoon and afternoon on Sunday, ye 30th of August, and died between twelve and one of the clock on the Tuesday night following, and buried Sept. 4.*"

Of his sons, John, Charles and Nicholas and perhaps the others were at the

Bury Grammar School. Samuel went up to Christ Church College, Oxford in 1733 and took his B.A. degree in 1737.

William was curate of Mildenhall, where there is a slab to his memory stating that he died in November, 1767, aged 38 years.

Charles went up to University College, Oxford, in 1738, B.A. in 1742, was presented by the Crown to the living of Wetherden in Suffolk, afterwards to that of Hunston in Suffolk, and died at Wetherden in 1791, aged 72 years. Charles' son, Waldgrave Batteley, was curate of Shotley for 42 years, and died there in November 1813, aged 66 years. The present rector of Shotley tells me that when he first went to Shotley there were some still living there who remembered Waldgrave Batteley. He was not a total abstainer, and his advice to his people was, Do as I say but not as I do.

REV. WILLIAM BEDELL, BISHOP OF KILMORE. — This good man was rector of Horringer from March 1616 to June 1628, and resided in the rectory house there. Two lives of him written by those who had known him well have been published, so that it is not difficult to find plenty to say about him. The difficulty rather is to condense what there is into the small space that I can afford him. One of the lives was written by the Rev. Alexander Crogy who married his step-daughter, and was first published in 1862. The other was (almost certainly) written by his son William Bedell, rector of Rattlesden in Suffolk, and was first printed in 1872 for the Camden Society. The editor, Mr. Thomas Wharton Jones, has added a great deal of valuable information, to which I am greatly indebted. I shall tell the tale of the Bishop's life as much as possible in the very words of his son. All quotations that follow are from his memoir unless otherwise stated.

William Bedell was born quite at the end of 1571 at Black-Notley in Essex, where his father and grandfather were yeomen. He was apparently the second of three sons, his father's name being John and his mother's Elizabeth (Elliston or Aliston). "*They were both very charitable and mercifull; their house was seldom without one or two poor children, which they kept upon alms. Mrs. Elizabeth Bedell was very famous and expert in chirugery, which she continually practised upon multitudes that flocked to her, and still gratis, without respect of persons, rich or poor.*" William and his elder brother John were sent to school at Braintree, about a mile from their home. Though very fond of learning yet William "*on a*

"*time received such a blow from his cholerick master, that he was beaten off a pair*
"*of stairs, and had one side of his head so bruised, that the blood gushed out of*
"*his ear, and his hearing was in consequence so impaired, that he became in process*
"*of time wholly deaf on that side.*" Before he was fully 13 years of age he went up to Emanuel College, Cambridge, and was soon chosen scholar. After a studious career he took his degrees, B.A. in 1588, M.A. in 1592, and in 1593 became a fellow of his college. Early in 1597 he was ordained a priest, and there ends the first chapter in his life. It may be summed up in the words of his son, "*A great student he was and a great proficient, as in all kinds of learning, so especially in Divinity. He did not only tast the liberal arts, or give them a short visit by the way, but thoroughly studied them.*" So he sallies forth from the University and makes his start in life well equipped.

In January, 1602, he was appointed preacher or lecturer at St. Mary's Church, Bury St. Edmunds. "*His first call to the ministerial work was to St. Edmundsbury in Suffolk, where the great esteem he gained for his grave, humble and diligent discharge of that employment is yet surviving in the mouths and memories of many. His auditory there was very much consisting of men of the best quality and best abilities of judgement and learning, who yet ever received ample satisfaction in his sermons.*" "*His prayer before sermon was not set nor fixed allways to the same form of words, but various in expressions as the time and present occasions most required; but ever in the plainest and easiest phrase of the English tongue, according to the capacity of the weakest understanding: so as the most unlearned hearer might say Amen.*" "*His voice was low, his action little, but the gravity of his aspect was great, and the reverence of his behaviour such as was more affecting to the hearers than the greater eloquence and more pompous pronunciation of others.*" He was said to excell in explaining the Scriptures, and was contrasted with his successor at St. Mary's, the one making the obscurest passages very plain, the other making the plainest passages very obscure. "*He had not been long there (at Bury) ere he had gained a great reverence as well from all that savoured of the power of godliness as from the gallants, knights and gentlemen, who reverenced him for his impartial, grave and holy preaching and conversation, and heard him gladly.*"

After five years at Bury he was appointed chaplain to the English Embassy at Venice, our ambassador being Sir Henry Wotton. He went there in the early summer of 1607. I must skip over the time spent there. It must be enough to say that he earned the respect of the most eminent Venetians, formed friendships there which lasted for life, studied hard at the Italian and other languages, and came back to Bury after an absence of nearly four years. He was probably back in Bury by March 1611.

He had formed a friendship at Venice with an eminent Venetian physician, Dr. Jasper Despotine. [See Despotine in these Notes.] This gentleman returned to England with Sir Henry Wotton and Dr. Bedell, and came to Bury with Bedell and started a practice there. They lodged together "in the house of one Mr. Nunne," and Bedell taught the Italian doctor English. Bedell's friends at Bury were very well pleased to see him return to his duties in St. Mary's Church. I don't know whether Mr. Nunn's house can be identified or not.

About a year after his return from Venice, on Jan. 29, 1612, Bedell was married in St. Mary's Church to Leah Mawe. She was the widow of Robert Mawe, Recorder of Bury, who had been buried at St. Mary's in June 1609. Mrs. Mawe had five children by her first marriage, of whom the eldest was now only seven years old. He must have left Mr. Nunne's now, and one would like to know where in Bury he did live. Of the five little Mawes, the eldest, Nicholas, was sent to Bury Grammar School and became a physician. John and Robert died young. Leah and Edward afterwards came with their mother and step-father to Ireland.

In March 1616 Sir Thomas Jermyn of Rushbrook presented him to the living of Horringer. He accepted it gladly because he felt that his voice was too weak for so large a church as St. Mary's. "*The place being near Bury and the congregation there not very great, but such as his voice might reach, he accepted the presentation.*" There was a little hitch at first. The fees for institution payable to the Bishop of Norwich's officials were then very high, and Bedell absolutely refused to take the living if he had to pay them, as he considered practically it would be buying his preferment. Eventually the Bishop, Dr. Jegon, gave way and left it to him to pay what he thought fit.

His son gives us an account of his manner of life at Horringer. "*His manner was to rise very early (commonly at 4 winter and summer), and so to retire presently to his study; where he would be so fixed till prayer-time, that if anything . . . did happen to call him down, he would be even angry with the messenger (wife, child or servant) of any such occasion of interruption.*" He had three seasons for prayer, morning, noon and evening. At noon he read and expounded a chapter before prayer. Some little time was devoted to the education of his children, as well as to his own studies and duties. "*Some little recreation he used to take before dinner or supper; which for the most part was planting, transplanting, grafting, and inoculating, and sometimes digging in his garden."* *"In his dress he was a great lover of plainness, both for the matter and fashion; never changing the fashion in all his life. His rules were easiness for the stirring of his body and serviceableness, avoiding all vanity and superfluity."* He wished his children to be dressed according to the same rules as himself, while his wife preferred them to be smarter; but he got his way. His son tells us of *"his behaviour to the beggars, bedlams and travellours that use to come to men's doors. These he would not fail to examine, mixing both wholsom instructions and severe reproofs. Nor rested he there; but if they had any passes to travel by, he would be sure to scan them throughly, and finding them false or counterfeit, his way was to send for the constable, and after correction given according to law, he would make them a new pass and send them to the place of their last settlement or birth. This made him so well known among that sort of people that they shunned the town (Horringer) for the most part; to the no small quiet and security of him and all his neighbours."* We are then told how the Lord's day was kept, and of his sermons forenoon and afternoon, and of the public catechizing of the young whereby both they and their elders profited alike. And we are told *"of his constant use of private admonitions and reproofs, which tho' some stomacked at, yet they durst not openly despise. The poorest of all he had a tender care over in this respect, whom he used bountifully to relieve every year. The others he entertained at his table once a year all through the whole parish, with whom he would be very cheary, and yet in so pious and profitable a manner that their minds and souls were no less feasted than their bodies."* He was most particular about preserving the rights of the Church and keeping all rectorial buildings in good repair. *"He left behind him a book to his successours, giving them a clear and exact "account what dues to expect from the parishioners, and some light for clearing "of controversies and difficulties about tithing that might afterward arise."* He had a long lawsuit with Mr. William Lucas of Horscroft, *"one of the chiefest of his parish."* He was given to understand that Mr. Lucas had certain pieces of ground in his possession which rightly belonged to the rectory of Horringer. He was told so by some who could remember when the grounds did do so, and he proved it by searching the rolls and records of the manor, the lord of the manor having given him leave to do so. But when he told Mr. Lucas of this, Mr. Lucas denied the right of the Church and refused to give them up. The suit began and lasted ten years. In the end the award was favourable to the Church. Not the same land, but the same amount of land more conveniently situated for the rector, was given up by Mr. Lucas. This lawsuit caused Mr. Bedell to make some study of the law, and in consequence he was often chosen as arbitrator by his neighbours in their disputes. (See Lucas.)

A Parliament being called while he was at Horringer, two ministers had to be chosen to represent the diocese of Norwich in Convocation, one for Suffolk, one for Norfolk. Whilst many were scheming to get themselves elected, Bedell refused to move in the matter. In spite of it he was chosen. He was sorry when he heard of it, saying that "*he knew he should but loose his time, and sit* "*there and tell the clock, without doing any good as to what the present exigencies of* "*the Church did most require.*"

But the time is now coming when he must say Good bye to Horringer, and not to Horringer only, but to Suffolk and England. The next fifteen years of his life are given to Ireland, and this last chapter in his life I must run through very quickly.

In May 1627, by mandate of King Charles I, he was nominated Provost of Trinity College, Dublin. Probably Sir Thomas Jermyn, who had sat under him in St. Mary's Church at Bury, and who had presented him to the living of Horringer, had something to do with this appointment. In July 1627 he started for Dublin and was admitted to the office. He returned to Horringer in September to settle his affairs there and to fetch his family. In June 1628 he resigned Horringer and quitted it and England for ever.

They were in all seven souls who moved from Horringer Rectory to Trinity College, Dublin. There were himself and Leah his wife; there were his two step-children Leah and Edward Mawe; there were his own three children, William, John and Ambrose. William and John had been born in Bury, and are in St. Mary's Registers; Ambrose was born at Horringer and will be found in these registers. The oldest of these five was Leah Mawe, 22 years, the youngest was Ambrose Bedell, 9 years. One child, Grace Bedell, was left behind, in Horringer Churchyard; she had died in 1624 just under 10 years of age.

Just two years after his first nomination to the office of Provost, but only one year after he had settled down at Dublin, he was through the efforts of Sir Thomas Jermyn appointed to the united Bishopricks of Kilmore and Ardagh. That was in May, 1629. He was not anxious to be promoted and hesitated before he accepted the offer. It troubled him that he would have now as a Bishop to use more state. "*His own wisdom prompted him to some conformity to the Episcopal rank, and his friends were sollicitous lest he should render himself contemptible or lie under sinister censures by coming too much behind other Bishops in state and gallantry. And therefore he took a middle way, rising a little but differing very much in outward splendour from the rest of his order. He never wore silk, only his girdle, chimier and tippet were of that material. Never wore bever, castor or demi-castor, but allwaies felts. He used not to ride up and down the streets of Dublin about his occasions, with his three or four men attending, as was the common usage of the Bishops there, but allwaies walked with only one man. And tho' in this practice he did discontent some, and suffered the gibes of the more lordly prelates and their followers, yet he could not be altered.*"

Mr. Clogy, who did not know him till he became a Bishop, but lived a good deal with him from then to his death, says, "*When others of his order were either galloping in their coaches or prancing upon their vaporing stone-horses through the streets of Dublin, he was never seen in a coach in city or country, nor a horse-back in the city; but walking with his servant after him, save when he rode publiatus in his scarlet robes in Parliament, or attended the Lord Deputy to church upon the Lord's day, as the manner of all prelates was in their pontificals. . . His habit was grave, in a long stuff gown not costly but comely; his stockings wollen; his shoes not much higher behind than before.*"

My limited space only allows me to say of the next 14 years that all through them he followed the same simple and fearless course of conduct. There were many evils to be attacked and reformed, and he went at them in his gentle but determined way without fearing any man. He incurred some opposition, but he incurred a great deal more of love and respect from all sorts and classes of people, Roman Catholics as well as Protestants.

Writing to a friend soon after his appointment he says of Kilmore, "*My cathedral church is such another as Horningerth was, but without steeple, bell or font. You can imagine the rest.*" His son describing Kilmore says, "*Kilmore itself was but a meer country village, of good large bounds, but so thinly inhabited that no where in the whole parish was any street or part of a street to be found. There was a competent number of English, but the Irish were more than five times their number, and all of them obstinate Papists. The Bishop's house joined close to the church, being built upon one of the highest hills in the countrey; not near any neighbour of any quality by a mile.*"

After about three years he resigned Ardagh and was Bishop of Kilmore only. So little in sympathy was he with the idea that Ireland was merely to exist for the benefit of England, so little did he approve of the English-made law obliging the Irish to learn English, that as soon as he got into Ireland he set to work to learn the Irish language himself, he taught it to his own children, he tried to get his clergy to set up Irish schools in their parishes, he was careful to place clergy who could speak Irish in all those places where Irish was the language known, he printed a summary of Christian doctrine in Irish, and then he had an Irish version made of the Old Testament. Up to his time there was only an Irish version of the New Testament. In all things he tried to act for Ireland as an Irish Bishop should act, and not merely as an Englishman imposed upon the Irish by England and acting solely for England.

Mr. Clogy describes his hospitality which was of a genuine though not showy kind. "*His castle was furnished with things not superfluous, ornamental and splendid, but good and necessary for common use. His table with plenty of good provision at all times; whereunto there was great resort, as to a place of greatest hospitality in all that county; half an Irish beef a week, besides other provision, a great part whereof was given to poor Irish families. At Christmas he had the poor Irish as well as rich British to sit and feast about him, both men and women, that dwelt next unto him, that scarce had any whole clothes to their back, nor could understand a word of English, and were strangers to such civil and plentiful entertainment.*"

In October 1641 the rebellion broke out in Ireland suddenly and with great fury. At first nothing of the Bishop's was touched, he being greatly respected. A great multitude of English fled to his house at Kintore, and there he kept them, having much cattle and much grain. After a time the rebels, if that is the proper name to give to those who are contending against intolerable tyranny, drove the English refugees away and seized the Bishop's cattle. The Bishop was allowed to stay in his own house till about Christmas, when he and his two sons were carried away by the rebels to Loughwater Castle, where there were neither glass windows nor wooden shutters. After about three weeks there they were set free. The Bishop could not return to his own house at Kilmore because the Roman Catholic Bishop had stepped into it and was occupying it. But a Mr. Sheridan whose house was a mile off from it kindly took him and his sons in. At the end of January, 1642, the Bishop was taken ill, probably in consequence of the hardships of the last few months, and on Feb. 7 he died. He was buried at Kilmore, the rebels attending the funeral and firing a volley over his grave, and showing various marks of respect.

He was a little over 70 years of age at his death. Mr. Clogy, his step son-in-law, who was with him up to the last as well as his own two sons, says in his memoir, "*His eye was not dim nor his natural force abated; only he had some kind of deafness in his left ear, occasioned by a fall down stairs in his childhood. I remember that when walking abroad with him and his two sons the week before he sickened, in returning back he leapt so nimbly and vigorously over a broad ditch that amazed us all, and put us to a stand to follow him. He never used spectacles; nor lost one tooth; nor any decay of his hair, save in the colour; his gray hairs being found in the way of righteousness were as a crown to him; his beard was long and broad. I never knew any razor to pass upon his face, which was beautiful, with more majesty and gravity than my tongue can express.*"

Mr. Clogy says elsewhere, "*Though his stature was tall his voice was low and mournful, both in praying and preaching.*"

We have already seen him digging in the garden at Horringer. The digging went on after he became a Bishop. Mr. Clogy says that though otherwise of great strength and health of body, above many, yet during the last few years he had occasional attacks, which he endured with great patience. "*The greatest antidote against it, which he found by experience to do him most good, was digging in his garden in a morning. Laying aside his gown he would dig for half an hour or thereabouts; and being a little heated he found mitigation of his pain. . . . . He had brought with him out of Italy such curious instruments for racemation, engraffing and inoculating, that I saw him once teach his gardener how to use them; and when he put the graft into the stock most neatly only tied it about with a seare cloth.*"

The seven souls who had moved from Horringer to Dublin in 1628 had been made less in number by death before these last troubles came. At Christmas, 1634, his second son John had died. Soon after Christmas, 1637, his step-daughter Leah Clogy had died, about a month after her marriage to Mr. Alexander Clogy, one of the Bishop's biographers. In March, 1638, his wife had died. So that there were left only Edward Mawe, his stepson, and William and Ambrose, his own sons.

Edward Mawe was ill when the Bishop was dying, and whether he died also or recovered is not known.

Ambrose Bedell, the only one who was born at Horringer, married in Ireland before the rebellion broke out; his wife was Mary, daughter of Peter Hill, Sheriff of Down; he served as a Captain in Col. Arthur Hill's regiment, who was his wife's uncle ; after the Restoration he had a grant of lands made to him in Cavan and Antrim, and died there in 1683. He left no surviving children.

William Bedell, the biographer and eldest son, was born in Bury early in 1613. He was ordained by his father in 1634 and presented by him to the Vicarage of Kinawley in the diocese of Kilmore. After his father's death he left Ireland for good and returned to England. He first went to visit his uncle at Black-Notley, and then he went to stay with his father's old Venetian friend at Bury, Dr. Despotine. Whilst there Mr. Hinde, the rector of Whepstead, disappeared in a curious way and left no one to take his duty. He furnished himself with horse, pistolls and sword, and borrowed some money, and went on a journey proposing to return before long. But he did not come back, and so there was no one to take the duty at Whepstead. William Bedell was asked by some of the Whepstead people to preach there, and he was appointed by Parliament to do so, this being during the Commonwealth. After doing it for about a year he was appointed Minister of Rattlesden, and there he remained for 26 years, being buried there in March, 1671.

Mr. T. W. Jones,* the editor of his memoir of his father, says his wife appears to have been a Mary Barber, but he could not find out much about her. I think that she must be the Mary, daughter of Nicholas Barber gent, whose baptism on April 4, 1620, is in the Horringer Registers. (See Barber.) It look as if the attachment, or at any rate acquaintance, had begun when they were children together at Horringer, and his moving into Ireland had not caused him to forget her, but he had seized the opportunity of a visit to England to make her his wife. As they were married before the rebellion broke out in Ireland in 1641, she could have hardly been out of her teens before she became Mrs. Bedell. I cannot say where the Barbers lived in Horringer, but her father appears soon after her birth to have been living in Chevington. And as subsequently one of the Barbers was married at Whepstead, there may be some connection between that and the previous fact that some of the Whepstead people had asked William Bedell to come and preach to them.

*While expressing my great obligation to Mr. Jones' careful and thorough work, I will take the opportunity of correcting a small error. In a note at p. 130 he says that Sir William Hervey married Suzan, daughter of Sir Robert Jermyn, and that this marriage brought the Jermyn property, including Horringer, to the Herveys. But in reality this marriage had nothing to do with it. How the Jermyn property did eventually come to the Herveys will be seen in the preface to this volume.

William and Mary Bedell had eight children, of whom the eldest, Leah, was baptized at Whepstead in 1643, and the other seven at Rattlesden, viz., William, John, James, Ambrose, Penelope, Agnes, Isabella. John succeeded his father as Rector of Rattlesden, but died the following year, 1672. Mr. Jones has gone very fully into the history of the Bishop's descendants, and it appears that there are none now of his name and lineage.

GEORGE INNES BEVAN came to live at Horringer house about the year 1840. He was the only son of George Bevan, and married his first cousin, Rachel, daughter of Robert Bevan of Rougham. Several children were baptized here, of whom George, 1842, went into the army, attained to the rank of General, and died in 1898. Mr. Bevan left Horringer in or about 1860 and went to live at Godmanchester.

DOROTHY BLAGGE.—The Blagges came to Little Horringer hall in the reign of Queen Elizabeth, in or about 1570, and they remained there about 70 years; two generations of them were baptized here. Some little account of them must therefore be given.

There was in the reign of Henry VIII an Essex family named Badby. One of them, Thomas Badby, lived in St. James's parish at Bury, and for a short time possessed the site of Bury Abbey, which had not long before been abolished. He was the son of William, and had a sister named Dorothy, who was a maid of honour.*

Dorothy Badby was married three times.

Her first husband was Sir George Blagge, the son of Robert Blagge. Robert was a Baron of the Exchequer in the early part of the reign of Henry VIII, and some account of him will be found in the Dict: of Nat: Biog:. His son George by a second marriage was a great favourite with Henry VIII, and was knighted; he was nearly killed at the siege of Landreci, and nearly burnt afterwards as a Protestant heretic. He died in 1551.

Her second husband was Richard Goodrick, a native of Yorkshire and nephew of Thomas Goodrick, Bishop of Ely. Richard Goodrick will be found in the Dict: of Nat: Biog:. He died in 1562.

* A pedigree in the Jermyn MSS at Bury makes out Dorothy to be granddaughter of that William and niece of Thomas, but that is obviously impossible.

Her third husband was Sir Ambrose Jermyn of Rushbrook, who had lately obtained the manor of Great Horringer. Sir Ambrose died in 1577, and last of all Dorothy died also. She was buried at Rushbrook in 1594. Sir Ambrose had purchased Little Horringer in 1562 from the Lucas family of Horsecroft.

By his first wife Sir Ambrose had had a son Robert, and a daughter Hester. By her former husband, Sir George Blagge, Dorothy had had a son Henry and a daughter Judith. Robert Jermyn married Judith Blagge, and Henry Blagge married Hester Jermyn, which made a very pretty complication.

Sir Robert Jermyn, who succeeded Sir Ambrose in 1577, settled Little Horringer upon Dorothy for her life, she being both his step-mother and his mother-in-law. Soon afterwards Little Horringer is found to be the property of her son Henry Blagge, who had married Hester Jermyn. Apparently he was living there before that, as he was married here in 1571. It is not quite clear how he came into possession of it; but as the site of Bury Abbey had come to him from his mother's family, the Badbys, and as that site is afterwards found to be the property of Sir Robert Jermyn, Mr. Gage guesses that there may have been an exchange of properties, Henry Blagge taking Little Horringer and Sir Robert Jermyn taking Bury Abbey. At any rate, however that may have been, Henry Blagge was settled there before 1574.

HENRY BLAGGE had two children baptized here, viz., Dorothy in 1574, and Thomas in 1579, who died an infant. Another son, Ambrose, was not baptized here. Henry was buried at St. Mary's in Bury in 1596.

AMBROSE BLAGGE was married here in 1608 to Martha Barber of Bury St. Edmunds. (See Barber.) She was buried here in 1624, and he married secondly Margaret Snelling, a widow. That he resided here continuously is proved by his having twelve children baptized here between 1609 and 1635, viz., Harry, George, Thomas, Katharine, Ann, Martha, Judith, Humphry, by his first wife, and Ambrose, Henry, Edmund, Margaret, by his second wife. Of these Harry, Humphry, and Edmund died in infancy. George died in 1611, aged 20. Martha married her first cousin, Edmund Barber. Judith married Thomas Covel of Great Horringer. (See Covel.) Margaret, the youngest child of all, died with her name unchanged in 1720, aged 85. Her tombstone is in the church, No. 18, but her age and date of death are there left blank. Thomas

T

heads the next paragraph. Ambrose himself, the father of all these children, died in August, 1662, when he must have been 80, if not 90. He was not buried here.

THOMAS BLAGGE, the third but eldest surviving son of Ambrose and Martha, was baptized here in 1613, and married Mary North of Mildenhall. He was a groom of the bedchamber to Charles I, and when the civil war broke out in 1642 he at once raised a regiment for the king's service. Probably his native village and the neighbourhood largely helped to fill the ranks of this regiment. His regiment suffered at the battle of Naseby in 1645. He afterwards was Governor of Wallingford, which after a long siege surrendered to the Parliament army but obtained very good terms. After the death of Charles I in 1649 he joined the young Prince Charles. After the battle of Worcester in 1651 he fled with Prince Charles and about sixty others. Having fled about 25 miles they reached John Penderel's house at Boscobel. Here they separated. Charles entrusted his watch to Lord Wilmot and his diamond badge as a Knight of the Order of the Garter to Col. Blagge, and after climbing up trees and many narrow escapes managed to take ship at Shoreham and get out of the country. Col. Blagge pursuing his flight in another direction hid the badge for safety sake; but was soon taken prisoner and carried to the Tower of London. Whilst there somebody managed to find the badge and bring it to him. Not long afterwards he managed to escape from the Tower and was able to restore the badge to Prince (or King) Charles. The badge was a sacred thing in the eyes of every Knight of the Garter, and honour was concerned in the keeping of it. This particular badge had probably an additional sacredness from having been the one worn by Charles' father at his execution. Hence Col. Blagge's responsibility was great.

The Colonel died within 6 months of the Restoration, on Nov. 14, 1660, and was buried in the north transept of Westminster Abbey. There was formerly a monument to him there, but it no longer exists. The long Latin inscription on it has been preserved.

He left a widow, who survived him about 10 years, and four young daughters. Charles II and his brother, the Duke of York, do not seem to have forgotten the services of Col. Blagge after his death. His two daughters, Mary and Margaret, both became Maids of Honour to the Duchess of York, and after her death in 1671 Margaret became Maid of Honour to Queen Catharine.

MARGARET BLAGGE.—Any temptation to give an account of her must be resisted, because strictly speaking she does not belong to Horringer, and I do not know that she ever could have been there. She was born in 1652, after that her father had left Horringer for court and camp. It must be enough to say that she must have been of a really excellent character. Brought up from early girlhood in the not very healthy atmosphere of the Court of Charles II, she laid down for herself the strictest possible rules of conduct and managed to conform to them with undeviating steadfastness. In 1675 she quitted her post as Maid of Honour to the Queen of Charles II and married Mr. Sidney Godolphin. Three years afterwards, Sept. 1678, she died a few days after the birth of her first child. She was buried at Breage in Cornwall. Her husband was afterwards created Earl of Godolphin. The child who lost his mother at his birth was Francis, 2nd Earl of Godolphin. Both father and son were distinguished statesmen.

The life of Mrs. Godolphin (Margaret Blagge) was written by her great friend and admirer, John Evelyn the diarist; it remained unpublished till 1848, when it was edited by Bishop Samuel Wilberforce. The continual stream of exaggerated praise which runs through the biography spoils it. It would have been better if more facts had been given and left to speak for themselves. To this life and its notes I am chiefly indebted for the account I have given of Col. Blagge. Mary, the daughter of the 2nd Earl of Godolphin, and granddaughter of Margaret Blagge, married the Duke of Leeds. The present Duke of Leeds is consequently descended from the Horringer Blagges. A portrait of Col. Blagge was at Gogmagog Hills near Cambridge in 1848, and a portrait of Mrs. Margaret (Blagge) Godolphin was then at Wootton, the property of Mr. Evelyn, the descendant of the diarist.

I have had no opportunity of examining title deeds, and so I cannot say exactly how or when Little Horringer passed from the Blagges to the Gipps's. I presume it was by purchase. The latest baptism of a Blagge here was in 1635; the earliest baptism of a Gipps was in 1645. I presume that the Blagges went and the Gipps's came between those two dates; but it is only a presumption, and there is slight evidence that Margaret Blagge's mother may have been here in 1651, when her husband was fleeing after the battle of Worcester. It is this.

Thomas Hervey, the father of the first Earl of Bristol, was courting Isabella May for 10 years before their marriage, which took place in 1658. Seventy-three of his letters to her during this long courtship were copied by him into a blank book which remains at Ickworth.* His letters were mostly written from Hengrave, where his father, Sir William, was then living, Ickworth being then in an uninhabitable state, whilst she was generally staying with one or other of her relatives at Bury, Boxted, Rushbrook, or somewhere near. The correspondence and the interviews between them had to be secret and stolen, because her mother opposed the match. In one of these love letters, written I think in 1651, he says he wants her to write down something for his information and to let him have the letter as she let him have a former one, "*which will not be hard to do if you will be at Mrs. Collonel Blaggs about five of ye clock on Tuesday night next, where I will not faile to meet you.*" But I do not know how to reconcile her being there in 1651 with the Gipps Baptisms beginning in 1645. Possibly Mrs. Collonel Blagg's means a house at Mildenhall, she being a daughter of Sir Roger North of Mildenhall; or it may mean a house at Bury or somewhere near. Or possibly the Gipps's came to some other house in Horringer before they got into Little Horringer hall. In another of these letters written during courtship, dated June 28, 1652, Thomas Hervey tells Isabella May that he had made a plot to come and see her at Bury, but that it was given out that she was gone to Horringer, so he did not go. Now if Mrs. Col. Blagge was living at Horringer in June, 1652, her daughter Margaret, born Aug. 2 in that year, would probably have been born there; but she does not appear in the Registers. However, the Registers being often defective, she may after all be a native of Horringer, in which case her biography here should have been fuller. It is very aggravating of Evelyn not to have told us.

BOKENHAM.—The family of Bokenham or Buckenham possessed manors in various parts of Suffolk from early times, as a reference to the Supplement to the Suffolk Traveller or any County history will show. One branch preceded the Drurys at Hawsted. The Horringer Registers show a John Bokenham, clerk, buried at Horringer in 1595, his wife Isabel being buried there in 1587. This must be he who was rector of Ickworth from (I think) 1566 to 1595. He may have resided at Horringer for the same reason that Mr. Alexander did just 100 years later, viz., the dilapidated state of Ickworth parsonage house; or he may have been a relic of the family who preceded the Drurys at Hawstead and whose possessions extended into Horringer, and may have lived on his own estate.

* These letters were published in 1891 with the letters of his son, John, Lord Bristol.

Others of the name besides this John will be found both in the Ickworth and Horringer Registers, but I cannot connect them.

There was another clerk or clergyman of the name buried at Horringer, viz., Nicholas in 1634, but I have not been able to find out what living he held.

BROOK.—For some years in the last century two brothers were respectively occupying Great and Little Horringer hall farms, William and Isaac Brook.

WILLIAM, the eldest of the two, succeeded the Goodchilds as tenant of Little Horringer hall in or about 1785. He died in 1795 aged 75 years, and was succeeded there by Isaac his son, who remained there till about 1810, when it became the home farm of the Ickworth estate. Isaac died in 1812 aged 50. Both are buried at Westley.

ISAAC senior, the brother of William, was occupying Great Horringer hall farm, then the property of the Davers family, for 30 or 40 years in the last century, and died in 1801 aged 71, and is also buried at Westley. He had several children baptized at Horringer between 1764 and 1780.

One of them, ARTHUR, succeeded his father at Great Horringer hall and remained there till about 1814, when I imagine that he moved into the new house, Brooke House, which he had just built on his own property. An inscription in the church tells us that he munificently restored it. He was buried at Westley in 1859 aged 86 years. Though he was a native of Horringer, and had spent the whole of his long life there, and had built a house there and restored the church there, yet he was taken to Westley for burial. I am told that the reason was that he objected to the water which lay in the vault at Horringer church.

Another son, THOMAS, lived to a great age and was buried at Horringer in 1869 aged 91 years.

Another son, STEPHEN, died in 1798 aged 32 according to his tombstone. It was he who for some reason or other had the marriage service repeated. (See page 129, note.)

The name is spelt sometimes Brook, sometimes Brookes. There was a John and Carr or Carolina Brook having children baptized here in 1703 and following years, but I do not see any connection between them and the two brothers, William and Isaac, who first came to reside here 60 or 70 years after that, and who were not baptized here.

REV. RICHARD BURGESS was presented to the rectory of Ickworth and Horringer by the Crown in 1869 on the promotion of Lord Arthur Hervey to the bishoprick of Bath and Wells. He was born in 1796, educated at St. John's College, Cambridge, ordained in 1820, chaplain to English residents at Geneva in 1828, and to those at Rome in 1831. In 1835 he took his D.D. degree. In 1836 he was appointed rector of Upper Chelsea, where he remained for twenty-five years. He was a prebend of St. Paul's Cathedral, and died in April 1881 at Brighton aged 85. He was the author of many publications, including sermons and works on the antiquities of Rome and a tour in Greece. A memoir of him will be found in the Dict : of Nat : Biography.

CHERRY.—See Appendix XI.

COVELL.—The Registers show that the Covells were in Horringer before the year 1600. Their estate was at the south end of the parish, where Horringer house now stands. Apparently they came to an end in the male line with Thomas Covel who died in 1715, and the estate passed to John Kettle, who (I think) had married Elizabeth Covell. His son, John Kettle, sold it in 1737 to Valentine Mumby or Mumbee of Ixworth, whose son Valentine in 1768 sold it to John Everall. It, or a part of the Covell estate, has been successively owned since then by Mr. Charles Hill Hall, Mr. George Bevan, Mr. Marriot, and is now the property of Mr. Lainson. There does not appear to be anything left of the house that the Covells lived in, the present house being the work of Mr. Mumbee with subsequent additions.

In 1599 there was baptized William the eldest of the two sons of William Covell. William sen. died in 1625, and William jun. married Alice ——— very soon afterwards. Between 1627 and 1638 six children of William and Alice are brought to the font, three sons and three daughters. Something can be seen and said of all the three sons, William, Thomas and John. William, the father of these three sons, died in 1661. See tombstone No. 15.

WILLIAM COVELL, the eldest, was baptized in 1627. From his being afterwards called Capt. Covell I imagine that he took a part in the civil war which broke out in 1642. Very probably he served in the regiment which was raised by Col. Blagge of Little Horringer hall. (See Blagge.) He is not down in Doyle's Army Lists beginning at 1661, so that apparently by the time that the war was over he had had enough of it and came back to Horringer. Between 1662 and 1671 five children of him and Mary his wife are brought to the font in Horringer church, viz., John, Ann, Thomas, Richard, Richard. Thomas and the two Richards all died unmarried, and John had only one daughter.

In 1695, when John Hervey, afterwards 1st Earl of Bristol, had lately succeeded to the Ickworth estate on the death of his father, Sir Thomas, he was acting as his steward. Whether he had been so in the time of Sir Thomas, I know not. There is a long letter written to him by John Hervey dated Jan. 1700, and beginning "Honest Will Covell." It is only interesting as showing the old manor house at Ickworth near the church tumbling to pieces, and as mentioning a meeting at the Red house, which I presume to be the Horringer inn. (Letter 190.)

He does not appear to have been a very businesslike steward. In 1702, when John Hervey was turning a farm house, the present Ickworth Lodge, into a mansion for himself, he writes to his wife to say that he cannot join her in London, because the head brick-burner at Ickworth has run away, the men can't get their wages, Will: Covell has done nothing that he ought to have done, and everything is in a state of chaos. He says that "*the poor workmen follow me about in shoales, crying, We are ready to starve and can gett no money of the noble Captain: so that I've been forced to pay off all their bills myself and write all their acquittances for them.*" Letters 204, 206.

Apparently William Covell had a tongue, as John Hervey writing to Lady Gipps of Little Horringer hall, with whom he had lately made an exchange of land, assures her that no complaint about the terms had been made, "*unless by Mr. Covell, whose tongue, Madam, I've no more command of than himself.*" Letter 260.

That is as much as I can glean of William, except to say that in spite of his supposed unbusinesslike ways he seems to have earned his employer's regard. His death is recorded in John Hervey's diary. "*1707. April 9. Wednesday, my steward Will Covell dyed.*" His tombstone, No. 15, tells us that he was 79 years of age.

THOMAS COVELL, the second son, was baptized in 1634. There is a beautifully executed Survey of Ickworth done by him in 1665, and showing exactly the extent and the boundaries of eighteen farms among which the present park, being temporarily disparked, was divided.* The map made to accompany

* This Survey has lately been beautifully printed in fac-simile under the editorship of Lord John Hervey.

this Survey most unfortunately cannot be found. The John Hervey for whom this Survey was made held office in the Court of Charles II, and was uncle to the John Hervey who was created Earl of Bristol and from whose Letters and Diary I am frequently quoting. Whether Thomas Covell acted as his steward or not I do not know. I presume that he did. There is also at Ickworth a beautifully executed map of Little Saxham hall, then the property of the Crofts, made by this same Thomas Covell.

The only allusion to him that I can see in Lord Bristol's Diary is under 1704. April 24. "*Thomas Covell and myself executed ye deed for exchange of land in Buckstal.*" Buckstall is also mentioned in an account of the admeasurement of Ickworth park pale, entered into the above Survey book in 1702. "*From the old gate way of Mr. Thomas Covels back lane end round Buckstall to Covels corner at the market stile is 175 rods.*" I take it that Buckstall is somewhere near the gate called Hammond's gate and the old brick-field. It would also appear from these last two quotations as if Thomas Covel occupied the Covel family estate, though he was the second son. Where William lived I know not. It is unfortunate that the rates printed in Appendix VI should be torn off just as they reach the Covels. In 1664 Thomas Covel married Judith Blagge, sister of Col. Thomas Blagge. (See Blagge.) As the Gipps's had before this arrived at Little Horringer, the Blagges must have left it, so I do not know where Judith Blagge could have been living at the time. But at any rate Thomas Covel and Judith Blagge had both been baptized in the same church and had spent the days of their childhood within a mile of each other. They were married by license. The license was taken out in the Bishop of London's Office.* Both their ages are stated to be 30. In reality she was rather more, being 44. They do not appear to have had any children.

I have nothing more to say about them except that the inevitable end came to them in due course. He died in 1715 aged 81, and with him the Covells of Horringer came to an end; she died in 1707 aged 87. Both their names will be found on a stone within the church, No. 18.

JOHN COVELL.—We now come to the youngest and most distinguished

* This license is printed in Col. Chester's London Marriage Licenses edited by Mr. Joseph Foster. They take out a license to be married at Horningsheath, Westley or Rickworth. This last is an obvious mistake for Ickworth.

of the three brothers. A life of him will be found in the Dict: of National Biography, to which I am mainly indebted for the following account. His baptism will be found in these Registers under April 14, 1638. He first went to the Bury Grammar School, and then in 1654, when he was about 2 days short of 16 years, he went up to Christ's College, Cambridge. In due course he took his degrees and became a fellow of his college. Having taken orders he was appointed in 1670 chaplain to the Levant Company, and also acted as chaplain to Sir Daniel Harvey and Sir John Finch, successive ambassadors to the Porte. He resigned this appointment in 1676 and reached London in 1679, the intermediate time having been spent in travelling. His journals of his travels are in the British Museum. He was a botanist and sent home rare plants.

On getting back to England he resided at his college. In 1680 the Bishop of Ely presented him to the sinecure rectory of Littlebury in Essex, and in 1681 his college presented him to the rectory of Kegworth in Leicestershire. In 1681 he was also appointed to succeed Ken as chaplain to the Princess of Orange, and went to reside at the Hague. In 1685 an intercepted letter of his caused him to be instantly dismissed and sent back to England. In 1688 he was appointed Master of Christ's College, and there he remained till his death in 1722. That same year he had published a folio volume entitled, "Some account of the present Greek church," the result of his chaplain days at Constantinople.

One can imagine that he may sometimes have come over from Cambridge during the latter part of his life to see his native place and his kinsfolk who remained there, but otherwise Horringer could not have seen much of him after he had left the Grammar School. There are two letters written to him by John Lord Bristol in Dec. 1706 and Dec. 1707, but there is not much in them. From the first of them it appears that he had lately paid Lord Bristol a visit at Ickworth, and had afterwards composed some verses which he attributed to the influence of the air of Ickworth park, a little compliment which no doubt gratified Lord Bristol. The verses appear to have been in honour of some great hero of the day, probably the Duke of Marlborough. Letters 266.272. From the account of Dr. Covel in the Dict: of Nat: Biog: it appears that among his numerous journals and other manuscripts at the British Museum there are a few attempts at poetry.

He was buried in his college chapel where there is an inscription to him; and the college possesses two portraits of him, one painted by a German, Valentine Ritz, and the other by Sir Peter Lely. He was never married.

There was a family named Coel at Debden in the 17th century, but I do not think that they had anything to do with the Covells of Horringer, nor even that the name is the same.

REV. HENRY CRASKE.—In 1729 Rev. Henry Craske of Reed was married here to Elizabeth Ray of Bury. He was a son of William Craske, a brewer of Bury St. Edmunds; educated at Bury Grammar School and Caius College, Cambridge; ordained in 1715; presented by John, Lord Bristol, to the livings of Anwick and Brauncewell in Lincolnshire, and by Col. Norton, M.P. for Bury, to the rectory of Shotley in Suffolk in 1730. He was also Rector of Fordham in Essex. He was preacher at St. James' church, Bury, from 1723 to 1743. He was chaplain to Lord Bristol, and was one of the royal chaplains. He is mentioned now and then in Lord Bristol's letters, and appears to have committed the sin, which in Lord Bristol's sight was unpardonable, of not giving him political support in Bury.

The rectory of Shotley became vacant in 1730, and Lord Bristol applied for it for his own son Charles Hervey. Letter 917. But Alderman Ray of Bury had also applied for it for his son-in-law, Henry Craske. And the patron, Col. Norton, being M.P. for Bury, and not wishing to give any offence there, presented Henry Craske. In July 1733 Lady Bristol writes to her husband from Tunbridge-Wells and says, "*That wretched fellow Craske has preached here, but did not remember you in his prayer, which was taken notice of, but I suppose he forgot he was your chaplain or that you raised him.*" (Letter 967.) I presume that the prayer in which he should have expressly mentioned Lord Bristol was the bidding prayer, now seldom heard.

In Dec. 1738 Lord Bristol writes from Ickworth to his son Lord Hervey in London, and says, "*The present state of affairs in the Corporation of Bury being brought into great confusion by the imprudent, unpopular management of his Majesty's new chaplain, Mr. Craske, in favour of Col. Norton's interest.*" . . . . . He died in 1743.

DAVERS.—The family of Davers properly belongs to the volume which will contain the Rushbrooke Registers; but as they possessed and resided in Horringer, a short account of their origin must be given here. In the reign of Charles I the forced loans and other arbitrary measures were causing many people to leave the country and cross the seas in order to find a freedom which they could not find at home. A volume edited by Mr. Camden Hotten and published in 1874 gives several lists of those who went out, taken from MSS in the Public Record Office. There is one list giving the names and ages of 78 persons who went out to the Barbadoes in the ship Falcoln in April, 1635. They are mostly men under 30, many in their teens. Amongst them is Robert Davers, 14 years. There is nothing to show whether he was with friends or by himself. He is the only one of his name in the list.

Further on in the same volume is another list. It is 44 years later than the above list, being dated Dec. 23, 1679. It is a list of the owners of land in the parish of St. George's in the island of Barbadoes. They are 122 in number, owning between them 9569 acres, with 111 white servants, and 4316 negroes.

The first two names on the list are

Robert Davers Esq. 305 acres, 8 white servants, 200 negroes.
Mr. Robert Davers jun. 47 acres, — —

I take it that Robert Davers Esq. in the later list is the Robert Davers, 14 years, of the former list, and that in the course of 44 years the usual half-crown which the boy took out in his pocket had fructified into 305 acres and 200 slaves.

Very soon after the date of this last list he must have returned to England with young Robert, and bought Rougham, near Bury St. Edmunds, for he was made a baronet by Charles II in May 1682.

Burke (Extinct Baronetcies) says that he made a fortune in the Barbadoes and was made a baronet in consideration of his own and his father's losses for the royal cause. But I expect that is merely imagined in order to give him a more aristocratic origin. He went out before the civil war began, probably a friendless and penniless boy.

He died in or about 1688. His son Robert, the Mr. Robert jun. of the second list, succeeded him as second baronet. This Robert must have been born in the Barbadoes and have come home with his father. Whilst living at Rougham he married his next door neighbour, Mary Jermyn of Rushbrooke. They were married in Rushbrooke church in Feb. 1682. Mary Jermyn was the eldest of the five daughters and co-heiresses of Thomas, Lord Jermyn. This marriage eventually brought the Rushbrooke property to the Davers family, and the second Sir Robert Davers of Rougham became Sir Robert Davers of Rushbrooke.

This Sir Robert Davers of Rushbrooke had several children, two of whom were for a time resident in Horringer, viz., Admiral Thomas Davers, and Isabella. Isabella will be found in these notes under Moyle.

ADMIRAL THOMAS DAVERS.—We have seen that the Blagges had Little Horringer hall from about 1570 to about 1640. We shall see that the Gipps family succeeded them and had it from about 1640 to about 1720. Not having title deeds before me I cannot give exact dates. The next owner after the Gipps's seems to have been Thomas Davers. How he got it I don't know, but I presume by purchase. He seems to have done something to the house; probably he put in sash windows, which were then a comparatively new fashion; for in 1736 Lady Bristol was rebuilding the family house at Bury, now known as the Court House; and being in London she writes to her husband at Ickworth to ask him to get from Capt. Davers the agreement that he had made with his glazier to guide her in making an agreement with her glazier. Lord Bristol writes back that he has constantly asked Capt. Davers for it without effect. At last he is able to get it and send it to his wife. "*You have been so very urgent about the enclosed account, that I gave Capt. Davers no rest, wherever I mett him, till he found it for you.*" Letters 1022, 1023, 1025. Soon after 1751 George, Lord Bristol, bought Little Horringer from the widow and son of Thomas Davers for £6600. He pulled down the old hall, and a farm house arose in its place just outside the moat. (See Goodchild.)

Thomas Davers was born about 1689 and went into the navy. A short account of his professional life will be found in Charnock's Biographia Navalis. From this I learn that in 1734 he commanded the Grafton of 70 guns, one of the fleet under Sir John Norris. In 1739 during the war with Spain he was appointed to the Suffolk, and sent with Sir Chaloner Ogle to the West Indies on the expedition against Carthagena. After the failure of that enterprize he remained there. He returned to England in 1742, and in the course of the next two years became rear-admiral of the red and vice-admiral of the white. In the latter half of 1744 he was appointed commander-in-chief of a squadron ordered out to Jamaica, where he staid till his death. In April 1745 he was promoted to be vice-admiral of the red. He died at Jamaica of yellow fever on Sept. 16, 1746. (Charnock says 1747, but his tombstone says 1746.) He appears to have done what he had to do with zeal and ability, without doing anything very remarkable.

There is a letter from John, Lord Bristol, written to him in Oct. 1743, during one of his short stays in England. Lord Bristol says that he hears that the time is coming when justice will be done him and he will get a flag, "*and the bearer, my grandson Augustus, being more ambitious of being your Captain than of any other present preferment, if you would be so good as a neighbour and relation to think him worthy of that honour, the obligation would be too great to be ever forgott by, Sir, your most affectionate friend and humble servant, Bristol.*" Letter 1184. So we can picture young Augustus with this note in his hand walking over from his grandfather's house, Ickworth Lodge, to the Admiral's at Little Horringer hall.

Admiral Davers was buried in Jamaica, and there in St. Andrew's church is a monument erected by his wife with a very long inscription. The inscription is printed in Capt. Lawrence Archer's Monumental Inscriptions of the British West Indies. From it one learns that he died in his 58th year after 40 years of service, that he married Katherine, only daughter of William Smithson of Yorkshire, an heiress, niece to Lord Jermyn and Lord Dover, by whom he had three sons and twelve daughters, of whom only one son and three daughters survived him. It would appear from that that his wife was his cousin on his mother's side. Being a naval man his fifteen children will probably be found scattered about in a good many Registers. The Horringer Register of Baptisms has five of them, viz. Mary 1732, Mary 1735, Henrietta 1736, Mary 1738, Isabella 1742. Of these Isabella and the three Maries were all laid in Horringer churchyard within a year of their birth. Thomas was the one surviving son of the Admiral. He was educated at Bury Grammar School. Perhaps it would have been better for him if he too had been laid in some churchyard within a year of his birth. Like several of his Davers cousins, he seems to have been of an eccentric and unhappy turn of mind and to have come to an untimely end. The Gentleman's Magazine for 1767 says that he built at great expence a little fort on the Thames near Blackwall known as Davers' folly, and that shortly before putting an end to his own life he wrote this on a card: *Descended from an ancient and honourable family, I have for fifteen years past suffered more indigence than ever gentleman before submitted to; neglected by my acquaintance, traduced by my enemies, and insulted by the vulgar, I am so reduced, worn down and tired, that I have nothing left but that lasting repose, the first and dernier inheritance of all.*

The name Davers was sometimes written Danvers. It is so written on Admiral Davers' monument in Jamaica, and in some of the early volumes of the Gentleman's Magazine. Admiral Davers signs his name, T. Davers, in one of the Horringer Parish books as having attended a vestry meeting on Easter Monday, 1737. The letters are very large, each one as large as the initial one.

DEITON.—See Duke.

JASPER DESPOTINE.—This gentleman, a native of Venice and for many years a resident in Bury St. Edmunds, came to be married at Horringer church, and so a note must be made of him.

We have already seen how that when Bedell returned to Bury from Venice early in 1611, he was accompanied by an Italian physician named Despotine. He had begun a friendship with him at Venice which lasted through life. Despotine had become a Protestant, probably under his influence, and now came and started a practice at Bury while his friend was preaching at St. Mary's church. They lodged together at the house of Mr. Nunne, wherever that was. Bedell taught the Italian physician the English language, without which he could not have got on with his patients. Bedell was married in the following year, but remained in Bury four years more, when he was appointed to Horringer. Three years later, in 1619, Despotine was married at Horringer church, apparently coming there in order that the ceremony might be performed in the church of his old friend. His wife, Susan Brand, seems to have belonged to a wealthy clothier's family, who had property at Boxford and Edwardston in Suffolk. Dr. Despotine had three daughters baptized in St. Mary's church, and his practice in Bury prospered.

His will, dated Dec. 1648, proved July 1650, has been printed among other Bury wills by the Camden Society, edited by that useful local historian, the late Samuel Tymms. He there speaks of himself as "an alien borne, but divers yeares since by the king's favour made free denizen." He wishes his body to be buried in the night privately by the body of his daughter Isabel. His other two daughters and his wife were still living. He leaves £10 to the poor of Bury, £5 to the poor of Nedging in Suffolk, where he had an estate, and various other legacies, including £5 to William Bedell of Rattlesden, the son of his old friend.

Dr. Despotine's daughter Catherine was married to Sir John Poley, Knt. of Bury St. Edmunds, who was third son of Sir William Poley, Knt. of Boxted by his wife Ann, daughter of Sir Robert Jermyn of Rushbrooke. Sir John was buried at Boxted in 1664, and Catherine his widow in 1670. They had four sons and a daughter baptized at St. Mary's in Bury St. Edmunds. The second son was christened Despotine.

JOHN FOWLER DOVE succeeded Mrs. Gedge at the Hopleys (see Gedge) about the year 1834, and died there in Oct. 1866 aged 79 years all but three days.

See Tombstone No. 206. He had been a London printer and publisher. Pitman's School Shakespeare and Pitman's edition of John Lightfoot's works were amongst others printed by him at St. John's Square, London, in and about 1820.

DUKE.—Only one of this name enters into the Horringer Registers, viz., Jermyn Duke, baptized in 1571.

The Dukes were settled at Brampton in Suffolk for 200 years or more till a little before 1600, when they moved to Benhall.

The above Jermyn Duke, whose parents names' are not given, must be a younger son of Edward and Dorothy Duke.

Edward Duke was the last of Brampton and the first of Benhall, which he bought. He died in 1598. Dorothy his wife was a daughter of Sir Ambrose Jermyn of Rushbrooke who married Dame Blagge (see Blagge), and sister of Sir Robert Jermyn who married Hester Blagge, and aunt of Sir Thomas Jermyn who befriended Bishop Bedell. There is a very good brass of Edward and Dorothy Duke in the chancel of Benhall church. Sixteen children are represented on it, marching two and two. Jermyn Duke seems to have been the sixth of eighteen children. The eldest was Ambrose, whose son Edward, created a baronet in 1661, is said to have had twenty-nine children, in spite of which the baronetcy became extinct on the death in 1732 of Edward his grandson, the third baronet.

Ann Jermyn, a sister of the above Dorothy Duke, married William Tyndale, son of Sir Thomas Tyndale, a Norfolk knight, and she was buried at Horringer in 1574.

Another sister, Margaret Jermyn, was married in Horringer church in 1569 to Thomas Dyton, a Lincolnshire gentleman. A child of this marriage was baptized at Rushbrooke.

Another sister, Hester, as we have already seen (under Blagge) married a sort of half-brother, Henry Blagge of Little Horringer hall.

Where these other connections of the Jermyns lived, Duke, Dyton and Tyndale, who seem to have dropped into Horringer and out again directly afterwards like falling stars, I don't know. But it is possible that they may have occupied the late Abbot's house, Great Horringer hall, before it became a farm-house. Or if that had already been a farm-house in the Abbot's time on account of the nearness of Little Horringer hall, which would have made another residential house unnecessary, then there may have been some other residential house in the parish belonging to the lord of the manor, who lent it or let it to one or other of his daughters or sisters.

SOPHY DUNCOMBE.—No Duncombes will be found in the Registers; but as a certain Sophia or Sophy Duncombe resided for a time in Horringer I make a note about her. She was the daughter of Sir John Duncombe, Knight, and her mother was Elizabeth, daughter of Sir Humphry May. Sir John was sent to Parliament to represent the Corporation of Bury from 1661 to 1679. Lady Duncombe was a sister of Isabella May, whom Thomas Hervey, then living at Hengrave, courted secretly for nine long years. During the courtship Lady Duncombe's house at Bury was one of the places where they contrived to meet without the knowledge of Lady May, who forbid the courtship. This was in 1651 and following years. The Registers of St. James' parish, and, I think, also those of St. Mary's, show Sir John and Lady Duncombe residing in Bury between 1650 and 1660. In 1661 Lady May, the enemy to the courtship, was buried at St. Mary's, Bury. As Thomas Hervey and Isabella May eventually married, their son John, first Lord Bristol, was first cousin to the children of Sir John Duncombe. There is frequent allusion to them in Lord Bristol's letters, and it is only from these letters that I know that Sophy Duncombe resided at one time at Horringer.

In 1718 Lord Bristol writes from Ickworth to his wife in London, and says he has not time to write much, because Sir John Holland from Bury had dined with him and stayed till near night, and after he was gone he and his daughter Betty had walked over to take leave of Mrs. Duncombe, and came home by moonlight. And Lady Bristol answers that she is much hurt, because instead of telling her how miserable he is without her, he only tells her how agreeably he is spending his time "*with polite Sir John all day and mad Sophy at night.*"

In 1720 Sophy Duncombe seems to have been still at Horringer, as he writes from Ickworth that "she has been here all this evening." In 1731 she was no longer there, as he writes to his cousin saying that the only thing wanting to make Ickworth perfectly pleasant "*is to have you again in our neighbourhood at Horringer;*" but apparently she had then left it for good. She led a gay life at Court and elsewhere, and some letters from her to Lady Sundon will be found printed in the Sundon Correspondence. In 1749, 1750, when Lord Bristol was past 80 and she could not have been less, there are letters from him to his son

Felton, from which it appears that she was then in great poverty. She died with her name unchanged. Where she lived in Horringer I cannot say. She probably was not a tenant of Lord Bristol's, as very little indeed of Horringer at that time belonged to the Ickworth estate. It has mostly been acquired since then. (Letters 524, 526, 598, 937, 1323, etc.)

EWIN.—This family lived in Horringer for 111 years, from 1634 to 1745, and then the place knew them no more. There were three successive John Ewins, father, son, and grandson. The first one came here in 1634, was married here in that year and again in 1645, and died, both he and his wife, in 1675.

The second John was born in 1634 and died in 1703.

The third John was born in 1669 and died in 1745. His two sons, John and William, had both died before him, and only daughters survived him, so that the name died out here.

The second of these three Johns occupied Great Horringer hall farm (see Appendix IV), and I have little doubt but that they all three did in succession, though there are no lists of ratepayers to prove it. Possibly the first John was the first tenant of Horringer hall after it became a farm-house. The owner of Rushbrooke, to whom it had come soon after the Abbot of Bury had been extinguished for ever, would not want another residential house so near Rushbrooke, and it would be found more convenient to turn it into a farm-house, and possibly John Ewen No. 1 was the first farmer who lived there.

Susan, a daughter of the third and last John Ewen, married Castell Goodchild, who was the first tenant of Little Horringer hall after that became a farm-house. (See Goodchild.)

Another daughter of the third John Ewen had the name Delariviere, or Dyllavera as it is written. For the origin of this christian name in Horringer see Appendix XII.

The name Ewin is occasionally in the Registers spelt Eurn.

There is a picturesque group of tombstones belonging to this family between the two paths on the south side of the church, Nos. 23 to 29.

SAMUEL FIRMIN.—In Feb. 1738/9 will be found the baptism of Thomas son of Samuel and Sarah Firmin. From the Jermyn MSS in the library of the Suffolk Archæological Institute I learn that in 1830 there died aged 93 years John

U

H. Firmin of Bricked house, Hawkedon. He gave Dr. Jermyn, who had been curate at Hawkedon, a pedigree of his family. From this pedigree it appears that there was a Rev. John Firmin of Stanstead, who amongst other children had a son Samuel who lived at Dean farm, Hawkedon. This Samuel had a son Samuel who lived at Horringer and was buried at Bury. Thomas whose baptism was at Horringer in after life lived at Hatfield Broad Oak. John of Bricked house, brother to the elder of the two Samuels, was father of John who gave the pedigree to Dr. Jermyn.

REV. EDWARD FORSTER.—In 1702 will be found the marriage of Richard Forster and Hester Ernesby. Richard is there a mistake in the original register for Edward. His death at the age of 37 happened in 1704, hers in 1717. Their gravestones are Appendix II, No. 5.

He was of Queen's College, Cambridge, B.A. in 1689. In 1690 he was appointed to the living of Badley near Stowmarket, the old possession of the Poleys, which was just then passing by inheritance from them to the Gipps family of Little Horringer hall. (See Gipps.) I notice in the Graduati Cantabrigienses that Queen's College was the college to which many of the Poleys went. Therefore some college acquaintanceship may have led to Edward Forster being appointed to Badley. And as Lady Gipps, the widow of Sir Richard Gipps and the daughter and heiress of the last Poley of Badley, was at this time residing at Little Horringer hall, that may be somehow the cause, direct or indirect, of his living at Horringer.

His wife, Hester Ernesby or Arnsby, seems to have been one of a family that was connected with Horringer for a short time. She could hardly be the Hester daughter of Richard who was baptized in 1687, but she might be a daughter of John Ernesby whose name is on tombstone No. 20. That John appears to have come down in the world, but he married the daughter, probably more or less of an heiress, of Josias Wright, and Mr. Forster may have lived on his wife's copyhold or lifehold estate. Josias Wright's lands are mentioned in Thomas Covel's Survey of Ickworth made in 1665, and a careful examination of that Survey might locate them exactly. They seem to have lain on the Horringer side of Ickworth and the Ickworth side of Horringer. Possibly he was in part a tenant of the Gipps's.

Edward Forster seems to have been a man of studious habits, and though dying at the early age of 37 he held the living of Badley for 14 years. Badley is a picturesque little church, both in itself and in its situation. It has not yet been ruined by a hard, unfeeling, priggish kind of restoration, as many Suffolk churches have, and its flat monuments have not yet been covered over with encaustic tiles, as they have been in St. James' Church, Bury St. Edmunds!!!

REV. JOHN FRENCH.—He was educated at Christ's College, Cambridge, B.A. in 1712. In 1721 he was appointed rector of Great Saxham, which he held till his death. From 1727 to 1745 he was reader at St. Mary's, Bury. From 1744 to 1758 he was preacher or lecturer at St. James'. In Feb. 1758 he was appointed by Sir Robert Davers to the rectory of Horringer on the death of Dr. Symonds. He held it till his death, but never resided here. He died in Jan. 1767, aged 77 years, and was buried at Great Saxham, where there is a gravestone for him, for Elizabeth his wife who died Aug. 1772, aged 77, for Rev. Robert French, his son, an old Bury Grammar School boy, who died June 1771, aged 42, and for Christina Parkinson, his daughter, who died Oct. 1802.

PETER GEDGE.—On Thursday, July 11, 1782, appeared No. 1 of the *Bury Post and Universal Advertiser*. It opened with an address from the proprietors, signed Green, Gedge, Deck & Co.

Green was William Green, a printer and bookseller in Cook Row. He also sold medicines which were largely advertised.

Deck was Philip Deck, a book and print seller at the Post Office in Bury. He had "a pleasing collection" of some thousands of volumes, and printed a catalogue. He also sold coins, seals, paintings, etc. I regret to state that he also sold medicines.

Gedge was Peter Gedge, a young man lately come to Bury from Norwich, and nephew to William Green. As he afterwards became a resident in Horringer he must have a note. He was the grandson of Peter Gedge of Old Buckenham in Norfolk, and son of Peter Gedge, a manufacturer, of Norwich. His mother was Alice Chase, daughter of William Chase, the first publisher and proprietor of the *Norwich Mercury*, and the ancestor of many journalists.* Sarah Chase, sister to Alice Chase, was married to William Green, the Bury bookseller.

* I am indebted to Mr. Arthur Johnson Gedge of Baldock for Gedge pedigrees. He tells me that as late as 1864 the *Worcester Herald*, the *Norfolk Chronicle*, and the *Bury Post* were all owned and conducted by descendants of this William Chase. I am also indebted to Mr. H. R. Barker for a reference to Rev. F. S. Growse's History of Bildeston, which contains a Gedge pedigree.

Peter Gedge was born in August, 1758, and so was under 24 years at the time of the starting of the *Bury Post*. In Oct. 1784 the death of William Green was announced at the age of 52. He left two daughters, Margaret and Sarah. In March 1785 Sarah Green was married to her first cousin, Peter Gedge, who immediately afterwards is announced as printer of the *Bury Post* and as succeeding to William Green's business. At the same time the title of the paper is changed to the more modest one of *Bury Post or Suffolk and Norfolk Advertiser*, and the day of issue is changed from Thursday to Wednesday.

Sarah Gedge died on Dec. 3, 1793, aged 31 years. Her mural tablet in St. Mary's Church tells us that "*she was a mirror in which personal beauty was seen only to reflect the still more resplendent qualities of her mind.*" Mr. A. J. Gedge tells me that he recollects a portrait of her by Gainsborough (?), representing "a most fascinating and charming personality."

Peter Gedge married secondly Ann Johnson. She was the only child of James Johnson of Bury St. Edmunds, 1723-1791, a former Alderman of Bury. Her grandfather James Johnson, and her great grandfather Jacob Johnson, were both mercers of Bury. By this second marriage he had several children. (1) Ann, 1797 to 1824, when she was buried at Horringer. (App: II, No. 1; App: III, No. 143.) (2) Rev. Joseph, 1799 to 1893, rector of Bildeston. (3) Johnson, 1800 to 1863, who succeeded his father in the conducting of the *Bury Post*. (4) Rev. Sydney, 1802 to 1883. Of this last there is a memoir in the Dictionary of National Biography, from which I learn that after being educated at the Bury Grammar School and St. Catharine's Coll: Cambridge, he became curate of Runcton in Norfolk; from 1835 to 1859 he was second Master of King Edward's School at Birmingham; from 1859 to 1875 he was vicar of All Saints, Northampton. He was a Liberal in politics and a great supporter of the C.M.S. His name will sometimes be found as officiating in Horringer Church. His son, Sydney Gedge, now represents Walsall in Parliament.

What year Peter Gedge came to live at the Hopleys in Horringer I have not been able to find out. He first appears in 1806 as paying a yearly rent of £8 10s. to the Ickworth estate, which in 1815 was increased to £28 19s. In the Horringer Rate-book for 1813 he is rated at £34 a year, and in 1815 at £48. Earlier rate-books do not appear to exist. He was present at a vestry meeting at Horringer on Dec. 18, 1817, when it was decided to accept Mr. Arthur Brook's offer to restore the church at his own expense. On Jan. 7, 1818, he died "suddenly at his cottage at Horningsheath," aged 59 years. His political principles were those of Charles James Fox, whom he is said to have resembled in personal appearance. Though buried at Horringer a tablet was put up to his memory in St. Mary's Church at Bury with this inscription, "*To the memory of Peter Gedge, printer, who first established the newspaper published in this town. He died Jan. 7, 1818, aged 59 years. Like a worn-out type he is returned to the Founder, in hopes of being recast in a better and more perfect mould.*"

I imagine that his widow, Ann Gedge, continued to occupy the Hopleys till 1833, as her name is in the rate-book till then. In 1834 it is gone, and that of John Fowler Dove takes her place. In 1829 Johnson Gedge was appointed churchwarden of Horringer. Ann Gedge died at Bury in April 1840, aged 70 years, but was brought to Horringer for burial.

There had been a family named Gedge living in Horringer 180 years before Peter Gedge came there, but I do not know if they were of the same stock. The descendants of Peter Gedge appear to be very numerous now.

GIPPS.—The Gipps family succeeded the Blagges at Little Horringer hall. I have already said (see Blagge) that as the Blagge baptisms leave off at 1635 and the Gipps baptisms begin at 1645, the one must have gone out and the other come in between those two dates, unless the new-comers had some other house in the parish for a time and so they over-lapped. I don't know that it was so nor that it wasn't. Not having title deeds before me I am rather in the dark. But as Mr. Gage had title deeds before him and does not temporarily put them anywhere else, I presume that they came straight to Little Horringer hall not long before 1645, the Blagges having by that time sold it and gone.

RICHARD GIPPS.—The first to come was Richard, who according to Mr. Gage was the son of Richard of London, Judge of the Sheriff's Court. The wife of Richard the Londoner was Margaret, daughter of Valentine Pell. The wife of young Richard of Horringer was Martha Seaman of Yarmouth.

Richard and Martha had nine children baptized here between 1645 and 1657, viz., Margaret, Richard, John, Thomas, Elizabeth, George, Martha, Mary, Elizabeth. He was buried here in 1663.

SIR RICHARD GIPPS.—Of those nine I can only follow the path of Richard. He was baptized in June, 1646. I see no more of him till 1676, when

Charles II came to pay his third visit to Lord Crofts at Little Saxham. Richard Gipps went there to meet him and came back Sir Richard, having been knighted. In November of that same year he was married by licence at St. Martin's-in-the-Fields to Elizabeth Poley, he being 30 and she 22. Elizabeth Poley was the daughter and heiress of Sir Edmund Poley of Badley. Her father was already dead. Her mother, Lady Poley, was a Crofts of Little Saxham. Apparently that visit to Little Saxham had brought him a wife as well as a knighthood.

Sir Richard had three children baptized here, viz., Richard in 1677, Elizabeth in 1679, Katharine in Jan. 1681/2. Katharine was a posthumous child, as Sir Richard had died in the previous September, aged 35. Lady Gipps survived him over 30 years, dying in 1715. Her mother, Lady Poley, had died at Badley in 1714, when she must have been of a great age.

Elizabeth, the daughter of Sir Richard, married her cousin Anthony Crofts of Little Saxham, and was buried there in 1753.

MAJOR RICHARD GIPPS.—This Richard, the only son of Sir Richard, and the fourth consecutive Richard counting the Londoner, was baptized here in 1677. If he inherited his father's estate at Little Horringer and his mother's at Badley, he ought to have been well off. But judging from his selling everything he was not. In the account of The Ancient Families of Suffolk by Sir Richard Gipps of Welnetham, who was a distant cousin of Sir Richard of Horringer, this is what he or his editor says of the Horringer Gipps's. Having said that the Gipps family was antiently seated at Ipswich, but afterwards divided into two branches, he says, "*Sir Richard Gipps of Horningsheath in Thingo Hundred was of the younger house; but sold his estate. Upon which his son Richard Gipps Esq. went into the army, and proved a brave officer; but was basely discharged upon party-pique, and is now seated at Badley in Bosmere Hundred.*"

I do not know anything of Richard Gipps' military career except that he seems to have attained to the rank of a Major. According to Mr. Gage and the Supplement to the Suffolk Traveller he sold land at Fornham All Saints and Fornham St. Genoveve, the latter being the estate afterwards acquired by the Duke of Norfolk. The above quotation represents Horringer as having been sold by his father. But I do not see how that could have been, as Lady Gipps continued to reside there for more than 20 years after her husband's death, and Lord Bristol's letters show him exchanging land with her and her son. Letters 226, 242, 260.

With regard to Badley, the Supplement to the Suffolk Traveller says that Major Richard Gipps sold it to Ambrose Crawley; but Lord Arthur Hervey, in a paper on the Poley family read before the Suffolk Archæol: Institute in June 1859, mentions a letter at Boxted written by a Poley to a Croftes in 1767 as saying that Badley passed by inheritance to William Crofts, son of Anthony who married Elizabeth Gipps, Major Richard's sister. No two statements ever seem to agree together, and unless one has actual title deeds before one it is difficult to say what did happen, and not always easy even then.

The Registers of Fornham All Saints contain an entry of the baptism of Edmund son of Richard Gipps in Jan. 1711/12. I imagine that Richard to be the Major, and that this Edmund died young, and that the line of Sir Richard of Horringer came to an end with his son the Major. He is mentioned as living at Badley in 1722, but that is the last that I know of him.

Badley is well worth a visit. Its church, between Stowmarket and Needham Market, is placed in green fields far away from any road; it has not yet been unfeelingly and priggishly restored like many Suffolk churches, and its flat monuments have not yet been broken up or covered over with new encaustic tiles. I suppose they will be some day.

But I have not quite done yet with the Horringer Gipps.

VALENTINE GIPPS.—Directly Richard Gipps, the father of Sir Richard, left off bringing his children to be baptized, Valentine began to bring his. He brought two, viz., Sulyard in 1659 and George in 1661, in which year he lost his wife Jane. Who this Valentine was I don't know, but I imagine from his christian name that he must be a son of Richard the Londoner, and uncle of Sir Richard. Where in Horringer he lived I can't imagine.

JOHN GIPPS.—Much earlier still, sixty years at least before Richard the son of the Londoner first came to Little Horringer hall, viz., in 1580 and thereabouts, there was a John Gipps bringing his children to be baptized here; but who he was and where he lived I know not. I imagine that he must be an ancestor of Sir Richard of Horringer, because in the herald's Visitation of Suffolk, 1561 (edited by Mr. Metcalf in 1882), I see an account of the Moore family of Stansted. It is there stated that John Moore, grandfather of Christopher Moore who represented the family in 1561, married Margaret Poley of Badley, and that their daughter married John Gipps of Horringer. So this early marriage of a

Gipps with a Poley of Badley makes it likely that Sir Richard who married a Poley of Badley was a descendant. I have often noticed that in early times, when there was less freedom of movement, a connection by marriage between two families has generally been preceded by a still earlier connection, or in other words they married cousins of some degree or other. I have nothing to do here with Sir Richard Gipps of Great Welnetham except to say that he must not be confounded with Sir Richard of Little Horringer. As they were born within two years of each other, were both knighted by Charles II, and both lived within three miles of Bury, it is easy to mix them up. They were cousins, but I don't know how near. A short account of Sir Richard of Welnetham will be found in the Dict: of Nat: Biography. He was born in 1644 and died in 1708. The latter part of his life was spent in Suffolk in genealogical pursuits. There is a good engraved portrait of him in the library of the Suffolk Archæological Institute. He was on very bad terms with his neighbour, John Lord Bristol, he being a high Tory and Lord Bristol a Whig. There was a desperate quarrel in 1702 about a may-pole and politics. See Lord Bristol's letters, Nos. 209, 210, 211, 213. There was another political quarrel with Mr. Richard Gipps in 1710, after both Sir Richards had passed out of reach of politics. See Letter 325. And as both Sir Richards had a Richard for son and heir and successor, it is a little difficult to say whose this was. But as the Richard of Welnetham would have been only about 18 at the time, it is probably the son of the other Sir Richard, viz., the Major.

The "old Mrs. Gipps" who is mentioned in letters dated 1734 from Lord Bristol to the Bishop of Norwich (Nos. 991, 996) must I think be the widow of John Gipps, rector of Brockley in 1686, a non-juror of 1689, and consequently deprived and reduced to great poverty, and brother to Sir Richard of Welnetham. If so she was aunt to John Giles Gipps, rector of Brockley and Chevington from 1726 to 1734, in which year he died.

There is a letter to Lady Gipps, No. 260, from which I have already quoted (under Covel), about an exchange of land that Lord Bristol had made with her. This would be the widow of Sir Richard of Horringer.

It is curious to notice what a very favourite name Richard was in both branches of the Gipps family, Welnetham and Horringer. Generation after generation kept it up.

CASTELL GOODCHILD.—Admiral Thomas Davers died in 1746. Soon after 1751 his widow and son sold Little Horringer to George, Lord Bristol, who gave £6,600 for it. He pulled down the hall, and a farm-house arose just outside the moat, probably built with the old materials of the house in which the Abbots of Bury, the Blagges, Gipps's and Davers's had successively resided. The first, or at any rate an early tenant of this farm-house seems to have been Castell Goodchild of Nowton, who in 1739 had married Susan Ewin, daughter of the tenant of Great Horringer hall. As he was churchwarden of Horringer in 1745, he must either have occupied the Little Horringer hall lands before Lord Bristol bought them and pulled down the hall, or possibly he may have succeeded his father-in-law, John Ewin, at Great Horringer hall farm, who died in 1745, and then afterwards shifted to Lord Bristol's new farm-house at Little Horringer. Between 1745 and 1778 he constantly served the office of churchwarden. He seems to have had only one daughter, Bridget, who in 1774 was married to Thomas Orbell of Risby. Castell Goodchild died in April, 1782, aged 61 years. His widow carried on the farm for another two years and died in July, 1784, aged 73 years. The yearly rent of the farm in 1782 was £180. The next tenant was William Brooks, who paid yearly £270.

From the Ickworth Survey of 1665 and from the Ickworth Registers there would appear to have been three successive generations of Goodchilds occupying a farm in Ickworth park between 1640 and 1720, *i.e.* during the time when the old manor house near Ickworth Church was gradually falling to pieces from neglect, and while the park was disparked and divided into eighteen farms. Of these eighteen farms Arthur Goodchild's was the largest, containing 159 acres. These farms disappeared when John Lord Bristol came to live at Ickworth and recreated the park. On June 4, 1723, Lord Bristol writes from London to Lady Bristol at Bath, and says that he has heard from William Oliver, his land steward, that the cheese chamber at Ickworth has been broken into, and upon search being made fifteen cheeses had been found in Larner's house, "*who conscious of his guilt has made his escape out of our poor old Constable Goodchild's hands, and left his wife and children to be maintained by your most affectionate longing husband, Bristol.*"

I do not know that Castell Goodchild was a descendant of these early Ickworth Goodchilds. Another Horringer Goodchild was James, who married Mary Eagle in 1791 and died in 1815 aged 52. He had several children, one of whom, Thomas, was for many years gardener to Lord Arthur Hervey at Ickworth Lodge, and died in 1876 aged 73.

REV. ROBERT GOODRICK.—He was appointed rector of Horringer in 1629, and was buried there in 1660. By his wife Margaret he had ten children baptized here between 1637 and 1653. As the patronage of Horringer at this time belonged to the Jermyns, and as the thrice-married Dorothy Badby had brought about a connection between the Goodricks and Jermyns (see Blagge), I imagine that this Robert was a connection, perhaps a descendant, of Richard Goodrick or Goodrich, Dorothy's second husband. The Commonwealth brought evil days upon him. This is what we are told of him in Walker's Sufferings of the Clergy, 1714, "*Robert Goodrick, Horninger, R. He also suffered much in other kinds, and dying before the Restoration left 6 or 8 small children and a very disconsolate widow, who was afterwards relieved by the charity of the Corporation for Ministers' widows.*" Walker is not quite correct in saying that he died before the Restoration, as he died about four months after it. After the entry of his burial in the Registers there is a word written that I could not at first make out, and printed it with a query. I have since made out that it is satus, an abbreviation of sequestratus. I imagine that two of his sons, Robert and Henry, went up to Pembroke College, Cambridge, and took their degrees, Robert B.A. 1660, D.B. 1671, Henry B.A. 1666. Another son, Nathaniel, had children baptized here, and another son, John, was buried here in 1702.

LYON GOODRICK.—In 1578 will be found the baptism of Lyon, son of Richard Goodrick, gent. I take it that this Lyon was a grandson of the thrice-married Dorothy by her second husband Richard Goodrick, and therefore was brought to Horringer Church from Little Horringer hall. In Mr. Venn's Biographical History of Caius College is a Lionel son of Lionel Gooderick, of North Creak, educated at Ely School, admitted to Caius College in 1623. The elder of these two Lionels must be the infant Lyon of the Horringer registers. Thomas Gooderick, Bishop of Ely, who died in 1554, was uncle of Richard Gooderick who married Dorothy Blagge, and that accounts for young Lionel being educated at Ely School. A memoir both of Thomas Gooderick the uncle, and of Richard Gooderick the nephew, will be found in the Dict : of Nat : Biography.

GOULD.—See Appendix XI.

GRIGBY.—Joshua Grigby seems to have resided here for a short time, as his daughter Lucy was baptized here in 1763.

There were four Joshua Grigbys in succession, father, son, grandson and great grandson, so that it is easy to confuse one with another.

Joshua No. 1 was a solicitor at Bury St. Edmunds, and was buried at St. Mary's in 1725, aged 66.

Joshua No. 2 was a solicitor and town-clerk of Bury and died in 1771, aged 80 years. He was buried at St. Mary's. His wife was Mary Tubby of Norfolk, whose mother was niece and co-heiress of Archbishop Tenison. This Mr. Grigby bought lands at Whepstead and thereabouts, some of which (Westwood etc.) he immediately sold to John, Lord Bristol, and some of which (Plumpton etc.) were eventually sold to General Sir Thomas Hammond.

Joshua No. 3 was educated at Bury Grammar School, became a barrister, married Jane Bird of Coventry, built the present mansion at Drinkstone, was M.P. for Suffolk from 1784 to 1790, died in 1798 aged 67 years, and was buried at Drinkstone. His address to the electors will be found in the *Bury Post* of April 1, 1784. From his remarks on the need of reform I imagine he was a liberal.

Joshua No. 4 was twice married but died without children in 1829, and was succeeded at Drinkstone by his nephew Thomas Harcourt Powell.

The above Lucy who was baptized at Horringer was daughter of No. 3 and sister of No. 4. She married Mr. Powell, and their son Thomas Harcourt Powell succeeded his uncle, the last Joshua. Thomas Harcourt Powell, late of the Scots Guards, died Aug. 1892 aged 71, and was buried at Drinkstone. The generation to which his mother, Lucy, belonged was an unfortunate one. Her sister Elizabeth married John Wombwell and died in July, 1784, aged 25 years, from injuries received in a crowd in Westminster Abbey. Her brother George, Captain in the 11th Regiment, was on board a transport ship which was run down off Falmouth in 1811, and he perished with 233 others. The fate of her brother Charles is unknown.

My authorities for these statements are the Jermyn MSS., Tymms' History of St. Mary's Church, Supplement to the Suffolk Traveller, Lord Bristol's Letters, Nos. 1285, 1288, 1292, 1306.

MARY HANDS.—She was the daughter of Thomas Moyle (see Moyle), one of the many Jermyn and Davers cousins who for a time found a home in Horringer. All I know of Benjamin Hands, her husband, is what I learn from her tombstone, No. 97. What she had to do with the Spencelys who share that tombstone with her, I do not know.

REV. JOHN HARRISON.—I have nothing to say of him except that he was appointed Rector of Horringer in 1558, and buried there in 1581. Mr. Gage has got the date of his appointment quite wrong, being misled by a mistake in the Tanner MSS.

Being the first rector presented after Bury abbey had come to an end, he may be looked upon as the first Protestant rector. He was presented by Ambrose Jermyn. He was also the first rector appointed after the consolidation in 1548 of Great and Little Horringer.

TOM HARVEY.—On pulling tombstone No. 87 up out of the ground into which it had sunk, I found it had an inscription stating that Tom Harvey died on May 12, 1752, in his 54th year, after having served John, Lord Bristol, upwards of 45 years. He appears to have been a native of Westley, though more than one of the family will be found in the Horringer registers. He must have entered Lord Bristol's service when only 8 years old, and succeeded Robert Wildman as coachman in 1721 when he was about 22 years old, and remained till Lord Bristol's death in 1750. His wages were £7 a year. Lord Bristol left him by will a year's wages and an annuity of £5, but as he only survived his old master about 16 months he did not get much benefit from it. He and Robert Wildman were coachmen to Lord Bristol and his father for 71 successive years. Tom Harvey is frequently mentioned in Lord Bristol's letters as the bearer of letters, and must have known the road between Ickworth and London pretty well. When Lady Bristol or anybody else had to be fetched from London or sent there, they seemed to have thought no more of sending a great lumbering coach all the way from Ickworth than we should think of sending a dog cart two or three miles to a railway station. Letter 572 shows the danger of the journey. In Oct. 1719 Lady Bristol has got to be fetched from London. Lord Bristol writes from Ickworth that Tom Harvey has orders to start on Friday morning, and Welch Tom and Mr. Morris will go too and return with her on Monday. "*I can never consent to have you attended by two horsmen only ; . . . . three horsmen will deterr any band of highway men from attempting you, wheras having but two may invite one.*"

REV. HENRY HASTED was the son of Roger Hasted of Bury St. Edmunds, surgeon, by his wife Elizabeth (Craske). He was born in 1771 and educated at the Bury Grammar School and Christ's College, Cambridge, 6th wrangler, B.A. in 1793. In October, 1802, he was elected preacher or lecturer at St. Mary's Church, which office he held for 40 years, resigning it in 1842. In March, 1803, he was appointed to the rectory of Ickworth-cum-Chedburgh, which he resigned in 1832. In 1808 he was appointed to the rectory of Bradfield Combust, which he resigned in 1832. In 1812 he was appointed to the rectory of Braisworth, which I believe he held till his death. In April 1814 he was appointed to the rectory of Horringer, which he held till his death in 1852. He married Mary Ann only daughter of Rev. John Ord, D.D., of Fornham St. Martin, who died Oct. 2, 1810, aged 34 years. By her he had two children, viz., Henry John, who was appointed to the rectories of Bradfield Combust and Little Welnetham in 1832, and afterwards to the rectory of Sproughton;* and Mary Ann Elizabeth who married Capt. G. H. Heigham, 4th Dragoon Guards.

Mr. Hasted seems never to have resided at Horringer, but lived in his own house at Bury, No. 108, Northgate Street. His portrait by J. G. Strutt, now in the possession of his granddaughter, Miss Heigham, was engraved by C. Turner. In Feb. 1852 he published a volume of "Sermons for Lent and Easter." "*To my parishioners, whom from age and infirmities I am now no longer able to address from the pulpit, or administer to in the church, I dedicate these sermons, as a token of my continued remembrance, and of my affectionate solicitude for their welfare.*"

He died that same year, Nov. 26, 1852, aged 81 years, and was buried at St. James'. He was greatly beloved in Bury and the neighbourhood, and £1,400 was raised by public subscription for the endowment of a ward in the Suffolk General Hospital to be called by his name, and for the erection of tablets in the the churches of the town.

NICHOLAS HEATH or HETHE.—He was presented to the rectory of Great Horringer in Sept. 1393 by the Abbot of Bury, but held it for less than a year. I presume that he was a member of the family of de Bruario or de Hethe, who held Little Saxham for seven generations, from about A.D. 1200 to about 1400. Branches of the family were also at Bury, Mildenhall, and elsewhere in the neighbourhood.

* To whose son, the Rev. H. Hasted, I am indebted for some information.

A certain Agnes Tamworth, who died in 1437, was successively the wife of Thomas de Ickworth who owned Ickworth, Nicholas Heth of Bury St. Edmunds, and Edmund Lucas of Westow. She had Ickworth till her death. Her only son Ralph de Ickworth dying young, there was a dispute as to whose Ickworth should be after her death. The Abbot of Bury, the Heth family, John Brockley and Sir William Drury all put in their claim. The matter was submitted to arbitration and decided in favour of Sir William Drury. His cousin, Henry Drury, somehow became possessed of it, whose daughter and heiress marrying Thomas Hervey brought it to the family which still possesses it just 490 years after the award of the arbitrators. I do not know that Nicholas Hethe, the rector of Great Horringer, was the same man as the second husband of Agnes Tamworth, but it is possible that he was. He was only an acolyte when presented to Horringer, and may not have proceeded any farther.

REV. ARTHUR L. C. HEIGHAM was appointed to the rectory of Horringer and Ickworth in 1881, which he resigned in 1883. Being a son of Capt. G. H. Heigham who married Miss Hasted he was a grandson of a former rector. Since leaving Horringer he has been rector of Englefield in Berkshire.

HON. and REV. FREDERICK HERVEY, Earl of Bristol and Bishop of Derry. This very extraordinary man was a resident in Horringer for a few years, and therefore a note must be given him.

He was the third son of John, Lord Hervey, by his wife Mary (Lepel). This is the announcement of his birth and baptism in the Diary of his grandfather, the first Earl of Bristol. "*1730. Aug. 1. Saturday. My daughter in law Lady Hervey was delivered of a son. The Prince of Wales, the Duke of Richmond and the younger Dutchess of Marlborough answered for him on ye third of September following, and named him Frederick.*"

The obituary notice of him in the Gentleman's Magazine, 1803, says that he was educated at Mr. Newcome's school at Hackney. He was also at Westminster school, where his father, uncles and elder brother had been before him. There is a letter to him from his grandfather, dated Ickworth Park, Dec. 13, 1746, beginning, "*My very hopefull Grandson,* and saying, *you need make no question of my being glad to see you at every breaking up of your school; and if I cannot say the same as to your brother William, tis not for want of having an equal natural affection for him.*" But there is nothing in the letter to show at what school he then was. Whilst school boys he and his brother William had for tutor Mr. Edmund Morris, afterwards Rector of Nutshalling or Nursling in Hampshire. Lady Hervey's Letters to Mr. Morris were edited by Mr. Croker in 1821. In a letter dated Ickworth, April 25, 1744, she says to him, "*I am extremely pleased with all you say of Frederick, for I value your judgement ; . . . . . he has certainly very good parts and great application, and will, I am persuaded, make a considerable figure in the world. I have heard from him of late pretty often ; he is a very agreeable, entertaining correspondent. His scheme of study and travelling, as you relate it to me, seems to be a very good one.*" He is only 13 years old when he makes these schemes of study and travelling.

In 1747 he proceeded to Benet alias Corpus Christi College, Cambridge, his younger brother William being there with him. His grandfather's letters to him show him still there in April 1750. The Dean of Hereford was master of his college, and Mr. Castle I imagine to have been his college tutor. On asking his grandfather to allow him 20 guineas to get the services of an additional tutor, it was granted. Mr. Heaton was the additional tutor. The 20 guineas were always sent from Ickworth to Cambridge "by the carrier."

Carriers in old days were used for more various purposes than they are now. I have heard my father tell a story, which I think he had from Mr. Hasted, of a countryman who had made a proposal of marriage to a young woman in a neighbouring village, and who said that he had told her that he did not care much which way it was, but she was to send him word how it was to be "by the carrier."

A letter from Lady Hervey to Mr. Morris gives additional evidence of his studies at this time. Writing from Ickworth on Aug. 23, 1749, she says, "*Frederick is with them (the Phipps's) for a few days ; I believe he studies very hard, and I am glad of it ; but I agree with you there should be a mixture of amusements with it, otherwise he may be a deep scholar, but never an agreeable companion.*" The Phipps's were then living at Horringer. (See Phipps.) Whilst at Cambridge Frederick thought he had discovered an original portrait of his grandmother by Vandyke. Lord Bristol was rather sceptical about it, and as the picture is not at Ickworth I presume that its authenticity was not proved and that he would not buy it. Letter 1354.

He must have left Cambridge in 1750 without taking a degree, and one loses sight of him till Aug. 10, 1752, on which day he was married in Rushbrooke Church to Elizabeth Davers, daughter of Sir Jermyn Davers of Rushbrooke. He was just 22, and she was 19.

I have already given some account of the Davers family (see Davers), but they belong properly to the Rushbrooke Registers and not to those of Horringer. It must be enough to say here that Elizabeth Davers was niece to Admiral Thomas Davers of Little Horringer hall, and that her father, Sir Jermyn, was grandson to the first baronet, who I have supposed to have gone out to the Barbadoes in 1636, a little boy of 14 years, friendless and with only half-a-crown in his pocket. The prosperity which attended the Davers's in the middle of the 17th century deserted them in the middle of the 18th century, and one after another they came to untimely ends, so that a Bury lady writes to her friend, 'Tis surprising how that family goes off. (See Symonds.) This marriage added a considerable estate to the Ickworth property. But that result did not come about till 50 years afterwards, and I do not think it could possibly have been foreseen at the time. For Frederick had two elder brothers, and Elizabeth Davers had four brothers and an elder sister. Of her brothers,* Robert went to America in a pique, courted death and got killed in a boat by some Indians in 1763. Henry shortly before that shot himself on board ship. Thomas, rector of Little Whelnetham, shot himself in 1766 in his mother's house on the Angel Hill, I think the house near the Abbey gate, now occupied as a young ladies' school. Charles succeeded to the estates and baronetcy and died without legitimate issue in 1806. Mary died unmarried in the house near the Abbey gate in 1805. On the deaths of these last two the Rushbrooke property, including the manor and advowson of Horringer and the site of Bury Abbey, passed to their nephew, Frederick William, afterwards first Marquis of Bristol. But in 1752 it would have been impossible to have foreseen that Frederick would have succeeded to the Ickworth estate, or that his son Frederick William would have succeeded to the Davers' estate, and so brought the two estates into one. So the marriage must have been for love and not for the sake of joining two neighbouring estates. One may hope that there was some love at first, as there was very little afterwards.

After his marriage in 1752 the next thing I know about him is that he became M.A. in 1754. He had left Cambridge without a degree, but as a nobleman's son he had the right to one without examination, and he now took it. He had been intended for the Bar, but had changed his mind and gone into the Church. He

* My authority for the untimely deaths of Robert, Henry, and Thomas, is a folio MSS. volume given to my father by Archdeacon Jermyn. Burke in Extinct Baronetcies leaves out Robert, and makes Charles successor to Sir Jermyn, which is wrong. Robert came in between.

was ordained in July, 1754. Lady Hervey writes to Mr. Morris from Lord Stanhope's at Chevening on July 18, 1754, saying, "*Your old friend Frederick is this day come from Ely the Reverend Mr. Hervey.*"

And now must have begun his residence in Horringer judging from the date of his children's baptisms. He had four children baptized at Horringer, viz., George in 1755, John Augustus in 1757, Elizabeth Christian in 1758, Frederick Clayton in 1761. Three other children were born after these, and not baptized here. So one may fix his residence here as being from the time of his ordination in 1754 to 1761 or soon afterwards.

I have tried to make out for certain where his house was, but have hardly succeeded. My mother tells me that Mr. Hasted used to say that it was a little to the right directly after you have entered the park through the Horringer gate, near a pond which is still there. There are now no sure signs of a house having stood there, though there are signs of old enclosures. If it stood there, its position near the church would make it look as if it were the old Great Horringer manor house. But I have always understood that the old hall or manor house was the farm-house on the Bury road. It might have been a house belonging to his brother George, who was then the owner of Ickworth, or it might have been a house belonging to his wife's brother, Sir Robert Davers, who owned Horringer manor. If it stood near this pond, though it would have been within Ickworth park pale now, it would not have been within Ickworth park pale then, for the park has extended in that and in every other direction since then, and swallowed up fields and houses which formerly lay outside of it. It might have been the house which the Phipps's had lately been occupying, and in which as an undergraduate he had stayed with them, though that does not make one much wiser, as one does not know where their house was. (See Phipps.)

Of the above four children who were born in this house and baptized at Horringer, George died in boyhood and was buried at Spa. Some years ago his brother tried to find out the exact spot of his burial, but could not, as apparently the burial of Protestants was not recognized. Frederick Clayton must have died before 1769, when another Frederick was baptized, who was afterwards first Marquis of Bristol. Of John Augustus and Elizabeth Christian I give some account below.

Whilst residing at Horringer, say from 1754 to 1762, he does not appear to have had any post or duties whatsoever; and no doubt while Horringer was his headquarters, some time was given to foreign travel. We have already seen him making out a scheme of travel when only a boy of 13; and in the Life of Alexander Humboldt we see him as keen as ever in his travelling schemes when little short of 70 years of age. So it is not likely that he stayed at Horringer doing nothing. In 1756 he was made a clerk of the privy seal, which is a lay office. In 1763 he was made a chaplain to the king. In 1766 he was at Naples during an eruption of Vesuvius, and going to look too close was hit by a stone. In 1766 his eldest brother George, second Earl of Bristol, was appointed Lord Lieutenant of Ireland, which he resigned a few months later without ever having gone there. He just held the post long enough to be able to nominate Frederick to the bishoprick of Cloyne. That was in Feb. 1767. So his first parish was a diocese. Exactly a year afterwards he was promoted to the rich bishoprick of Derry.

I have no space to give details of his life in Ireland and must pass them over. But as we have already had one Irish bishop in these notes, Bedell, I can't resist comparing or rather contrasting the two. Probably they were as different from each other as any one man can be from any other. I gave some extracts showing Bishop Bedell dressing with almost an excess of plainness and simplicity; and when the offer of a bishoprick was made to him he was unwilling to accept it, because he feared lest he should have to part with some of his simplicity and plainness of life.

Frederick Hervey had no such fears. Here is Mr. Lecky's account of one of his appearances at Dublin: "*Dressed entirely in purple, with diamond knee and shoe-buckles, and with long gold tassels hanging from his white gloves, he sat in an open landau drawn by six noble horses caparisoned with purple ribands. Dragoons rode on each side of his carriage which proceeded slowly through the different streets amid the cheers of a large crowd, till it arrived at the door of the Parliament house. . . . . The Volunteers presented arms; the bands played the Volunteer march, then with a defiant blast of trumpets the procession proceeded on its way.*"

The one revelled in simplicity, the other revelled in show. That is only one difference out of many. But with all their differences one can't help seeing something that was common to both. By different routes, by different processes of thought, they sometimes arrived at a common end. If they had been contemporary, one can imagine the Bishop of Kilmore and the Bishop of Derry taking the same views, giving the same votes, on some questions. They were poles asunder in nature and constitution, and yet they might have agreed together while disagreeing with others from whom they differed less. I imagine that both went to Ireland to do their best for Ireland and not for England, though really what was best for Ireland would be best for England. Both accepted a post in Ireland, both were sent to Ireland by England, and when they got there did their best for the country to which they were sent without considering only the interests of the country that sent them. I don't think that either of them would have sympathized with the idea that any one country is only meant to be an appendage of another, or only meant to exist for the sake and for the glory of another, or that the wishes and interests of one are to be subordinated to those of another. Such an idea is only a modified form of the idea that the black man is meant to be the slave of the white.

And another point common to these two Irish bishops is that both to an extraordinary degree won the regard of all sorts of men. The rebels coming to fire a volley at the funeral of Bishop Bedell with the very guns that they had got to shoot down his fellow countrymen has its parallel in Roman Catholics uniting with Churchmen and Protestant dissenters to set up a monument in Ickworth park to the Bishop of Derry. When one thinks of the last fifteen years of the Bishop's life, one may well wonder how ever that monument got to be set up. However, there it is. And it is a testimony to the fact that while he was at his best, though there was something shabby and shady even then, yet there was also something broad and liberal and far-seeing. For whilst the narrowest and blindest of men may get the applause of one sort, they cannot unite the applause of opposite extremes. Only men of some breadth can do that. But of course any comparison between the two is only possible when Frederick Hervey was at his best. And his best, such as it was, did not last long. He deteriorated, and then no comparison is possible. I must hurriedly set down the remaining dates of his life.

He went, as I have said, to Derry in the early part of 1768. For the next few years he was in Ireland, and threw himself into his work with great zeal. He showed much public spirit in reclaiming bogs and making roads; he tried to make the clergy reside in their parishes, and he showed care for superannuated curates. He also began to build two enormous palaces in his diocese, at Downhill and Ballyscullion.

His and his wife's letters recently published in "The Two Duchesses," edited by Mr. Vere Foster, show that from June 1777 to the end of 1779 he was abroad. In December, 1779, by the death of his brother Augustus, Lord Bristol, he became Earl of Bristol and owner of Ickworth.

Soon after this there arose the Volunteer movement in Ireland. The American war had caused the English troops to be withdrawn from Ireland. The Protestants in the north asked for more to be sent to safeguard the country against the French. More could not be sent. Thereupon Volunteers sprung up. In a little while the movement spread through the country, and there were 100,000 of them, Roman Catholics and Protestants, united to maintain the freedom of their country and to reform its Parliament. The Bishop of Derry of course became a Volunteer. He was desirous to be elected President of the Volunteer convention, but just failed. If he had been elected, war with England would probably have been the result, as he was utterly reckless and very ambitious. A satirical engraving of him published in 1784 represents him as The Irish Patriot, with a fire brand in his hand and the devil sitting on his shoulder. During 1781 and 1782 he seems to have been chiefly at Ickworth. It was in 1782 that the scheme of the Suffolk ship was being pushed forward, which he warmly supported. (See App: IX.) Arthur Young tells us in his autobiography that he had a general invitation to dine with him every Thursday the whole time he was there, which he did. Professor Symonds, son of the late rector of Horringer (see Symonds), Sir John Cullum, and the Rev. G. Ashby, rector of Barrow, were often there too. No two men could be more different than the Bishop and Arthur Young, but their common interest in agriculture, and the Bishop's power of being agreeable when he chose, enabled them to be very friendly together. Young says, "*In my life I never passed more agreeable days than these weekly dinners at Ickworth. The conversation was equally instructive and agreeable.*"

When the Bishop returned to Ireland, I think quite at the end of 1782, Lady Bristol did not return with him, and I think they can seldom have met again. She lived henceforth chiefly at Ickworth. It was just 30 years since they had been married in Rushbrooke church, and the wonder is not that they separated now, but rather that they had gone on together for so long. For the Bishop's virtues, such as they were, were of a public and not of a private kind. They consisted of enlightened views on public questions rather than of those virtues which conduce to the happiness of a home. And whilst he could be profusely liberal in public gifts, he could be incredibly mean at home. And probably whilst he could be charming in society, he could be odious at home. So there is no need to find any one single quarrel, any one single act or word, to account for their henceforth walking apart, and parting from one another 17 years before death parted them. But tradition enables one to see what was the talk of the household at Ickworth and the village of Horringer at the time.

Some years ago there was living at Horringer a worthy couple, Mr. and Mrs. James Byford. They had been married in Ickworth church in 1826, and occupied a small farm of Lord Bristol's in Sharpe's lane *alias* New road, which took its name from the former tenant who was Mrs. Byford's uncle. Mrs. Byford had been a servant girl at Ickworth as her mother had been before her; and I recollect hearing her say forty years ago or so that her mother used to say that whilst she was living in service there the Bishop and his wife went out for a drive together, and in the course of the drive something was said, something passed between them, and they came home and never spoke to each other again. And the coachman alone knew what was said, and her mother was always trying to get him to tell, but he never would.

Looking at these Registers to see how far they supported the possibility of that story, I find that Susanna Lanham (Mrs. Byford's maiden name) was baptized in 1801, and that Elizabeth Sharpe (her mother's maiden name) was baptized in 1762; so that in 1782 or 1783, the year of the Bishop's sojourn at Ickworth and separation from his wife, she probably would have been in service there.

The Bishop then early in 1783 returned to Ireland alone, and for a time found something to interest him in the Volunteer movement and in politics of a stormy kind. I imagine that by this time mere episcopal or diocesan work had completely lost any attraction for him. In 1785 he was at Bath, being a sufferer from gout. In 1786 he was abroad for a year or two. In 1790 he was back in Ireland, and received addresses from the Corporation, Citizens, and Volunteers at the opening of the bridge at Derry. In 1792 he paid a visit to Ickworth to see after the new house which he was just beginning to build there, and which an Irish clergyman, Rev. Joseph Sandys, was appointed to look after. In 1793 he went abroad and never came back alive. In November 1797 he proposed to Alexander Humboldt an elaborate expedition to Egypt. Humboldt considered him half mad, though he recognized his great abilities, and gladly accepted the proposal. War prevented its being carried out. In 1798 he was arrested by the French republicans in Italy. Two large portmanteaus of suspicious papers being found in his rooms he was thrown into prison at Milan. His enormous collection of works of art at Rome which were intended for his new house at Ickworth were seized. 343 artists of all nations signed a petition to the French, asking that in consideration of the Bishop's services to art and artists these might be restored to him. But in spite of it Ickworth never got them. He died at Albano on July 8, 1803; his body was brought to England, and the Ickworth registers record his burial on April 21, 1804.

There is a whole length portrait of him, seated, at Ickworth, by A. Kaufman, which has been engraved for Gage's History of Thingoe Hundred. There is an odious one at No. 6, St. James' Square, with Vesuvius in the distance, by Madam Le Brun. There are several of him at Downhill, belonging to Sir Hervey Bruce, one of them representing him as presenting his eldest son, John Augustus, to Lord Chatham, of whom the Bishop was a great admirer. Lady Arthur Hervey has a miniature of him, holding a plan of Ickworth, with Vesuvius in the distance. I do not imagine that he was in the least good-looking; tradition and the satirical engraving of him that I have already mentioned give him a good calf to his leg. He appears to have been not tall or stout, but active and strongly made. As portraits are intended to hand down a man's likeness to those who have never seen him, I think it is a very great fault in them that they do not give one any idea of a man's height. And if it would be too inartistic to have a small scale in the corner, as in a map, would it not be possible that every man's name should be on his portrait, with his age, height, and weight at the time when the portrait was taken?

The authorities for the Bishop's life are of course various contemporary magazines, newspapers, memoirs, and histories. Mr. Peter Gedge, the editor of the *Bury Post*, naturally kept his eyes open to the Bishop's proceedings in Ireland, and reported them for the benefit of the Bury public. The Dictionary of Nat: Biog: has an article on him, and one will be found in the Edinburgh Review for July, 1898, and in Temple Bar, September, 1898. To all of these I am indebted in varying degrees. The article in the Edinburgh is the fullest.

Lady Bristol had pre-deceased her husband by under three years. She was buried at Ickworth on Dec. 27, 1800. From her letters that have been lately published in Mr. Vere Foster's The Two Duchesses she would appear to have been a quiet and sensible woman. There was undoubtedly something very cranky, or at least unfortunate, in the Davers's of her generation, but one cannot perceive anything cranky in her. After the separation from her husband she appears to have lived chiefly at Ickworth with her youngest daughter Louisa, afterwards Lady Liverpool, and they both busied themselves in good works in Horringer and Ickworth. The debtors in the Bury gaol were indebted to her for an annual guinea, and a school was provided for Horringer. She appears to have died suddenly. A letter from her daughter, Lady Erne, announcing her death to young Frederick Foster is given in The Two Duchesses. Lady Erne says, "*It happened early yesterday morning from a spasm in her stomach. What my grief and suffering is no words can say, as no mother could be a greater loss to a daughter than she is to me.*" The letter is dated Oct.* 20, 1800. The suddenness of it agrees with what I have said under Howe. There is a portrait of her at Rushbrooke, but none at Ickworth. Apparently this was painted at Rome in 1778, and given to her brother, Sir Charles Davers.

JOHN AUGUSTUS, LORD HERVEY, the second but eldest surviving son of the Bishop of Derry, was baptized at Horringer in January, 1757. He went into the Navy, and in Dec. 1778 his mother writes to her married daughter, Mrs. Foster, saying that Jack was on a cruise, was delighted with his station, and was determined that Captain Hervey should be as a great a man as his uncle, the Admiral. I cannot here follow him in his naval career. He was married in October, 1779, at Quebec to Elizabeth Drummond, whose kinsfolk lived at Megginch in Perthshire. In June, 1783, he had to suppress a mutiny on board his ship, the *Raisonable*. The *Bury Post* for Oct. 9, 1783, prints a very blunt outspoken letter from him to the Admiral Lord Howe, dated *Raisonable*, St. Lucia, April 10, 1783, in which he criticizes Lord Howe's conduct. It is followed by another one to Lord Howe written when he reached London in the following August, and in which he more or less apologizes. A long letter from Lord Hervey to a London paper qualifying or denying his apology is given in the *Bury Post* for Oct. 16, 1783. In 1787 he was appointed envoy extraordinary to the Grand Duke of Tuscany. In 1791 he was promoted from envoy extraordinary at Florence to be minister plenipotentiary there. In August, 1794, a pension of £1,500 a year was granted to him for his services at Florence. He had a house at Valintine in Hertfordshire. He died on board the *Zealous* which he commanded,

* But this must be a transcriber's or printer's error for December.

June 10, 1796, and was buried at Ickworth, Sept. 26th. Among the "Letters to Lady Hamilton," 1814, will be found one to her from the Bishop of Derry announcing his son's death. "*My dearest Emma, The very unexpected intelligence, which Prince Augustus has most delicately communicated to me, of poor Lord Hervey's decease, has quite bouleversée my already shattered frame. I would not allow your friendly mind to learn an event so interesting to me from any other hand than that of your affectionate and devoted friend, Bristol.*"

Lady Hervey survived him till 1818. They had an only daughter, Elizabeth Catherine Caroline, baptized at Ickworth in Sept. 1780. She married in 1798 Charles Rose Ellis, first Baron Seaford, and died in Jan. 1803. When the Bishop of Derry died in July 1803, the Earldom of Bristol and the estates thereto belonging passed to his younger son Frederick William, while the barony of Howard de Walden passed to Charles Augustus Ellis, the grandson of his elder son, John Augustus.

There is a whole length portrait of John Augustus, Lord Hervey, at Ickworth by Gainsborough, from which he appears to have been a very handsome man.

There are two portraits of his wife, both by Angelica Kaufman, one at Ickworth, and the other at Megginch.

ELIZABETH CHRISTIANA HERVEY was baptized at Horringer in May, 1758. When only 18 years old she was married to John Thomas Foster of Co. Louth. The marriage was not a happy one, and after a time they parted, he refusing even to support her. There were two sons by this marriage, Frederick and Augustus. Frederick was a wit. My mother tells me that he made the servants laugh so by his jokes at dinner that they could scarcely wait at table. John Thomas died in 1796.

Lady Elizabeth Foster married secondly in Oct. 1809 William, fifth Duke of Devonshire. He died in August, 1811. She is the second of the Two Duchesses from whom the volume so called, published in 1898, takes its title. In it will be found many letters to and from her. She must have been beautiful, clever, and perfectly charming in her manner. She inherited all her father's love of travelling and also of antiquities and works of art. She had lived abroad a good deal before her second marriage; and after the death of the Duke of Devonshire she went abroad again. From 1814 till her death in 1824 she lived almost entirely abroad, chiefly at Rome. She carried on excavations there in the Forum, and she had a machine made for dredging the Tiber, in the hope of recovering the statues which had been thrown into it from time to time. She was an artist herself, and a liberal patron of artists. Portraits of her are numerous, at Ickworth, Chatsworth, and elsewhere. Medals in her honour were struck at her death. The Elizabeth grove in Ickworth park, sown in 1786, near the park pale on the right hand side as you come in through the Horringer gate, and therefore not very far from where the house probably stood in which she was born, is called after her. She died on March 30, 1824.

The account of her in the Dictionary of National Biography has three mistakes. (1) It gives 1759 as the year of her birth instead of 1758. (2) It represents her as a widow in 1787 and receiving a proposal of marriage from Gibbon, whereas John Thomas Foster did not die till 1796. (3) It gives 1814 as the date of the death of the Duke of Devonshire instead of 1811. A volume called Anecdotes and Biographical Sketches, by Elizabeth Duchess of Devonshire, was privately printed in London in 1863. A short memoir of her in French, by Monsieur Artaud, which is prefixed to the Anecdotes, wrongly gives the date of her second marriage as 1812.

REV. LORD ARTHUR CHARLES HERVEY.—A short note must be given to Lord Arthur Hervey as being one of Horringer's rectors. He was a grandson of the Bishop of Derry, who dying in 1803 was succeeded in the earldom of Bristol by his eldest surviving son, Frederick William, Lord Hervey. This Earl of Bristol was created Marquis of Bristol in 1826, and Lord Arthur was the fourth of his six sons. He was born in his father's London house, No. 6, St. James' Square, on Aug. 20, 1808. His mother was Elizabeth Albana, daughter of Clotworthy Upton, first Baron Templetown. He remembered a breakfast given by his uncle, Lord Liverpool, in 1814 to the allied sovereigns at Combe Wood near Kingston, when the Emperor of Russia put out his hand and said to him in good English, Give me a good spank. He remembered the opening of Waterloo bridge in 1817, when the Duke of Wellington was present with a bag of silver medals, of which he gave one to each of those who were privileged to be present. The small boy secured two, which I now possess. Soon after that his father and all the family travelled abroad for five years, whilst the building of the great house at Ickworth went on. The agricultural depression which was affecting landed proprietors then as it is now was also a cause of their going abroad.

Coming back to England in 1822 he went to Eton, Yonge being his tutor, and stayed there till 1826. In 1828 he went up to Trinity College, Cambridge, and in 1830 he took his degree. Though as a nobleman's son he had and used the privilege of being only two years at the University, yet he obtained a first class in the Classical Tripos. In Oct. 1832 he was ordained deacon at Norwich, and priest (by letters dimissory) at Peterborough immediately afterwards, and in Nov. 1832 was instituted to the rectory of Ickworth-cum-Chedburgh, which Mr. Hasted had resigned. He took up his residence at Ickworth Lodge. Ickworth Lodge was a farm-house till 1702, when John, Lord Bristol, turned it into a temporary mansion house for himself, as the old mansion house near the church had more or less tumbled down. It remained a temporary mansion house rather longer than he expected, viz., till about 1830, by which time the round house, begun in 1792, being sufficiently advanced to be habitable, Lord Bristol moved into it. The Lodge becoming vacant near about the time when Lord Arthur became rector of Ickworth, it became his residence. Not long afterwards Ickworth and Chedburgh were separated at his request. They had been united in 1712 in the time of the first Lord Bristol, because he wanted to get rid of the old rectory that stood in the park near Parson's pond. Lord Arthur, now holding Ickworth only, became in 1844 curate of Horringer to Mr. Hasted. He was also chaplain to the Thingoe Union Workhouse at Bury. On the death of Mr. Hasted in 1852 he became rector of Horringer, which was then united to Ickworth. In 1862 he was appointed archdeacon of Sudbury. In the latter half of 1869 Mr. Gladstone offered him the bishoprick of Bath and Wells, which he accepted, being consecrated on St. Thomas' day, 1869. This took him away for good from the county to which (to use his own words in an archæological address) his "*affections were linked by a family residence of more than four hundred years.*" He had been 37 years rector of Ickworth and 17 years rector of Horringer. But his work was not yet over. He held the office of Bishop for just under 25 years, and died on June 9, 1894, aged 85 years and 9 months. He was buried in the graveyard of Wells Cathedral, his son Arthur, a Captain in the Rifle Brigade, having been already laid there in 1889. The diocese has shown its appreciation of his work and character by a noble monument placed in the south aisle of the choir of the cathedral.

Lord Arthur was a man of great industry and energy, doing whatever he did do with his whole heart and with great delight. His place in the first class of the

Classical Tripos after only two years at the University shows that he made a good use of his time and was a good scholar. His taking a part in the chief biblical works of his day, *e.g.*, The Revision of the Old Testament, Dr. Smith's Dictionary of the Bible, the Speaker's Commentary, the Pulpit Commentary, and others, show that he retained his industry and scholarship right to the very end, to the very last week, of a long life.

But he was not only a classical and biblical student. He had a great delight in all archæological studies, and there was hardly any branch of learning that did not interest him. The same genealogical tastes which led him with the help of his eldest brother to write an elaborate history of the Hervey family, led him also to write a volume on the apparently contradictory genealogies of Jesus Christ in the Gospels of St. Matthew and St. Luke; and it also led him to pay more attention than had been paid before by biblical scholars to the numerous genealogies given in the Old Testament, and to use them for settling points of chronology.

But he was not a mere student of any sort. As a young man he had been good at high jumping, and was also one of the very best amateur tennis players of his time. He won a challenge silver racket three years following, and so kept it, and one of his sons has it now. Long before lawn tennis was ever invented he played it on his lawn at Ickworth; and long after he was three score and ten years of age he would come out and play a set on his lawn at Wells with amazing activity. He was a good rider, and a dashing driver, and enjoyed a good long spell in the open air and on the hills as much as he enjoyed his literary studies.

He was very keen, not only in acquiring knowledge for himself, but in promoting institutions which might help to spread it amongst all classes and conditions of men. He had no fear of knowledge, neither for himself nor for any one else. In 1855 he published a pamphlet, "*A suggestion for supplying the Literary, Scientific, and Mechanics' Institutes of Great Britain and Ireland with lecturers from the Universities.*" This suggestion has since ripened into the system of University extension, whereby through their lecturers the Universities have as it were gone forth into the country instead of merely waiting for students to come to them. The Athenæum at Bury St. Edmunds being largely educational in its object, it is no wonder that Lord Arthur threw himself into it heart and soul from its very first beginning. Harrod's Directory of Suffolk, 1864, says that the Athenæum was established in 1853 for fostering literature, art, and science. It purchased the old Assembly-room from the shareholders for £2,500, and amongst its institutions were reading rooms, courses of lectures, concerts, a museum of antiquities and natural history, a reference library, classes for elementary instruction, and an observatory for astronomical purposes. And it adds, "*The high position which the Athenæum has attained among kindred institutions of the country is attributable in a great degree to the untiring interest which its noble president, the Rt. Hon. and Ven. Lord Arthur Hervey, has displayed in its behalf.*" Lord Arthur frequently lectured there himself, besides getting many of the most eminent men in the country to do so.

With regard to his character, I would say that he was just and considerate to others, straight and incapable of scheming or of duplicity, always self-controlled, thoroughly reasonable and practical, possessing tact and good judgment, liberal, hospitable, and kind-hearted. I am not merely stringing together all the good qualities that I can think of, but am only setting down such as I think he possessed in a high degree. In his church views and in his political views he was moderate. You might with equal truth have called him a moderate high churchman or a moderate low churchman. Perhaps, to be more exact, the former term would describe him as a Bishop, the latter as a Suffolk clergyman. But he was always free from anything like mere partizanship, and could always appreciate good wherever it was. In politics he had conservative views with liberal tendencies, but in most cases the views would have decided his vote rather than the tendencies. His manners with their mixture of natural dignity and ease were perfect. He was five feet, ten inches, in height, and always looked his full heighth. He was active and well made, and he seldom had a day's illness.

In July, 1839, he was married to Patience, daughter of John Singleton of Hazely heath, Hants, and Mell, Co. Louth. Twelve children were born, and the golden wedding was celebrated at Wells in 1889.

Lord Arthur was crippled by rheumatism during the last few years of his life, but his mind retained its youthful vigour up to the very last. He was engaged in literary work up to within a day or two of his death, the illness which terminated in a painless and peaceful death being very short. He died when on a visit to his son-in-law, Mr. Charles Hoare, at Hackwood near Basingstoke, on June 4, 1894, being about 10 weeks short of 86 years.

The chief painted portraits of him are a miniature by Ross belonging to Lady Arthur; two portraits painted by Graves when he left Suffolk in 1869, one of them now at the Athenæum at Bury St. Edmunds, the other presented to Lady Arthur by the clergy and laity of the archdeaconry of Sudbury; a portrait painted by Sir W. B. Richmond in 1889 at the request of the city of Wells and its neighbourhood, and now hanging in the town hall at Wells.

A memoir of him by his eldest son, Rev. John Hervey, was printed for private circulation in 1896, and a forthcoming volume of the Dictionary of Nat: Biog: will contain a sketch of his life.

JAMES HOWE.—In 1742 was baptized Rebecka daughter of Thomas and Rose Gardiner. In 1764 she was married to James Howe, and in Dec. 1765 was baptized James their child. This young James was afterwards footman to Lady Bristol, wife of the Bishop of Derry, and was living in service at Ickworth Lodge when a violent ringing of the bell one night summoned him to find his mistress dying. This was in the middle of December, 1800. A letter from Lady Erne to Frederick Foster, printed in "The Two Duchesses," confirms this account of the suddenness of Lady Bristol's death, but by a transcriber's or printer's error the letter is dated October.

James Howe afterwards went to live in a cottage near Ickworth park pale and near the Bishop of Derry's monument, and there he died in 1848 aged 84 years, and was buried at Ickworth.

JERMYN.—Two members of the Jermyn family of Rushbrooke will be found among the Marriages, viz., Margaret who married Thomas Dytun in 1569, and Hester who married Henry Blagge in 1571. They were both daughters of Sir Ambrose Jermyn, sisters of Sir Robert, and aunts of Sir Thomas who sent William Bedell to Horringer and befriended him all his life. See Blagge and Duke.

Two others will be found bearing the surname Jermyn of a later date and in poorer circumstances, viz., in Marriages 1747, Baptisms 1814. They may be of the same stock, but not necessarily. The history of the Jermyn family belongs to the volume which will contain the Rushbrooke Registers.

REV. THOMAS KERRICH.—He was curate of Horringer in 1783, and rector of it from May, 1784, to his death in Jan. 1814. He was also rector of Wendens Ambo in Essex from August, 1783, till his death. Both livings were in the gift of Lord Bristol. Mr. Kerrich seems to have been educated at Trinity

Hall, Cambridge. The only degree given him in the Graduati Cantabrigienses is that of LL.B. in 1780, when he must have been about 40 years of age. In the Biographical history of Caius College Mr. Venn has confounded him with a Thomas Kerrich, rector of Banham in Norfolk. I believe them to be two different men, though contemporary. The register and the tombstone, No. 137, do not agree as to Mr. Kerrich's age at the time of his death. In the register he is entered as 73 years of age and 28 years rector, on the tombstone 76 years of age and 32 years rector. He was really rector for 29 years and 8 months.

There was a John Kerrich, a medical man of Bury St. Edmunds, who died in 1762 aged 70 years, and was buried at St. Mary's. He was of the right age to have been the father of the rector of Horringer, but I have not made out for certain whether he was so or not. For other members of the rector's family see Register of Burials and tombstone, No. 137. Mr. Kerrich was about the first to be buried on the north side of the church. There is everywhere a feeling against being buried on the north side of a church unless circumstances allow no alternative.

LUCAS.—In his History of Thingoe Hundred Mr. Gage tells us that in the reign of Henry VII, about 1505, Thomas Lucas, Solicitor General, purchased Little Saxham and built the hall. He was the son of John Lucas and grandson of Edmund Lucas, both of Westow, and further back still several of his forefathers had been Aldermen of Bury St. Edmunds.

The Solicitor General had three sons, Jasper, Henry, and John, and died in 1531. With Henry of Bury St. Edmunds, who lies buried in St. Mary's Church there, and with John of Colchester, the ancestor of Sir Charles and the three barons in the 17th century, we have nothing to do. But Jasper, the eldest, dying before his father, left a son Thomas who was grandson and heir to the Solicitor General.

THOMAS LUCAS, grandson of the Solicitor General, married Mary daughter of Sir Thomas Jermyn of Rushbrooke, sold Little Saxham to Sir John Crofts of Westow, bought Horscroft and other lands in Great and Little Horringer, and so finds his way into these Registers. He was buried here in 1595.

CLEMENT LUCAS, son of Thomas, succeeded him at Horscroft, and was buried here in 1603. He married first Mary Kempe, secondly Mary Barker of Bury St. Edmunds.

WILLIAM LUCAS, son of Clement, succeeded him at Horscroft. He married Christian, daughter of Thomas Gibson, Alderman of Norwich, and had eight children baptized here between 1609 and 1626. This is he who got possession of some Church lands, and after a lawsuit with William Bedell the rector, which ran through ten long years, was compelled to make compensation for them. (See Bedell.) His eight children were Lucy, Christian, Thomas, Gibson, William, Lydia, Jasper, Mary. I cannot follow all their careers in these short notes, but must confine myself to the successor. (For Lucy's tombstone see p. 217. Thomas, the eldest son, died in 1637 aged 24.) William was buried here in 1639/40, but Christian, his widow, survived him and married secondly Thomas Sache of Great Horringer. For her tombstone, not now visible, see p. 217. For William's see App. II, No. 3.

GIBSON LUCAS, second but eldest surviving son of William, succeeded him at Horscroft. He was baptized here in 1615 and called after his mother's maiden name. He was educated at Bury Grammar School and Caius Coll:, Cambridge. I presume that, like his father who took the Church lands, he was not a very good churchman, and that in the civil war he was a Parliamentarian, though his Essex cousins were strong Royalists. For in a tract printed in 1647, "The County of Suffolke divided into fourteene precincts for classicall Presbyteries," giving the names of the committees for each division with the names of the ministers and others, I find his name on the committee for the eleventh division, which included the Hundreds of Thingoe, Lackford, and Thedwastry, with the Corporation of Bury. But, if a Parliamentarian, I presume he became a penitent one, as in 1661 he had the degree of S.T.P. (Sacræ Theologiæ Professor) conferred upon him at Cambridge "per literas regias."

By his first wife, Elizabeth, daughter of Richard Gipps of Welnetham and aunt of Sir Richard the genealogist, he had twelve children baptized here between 1643 and 1665, viz., William, Gibson, Christian, Richard, Thomas, Christian, John, Clement, Sache, Charles, Clement, Mary. She died in 1668, and in the same year he was married at Little Saxham to Mrs. Capell, widow, of Bury St. Edmunds. From the rate for 1693, which I have printed in App: IV, it would seem that he gave up Horscroft to his son William during his life time, and lived himself at the College, which I presume is the present College farm in Horringer. He died in 1698 aged 83. For his tombstone see App: II, No. 3.*

It appears from Dr. Gibson Lucas' will that there was a portrait of him in his scarlet robes, which he left to his daughter-in-law, the wife of William Lucas, for her life, and then to be handed down.

WILLIAM LUCAS, eldest son of Gibson, succeeded him at Horscroft, which he appears to have occupied during the last few years of his father's long life. He was baptized here in 1643. In the rate for 1699 (App: IV) he is always called Captain Lucas, but I do not find his name in Doyle's Army Lists from 1661 to 1694. His first wife, Margaret, daughter of James Cobbs of Bury St. Edmunds, died immediately after the birth of her first child Gibson, in March 1674/5. By his second wife, Ann, he had four children baptized here, besides three others buried here in infancy. With him the Lucas family came to an end so far as Horringer is concerned. Mr. Gage says that he sold Horscroft in 1706 to William Turnor of Bury St. Edmunds, from whom it has come by inheritance to the Wigsons. (See Wigson.) William died in 1716, his wife Ann having died in 1715. Those are the two last entries of Lucas in the Horringer Registers. Probably the deaths of all his nine children in his lifetime, most of them in earliest infancy, was the cause of his selling Horscroft.

From the Visitation of Suffolk, 1561, edited by Dr. Howard, I learn that John, younger brother of the Captain, was a merchant of Norwich, where he died in 1696 aged 44 years, and was buried in St. Peter's Mancroft Church. He left children whose descendants are living to-day. From this John were descended several successive Gibson Lucas's, so that both names of the divinity doctor and penitent presbyterian have been carried well into this 19th century.

* Since writing this account of Gibson Lucas I have come across Mr. Venn's Biographical History of Caius College, Cambridge, in which my suspicions of his penitence are confirmed. Mr. Venn says that he was at first a Presbyterian minister in Norwich, and afterwards conformed. And he quotes a letter from H. Paman of St. John's to William Sancroft, dated Nov. 19, 1655, saying, "Mr. Lucas is become a zealous man for the Church of England, and upon profession of his hearty repentance for what he has done against it and his resolution to preach up what he before persecuted, was ordained priest by my Lord Bishop of Norwich. . . . . The Presbyterians of Norwich in the meantime being full of rage to have lost a brother, I wish heartily we may have any cause to brag of the proselyte."

The house in which the Lucas family lived has been pulled down. The present house at Horscroft is modern ; the old house, Mr. Gage says, stood north-east of it.

MANTUA.—In the Register of Baptisms this name is written Manteau, in that of Burials Mantua. John and Mary Mantua had three children baptized here, viz., John in 1655, Sherman in 1658, Mary in 1662. John the father was buried in 1671, Mary his widow and the boy Sherman in 1677. That is the whole history of the family as far as the Registers tell it. The name is apparently foreign, and I have already suggested that John Mantua may have been one of the retinue of the Earl of St. Albans, or of Queen Henrietta Maria whom he is supposed to have married, and have been settled in one of the houses in Horringer belonging to the Jermyns of Rushbrook. The date agrees very well. I have also made the rather wild guess that when the foreign John Mantua was asked by the minister, Name this child, he said Sherman, meaning to call the child Jermyn after the name of his patron, which the minister did not understand. The owner of Rushbrook at the time when John Mantua came to Horringer was Thomas Jermyn, elder brother of the Earl of St. Albans.

MOYLE.—In the Register of Baptisms will be found that of Thomas Coppinger Moyle in 1747, Isabella Moyle in 1749, children of Thomas and Sarah Moyle.

Sir Robert Davers, 2nd baronet, married Mary Jermyn, one of the five daughters and co-heiresses of Thomas, Lord Jermyn. This marriage brought Rushbrook to the Davers family. Of the ten children of this marriage Robert and Jermyn became successively 3rd and 4th baronets, and Thomas was the admiral who had Little Horringer hall. (See Davers.) Another of the ten children was Isabella, who married General Moyle. General Moyle amongst other children had a son Thomas, who in 1745 married Sarah Coppinger, and it is they who for a time lived in Horringer and had two children baptized here. Thomas was admitted at the Bury Grammar School at midsummer, 1730, and died in 1766. Sarah his wife died in 1764.

Of the two Moyle children baptized here there is not much to be said. Thomas Coppinger became a Lieut.-Colonel, died unmarried in 1788 aged 41 years, and is

W

buried at Lichfield. Isabella also died unmarried. There was another sister, Mary, not baptized here, who married Benjamin Hands, and was buried here in 1820 aged 65 years. See tombstone No. 97.

Where the Moyle's house in Horringer was I have not been able to make out. I imagine that it was on the Ickworth side of Horringer, somewhere between the present Horringer gate and Hammond's gate, on ground that is now either wood or just inside the park. George, Lord Bristol, who succeeded his grandfather in 1751, has entered in a book purchases made by him since his grandfather's death. Amongst them is this, "*To Mr. George Boldero for house and lands belonging to Mr. Moyle in the parish of Horringer, £840.*" We may notice what a nest of cousins there was at Horringer while Dr. Symonds was at the rectory, Admiral Davers at Little Horringer, Mr. Moyle in his house, with Sir Jermyn Davers as patron and lord of the manor.

In vol. 3 of the Proceedings of the Suffolk Archæological Institute is a paper by Mr. Samuel Tymms on the old house in the Meat Market, Cupola house, formerly belonging to the Macro family. Mr. Tymms says, p. 379, that in 1745 it was bought by Thomas Moyle and settled according to the uses of his marriage settlement, and that it was sold by his son Thomas Coppinger Moyle to Robert Hockley, grocer.

VALENTINE MUNBEE.—Mr. Gage says that soon after 1730 John Kettle sold his copyhold estate at Horringer to Valentine Mumby (sic) of Ixworth, who built a house on it, which his son Valentine sold in 1768 to John Everatt. Everatt is an error of Mr. Gage's for Everall. This was the old Covel estate, and the house is now called Horringer house. The only Munbee or Munby who enters into the registers is the first of the above two Valentines, who was buried here in 1750. His tombstone is App: II, No. 10. The younger Valentine was educated at Bury Grammar School and Caius College, Cambridge, and admitted at the Middle Temple in 1758. About 25 years ago I recollect seeing the announcement of the death of Valentine Munbee in the newspapers. He died at Weston-super-Mare, and was, I think, a General, and over 80 years of age, so that he might have been a grandson of the Valentine who sold Horringer house.

NOILLE *alias* REVE.—See Reve.

WILLIAM OLIVER.—In 1712 William Oliver was appointed to be Ickworth land-steward. He had been in Lord Bristol's employ for several years previous to that. His predecessor as steward, William Covell, had died in 1707. (See Covell.) In 1720 William Oliver was married in Ickworth church to Ann Webster of Newmarket. After his marriage he lived in Horringer. Six of his children were baptized in Horringer church, viz., John in 1721, William and Ann, twins, in 1722, Thomas in 1724, Isabella in 1725, George in 1727, buried in 1730. Where William came from originally I do not know, nor where he was buried. Not at Horringer. He was still Ickworth land-steward in 1748, and I know not how much longer. Probably he came from Bury, and went back there to die when his life's work was ended.*

REV. JOHN OLIVER.—John, the eldest son of the above William Oliver, was godson of John, Lord Bristol, who at any rate looked after his material interests. In the summer of 1730 he went to the Bury Grammar School. In Aug. 1731 Lord Bristol writes from Ickworth to his son Lord Hervey who was at Court, and says, "*Will Oliver's son will be of age fit for ye Charter-house on ye 9th of Nov. next, and if you could get but one turn for him from ye King, Queen, Prince, or any other of your great friends, I would never trouble you or them any more.*" Letter 931. I have not found out whether he went to Charter-house School or remained at Bury. In 1738 he went up to Trinity College, Cambridge, Lord Bristol giving him £15 to pay for his caution money and for the furniture of his chambers. In 1742 he took his B.A. degree. I suppose he was then ordained and had a curacy somewhere not far off. One day in April, 1749, he came running over to Ickworth from Bury to tell Lord Bristol that "Mr. Davis, rector of Tuddenham dyed this morning." Lord Bristol presented him to Tuddenham, and also tried hard to get the Lord Chancellor, Lord Hardwick, to appoint him to Cavenham, that he might hold the two together. Letters 1332, 1334, 1339. But the Lord Chancellor would not consent. John Oliver remained rector of Tuddenham from 1749 to 1786. He also held the living of St. James, Icklingham, from 1767 to 1786. I presume he died in 1786. His subscription of one guinea to the Suffolk Ship (App: IX) in 1782 is printed under Icklingham, but he was not buried there.

*I am indebted to Alderman J. G. Oliver, whose fathers have lived in Bury for many generations, for help in trying to connect William Oliver with them; but we could not get quite evidence enough to prove it. It therefore remains only an unproved probability.

THOMAS OLIVER.—Thomas, the second son of William Oliver, went to Bury Grammar School in Oct. 1734. Apparently his father was then living in Bury, as he is described in the Admissionum Catalogue as being of St. James' Parish in this Burgh. I don't suppose he stayed there long, as he went into the Navy. In 1740 Lord Bristol mentions him as being in the same ship with his grandson Augustus (afterwards Admiral and 3rd Earl of Bristol); and in 1748 Lord Bristol writes to his son Felton Hervey, then M.P. for Bury, asking him to use all his influence to get Thomas Oliver a lieutenancy. "*He hath been 12 years at sea, four years whereof he hath been a midshipman on board the Hampton Court, Commodore Mostyn, commander, and is now at Portsmouth. He hath passed his examination at the Admiralty and obtained a certificate in form of his being qualified for promotion. His father hath been above fourty years in my service.*" Letters 1140, 1275. There I must drop him, not being able to follow his career any further.

WILLIAM OLIVER, JUN.—This boy went to the Bury Grammar School in Oct. 1734, at the same time as his brother Thomas, but that is all I know about him.

PEYTON.—See Skelton.

PHIPPS.—On Aug. 6, 1748, will be found the baptism of George William, son of Constantine and Lepel Phipps. This child was privately baptized at Horringer where his parents were then staying, and received into the church a month later at Ickworth, and is entered in the registers of both parishes. Nevertheless his birth seems to have been unknown by the compilers of peerages, who do not mention him. I presume that he died quite young, so that there is nothing more to say about him.

His father, Constantine, was the son of William Phipps and grandson of Sir Constantine Phipps, who was appointed Lord Chancellor of Ireland in 1710. Nineteen years after the birth of this child he was created an Irish peer, Lord Mulgrave of New Ross, and died in 1775. His mother, Lepel, was the eldest daughter of John Lord Hervey. Horace Walpole describes her when she was Miss Hervey as "*a fine black girl, but as masculine as her father should be.*" Corr: I, 113. She died very suddenly in 1780 at the Admiralty.

This child was their second child. The eldest, Constantine John, was a distinguished naval officer, and commanded an expedition to discover a north-east passage to Asia. Had this child lived, he might have been numbered among the distinguished natives of Horringer, as on his father's side alone he had two brothers, three nephews, and a great nephew, besides a great grandfather and his cousin, who have all got a place in the Dictionary of National Biography.

The Phipps's came occasionally to stay at Horringer, though I cannot make out where the house was. Possibly it was the same house as that in which the future Bishop of Derry spent the first few years of his married life. I think Dr. Malfalguerat, an eminent accoucheur of Bury St. Edmunds, was partly the attraction. The nearness to Ickworth was of course another. They seem to have been here again the following year, for Lady Hervey writes from Ickworth to Mr. Morris on Aug. 23, 1749, and says, "*Mr. and Mrs. Phipps are now so near me, that I see them almost every day, which is a great satisfaction to me. They are both most agreeable people, and she is the best, the most amiable child that ever any parent was possessed of.*" p. 160. On this occasion Mrs. Phipps's brother, a Cambridge undergraduate, was staying with them and apparently studying very hard. His name was Frederick Hervey, and he was afterwards Bishop of Derry. Apparently the house, wherever it was exactly, was only a small one, as Lord Bristol writing to his granddaughter, Mrs. Phipps, just after she had left, viz., on Sept. 19, 1748, says that Lady Hervey had suggested their coming there, but "*I as constantly dissuaded it, foreseeing the many inconveniences you woud necessarily undergo from the incapacity of my poor cottage to receive you as I ought.*" Letter 1302.

THOMAS REEVE *alias* NOILLE.—The *alias* is also written Newell and Noel. He was rector of Horringer from May, 1520 to 1528, when he resigned. He was presented to the living by the Abbot of Bury. As the Abbot who presented him was John Reeve *alias* Noel, very likely they were brothers. Abbot Reeve, the last of the Abbots of Bury, was a native of Melford; he was elected Abbot in 1514, and in Nov. 1539 he was compelled to surrender the monastery and retire on a pension. He died four months afterwards at Bury and was buried in St. Mary's Church.

REV. THOMAS ROGERS.—A memoir of him will be found in the Dict: of Nat: Biography, but there is not much to say about him except dates. He is supposed to have been a native of Cheshire, and was a student of Christ Church, Oxford, B.A. in 1573. He was presented to the rectory of Horringer in Dec. 1581 by Queen Elizabeth. I presume that she presented him on account of the old Bury Abbey property having not yet got settled down in the hands of its new lay possessors. In Aug. 1588 he was married in Horringer Church to Bridget Wincol. The Jermyn MSS in the library of the Suffolk Archæological Institute give a pedigree of the Wincol family, from which it appears that she was one of seven children of John and Margery Wincoll of Netherhall in Little Waldingfield, in which parish her grandfather Roger Wincol and his father had been clothiers. Her brother Isaac, also of Netherhall in Little Waldingfield, married Mary, daughter of Sir Thomas Gawdy, Judge of the Queen's Bench.

Thomas and Bridget Rogers had one child, Robert, baptized here in Oct. 1589, of whom I know nothing more.

Thomas Rogers was the author of several theological works, which were much read in their day, but for which I expect there is little demand now, and one can only marvel how anybody ever got through them. The chief of them is an exposition of the 39 Articles. He was the opponent of Dr. Bound on the Sabbatarian question, which was one of the earliest points on which the Puritans diverged from the High Church party. Dr. Bound, who was rector of Norton near Bury St. Edmunds, took the Puritan view of the Sabbath, while Thomas Rogers laid on for the High Church view. He had at one time been chaplain to Bishop (afterwards Archbishop) Bancroft.

He was buried at Horringer in Feb. 1615/6, and his wife Bridget joined him ten days later. Antony Wood says that "he was buried in the chancel of the church there, under a rough, unpolished and broken gravestone without name or epitaph."

REV. GEORGE ROGERS.—He was appointed to the rectory of Horringer just 150 years after the death of the above Thomas Rogers; but I do not expect that there was any connection between them, *i.e.*, not more than there is between all the sons of Adam. From the Supplement to the Suffolk Traveller I learn that he was a native of Bury St. Edmunds and educated at the Bury Grammar School. From there he went to Trinity College, Cambridge, was elected a fellow of his College, and took his B.A. degree in 1764. In 1765 he became curate at Horringer. In 1766 he was presented by Sir Charles Davers to the rectory of Little Welnetham, which he resigned in 1767 on being presented by Sir Charles to Horringer. He held Horringer till May 1784, when the Earl-Bishop of Derry presented him to Sproughton. He remained there over 50 years, and died in December, 1835, aged 94. If he had stayed on at Horringer till his death he would have held it for 68 years. In that case neither Mr. Kerrich nor Mr. Hasted would have come here, and he would have been succeeded by Lord Arthur Hervey, who was already rector of Ickworth. If Lord Arthur had likewise remained at Horringer till his death in 1894, he would have held it for 59 years, and the two together would have held it for over 127 years. During the course of 125 years there would have been only once a vacancy, only once a new rector.

In May, 1768, he was married in Horringer Church to Elizabeth Drew of Horringer, by whom he had nine children baptized here between 1769 and 1783, and possibly there were others born at Sproughton. George, Elizabeth, Peter, Edward, Thomas, Lucy, James, Robert, Martha Maria, were born here, of whom Edward, Thomas, and Robert died in infancy.

He published and edited some sermons. His portrait by W. M. Bennett has been engraved.

Elizabeth Drew was the daughter of Edward and Suzan Drew. She was one of four sisters who were all married in Horringer Church respectively to Rev. George Watson of St. Mary's, Bury St. Edmunds, James Scarlin of Sudbury, and Samuel Burroughs of Stowmarket.

RUSHBROOK.—This name is fairly common in the neighbourhood of Bury. The different families who own it need not be related to each other, though they all originally took their name from the same village. The first vowel is frequently changed, and the forms Rashbrook, Risbrook, and Rosbrook are more common than Rushbrook. There is only one entry in these registers that belongs to the family of Rushbrook that now owns Rushbrook, viz., the baptism in 1849 of William Henry son of William Henry Rushbrooke. The latter, Commander R.N., was a son of Col. Rushbrook, M.P., and died in 1883 aged 68 years.

THOMAS SACHE.—He was buried here in May 1661. I know nothing more about him except that he married Christian Lucas, widow of William Lucas of Horscroft, and thus was stepfather to Gibson Lucas, D.D., the parliamentarian who turned royalist, and presbyterian who turned episcopalian. (See Lucas.)

SANCROFT.—There seems to have been one generation of a family of this name resident here at the opening of the 18th century. The name is generally spelt Sandcroft and Sondcroft. As Archbishop Sancroft was of a Suffolk family that had lands at Fressingfield, it is very possible that the Horringer Sancrofts were kinsfolk of his. His life lasted from 1617 to 1693.

SCARLIN.—In July, 1774, James Scarlin of All Saints, Sudbury, was married here to Suzan Drew, whose sister Elizabeth was already married to the Rev. George Rogers, rector of Horringer. There was a Samuel Scarlin of Sudbury, M.D., of the right age to have been his father, but I have not made out whether he was. James was buried at Horringer in 1825, aged 87 years, and Susan his widow lived on till 1844. The register of burials gives her age as 99, her tombstone gives it as 98. The epigrammatic epitaph on it, "*She thought the world was like herself sincere*," records two virtues on her part, and seems to have a hit at the world as well. From there being no entry of baptism of any child of theirs, I imagine they only came to live in Horringer late in life, perhaps when a Drew estate came to their possession. Tombstone No. 153.

Their son James, No. 2, married Martha Fuller, and lived here and had two children baptized here, James Mathew and Martha Susanna, which last died in infancy. James died in 1854 aged 85, and Martha in 1859 aged 80. Tombstone No. 165.

Their son James Mathew left Horringer some years before his death. His children by both marriages mostly died young. He died in 1890 aged 80 years. Tombstone No. 195.

The Rev. Walter James Scarlin, of John's Coll: Cambridge, B.A. 1867, at present represents the family, being a son of James Mathew.

SIR JAMES SIMPSON.—His name does not appear in the printed registers, as his death occurred after 1850, which is my stopping point. But as his tombstone, No. 209, is among those whose inscriptions I have recorded, I must make a note about him. He came to spend the evening of his life here, renting Brook house. From the Memoir of him in the Dict: of Nat: Biography, and from the sermon preached in Horringer Church on the Sunday after his funeral by Lord Arthur Hervey, I take the following particulars.

He was born at Edinburgh on Feb. 12, 1792, and educated at Edinburgh University. He was the son of David Simpson of Teviotbank, Roxburghshire. His military career began as early as 1808 in the Madras Cavalry. After a year or two he gave that up and returned to England. In 1811 the Duke of York gave him a commission in the 1st (Grenadier) Guards. In 1812 he was sent to Spain, and took a part in the defence of Cadiz, the relief of Seville, and the retreat from Burgos. In 1813 he returned home with his regiment. In 1815 he was ordered out again, was severely wounded at Quatre Bas and invalided. In 1826 he was appointed Lieut.-Col. of the 29th Foot, took it to Mauritius and stayed there till 1837, when he returned to England. In 1838 he became Colonel in the Army. In 1842 he was re-appointed to the 29th and took it to Bengal. In 1845 he was appointed second in command to Sir Charles Napier in Scinde. In 1846 coming home in bad health he was appointed Commandant of Chatham, and afterwards Commander-in-Chief at Portsmouth. When the Crimean War broke out in 1854 he was appointed by Lord Raglan Chief of the Staff. On the death of Lord Raglan in 1855 he succeeded to the chief command. After the fall of Sebastopol he resigned the command and returned to England. He was a brave man and one who would neglect no duty, but he was better qualified to act as a second in command than as a chief. He took Brook house in Horringer in 1860, and there he resided till his death in April, 1868, aged 76 years. In 1839 he had married Elizabeth, daughter of Sir Robert Dundas of Beechwood, Midlothian. She died in 1840.

Having run through his military career there only remains to give one or two extracts from Lord Arthur's sermon to show him from another point of view. "*The greater part of this peaceful close of an active and eventful life he passed among us at Horringer. And to see his gentle presence and humble bearing and quiet demeanour, as he went in and out amongst us, who would have thought that he was familiar with rough war and its terrible glories, and had commanded armies on the battlefield. You know how kind and friendly and neighbourly he was in all his dealings with rich and poor; you know too how constant he was in his attendance in this house of prayer as long as his health made it possible for him to come to church, and what a consistent example he set us of christian virtue in all the arrangements of his life. As far as my own personal observation of his character went, and I had great opportunities of judging, I should say of him that he was pre-eminently a fast and true friend to those whom he called his friends; that he was a man of tender heart and kind deep feelings; that he was singularly upright, sincere, true and just in all his dealings; that he was remarkably pure-minded, and that the purity of his speech corresponded thereto; that he had a genuine humility and simplicity of character which prevented his ever speaking of himself or magnifying his own achievements.*"

One extract more as to "*his intense and childlike love of nature.*" "*That was a book of beauty which his eyes ever loved to look upon: and I verily believe that no child ever took more delight in spring flowers and the notes and nests of birds and the other simple pleasures of the country than did this veteran commander of great armies, to whom all the pomps of oriental splendour were familiar. . . . . To see him watch the rooks and mark their voice and their ways at the return of spring, to see him walk through the lanes watching the white-thorn as it began to bud, or to hear him discourse of some rare songster whose note had attracted his ear, you could hardly think it was the same person who had stormed the strongholds of the Boogtie tribes, or faced a thousand deaths in the trenches of Sebastopol.*"

SKELTON.—In Dec., 1675, will be found the baptism of Katharine, daughter of John Skelton, Esq., and the Lady Payton, his wife. What they were doing in Horringer, whether residents or visitors, I have not been able to make out. But as the rector of Horringer was also rector of Boxford, Lady Peyton's old home, that may somehow account for it. (See Womack.) Sir Algernon Peyton of Peyton hall, Boxford, Co. Suffolk, and of Dodington, Co. Cambridge, succeeded to the estates on the death of his brother, Sir John, in 1660, and in 1667 was made a baronet, the former baronetcy having become extinct at his brother's death. Sir Algernon was married to Frances, daughter and heiress of Sir Robert Sewster, Knt., of Ravely, Co. Huntingdon. She is the Lady Peyton mentioned above. She survived Sir Algernon and was married secondly to John Skelton, who was a soldier. Unfortunately there were two John Skeltons in the Army at the same time between 1670 and 1690; the numerous regiments in which they served and the successive steps which they gained are given in Doyle's Army Lists for that period, but I have found it impossible to distinguish between them, and to say which was ours and which was the other. One of them was a son of Sir John Skelton, Lieut.-Governor of Plymouth, and brother of Col. Bevil Skelton who was a man of some note. Bevil and one of the two Johns were both adherents of James II after his deposition, *i.e.*, high Tories. The memoir of Bevil

Skelton in the Dict: of Nat: Biography says that he married firstly Frances, daughter of Sir Robert Sewster and widow of Sir Algernon Peyton. But that must be a mistake. The above entry in the Horringer register makes it clear that John Skelton married Lady Peyton. Probably Bevil and John were brothers.

REV. THOMAS SMITH.—Sometimes written Smyth. I do not know anything of his parentage. In June, 1683, he was presented to the rectory of Horringer by Robert Sharpe, patron for this turn. As the register records the burial here in 1713 of Mrs. Judith Sharpe, mother of Thomas Smith, possibly Robert Sharpe was his stepfather and bought the next presentation from the Jermyn family for him. In 1685 Thomas Smith was presented by Thomas, Lord Jermyn, to the rectory of Nowton. He held Nowton and Horringer till his death in 1725. He resided at Horringer, and had six children baptized there between 1684 and 1695, viz., Mary, Thomas, Robert, Antony, Mary, Jane, of whom Mary, Antony, and Jane died in infancy. His first wife, Eleanor, was buried here in 1706; his second wife, Elizabeth, survived him and was buried here in March 1736/7. He was buried here in April 1725. Mr. Gage mentions a gravestone in the chancel of Horringer Church giving his age as 68. This is not now visible.

In 1712 was married at Horringer Thomas Smith, rector of Rougham, and Suzan Wiseman. I imagine that this Thomas was son of the rector of Horringer, baptized here in 1686.

In 1743 was married at Horringer Rev. Thomas Smith of Pakenham and Mrs. Mary Ellis of Horningsheath. He was rector of Pakenham from 1742 to 1763, and rector of Stowlangtoft from 1748 to 1763. I imagine that he was son of the rector of Rougham and grandson of the rector of Horringer. The patronage of Horringer, Rougham, Pakenham, and Stowlangtoft all belonged at this time to families that were closely connected with each other, so that it is not unlikely that a son of the rector of one should be appointed to the rectory of another. The Smiths are not an easy family to track.

THOMAS STANTON.—In 1602 Hardwick was purchased by Thomas Stanton of Bury St. Edmunds, mercer. In 1610 he sold it to Sir Robert Drury of Hawstead for 1100 pounds, who rebuilt the house, which was again rebuilt in 1681 by Sir Dudley Cullum. Hardwick being extra-parochial, Thomas Stanton seems to have made use of Horringer Church. His daughter, Margery, was baptized here in 1602, and his son Henry in 1608, and he himself was buried here in 1634. In 1661 was buried here Thomas Stanton, who I presume was a son of the former owner of Hardwick. From his tombstone, which is not now visible but is described in Gage's History of Thingoe Hundred, we learn that he was a Major, that he was 61 years at the time of his death, and that he was of Mildenhall. He was not baptized here, having been born just before his father bought Hardwick. I presume that he took a part in the civil war. Mr. Gage says that he was a royalist who compounded for his estate in the sum of £160.

REV. JOHN SYMONDS, D.D., rector of Horringer from 1725 to 1758.* He was born in 1696, was educated at Bury Grammar School, and by parentage was thoroughly Buriensis.

For his grandfather was Henry Symonds, a rich clothier of Bury, who married Suzan, daughter of John Craske of Bury.

And his father was John Symonds of Bury, who died in 1704 when young John was only 8 years old. And his mother's maiden name was Ann Hovell, and she was sister to Richard and Thomas Hovell, two active members of the Bury Corporation.

These two uncles are now and then mentioned in the letters of John, Lord Bristol, and not being political friends or supporters of his were regarded by him with great indignation.

In Sept., 1713, Lord Bristol writes from Bath to Mr. Richard Hovell, Alderman of Bury, to thank the Corporation for returning his son and brother-in-law (Porter) as their representatives in Parliament. (Letter 436.)

In Aug., 1721, Lord Bristol writes from Ickworth to his wife in London, and says, "*Yesterday I dined with ye Corporation, who received me with more universal kindness and respect (if possible) than ever, except ye two Hovells.*" (Letter 619.) A week later he writes again to his wife, "*On Thursday next I am to treate the Corporation at the Angel in Bury: they have given the Hovells a fresh mortification by choosing a kinsman of Mr. Macro's for their Preacher in exclusion of their nephew Symonds; this, they say, they may take for offering to sett up an interest in opposition to Lord Bristol's.* (Letter 627.)

In Oct., 1723, one of the two Hovells had lately passed out of reach of Lord Bristol's indignation, for writing then from Bath to Alderman Ray he says,

* For much information, genealogical and otherwise, about Dr. Symonds I am indebted to Rev. William Symonds, vicar of Frocester in Gloucestershire.

"*Alderman Hovell being called to give an account of his past conduct, I shall leave him to that great tribunal with this short remark, that I have been young and now am old, yet did I never see any man prosper after deserting truth or his professed principles for any worldly interest whatsoever, an observation honest Mr. Hall would do well to consider of in time.*" (Letter 783.) But we must leave the uncles and go back to the nephew, merely expressing the hope that honest Mr. Hall was not too late.

After leaving Bury Grammar School young John Symonds, who lived with his mother at Bury in Eastgate Street, went up to St. John's College, Cambridge, where he was admitted in 1712. He was Spalding scholar and Symonds exhibitioner, and in 1716 took his B.A. degree, M.A. in 1720. In 1718 he became a fellow of his college. In Bishop Monk's Life of Bentley, p. 456, it is told that there was much heat shown in the appointment of Dr. Conyers Middleton to be librarian of the University library, and that the indignation against Symonds and another member of his college who had voted against Middleton was so great, that they were hooted the whole way back from the Schools to St. John's College.

Having survived the hooting he was in August, 1724, presented by Sir Jermyn Davers to the rectory of Rushbrooke, which he resigned in 1726. In June, 1725, Sir Jermyn presented him to Horringer and Nowton, which both became vacant by the death of Rev. Thomas Smith. (See Smith.) About 6 months afterwards, in Jan., 1725/6, he was married in Hengrave Church to Mary Spring. This marriage connected him with several of the big houses in the neighbourhood of Bury, *e.g.*, Hengrave, Rushbrook, Pakenham and others, and surrounded him with cousins and connections of all sorts at Bury, Horringer and elsewhere, and eventually brought lands and houses to him and his children. So we must see who Mary Spring was.

She was the daughter of Sir Thomas and Merilina Spring. Sir Thomas Spring of Pakenham, 3rd baronet, was the descendant of Springs who were wealthy clothiers at Lavenham three hundred years before this, and to whom Lavenham Church owes some of its stately beauty. His wife Merilina was one of the five daughters and co-heiresses of Thomas, Lord Jermyn, of Rushbrook. As another of those five daughters had married Sir Robert Davers of Rushbrook, and was the mother of Sir Jermyn Davers, it follows that Sir Jermyn, the patron of Horringer rectory, and Miss Spring, who was now going to be married to the new rector of Horringer, were first cousins. Merilina, Lady Spring, survived Sir Thomas and married secondly Sir William Gage of Hengrave, where she was living at the time of this marriage, which consequently took place in Hengrave Church.

Miss Spring, now become Mrs. John Symonds, was evidently a smart woman. A letter from a Bury lady to Mrs. Ross of Helmingham, dated Feb. 4, 1725/6, says,* "*Mr. Symonds was married to the gay, the admired Molly Spring last week; they are yet at Hengriff, are expected to spend some time at his mother's [in East-gate St.] before they go to housekeeping; if so we must do ourselves the honour to visit these great people, but I'm determined not to go to see 'em at Horringer till I've a coach, you may guess when that will be. Her first suit a pinke sattin lined with silver tissue, the next a chint silk lin'd with white tabby, and so on, have hired six servants, 3 men in liveries, a Berlin and four horses; they must have a great deal of Oeconomy to support this figure with their fortune. Poor Mrs. King, Sir Jermyn Davers' sister, died last week, a mighty pretty woman; tis surprising how that family goes off.*" If the writer of that letter had been writing about 40 years later, she would have had still more reason to say of the Davers family, Tis surprising how they go off. Mrs. Symonds had been before her marriage the object of several poems addressed to her by Col. Richardson Pack and printed in his miscellany.

She had one brother, William, and one sister called after their mother, Merilina. Merilina married Thomas Discipline, Alderman of Bury, and had two daughters; from one of whom are descended Le Heups and Cocksedges; the other married John Godbold, who lived for many years in Bury and died in Oct. 1822 in the 93rd year of his age.

Her brother William succeeded their father, Sir Thomas Spring, as 4th baronet in or about 1710, and died unmarried in 1737, when the Spring property at Pakenham came to his two sisters, Mrs. Symonds and Mrs. Discipline. This was divided between them, Mrs. Symonds having New hall and the great tithes, etc., Mrs. Discipline having the old hall or mansion and the advowson.

I must wander a little from Horringer to state a very shocking fact which I find recorded in a folio MS. volume by Rev. George Jermyn giving the history of certain families, and given to my father by his son Archdeacon Jermyn. Mr. Jermyn says that the old manor house of the Springs at Pakenham passed from Mrs. Discipline to her two daughters, Mrs. Le Heup and Mrs. Godbold, and was

* For this extract from a truly feminine letter and for much else in this memoir I am indebted to a great great grandson of the smart couple, Rev. William Symonds.

by them pulled down and the site sold: and when it was pulled down several of the family pictures in it were (apparently on purpose) burnt!!! However, Mr. Godbold preserved a few of them. One of Sarah (Cordell) Lady Spring he gave to Miss Casborne; another of Elizabeth (Le Strange) Lady Spring he gave to Mr. Jermyn.

To go back to the rector of Horringer. In 1737 his wife succeeded to her share of the Spring property at Pakenham. In 1738 he took the degree of S.T.P. or D.D., so that henceforth we may call him Dr. Symonds, but must not confound him with his son, the Professor. In or about 1738 his mother died at her house in Eastgate Street, Bury, and soon afterwards, I imagine in 1742, he left Horringer and went to live there. In 1742 he was appointed preacher at St. Mary's Church in Bury, having, as we have already seen, been disappointed twenty years before. He was also now made a J.P. for Suffolk.

He had eight children baptized in Horringer Church. Jermyn, the eldest, baptized in 1726, must have died young, though there is no known record of his burial. John and Thomas, twins, 1728, and Mary 1729, died in infancy. Of John, 1730, and Thomas, 1731, some account will be found below. Delariviere, 1732, married Rev. John Casborne, and their grandson, Rev. Walter John Spring Casborne, inherited the Symonds' share of the Spring property at Pakenham. Anna Maria, 1742, died in 1758 aged 16 years, and was buried in the same grave as her father.

I do not find much about Dr. Symonds in Lord Bristol's letters. There is one letter written by him from Ickworth in August, 1738, addressed to Mrs Henrietta Howard, who I think lived at Bury, and who had incurred Lord Bristol's anger by acquainting "*the whole company at Dr. Symonds'*" with something to his disadvantage. "*I must insist upon knowing who your informant was, or whether they will make good or retract their evidence.*" (Letter 1089.)

I have not much more to say about Dr. Symonds. So far as one can see at this distance of time he was a very prosperous man and things went well with him. With his own estate, with the two livings of Horringer and Nowton, with the preachership at St. Mary's, with his wife's share of the Spring property and of the Jermyn property, he must have been very comfortably off. He had an estate at Horringer which he sold soon after 1750 to George, Lord Bristol, for £4,500. This may have been part of the Jermyn property which his wife inherited from her mother, or it may have been bought by him. He kept the rectories of Horringer and Nowton and the preachership at St. Mary's till his death.

He died Oct. 12, 1757, in the 61st year of his age, and was buried in the chancel of Pakenham Church. The flat stone there tells us that "*he was a wise and an honest man, a tender master, parent and husband; and, without which none can be truly great, a charitable and a sincere Christian.*"

Another flat stone close by is sacred to the memory of Mary his widow, last surviving daughter of Sir Thomas and Merilina Spring, who was born in 1698, and died in the 67th year of her age.

Her sister Mrs. Discipline lies not far off. She died in Nov., 1761, aged 66 years.

Their mother Lady Spring, afterwards Lady Gage, also lies there. She died in Aug., 1727, aged 52 years.

PROFESSOR JOHN SYMONDS. 1730—1807.—He was the third, but eldest surviving, son of the rector of Horringer where he was baptized. He was educated at Bury Grammar School and St. John's College, Cambridge, and took his B.A. degree in 1752, being 4th Jun. Optime. In 1753 he was elected a fellow of Peter-house, and M.A. in 1754. In 1768 he was appointed Recorder of Bury. This office he resigned in Oct. 1801, when the Corporation voted him a piece of plate of the value of £50 for his long and eminent services. In 1771, probably through the influence of the Duke of Grafton, Chancellor of the University, he was appointed Professor of Modern History, succeeding Thomas Gray the poet, and in the next year was created LL.D. and migrated to Trinity College. He afterwards travelled in France and Italy, and on his return to England built the house on the east side of Bury St. Edmunds which he called St. Edmund's hill, though the name has since been changed to the Mount. He records in his diary that the foundation stone was laid on April 2, 1773. The architect was Adam. It was built on ground which was part of his maternal grandmother's share of the Jermyn property. He was one of the small party which dined weekly at Ickworth when the Earl-Bishop of Derry made his occasional stays there. He was also a great friend of Arthur Young, to whose "Annals of Agriculture" he frequently contributed articles. He is frequently mentioned in Arthur Young's Autobiography, who mentions paying him several visits at St. Edmund's hill during a very dangerous illness in December, 1805. He survived this illness rather more than a year, and died in Feb., 1807, aged 77 exactly, and was buried at Pakenham. He died unmarried. His house at St. Edmund's hill he sold to Mr. Cocksedge, whose son, Martin Thomas Cocksedge, married Mary Le Heup, who was granddaughter to Mrs. Discipline, the Professor's aunt. His property at Pakenham he left to the Rev. John Walter Spring Casborne, his sister's grandson.

His portrait was painted by George Ralph, and engraved in 1788 by J. Singleton.

There is a memoir of him in the Dict: of Nat: Biography, which wrongly gives the year of his birth as 1728/9 instead of 1729/30. It also wrongly gives the year of his mother's death as 1774 instead of 1763.

THOMAS SYMONDS. 1731—1792.—This was the younger brother of the Professor, and like him baptized at Horringer. He went into the navy himself, and among his descendants are a large number of naval officers. Looking at the pedigree as it lies open before me I see no less than six naval officers among his immediate descendants. As one looks at it and sees R.N. after R.N. the words of the Psalm come into one's head: "These men go down to the sea in ships and their business is in the great waters." Among his sons there were two Admirals and two Commanders. Among his grandsons there was an Admiral and a naval Captain, besides a General in the Marines, and an army Captain who was drowned off New Zealand. Apparently if they did not go to sea, the sea came and claimed them.

I cannot follow Thomas Symonds in his naval career, but must content myself with saying that he was twice married, firstly to Mary Noble, who died in 1771, and was buried in St. James' Church, Bury, secondly to Elizabeth Mallet.

By his first wife he had a son Jermyn John, Commander R.N., who, as we are told by a mural tablet in Pakenham Church, "*with his ship and whole crew was lost at sea in a gale of wind in October, 1796.*" There were also two daughters, Elizabeth who married Rev. Henry Heigham of Hunston hall, and Mary Ann who married John Benjafield of Bury St. Edmunds.

By his second wife he was the father of Admiral Thomas Edward Symonds, who died in 1868, and Admiral Sir William Symonds, who died in 1856, and Commander John Charles Symonds, who died s. p. in 1840.

x

There I must stop, as I have left Horringer far behind. Both the above Admirals had sons who followed their father's profession. Admiral Sir Thomas, son of Admiral Sir William, died in 1894, and it is to his son that I have already expressed my obligations. Memoirs of Sir William and of his son (not his brother) Sir Thomas will be found in the Dictionary of National Biography.

Captain Thomas Symonds died at his brother's house, St. Edmund's hill, on May 25, 1792, aged 60 years. He was buried at Pakenham and shares a mural tablet there with his son Jermyn John.

TINDAL.—See Duke.

JOHN WADKIN.—Under March 31, 1690, John Hervey (afterwards Lord Bristol) records in his diary, "*John Wadkins died 11 at night at London.*" I think John Wadkin was his coachman, and I presume he is the John, son of Thomas and Sarah Wadkin, baptized here in Sept., 1650.

WIGSON.—We have seen that the Lucas family parted with Horscroft soon after 1700. They sold it to William Turnor of Bury St. Edmunds. Mr. Gage tells us that from William Turnor it passed to his son Henry, who left it in 1764 to William Agor, who took the name of Turner. He by will dated 1771 left it ultimately to William Seaber of Colchester, merchant, and Elizabeth his wife. William Seaber died in 1784, and his wife, who survived him, left it to her niece, Elizabeth wife of William Wigson, whose son William Bacon Wigson inherited it and died in 1872, aged 85 years. Several children of his will be found in the Register of Baptisms. See also App: II, Nos. 14, 15, 16, 17. In the earlier entries the name is written Wigson, in the later ones it is written Wigston. I recollect perfectly when and why the change was made. In 1860 my father was writing a short account of the Felton family for a meeting of the Suffolk Archæological Institute, and in his researches for it came across a family of Wigston of Leicester in the 15th and 16th centuries, which took its name from a village in Leicestershire. He told the late Mr. William Bacon Wigson that that was the origin of his name, and so the dropped t was put in again.

REV. LAWRENCE WOMACK.—He was rector of Horringer from 1662, or perhaps a year earlier, to 1683, when he was appointed Bishop of St. David's. I presume that there will be a memoir of him in the Dict: of Nat: Biog:, but his name has not yet been reached. Mainly from Blomefield's History of Norfolk, Bentham's History of Ely Cathedral, and the Supplement to the Suffolk Traveller, I gather the following facts about him.

From 1595 to 1685 the parish of Fersfield in Norfolk had three successive Womacks for its rectors, viz., Henry from 1595 to 1609, Lawrence 1609 to 1642, Arthur 1642 to 1685. I presume that these were respectively father, son, and grandson. Lawrence was also rector of Lopham in Norfolk.

Francis Blomefield, the historian of Norfolk, was born at Fersfield in 1705, and was afterwards rector of it. His wife was Mary, daughter of another Lawrence Womack, rector of Castor, who was a cousin of the Womacks of Fersfield. He tells us that various charges were brought by the roundheads against Arthur Womack who held the living of Fersfield during the civil war and commonwealth. Amongst other things he was charged with speaking these words:

Here is a health unto his Majesty,
Pray God confound his foes,
And the devil take all Roundheads,
For we are none of those.

He was thrown into Ipswich gaol, but after a time set free. (Blomefield's Norfolk, ed. 1805, I, 112.)

Lawrence Womack, jun., the son of Lawrence and the brother of Arthur, was born in 1612, and educated at Corpus Christi College, Cambridge. In 1642 he succeeded his father Lawrence at Lopham, but was soon afterwards deprived of it. Before that he had been living at Quidenham as chaplain to the Holland family. In July, 1660, he was made a Prebendary of Ely Cathedral. In 1661 he had the degree of S.T.P. conferred upon him per literas regias, and was presented to the rectory of Horringer by Sir Thomas Jermyn. His institution is dated July, 1662, but his predecessor, Robert Gooderich, had died in 1660, and his name appears in the registers in Jan., 1661. He buried his wife Ann here in 1665. The child Ann, whose birth and her mother's death came together, died in Oct., 1685, aged 19 years. Another child, Mary, died in infancy. No children survived him, and his cousin Mary, who married Francis Blomefield, was his heir. In 1660 he was appointed Archdeacon of Suffolk (Gage says of Sudbury), and also made a Prebendary of Hereford Cathedral. He also had the living of Boxford in Suffolk. Boxford belonged for many years to the Peytons, and Sir Algernon Peyton lived there. So possibly Lady Peyton may have been on a visit to him when her child

Katharine was born, or she may have brought the child to Horringer to be baptized by her old friend. (See Skelton.)

Lawrence Womack remained rector of Horringer till 1683, when he was appointed Bishop of St. David's. He was the author of several controversial works directed against the Puritans. He died in March, 1686, aged 73, and was buried in St. Margaret's Church, Westminster, "where is a white marble monument affixed to one of the pillars at the west end of the church" with an inscription. So writes Bentham in 1812. I have not ascertained whether it is still there.

WYMARK.—This name must not be confounded with the preceding one, though when carelessly spelt Wymock it gets very like it. There appear to have been two generations of a family of this name living here from about 1730 to about 1780. Their farm-house seems to have been near Horringer Green, which I take to mean not what is called Horringer Green now, but the old sheep green towards Horringer house. In 1775 John Whymark, jun., rented 188 acres from Lord Bristol, paying yearly a gross rent of £130. By 1781 the farm was broken up and divided among several tenants. The house stood empty for a time, the window tax being paid by Lord Bristol as it was in his own hands. Seventeen shillings was the annual amount of that. The *Bury Post* for Aug. 19 and Sept. 9, 1784, gives details of the new window tax just then imposed. From this I gather that a tax of 17 shillings in 1781 would imply a house with 12 windows. The new window tax of 1784 would have increased this to 35 shillings. I think the house was then pulled down. While it stood empty horses coming to Horringer fair were turned into its yard the night before at a payment of 2 pence each. There were generally from 30 to 40. After a few years all traces of Wymark's disappears. The family seem to have gone into Reed and Whepstead.

In the late Mr. Beckford Bevan's little book about St. James' Church at Bury St. Edmunds, Edward Wymark, draper, is mentioned as giving £10 in 1521 to the glazing of the west window of that church.

INDEXES.

INDEX No. 1.

Being an index to Appendix II which contains the monumental inscriptions now visible within the church. The reference is to the numbers which I have given to the stones.

INDEX No. 2.

Being an index to Appendix III, which contains all the monumental inscriptions in the churchyard. The reference is to the number which I have given to each stone.

INDEX No. 3.

Being an index to the biographical and genealogical notes, p. 273 to 356.

INDEX No. 4. BAPTISMS.

BUCKENHAM George 1609.
— Henry 1586, 1589.
— Isabel 1583.
— Joan 1612.
— John 1568, 1581, 1614.
— Nicholas 1621.
BUCKLE George 1813, 1834.
— Sarah 1840.
— William 1836.
BUCKLEY Hercules 1843.
BUD Elizabeth 1578.
— Thomas 1577.
BUGG Eliza H. 1843.
— Emily 1848.
— Frederick 1848.
— Henry 1845
— John 1845.
— Kezia 1850.
BULL Alice 1621.
— Ann 1601.
— Bridget 1604, 1632.
— Elizabeth 1815.
— John H. 1806.
— Mary 1776.
— Robert 1607.
— Sarah 1605.
— Thomas 1614.
— William 1828.
BULLACE Charlotte 1813.
— Harriet M. 1840.
— Henry J. 1810.
— James 1816.
— John 1804.
— John A. 1828.
Marianne 1832.
— Mary E. 1819.
— Robert D. 1834.
— Sarah C. 1837.
— Thomas 1836.
— William 1800.
BULLY Margaret 1559.
— Stephen 1561.
BUMSTEAD John 1634.
BUNTING } Ann 1702.
BUNTON } Delarivier 1744.
— Elizabeth 1700, 1715, 1754.
— John 1745.
— Joseph 1698.
— Mary 1697, 1722, 1750.
— Samuel 1704.
— Susan 1727.
— Thomas 1718.
— William 1743, 1755.
BUTCHER Bet 1790.
— Jemima 1794.
— Martha 1788.
BUTCHER Susan 1805.
BUTLER Anthony 1566.
— John 1564.
BYFORD Emma 1836.
— Elizabeth 1838.
— Frances 1785.
— George 1844.
— Henry J. 1847.
— James 1797.
— John 1792.
— Margaret A. 1840.
— Maria 1832.
— Mary 1785, 1794.
— William 1783.
CADMAN —— 1653.
CADNEY George 1674.
— Grace 1679.
— Mary 1671.
CALE Edmund 1579.
CALOWE Margaret 1591.
CANDLER William 1777.
CANHAM George Will: 1834.
CATCHPOLE Mary Ann 1837
— Martha 1839.
— Sarah 1825.
— Sophia 1843.
— Thomas 1823.
CATER Amy 1821.
— Ann 1773, 1786, 1790.
— Charles 1775.
— Eliza 1847.
— Elizabeth 1743, 1754, 1777, 1798.
— Emily 1845.
— Francis 1743.
— George 1759, 1784, 1787, 1815, 1821.
— Hannah 1784.
— Harriet 1809, 1842.
— Henry 1746, 1779, 1780, 1800, 1826.
— James 1740, 1789, 1845.
— John 1748, 1768, 1783, 1847.
— Joseph 1677, 1737.
— Marianne 1849.
— Martha 1786, 1793.
— Mary 1750, 1751, 1782, 1787, 1793.
— Sarah 1756.
— Sophia 1824.
— Thomas 1675, 1745, 1748, 1771, 1786, 1787, 1849.
— William 1667, 1737, 1738, 1770, 1777, 1790, 1838, 1840, 1843.
CAWSTON } James 1783,
CORSTON } 1786.
CHALLICE } George 1764.
CHALLIS } Hannah 1769.
— John 1771.
— Sarah 1766.
— Susan 1773.
— William 1771, 1775.
CHAPMAN William 1630.
CHEAVELY William 1677.
CHERRY Emily A. 1826.
— Henry C. 1823, 1824.
CHESTON Bacchavil 1606.
— John 1618.
— Margaret 1608.
CHINERY Ann 1643, 1676, 1684.
— Elizabeth 1681.
— Hester 1685.
— Isaac 1691, 1716.
— John 1636.
— Mary 1674, 1675.
— Sarah 1678.
— Susan 1677.
— Thomas 1635, 1640, 1673, 1683, 1687, 1717
CHURCH Elizabeth 1618.
— John 1624.
CLARKE Emily 1838.
— John 1688, 1692.
— Jonathan 1700.
— Katherine 1704.
— Rachel 1696, 1720.
— Robert 1690, 1715.
— Susan 1693, 1701.
— Thomas 1691.
— —— 1722.
COBBIN } Abraham 1796.
COPPIN } Ann 1642.
— Charles 1840.
— Elizabeth 1564, 1742.
— John 1745, 1798.
— Mary 1843.
— Richard 1743.
— William 1803.
COCK Elizabeth 1576.
COCKEL } Emma 1850.
COCKEREL }
— George 1791, 1839.
— Harriet 1831.
— Jane 1830.
— Marianne 1836, 1850.
— Richard 1794.
— Sarah 1850.
— William 1833.
COE Ann 1780.
— Charles 1794.

*These are really Haywards, which name is written Howard in these registers from about 1670 to 1680

INDEX No. 5.—MARRIAGES.

*These are all (except William) really Haywards. The keeper of the Registers from about 1670 to 1680 always writes Howard.

INDEX No. 6.—BURIALS.

* These are really Haywards, which name is written Howard in these Registers from about 1670 to 1680.

ERRATA.

P. 2, l. 31.—Dele [Sargeaunt ?] The name is Largeaunt.

P. 91, l. 30.—For Seaven read Seaber.

P. 124, l. 2.—For Penson read Person.

P. 155, l. 16.—For sat.. : [?] read Sequestratus.

Zeitfracht Medien GmbH
Ferdinand-Jühlke-Straße 7
99095 Erfurt, Deutschland
produktsicherheit@kolibri360.de